FREUD'S PARANOID QUEST

FREUD'S PARANOID QUEST

Psychoanalysis and Modern Suspicion

• • •

John Farrell

New York University Press
New York and London

NEW YORK UNIVERSITY PRESS
New York and London

Library of Congress Cataloging-in-Publication Data
Farrell, John, 1957–
Freud's paranoid quest : psychoanalysis and modern suspicion /
John Farrell.
p.   cm.
Includes bibliographical references and index.
Contents: From primal father to paranoid—Paranoid logic—
Paranoid psychology—Before Freud—Freudian satire—Freud as
Quixote—The charismatic pararnoid.
ISBN 0-8147-2649-6 (cloth : alk. paper). —ISBN 0-8147-2650-X
(pbk. : alk. paper)
1. Freud, Sigmund, 1856–1939.   2. Paranoia.   3. Psychoanalysis.
I. Title.
BF109.F74F37   1996
150.19′52′092—dc20   95-50156
CIP

New York University Press books are printed on acid-free paper, and their
binding materials are chosen for strength and durability.

Manufactured in the United States of America

10 9 8 7 6 5 4 3 2 1

To Leo, Verna,
and Edward Farrell

I have succeeded where the paranoiac fails.
                                    —Freud

Contents

Acknowledgments   xi

Introduction   1

One · From Primal Father to Paranoid   10

Two · Paranoid Logic   28

Three · Paranoid Psychology   41

Four · Before Freud   66

Five · Freudian Satire   96

Six · Freud as Quixote   131

Seven · The Charismatic Paranoid   167

Conclusion   213

Epilogue   217

Notes   223

Works Cited   257

Index   267

Acknowledgments

An early version of the epilogue was published in the *Harvard Review* and is reprinted with the kind permission of Stratis Haviaris. Daniel Paul Schreber's *Memoirs of My Nervous Illness* are quoted with the permission of Harvard University Press. The Schmutzer etching of Freud is reproduced with the permission of Sigmund Freud Copyrights.

My turn to Freud as a subject was an unexpected development and came at the end of a much longer period of investigation than went into the writing of this book. During this period I acquired more debts of scholarship and friendship than I can possibly acknowledge. I mention only a few. To begin with, my decade-long conversation with Blanford Parker has been an education in itself. My thinking about the problems of modernity in recent years has been shaped and invigorated by the influence of Anthony Kemp, Robert Faggen, and Jeffrey Fergusson. And it was Glenn Kim who put me onto paranoia (and Thomas Pynchon) in the first place.

Murray Schwartz provided bibliographical guidance at an early stage. Ralph Ross provided fruitful resistance to my ideas at a talk given in Claremont. Langdon Ellsbree suggested the epilogue. Audrey Bilger, Maria Davidis, Granville Henry, Maureen McLane, John Rabbinowitz, James Rogers, David Venturo, and Charles Voinovich read all or part of the manuscript at various stages. All provided valuable encouragement and guidance, and Venturo, with characteristic alacrity, supplied an elusive epigraph. Yoon Sun Lee and Nicole Hamon checked my French. Frederick Crews and Louis A. Sass gave excellent counsel and criticism as peer reviewers for New York University Press. Crews and Faggen were particularly helpful in the crafting of the title. And I have been ably served by my editor, Tim Bartlett. To all I am more grateful than I can say.

Introduction

Society everywhere is in conspiracy against the
manhood of every one of its members.

—Emerson

Henry James spent his last afternoons as Napoleon, ordering furniture by
imperial fiat. Friedrich Nietzsche late in his career assumed the titles of
Caesar and of "The Crucified." August Strindberg, exhilarated by a letter
from "Nietzsche Caesar," signed his reply "The One and Only God."
Strindberg believed that the persecuted heroes in the plays of Henrik Ibsen
were disguised portraits of him, plagiarized, infuriatingly, from his own
paranoid self-portrayal. Ibsen, in turn, kept a portrait of Strindberg over
his writing desk, for inspiration.

Hobbes was pathologically timorous, given to sudden flights. Maupassant suffered from bouts of persecution, as did E. T. A. Hoffmann. Schopenhauer slept with a gun beside his bed. "Stendhal" kept changing his
name. Imaginary enemies pursued Hemingway. Jean-Jacques Rousseau
believed that he was being persecuted by the entire generation of living
Frenchmen, that his every move was being carefully watched, his mail and
publications controlled, to prevent him from having access to unprejudiced
posterity. The second half of his *Confessions* is taken up with the plots of
his enemies. He attempted to place the manuscript of *Rousseau, Judge of
Jean-Jacques*, in which he minutely weighs the charges against his name,
upon the high altar of Notre Dame. Thwarted even there, he recognized
that God too was against him; in his last work, *Reveries of a Solitary Walker*,
he attempted a final escape into the arms of nature.

The dominant figures of modern culture exhibit a strange susceptibility
to delusions of grandeur and fears of persecution upon imaginary grounds—
in other words, to paranoia. In many instances the condition remains within
the range of ordinary behavior. It is what may be described technically as
a 'paranoid slant', a penchant for over-estimating one's own importance, a

1

morbid concern with autonomy and control, and the finding of hostile motives in other people's behavior. But in a number of cases, such as those of Rousseau and Nietzsche—not the least important figures in modern culture—the condition reaches the level of a full-blown psychosis. Strindberg's diaries reveal him to be the maddest of authors who can still write with power.

The eminence of paranoid figures in modern philosophy and art might not be significant were it confined to the personal lives of the writers concerned. But this is hardly the case. For both Rousseau and Nietzsche, suspicion is a driving motive of the work, along with a hysterical individualism, a desperate assertion of the uniqueness, autonomy, and power of the self. The suspicious hermeneutic systems of Nietzsche, Marx, and Freud are among the most distinctive intellectual achievements of advanced modernity. And in the pages of modern literature, the peculiar slant of the paranoid character appears even more conspicuously than in the lives and writings of the philosophers. The modern novel begins with its greatest paranoid, Quixote. Grandiosity and persecution distinguish the characters of Swift's Gulliver, Stendhal's Julien Sorel, Melville's Ahab, Dostoyevsky's Underground Man, Ibsen's Masterbuilder Solness, and Joyce's autobiographical hero Stephen Daedalus, with his three weapons, "silence, exile, and cunning." Much of the work of Kafka is strikingly paranoid. Paranoia in an enlarged social form is the central imaginative concern of American literature since World War II. The all-encompassing conspiracy, very much in its original Rousseauistic cast, has become almost the normal way of envisioning American society and its institutions in this period, giving impetus to heroic plots and counter-plots in a hundred films and in the novels of Burroughs, Heller, Ellison, Pynchon, Kesey, Mailer, and others. Thomas Pynchon excels his paranoid generation with the wholeheartedness of his paranoid vocation, which has kept him hidden from public sight for over thirty years. No one who's willing to talk about it on the record even knows what he looks like.[1]

The inquiry that led to the writing of this book began as an attempt to understand the paranoid slant of modernity, especially as it was given imaginative substance in the novels of Pynchon. Its historical origins seemed to me clearly to spring from the seventeenth century and the transformation of medieval into modern intellectual culture.[2] In making this hypothesis I had another distinguished forerunner: Sigmund Freud believed that the modern susceptibility to neurosis and paranoia could be explained as a side-effect of the process of secularization that began with the scientific discoveries of early modernity. Paranoia, in his view, was a psychological substitute for religion. The energies that had once been directed into the great collective ideologies of the past, into traditional religious and political culture, had suffered in the Enlightenment and its aftermath the fate of a private immolation, leading to neurosis, or of a perverted, comical expression in suspicious megalomania. In Freud's analysis, this was the price that some of the vulnerable natures among us had to pay for being modern.

Freud's conjecture seemed plausible enough, but when I began to reexamine the details of his theory, a peculiar difficulty arose—Freud's own method of thinking seems to fall unambiguously within the category that he himself designates as paranoid. For Freud, in fact, we all participate in paranoid thinking: our very way of making sense of things is to him a manifestation of illness akin to paranoia: "The moment a man asks about the meaning and value of life, he is sick, since objectively neither has any existence."[3] This state of affairs causes Freud no discomfort. He appears to enjoy likening himself, and the rest of humanity, to the paranoid. He revels in the ironies of that reflection. Freud's paranoid has the character of an overly credulous intellectual, a religious zealot who can neither distinguish wish from reality nor preserve the proper level of skepticism toward his own thought. Freud knows himself to be smitten with the same curse as the paranoid, to be an irrational being of the same kind, only he, as a scientist, has kept his credulous tendencies moderately in check. What distinguishes the scientist from his paranoid patient is not so much a superior understanding of the world, or even of other people's motives, as much as it is a superior awareness of his own irrationally self-aggrandizing nature. It is the difference between naive and sentimental paranoia.

The gesture by means of which Freud establishes his kinship with the paranoid is one of definition. If we accept Freud's contention that our way of questioning existence for its meaning is akin to an illness, then we must accept our likeness to the paranoid, it being impossible for most people to avoid asking such questions, whatever the answers they may come to. But the likenesses between Freud and the paranoid are not limited to what is implied in this a priori technical distinction. Freud shares with the paranoid character an unabashedly heroic self-image tending, as he admits, toward megalomania; he sees the social world as being fundamentally hostile and as threatening specifically toward him; he excels at finding hidden, malignant significance in the behavior of others; above all, he is systematically suspicious. Whereas I originally turned to Freud for insight into the origins of modernity's paranoid slant, what I found, rather, was that Freud himself is one of the most flagrant cases of the paranoid intellectual. More important still, his awareness of his kinship with the paranoid is not such as to make him an authoritative source of illumination about the condition. On the contrary, that awareness forms, in Freud, an essential element of the condition itself, and is inseparable from it. This being the case, I have found it possible to clarify the relation between paranoia and modernity by taking up the case of Freud, along with his very personal intellectual creation, psychoanalysis. Psychoanalysis is a complex synthesis of the historical experience of modernity. It achieves a compelling recapitulation of the intellectual substance of that experience in logic, rhetoric, and psychology. The dominant tendency, rigidified and deepened in Freudian science, is one of systematic suspicion both of individuals and of society, self-conscious intellectual excess, hostile and reductive logic, and nihilating satiric irony modified by a kind of literary preservation of the discredited elements of culture in the psychological territory of the 'unconscious'. Above all, there is the interpretive system of psychoanalysis, a system that rests upon the paranoid axiom that human motives are almost never what they seem. For the archeologist of culture, all of modernity's paranoid qualities are here to be excavated and displayed.

The aim of this study, then, is to show how Freud's personal paranoia combined with the resources of suspicion dominant in modernity to produce the superbly persuasive intellectual and rhetorical structure that is psychoanalysis. My procedure has been to work within and reinterpret Freud's own theoretical vocabulary as it applies to paranoia and modernity: where Freud converted the history of culture into psychology, I have tried to resolve it, in some measure, back into history. In chapter 1, I have attempted to initiate the reader into Freud's thinking about the historical origins of paranoia by presenting a reconstruction of his evolutionary and cultural account of human development, from the formation of the earliest human groups to the delivery of that homely pair of twins, the scientist and the paranoid. In chapter 2, I analyze the logic of the theory itself and state a historicizing counter-theory. Chapter 3 attempts to show the results of paranoid logic in the paranoid psychology of which Freud is both purveyor and victim. In chapter 4, I give a rough inventory of the intellectual constituents of modern paranoia, with special emphasis on those most important for Freud: the Baconian psychology of suspicion, empiricist and Kantian epistemology, progressive historicism, and Hobbesian political philosophy. In the following two chapters I turn to the subject of Freudian rhetoric, which is generically that of the satiric romance. Freud believed the romance to be a product of paranoid consciousness: I have sought to reverse that formula. Since the first depiction of the paranoid character belonged to Cervantes, for whom Freud had a cult from the time of his adolescence, I have attempted in chapter 5 to show Freud's deep affinities with that author. Chapter 6 applies the understanding of Freudian rhetoric gained in chapter 5 to Freud's masterpiece, *The Interpretation of Dreams*, in which he makes his own megalomaniacal personality the object of a satiric spectacle as he guides the reader on a paranoid quest for the hidden significance of dreams. Finally, in chapter 7 I have taken up Freud's case history of the paranoid Schreber, which is also his central theoretical statement on paranoia. In Freud's infatuated relationship with Schreber we can see some of the existential consequences of his satiric, 'paranoid' self-conception.

Since the debate about the validity and value of Freud's contribution has been particularly heated in recent years,[4] I might as well state at the outset that the portrait I have given of Freud will not tend to confirm the views of those who admire psychoanalysis. I have attempted throughout to anticipate and engage their objections. At the same time, my chief concern has not been to add to the already substantial literature disproving or discrediting psychoanalysis, but to understand the sources of its appeal in a way that is revealing about the broader intellectual culture of modernity. Freud promulgated a psychology philosophically attuned to the scientific movement in its grandest ambitions; but over the long term the proponents of this psychology have been unable to demonstrate its scientific value.[5] And yet, despite the absence of clear and convincing proofs of its validity, psychoanalysis has proven one of the most durable and potent forces in modern culture. It is this phenomenon I have attempted to explain. If psychoanalysis is not a convincing, valuable explanation of the functioning of the human mind, then what, exactly, is it, and whence derives its appeal? What is psychoanalysis?

My approach to Freudian paranoia is not primarily biographical. Though I have made frequent use of Freud's published letters, my chief interest lies in his official writings. I have learned from E. M. Thornton's unjustly neglected work on Freud's cocaine addiction, which she believes to have caused a good deal of his paranoid behavior.[6] I do not possess the medical expertise to confirm her judgment, and I am cautious about medical diagnoses made on the basis of historical evidence.[7] The focus of my scrutiny has been toward the intellectual manifestations of Freud's paranoid slant, which

I see as resulting from a dynamic interaction of philosophical prejudice, cultural and political circumstance, and personality. Ordinarily I would scruple to judge the man by the theory and the theory by the man, but Freud made that inevitable when he took his own psyche as the chief exhibit for psychoanalytic interpretation. Indeed he made a display of his 'unconscious' megalomania and paranoid potential. In a sense I am actually confirming Freud's paranoid self-image while providing a new understanding of its motives and significance.

On the subject of the general relation between mental illness and modern culture, I have been much instructed by Louis Sass's work on the affinities between modernism and schizophrenia. Sass has clarified the phenomenological character of schizophrenia by showing the extraordinary likenesses between the products and explicit aspirations of post-Romantic, 'modernist' culture (primarily after 1800) and the self-described experiences of schizophrenics.[8] He illustrates these similarities in massive detail in order to show that schizophrenia is not the product of primitive or defective intellectual functioning, but rather a kind of hyperintellectual alienation similar to that courted by the modernist avant-garde. While Sass's first intention in making this connection is to show that schizophrenia has been misunderstood, he is acutely aware of the irony in the fact that the best and most helpful analogs to schizophrenic thinking are to be found among the most prestigious examples of modern art and thought. Thus Sass has his place among the psycho-satirists led by Freud.

I find myself participating in this genre while attempting to define its limits. It may be revealing to draw out the likeness between the observed behavior of mad people and the aspirations and assumptions of modern culture because there arises in this way a powerful intimation that the aspirations are unworthy and the assumptions doubtful. Particularly, insofar as the habit of suspicion among modern intellectuals has become so systematic and rigid that it resembles mental disease, we should reconsider how well it is justified. But what lesson should we draw, ultimately, from the observation that paranoids (or schizophrenics) accomplish the same things that normal people do when they think? The lesson I would draw would not be Freud's ironic lesson—that thought in general is closely akin to paranoia, the product of 'narcissism' and unconscious 'projection'—but only that paranoids can also think. Like the rest of us, they must discover order in the midst of phenomena. It is the way they go about this, however, that makes them paranoid. The meaningfulness of their experience carries them beyond what is evident to others into an excess of grandeur, suspicion, and ingenious delusion. It is evidence of the generally suspicious and satirical character of modern psychological thought that it takes the similarity between thinking per se and the thinking of the mentally ill as a strike against the normal operations of the mind. My intent has been to suggest that important modern intellectuals have come to share, by their own efforts, the aspects of so-called paranoid thinking that are truly undesirable and aberrant. They have made paranoia often the most attractive and persuasive stance for artists and intellectuals to take.

It is important for my readers to understand at the outset that I am not attempting simply to apply a term from clinical psychology to the makers of culture or to their work. My purpose is, rather, to illustrate the intellectual and psychological consequences of the tendency among some modern intellectuals to erase the difference between madness and the ordinary functions of thought. It is their willingness, out of profound suspicion, to see themselves as akin to the mad, and then to embrace this image with heroic self-assertion and irony, that is the object of my concern. My use of the term 'paranoid' often intends to emphasize its deliberately self-inclusive character, with the implication that the description *and* the condition are, for the intellectual, self-imposed or acquired by intellectual sympathy; the same is true of the vocabulary of 'narcissism' and 'projection' that support Freud's conception of paranoia. Since we must all suffer the fate of living out to some considerable degree our images of ourselves, I take paranoid self-recognition to be inherently self-fulfilling for those who adopt it. Further, once this heroically ironic and suspicious intellectual stance has been established, once the paranoid quest has become a visible part of the public domain, it naturally attracts those who have the temperament and powers to assume and sustain it. And so a recursive dynamic comes into force, unpredictably augmenting and elaborating itself.

This is a thesis I will have to defend in a much more comprehensive treatment of modernity. Here I have attempted merely to show how the logic, psychology, and rhetoric of paranoia combine in the intellectual outlook of a single, crucial figure. I sketch only the broader cultural elements that psychoanalysis calls particularly into play. The progress of the argument moves from the logic of reductive suspicion to paranoid psychology to satiric rhetoric because this seems to me to be the most clarifying manner of articulation. I do take logic—and therefore intellectual commitment—to be, in some sense, the most fundamental determinant. Others may privilege psychology or rhetoric, or choose to regard the three as complementary. I have not attempted to make a strong choice on this point. In the work of Sigmund Freud, who is surely a mature example of the paranoid slant, the logic, psychology, and rhetoric of paranoia seem to me perfectly integrated.

In the first chapter I will ask the reader to enter with me into the details of Freud's conception of paranoid psychology and its relation to the other psychological features of modernity. Before taking up that task, however, I wish to offer an anecdote to crystallize the image of Freud that this work will attempt to sustain. It has to do with a permanent rift that developed between Freud and his collaborator Otto Rank in the mid-1920s. For many years, Rank, a man of extraordinary talent and erudition, had served as Freud's secretary and intellectual majordomo. The friction between them had begun during an earlier period when Rank started to seek new means of support in what turned out to be a premature anticipation of Freud's death. As Paul Roazen tells the story, the younger psychoanalyst Helene Deutsch made a last, unsuccessful attempt to bring the two men together again:

She did it as much for Freud's sake as for Rank's, since Freud seemed deeply hurt. She explained that Rank's closeness to him had put the younger man in a state of extreme stress; patience and understanding were in order. She reminded Freud of Rank's attachment to him, and of how he had set out on his own in expectation of Freud's death. But none of this gave any comfort to Freud. He brushed aside her intercession with the final sentence from a Jewish story, "Then why isn't he kissing the hot stove!" Freud explained his meaning: The Rabbi has a beautiful young wife and many young students living in his house. One day the Rabbi returns home to find his favorite student kissing his wife. The Rabbi turns on his wife to accuse her, but she pleads with him that the pupil does not know what he is doing, he is sick. "Then why isn't he kissing the hot stove!"[9]

This story, it seems to me, epitomizes the paranoid slant both of Freud and of the psychoanalytic worldview. Freud had a special love of Jewish stories of this kind and considered their wisdom as being akin to his own.[10] "Then why isn't he kissing the hot stove!" The imperious question declares that behind the apparent irrationality and confusion of human behavior there is always a deeper, more purposeful selfish and hostile intention to be uncovered by the one who knows where to look. A student who was truly ill would do something arbitrary and meaningless, something irrelevant or even harmful to his interests. But this student, in his illness, finds himself inadvertently kissing a beautiful woman. The rabbi has a point—if only we could all be so besotted! The wife in the story plays the role of the censorship in the Freudian theory of dreams, attempting to distort and

disguise the true meaning of a guilty wish. It is her hypocrisy that makes
the rabbi's reply a joke: he has shown the pointlessness of her attempt at
concealment. In psychoanalytic thought, this fate always awaits those who
plead for the honor of human motives. Their secret wishes give them away.
For Freud, suspicion is always justified. Nothing is accidental, there is no
innocence. Inadvertency is a disguise of the unconscious, a form of hypocrisy, of mauvaise foi. And the purpose of psychoanalysis, like the purpose
of a joke, is to reveal all such disguises and hypocrisies. Only those actions
that overtly display their hostile or libidinous origins can be taken at face
value. The rest are worthy to be laughed at.

It is often appropriate, we must recognize, to view the motives of
our fellow human beings with suspicion. They are capable of a nearly
unfathomable deviousness involving things great and small, a deviousness
that goes beyond any imperatives of practical interest. This is why the
rabbi's remark is funny and true. But what would it mean to live one's
whole life in the bitter wisdom of the rabbi's unpleasant discovery systematically applied in the form of a science? As Freud employs them, the rabbi's
words suggest that Helene Deutsch, in her attempt to plead the case of
Rank, was covering over the secret pleasures of Rank's friction with Freud,
his betrayal of the father; there is a further suggestion of the insincerity of
Rank's protests of pain, and even of a conscious or unconscious complicity
between the outcast and his intercessor. It is implied that, like the wayward
student, both of them are taking advantage of the situation to carry out
wishes we all would like to gratify, giving the father pain being as attractive
a guilty pleasure as kissing his beautiful wife! Anyone familiar with the
practice of psychoanalysis would have grasped these implications with
ease. It was a startling rebuke to Deutsch. What chance, then, did her
mission have to succeed, what intellectual resources could she have drawn
upon to alleviate Freud's suspicions and convince him that Rank's motives
were not the worst, when the theory of psychoanalysis leaves no room for
such an interpretation? Its form of suspicion is not of a knowing, worldly
kind, but systematic and absolute. It leaves no room for error. The unconscious makes no mistakes!

Here, then, we have Freud in his maturity, a man who knew how to turn
a joke to his advantage, a genius of satiric rhetoric whose personal bent for
suspicion had evolved into a worldview expressed by means of a distinctive
literary sensibility, a system for decoding the motives of others, and an
unflappable method of self-justification—a chilling figure, perhaps, but
one, nevertheless, of great persuasiveness and uncanny fascination, one
whose continuing influence in our culture needs to be understood.

ONE

From Primal Father to Paranoid

For relaxation I am reading Burckhardt's *History of Greek Civilization*, which is providing me with unexpected parallels. My predilection for the prehistoric in all its human forms has remained the same.
                                                                    —Freud

The attempt to describe paranoid psychology began with a great work of comic fiction: an elderly and decrepit gentleman, crazed with the reading of vulgar romances, becomes suddenly convinced that he is a knight-errant born to restore a golden age of chivalry. Don Quixote's first adventures lead to a defeat so unambiguous as to defy explanation within the frame of his delusion, and Cervantes' story seems in danger of losing momentum within its first fifty pages. But then the hero's niece makes a saving suggestion— that Quixote's quest for glory is being thwarted by a swarm of malicious enchanters who persecute him at every step. These agents of persecution immediately become the key element in Quixote's thinking. The assumption of their existence allows him to preserve his exaggerated idea of himself and his powers while he suffers innumerable humiliations, drubbings, and defeats. For all of these his imaginary enemies are responsible.

And so the paranoid quest is capable of an almost endless satiric elaboration. It is important for our purposes to take account, as well, of the peculiar effects that Quixote's paranoid character tends to exercise upon those he encounters. First there are the ones ignorant enough to be taken in by his impersonation, which is maintained with perfect consistency. Then there are those who become infatuated with Quixote's heroic posture even though they know it to be grounded in madness. In this category we may place not only certain characters in the story but also Cervantes' Romantic and existentialist readers, who become enchanted with the absolute and self-sufficient character of Quixote's idealism; they admire the warmth, humanity, and grandeur of his delusion all the more for the fact that it stands in contradiction to banal reality. Finally, there are those leisured and cultivated characters within the story who become intoxicated with Quixote as a figure of mirth and give themselves over to the staging and execution of his adventures. These characters appear largely in Part Two of the book; many of them have become familiar with Quixote by reading Part One. They are the audience par excellence, and Quixote is for them virtually a creature of their own fancy. In these living readers he encounters the true enchanters whose power of manipulation he has always feared.

If Cervantes' elaborate fiction seems too whimsical or too artificial a source of examples to illustrate the dynamics of a commonly occurring psychological condition, there is no shortage of well-known examples from life exhibiting the identical features. Adolf Hitler, for instance, experienced the same misguided flights of self-denying idealism, the same megalomania, suspicion, and fear of persecution as Quixote. The power to infatuate and impel by the force of heroic delusion has never been more strikingly demonstrated than in the course of his career.

Sigmund Freud is still the most influential student of this chronically grandiose and persecuted state of mind to which modern psychology has given the name of paranoia. According to Freud, paranoia occurs when an adult regresses to an early stage of psychosexual development in which he has not yet distinguished the products of his own thinking from external reality.[1] In this state only he exists, his ego contains the whole world, and, insofar as he relates to a sexual object, that object can only be himself. Freud called the thinking characteristic of this stage of development 'narcissism'. Personalities that receive their decisive stamp at this stage will be homosexual, having taken themselves as the model for the object of love. In many cases, however, the homosexual desire will be repressed from consciousness, and it is in such cases that the groundwork for paranoia is established. If the person cannot sublimate or repress his homosexual urges, he may regress to the stage of narcissistic omnipotence and self-containment. He obliterates the existing world and replaces it with one that in some sense fulfills his desire. He becomes a hero, a king, or a god. But even after achieving this regression the paranoid continues to struggle against his homosexual urges. Because he cannot allow them to come undisguised into consciousness, he experiences them in a negative form as part of the external world. The libidinal interest originating in his unconscious appears as a hostility directed toward him by others. In Freud's formula, "what was abolished internally returns from without."[2] The "I love him" corresponding with his forbidden passion comes into consciousness as "He hates me."[3]

Freud's theory of narcissism also suggests an explanation for the way comparatively normal people respond to the paranoid. The paranoid's view of the world is bizarre and detached from reality. But it can charm and compel, because the narcissism of the paranoid resonates with the repressed narcissism active in each one of us. We have all passed through a narcissistic phase, and we all go on projecting our inner fantasies onto outer reality so long as we live. Freud believed that the subterranean narcissism of the average person was responsible for the attractiveness of artists, children, cats, great humorists, and even criminals, all of whom are figures of narcissistic self-absorption. Women, in his view, tend to be narcissistic as a rule, and this permits them to appeal to the repressed narcissism of the average male, a fact that Freud considered to be of the greatest importance for the ordinary life of the species.[4] Freud never extended his theory of narcissism to cover the attraction that could be exercised by the paranoid character; he does not seem to have taken note of this phenomenon directly, although, as we shall see in a later chapter, he was acutely susceptible to it himself; but it requires no bold extension of his theory to suggest that the narcissism of the paranoid would call up the same surges of repressed heroic fantasy as do other figures of exemplary self-sufficiency.

The theory of narcissism can even be made to yield a psychoanalytic explanation for the humorous qualities of paranoid delusion. Wit succeeds, according to Freud, when a repressed wish is given conscious expression in a sudden and unexpected way.[5] Quixote's improbable grandeur may be said to resonate with the latent narcissism of Cervantes' readers, giving to their buried heroic longings a surprising, pathetic, but still recognizable form. Furthermore, Cervantes' comical detachment and self-sufficiency in presenting the adventures of Quixote may be said to have prompted his readers to identify with him out of their own repressed narcissistic independence.

Taking all of this together, it is impossible not to admire the beautiful economy and completeness of the theory of narcissism with regard to the phenomena of paranoia. It accounts not only for the paranoid character itself but for the range of responses it evokes in others. The protean flexibility of the theory seems a little uncanny, and calls upon us to admire the mind that devised it. But this reaction too can be accounted for by the theory of narcissism itself. The sense of the 'uncanny', according to Freud, originates in the resonance of conscious events with historically repressed, unconscious motives, and the mastery of psychological researchers over their materials can be attributed to such motives of a narcissistic origin.[6] So even the theory of narcissism has a certain narcissistic appeal. This is plausible enough within the logic of psychoanalysis: making theories about paranoia, as we shall see, is one of the narcissistic alternatives to becoming paranoid.

An examination of Freud's thinking about the eccentric figure of the paranoid has led us directly to his conception of the ordinary human character. If he is right, we are all swollen with secret grandeur. Our delusion does not manifest itself only in the inflated moral image we have of ourselves: we are even prone to suspecting that the very structure of the world in which we live accords with our desire and that the thoughts and feelings comprising our mental universe actually constitute a part of the external world. Although most of us hold these grandiose feelings in check at the boundaries of the conscious mind, they give constant direction to our attention. They exert their influence in a multitude of forms—in daydreams, in religion, in fantasy, in humor, and in love. When a self-inflated being like Quixote appears, we laugh, admire, or become enthralled, and in so doing we betray a recognition of our essential selves. The apparent strangeness of the paranoid evokes a deeper recognition of common narcissism.

Freudians of the later twentieth century attribute the state of affairs I have been describing to the fixed nature of the human psyche and to the Oedipus complex, its signature. For them, the dialectic of narcissism and repression is nothing other than the standard operation of our human equipment.[7] Freud did not hold this view. For him, the Oedipus complex had been brought about by specific events within the course of human history. He believed that the dramatic tension visible within the psyche, the struggle for power between narcissistic and repressive impulses, was the residual effect of conflicts that had taken place between groups of men and great individuals in history. These conflicts, over the millennia, had left a permanent impression upon the human mind, an impression preserved from generation to generation through the mechanisms of biology and culture. As a consequence of this belief, Freud observed that the heroic and narcissistic impulses that still animate the psyche in our time are not entirely lacking in connection with reality, for they embody the memory of a historical reality that we continuously relive in psychological terms.[8] The condition of the paranoid, more than that of other neurotics, shows an obvious affinity with the historical struggles for dominance that produced the Oedipus complex. The paranoid's grandiosity and fear, originating in a disturbance of the psyche, give the clearest evidence of the memories of primordial heroism and strife that remain active in the species as a whole. We all bear within us, Freud tells us, "the impressions left behind by the personalities of great leaders—men of overwhelming force of mind or men in whom one of the human impulsions had found its strongest and purest, and therefore often its most one-sided, expression."[9] The paranoid's delusion and the social reaction that it produces are the aftereffects of these "impressions." In order, then, to understand the deepest social significance of paranoia in psychoanalytic thinking and to set the theory of paranoia into the widest perspective, it will be necessary to reconstruct from Freud's writings a consecutive account of human bio-history.

Freud presents the story of human origins in seemingly cautious terms, calling it a "scientific myth," a "Just-So Story."[10] As with all myths of origin, the early parts of the story remain fragmentary and obscure, while the later have the clarity of dogma. Although the events to which it refers are historical, the certainty of the whole was grounded, Freud thought, not in the evidence provided by history but upon what he had discovered from his patients about the course of individual development.[11] Freud believed, according to a mistaken assumption of Victorian biology, that the individual, in the process of maturing, recapitulates the development of the species. This assumption permitted him to extrapolate from clinical observation to universal history and to fill the gaps in the observation of clinical experience with the *Urphantasie* of the human race. What he set forth, then, was a double history—a historical narrative of evolution recapitulated in individual development from childhood to maturity.

Freud begins the "scientific myth" of human history by adopting Darwin's suggestion that the earliest human groups must have been dominated by a single father who suppressed the sexual activities of his male children in order to monopolize the supply of females.[12] This group, the 'primal horde', was held together in bonds of simple power, with no need for symbolic representations of authority. The father was simply the father, a figure of absolute self-assertion. In him we find the original instance of the psychology of narcissism:

The father of the primal horde was free. His intellectual acts were strong and independent even in isolation, and his will needed no reinforcement from others. Consistency leads us to assume that his ego had very few libidinal ties; he loved no one but himself, or other people only in so far as they served his needs. . . . Here at the very beginning of the history of mankind, was the 'superman' whom Nietzsche only expected from the future. Even to-day the members of the group [in typical group psychology] stand in need of the illusion that they are equally and justly loved by the leader; but the leader himself need love no one else, he may be of a masterful nature, absolutely narcissistic, self-confident and independent.[13]

It may seem surprising that the father, with his authentic power, should have been a figure of 'absolute narcissism', since we normally associate narcissism with a withdrawal of libido from the world. Presumably the primal father could sustain his narcissistic self-fulfillment while keeping a firm grasp upon reality because reality offered no checks to his desire. For him, ought was identical with is, his absolute narcissism coinciding with absolute power. The father experienced few libidinal ties with his slave family because ties of this kind are based upon a component of sublimation; such a diversion of libido would have been quite incompatible with the father's privileged state. Still more foreign to his nature would have been the conversion of sexual into social interest that sustains the psychology of the group. The father's mastery lay precisely in not having submitted to the social ties that give value to other people as objects of regard. The superhuman freedom of the father depended upon his being the sole object of regard in a world that could offer no resistance to his desire. Such was the perfect narcissistic self-enclosure and total sexual fulfillment of the primal human consciousness. It was the only true state of freedom Freud ever imagined.

In addition to the dominant consciousness of the father, Freud's description of the primal horde included, as the quoted passage makes clear, a second original psychology—the psychology of the sons.[14] The sons differed from the father in two ways. The first was in an absolute disadvantage of power relative to him, for he compelled their obedience by force and deprived them of all sexual satisfaction. The second difference was entirely a psychological one: the sons loved the father, and they loved their mothers, sisters, and each other. They had given up a part of their libido to social ties. This psychological surrender of libido to the sublimations of love and social attachment marks the enslavement of the sons fully as much as the sexual abstinence imposed upon them by the father through the use of force. In fact, their psychological attachment to others was created out of the energy diverted from sexual activity by the interdictions of the father. The experience of love in the children of the primal horde was the psychic equivalent of their disadvantage in power.

At some point, the sons banded together to kill the primal father. The motive for their action was simple—they wanted sexual access to their mothers and sisters, hitherto kept in a paternal harem. But the consequences of their revolt were complex, just as their enslavement had been. In the long run it was easier for them to destroy the physical might of the father than it was to escape from the repression of the libido that he had imposed by means of it. For as much as the sons hated their father and his rule, they had also come to love him. And so, along with the satisfaction of killing him and eating his body, there came a sense of guilt. And this guilt resulted in a stronger investment than ever before in the restrictions of social life. It gave rise to prohibitions against the repetition of the primal crime of murder and also of incest, its fruits.[15] In this manner was established the Oedipus complex, rooted in the repression of these two fundamental wishes. The unity of the group no longer depended upon the brute force of the father; from this point the group secured itself by means of the taboos and totemic rituals established in commemoration of his death: "Society was now based on complicity in the common crime" (146). The primal crime was not a single event; Freud believed that it must have occurred many times in order to have left such a deep impression upon human nature. The Oedipus complex, which resulted from the collective force of these experiences, formed the basis for civilization: "the beginnings of religion, morals, society and art converge in the Oedipus complex" (156). At the end of *Totem and Taboo* where he first described this sequence of events, Freud quotes Faust's revision of the Gospel of John: "In the beginning was the Deed" (161).

The brothers of the primal horde killed their father because they wanted to be like him; they wanted to enjoy the power to gratify their narcissistic fantasies as part of reality. But the guilt they experienced as a result of their psychological enslavement to the father forced them to suppress their own narcissistic urges. The pleasure-seeking part of the father in them led them to kill him, but this act left them prey to the guilt urged by the punishing part of the father, which had also become an ineradicable part of their nature. Thus, the antisocial and narcissistic motives of the primal crime led, paradoxically, to the strengthening of the social order. The structure of the primal horde gave way to a communal, democratic society based upon collective guilt and renunciation. Each of the primal brothers renounced the pleasures enjoyed by the father and the wish to be like him. It was even possible, Freud believed, that a period of matriarchy intervened. But the longing for the father could not be permanently repressed. Communism eventually gave way to a new patriarchal structure—the family as we know it, with its single father and mother. There was a great difference, however, between this new paternal regime and that of the primal horde: Oedipal restrictions remained in force, keeping the father and the sons from gratifying the urge to commit murder and incest. The "social achievements" of the fraternal clan were preserved. Furthermore, the return of patriarchy to the family did not remove the need for the totemic or religious reenactments of the primal murder that had developed in the wake of primal father's death: "the gulf between the new fathers of a family and the unrestricted primal father of the horde was wide enough to guarantee the continuance of the religious craving, the existence of an unappeased longing for the father." [16] The existence of the new family was sustained by a repression that now included fathers as well as sons.

In his early formulation of the return of the father, Freud emphasized the simple longing created by his departure as the cause of his return. But in his later work he emphasized, as I have noted, the effects of the individual heroism originating in the "personalities of great leaders." In his work on group psychology, which gives the fullest treatment of these themes, Freud particularly emphasizes the poetic origins of the father myth and the fact that, in restoring the father, the poet put himself in his place. In this version, Freud makes emphatic use of the idea of a transitional matriarchy presiding over a vague and weak family, setting the stage for the next decisive development:

It was then, perhaps, that some individual, in the exigency of his longing, may have been moved to free himself from the group and take over the father's part. He who did this was the first epic poet; and the advance was achieved in his imagination. This poet disguised the truth with lies in accordance with his longing. He invented the heroic myth. The hero was a man who by himself had slain the father—the father who still appeared in the myth as a totemic monster. [17]

The heroic myth invented by the first epic poet brought back the father in a double form, as head of the family and as hero. Oedipal desire thus attained satisfaction by two means: in the reconstitution of the family and in the new life of imagination. The creativity of the new family gave multiform expression to heroic projections of the 'family romance'. Freud and Rank traced the miraculous birth of the hero and his magical adventures in fairy tales and myths, romantic narratives and popular fiction.[18] In tragedy Freud found the reenactment of his death, the memory of the primal crime.[19] In religion the father-hero eventually achieved the status of God: "The lie of the heroic myth culminates in the deification of the hero."[20] The self-aggrandizing imagination of the epic poet thus produced the entire patriarchal culture that has come down to us through tradition. In the monotheism instituted by Moses the Egyptian among the ancient Hebrews, Freud discovered the final symbolic return of the father as a single, dominating force. The religion of Moses and his Egyptian predecessor, Ikhnaton, represents the most concentrated effort of the narcissistic impulse to reincarnate the primal father.[21]

With the return of the father and the arrival of the family and religion, the communal psyche of the fraternal clan was replaced by an individual psychology based upon social inequality. Each person felt a strong identification with the father of the family and with the father-God; each felt as well a strong libidinal bond with the other members of society based upon a shared, ideal image of the father. And the libidinal bond of the group operated as a limitation upon the narcissistic independence of its individual members.[22] The epic poet and his religious imitators exacted in the name of the father the most extraordinary sacrifices. These sacrifices constituted the basis of civilized life, for every achievement of civilization, in Freud's view, depends upon the denial of instinctual gratification. There is a paradox here, for was not the father myth itself a form of instinctual gratification? So it was, but the greatest pleasure accrued to the one who created it. For the rest, the followers, it demanded sacrifice in return for patriarchal love. Human progress actually depends upon this social inequality. The epic poet, having freed himself from the restraints of the group, reintroduced the double psychology of dominance and submission that had existed in the primal horde. He took for himself the place of the father-hero:

The myth, then, is the step by which the individual emerges from group psychology. The first myth was certainly the psychological, the hero myth; the explanatory nature myth must have followed much later. The poet who had taken this step and had in this way set himself free from the group in his imagination, is nevertheless able to find his way back to it in reality. For he goes and relates to the group his hero's deeds which he has invented. At bottom this hero is no one but himself. Thus he lowers himself to the level of reality, and raises his hearers to the level of imagination. But his hearers understand the poet, and, in virtue of their having the same relation of longing towards the primal father, they can identify themselves with the hero.[23]

This passage delineates the economy of social imagination as Freud understood it. A repression has occurred and been accepted by the group. One individual, the poet, frees himself in imagination and returns to a narcissistic state of gratification that appeals to others because of their own repressed narcissism. But the satisfaction gained by the poet far exceeds what is given to his audience. And when it comes to religion, the discrepancy between the poet-prophet and his followers widens immeasurably: out of his own sense of heroism, the religious leader demands an absolute renunciation from those who believe in him. All pleasures, all happiness must be delayed in anticipation of an ideal future. With the triumph of religious consciousness, humankind had achieved, according to Freud, a truly heroic level of renunciation.

In the passage on the 'first epic poet' that I have just discussed, Freud mentions that the heroic form of mythological consciousness instigated by the poet came long before the 'nature myth'. The 'nature myth' in question was animism, which Freud had earlier placed alongside heroic mythology as the most primitive social form of narcissistic thinking. Freud linked these two together in a typically positivist historical scheme, recognizing "three great systems of thought: animistic (or mythological), religious and scientific."[24] The precedence given to mythology in Freud's later work seems to stem from the fact that mythology shows the traces of its origin in an individual heroic fantasy and so is linked more closely with a heroic founder. Animism, on the other hand, is anonymous and does not suggest the inequality of the social order. It expresses the narcissism of the entire group, thus displaying in an uninhibited way the full cognitive potential of narcissistic thinking rather than simply its heroic tendency. This makes it for us an especially important object of study, for in animism Freud gives the fullest description of the unbridled narcissism of primitive social imagination. Of the three great systems of human thought, Freud writes, "animism, the first to be created, is perhaps the one which is most consistent and exhaustive and which gives a truly complete explanation of the nature of the universe. The first human *Weltanschauung* is a psychological theory" (77).

The reader should not be misled by this unexpected tribute to the completeness of animism as an explanatory system, for animism has a fundamental flaw: it fails to recognize the psychological origin of its materials. It is supremely guilty of the sin of 'projection'. Freud quotes the words of Sir James Frazer: "Men mistook the order of their ideas for the order of nature, and hence imagined that the control which they have, or seem to have, over their thoughts, permitted them to exercise a corresponding control over things" (83). Because primitive men could not distinguish the internal experience of thought from their perceptions of the outside world, their manner of conceptualization provides Freud with what he considers to be a unique example of the mind's own tendency of operation before a language of abstract thought had been developed to separate the outer and inner worlds: "Before that, owing to the projection outward of internal perceptions, primitive men arrived at a picture of the external world which we, with our intensified conscious perception, have now to translate back into psychology" (64).

There is much to instruct us in this account of animism. Let us first take up the question of its completeness. Animism is complete because it is based entirely upon psychological principles of causation, and because it makes no attempt to censor these on the basis of reality. Thus its picture of the external world is a mirror image of the psyche. In this sense it is "a psychological theory." But so, for Freud, are all other non-scientific theories, whether they know it or not. The true significance of the completeness of animism is that it is a mirror image of psychology itself and so testifies to its power.

The completeness of animism, its unawareness of limit, leads to a second point of interest. The very self-enclosed quality of animism that leads it to confuse thoughts with things, also provides the animist with his illusion of control. Freud, elaborating upon Frazer's initial formula, observes that in primitive magic,

relations which hold between the ideas of things are assumed to hold between the things themselves. Since distance is of no importance—since what lies furthest apart both in time and space can without difficulty be comprehended in a single act of consciousness—so, too, the world of magic has a telepathic disregard for spatial distance and treats past situations as though they were present. In the animistic epoch the reflection of the internal world is bound to blot out the other picture of the world—the one which we seem to perceive (85).

In animism Freud discovers the true psychological cause of human megalomania, which lies in the inability to distinguish thought from reality. The same dysfunction occurs in the thinking of paranoids and neurotics. The "Rat Man," one of Freud's famous patients, gave it a name. He called it the 'omnipotence of thoughts' (85). We can see that in this magical omnipotence the narcissistic fulfillment of the primal father is partly retained. For the father, as for the animist, wish is identical with act. But while the primal father's narcissism was enacted in reality, magical thinking preserves only the 'omnipotence of thoughts'. This same overvaluation of the intellect is visible in religion and in the systems of the philosophers. In all these forms of consciousness, the narcissist invests an excess of libido in the ego, with the result that he attaches too great a value to himself as a thinking being. The paranoid, we shall see, is a person who has reverted to the 'omnipotence of thoughts' that once belonged to the whole of humankind but that the majority have now renounced.

It is probable that Freud imagined animism as always coexisting with some type of father mythology or totemism. He recognized in it, nevertheless, a fully developed social narcissism, and considered religion to be a transformation from out of it. In religion, men transferred the 'omnipotence of thoughts' from themselves to their god (88). They revived the memory of the father in the form of a divine imago. We need not be concerned whether this occurred directly, as Freud first surmised, or whether the heroic action of the epic poet intervened, as he later thought. In either case, the arrival of religion depended upon a truly extreme repression. The submission exacted by the father-God was a small thing compared with the renunciation that brought him into being.

There was still, however, a third phase of renunciation to come. For as much as religion may have sought to curtail the satisfaction of desire, its view of the world still preserved the character of its origins in narcissistic projection. Humankind still lived at the center of a cosmos that the human mind had made. The race of beings that could do without such narcissistic comforts was a long time coming to birth. It was led by a new kind of hero — the scientist. While the primal father and the first epic poet retained the facelessness of myth, and while the true characters of Moses and of his precursor, Ikhnaton, the founders of monotheism, remained hidden in the obscurity of early times, these new heroes stood forth in the light of modernity. Freud identified Leonardo da Vinci as "the first modern natural scientist," the first man to free himself from narcissistic projections in order to adopt the study of nature on the basis of experiment alone and without the benefit of 'presuppositions'. In order to understand how this strange mutation of human nature could have occurred, Freud investigated the painter's psyche with special interest, devoting to him the most detailed of his case studies. He exerted all of his ingenuity and all of his literary gifts in the attempt to explain how the accidents of Leonardo's childhood could have freed him from dependence upon the myths of the father and actually allowed him to channel his narcissistic libido into the pursuit of knowledge. These accidents accounted, in Freud's mind, for the mystery and power of Leonardo and the incomprehension of his motives attributed to his contemporaries.[25] And Leonardo was only the first of the great and misunderstood revolutionary heroes of modern science:

In the course of centuries the *naive* self-love of men has had to submit to two major blows at the hands of science. The first was when they learnt that our earth was not the center of the universe but only a tiny fragment of a cosmic system of scarcely imaginable vastness. This is associated in our minds with the name of Copernicus, though something similar had already been asserted by Alexandrian science. The second blow fell when biological research destroyed man's supposedly privileged place in creation and proved his descent from the animal kingdom and his ineradicable animal nature. This revaluation has been accomplished in our own days by Darwin, Wallace and their predecessors, though not without the most violent contemporary opposition. But human megalomania will have suffered its third and most wounding blow from the psychological research of the present time which seeks to prove to the ego that it is not even master in its own house, but must content itself with scanty information of what is going on unconsciously in its mind. We psycho-analysts were not the first and not the only ones to utter this call to introspection; but it seems to be our fate to give it its most forcible expression and to support it with empirical material which affects every individual. Hence arises the general revolt against our science, the disregard of all considerations of academic civility and the releasing of the opposition from every restraint of impartial logic.[26]

In this reconstruction of Freud's account of human development, the scientific hero, and particularly the psychoanalyst, naturally falls into place as the successor of the primal father, the first epic poet, the religious prophets, and the great personalities of history. Freud never gave his myth such a systematic exposition and so avoided putting himself in quite so invidious a position. But in the passage I have just quoted, and in many other places in his work, he casts the scientist and, indeed, the psychoanalyst, in this heroic mold. The scientist determines the psychological character of the modern, scientific phase of social existence, just as the primal father and the epic poet had determined the psychological character of its precursors.

From the standpoint of the twentieth century, Freud could look back upon what he took to be the psychological effects of almost three hundred years of scientific revolution. What he saw was the progressive development of individual psychology at the expense of the social and religious institutions that sustained the patriarchal culture of the past. The scientist had brought these institutions under attack by uncovering their delusory underpinnings, the effect of scientific injunction being to force the educated members of society to detach themselves from religion and other forms of group idealization. We can see in the scientist's gesture of separation from the group a recapitulation of the gesture of the epic poet, who withdrew from the fraternal clan, then replaced its bonds with those of the new family and its patriarchal god. The scientist undid this second bond without attempting to replace it with anything but the pride of repression and adherence to the truth of reality. In exacting this final repression, the culture of science removed the protection that religion had furnished against neurosis. Religion is indeed, Freud tells us, the "most powerful protection against the danger of neurosis."[27] The reason for this is that the neurotic, deprived of religion, has to create "his own world of imagination, his own religion, his own system of delusions."[28] When he does so, the product shows its origin in neurotic destitution:

The neuroses exhibit on the one hand striking and far-reaching points of agreement with those great social institutions, art, religion and philosophy. But on the other hand they seem like distortions of them. It might be maintained that a case of hysteria is a caricature of a work of art, that an obsessional neurosis is a caricature of a religion and that a paranoiac delusion is a caricature of a philosophical system. The divergence resolves itself ultimately into the fact that the neuroses are asocial structures; they endeavor to achieve by private means what is effected in society by collective effort. If we analyze the instincts at work in the neuroses, we find that the determining influence in them is exercised by instinctual forces of sexual origin; the corresponding cultural formations, on the other hand, are based upon social instincts, originating from the combination of egoistic and erotic elements. Sexual needs are not capable of uniting men in the same way as are the demands of self-preservation. Sexual satisfaction is essentially the private affair of each individual.[29]

The scientist, with his capacity for heroic repression, created a perilous set of conditions for the individual. He undermined the emotional bases of social life by exposing the irrational origins of social institutions. At the same time, he enjoined a strict adherence to reality, a reality holding no attraction for the libido. To depart from reality was now to lapse into private delusion, for the public space of social imagination had been destroyed. Those who attempt to preserve it in a private form take on a comical character. We can see in their illusion the outline of the noble forms of culture that sustained the meaning and value of life in the past, but foolishly and selfishly distorted. And the resemblance works both ways, for the pathological distortions of neurosis, displaying their origins in sexual repression, reveal the libidinal character of the traditional institutions that they mimic. The "Just-So Story" has arrived at the modern culture of irony.[30]

This is the account of human evolution Freud contrived out of his experience analyzing a few dozen patients in late nineteenth- and early twentieth-century Vienna.[31] The movement out of idealistic or 'narcissistic' self-enclosure marks, he thought, both the progress of the species and of the individual. Its dynamic element is repression. Only by means of repression can power over others and over the natural world be gained. The heroism of repression was peculiarly symbolized for Freud in the myth of Prometheus. Prometheus' conquest over fire was in fact a great sexual repression because, as the works of Swift and Rabelais suggested to Freud, urinating on fire is a great megalomaniacal fantasy, rooted in homoerotic pleasure. The myth of Prometheus thus symbolizes the heroism of the first man to capture fire by restraining his homoerotic desire to put it out with his urine, as Gulliver did when he doused the burning chambers of the Lilliputian palace. In Prometheus' fate the myth also reveals the hostility that greets the heroes of renunciation among those weaker souls who would preserve their pleasures.[32]

Before we go on to reinterpret Freud's bio-history of the species, it is important that we should present his account of development and repression in individual consciousness, the object of study from which he originally devised it. Freud analyzed the dynamic of repression as it relates to the development of consciousness in a classic psychoanalytic essay, "Formulations on the Two Principles of Mental Functioning," composed during the same period as his theoretical analysis of paranoia.[33] In it he describes our early stage of mental development, the 'primary processes', which operate according to the 'pleasure principle', *'Lust-Unlust'*. The pleasure principle expresses itself merely in the seeking of pleasure and the avoidance of pain. "Our dreams at night and our waking tendency to tear ourselves away from distressing impressions are remnants of the dominance of this principle and proofs of its power" (219). Freud does not tell us so, but the narcissistic stage obviously comes under the pleasure principle, with its tendency to be content with ideal or hallucinatory satisfactions.

At a certain point in an individual's development, Freud goes on to say, the passive state of the pleasure principle can no longer satisfy, and a second principle emerges, the 'principle of reality'. This principle admits to consciousness whatever is real, whether it produces pleasure or unpleasure. It begins to mobilize the sense-organs toward the external world and to develop the function of attention, the active seeking of sense impressions, as well as a system of notation, or memory, to preserve the results of attention (220–21). The repression of unpleasurable ideas is now superseded by an impartial passing of judgment true or false based upon comparison with the memory traces of earlier impressions. At this point as well, action and the delay of action in deliberation become possible, and the individual has a fully developed capacity to test his or her ideas against reality (221).

The pleasure principle must sacrifice mightily in order that the reality principle can come into force. But the pleasure principle is not destroyed in the process. It maintains its strongholds in the domain of fantasy and also that of sexuality, a function that always preserves a strongly auto-erotic and infantile character (222). The purpose of the reality principle is not to supersede the pleasure principle but to safeguard it, to lead the organism to surer pleasures than it can achieve at the prompting of pleasure alone. The demand for renunciation, Freud tells us, made by the reality principle with the promise of future rewards, has been projected onto external reality in the form of religious myths, which, with the doctrine of the afterlife, seek "absolute renunciation of pleasure in this life." But it is science that comes closest to overcoming the "ancient pleasure principle." Science, not religion, furnishes the true institutional expression of the principle of reality (223). The culture of science provides the standard of reality for modern people. We can see, then, the perfect convergence of science as a historical movement and the reality principle as the outcome of individual mental development.

While science throws its weight behind the reality principle, the pleasure principle, it is not surprising to discover, also has a mature expression in culture, one that preserves its rights upon the higher ground of reality:

Art brings about a reconciliation between the two principles in a peculiar way. An artist is originally a man who turns away from reality because he cannot come to terms with the renunciation of instinctual satisfaction which it at first demands, and who allows his erotic and ambitious wishes full play in the life of phantasy. He finds the way back to reality, however, from this world of phantasy by making use of special gifts to mould his phantasies into truths of a new kind, which are valued by men as precious reflections of reality. Thus in a certain fashion he actually becomes the hero, the king, the creator, or the favourite he desired to be, without following the long roundabout path of making real alterations in the external world. But he can only achieve this because other men feel the same dissatisfaction as he does with the renunciation demanded by reality, and because that dissatisfaction, which results from the replacement of the pleasure principle by the reality principle, is itself a part of reality. (224)

In the role of the modern artist we recognize the pattern established by the epic poets and prophets of history. All of these figures separate themselves from the group in imagination. By means of this separation they reclaim for themselves some part of the primal father's narcissistic omnipotence. And with the force of their imaginings, they induce others to take as part of reality what they have only dreamed. Others participate in the father through them. The difference between the epic and the modern poet is that the epic poet presents his vision of the hero as a true one while the modern poet presents it as a fantasy, though a fantasy that will become a treasured addition to the real social world.

Freud explained in another classic essay how the artist goes about making his fantasies accessible to others. His "innermost secret," his "ars poetica," consists of divesting his erotic and ambitious wishes of all those qualities that reveal a personal origin. The artist softens the egotistical character of his daydreams and adds aesthetic enhancement, by this means preventing others from experiencing the shame and repulsion Freud expects private fantasies to evoke.[34] As the clearest example of the artist's technique, Freud cites the popular romances, with their indestructible and irresistible main characters. They are thinly disguised versions of "His Majesty the Ego, the hero of all daydreams and all novels" (149–50). Were the artist to fail in disguising the private, egotistical sources of his heroic fantasy, the results would be comical, a parody. We would laugh to see heroism and the 'omnipotence of thoughts' expressed in such an undisguised form. We would recognize with contemptuous pleasure our own egotistical wishes being given an outward expression we would not permit to ourselves. Such a failed artist would seem to be verging on paranoia, for it is the same narcissistic wishes that animate the paranoid's delusion and the artist's vision. The difference is that the artist knows his heroism to be nothing more than an illusion, while the paranoid, like the prophets of old, mistakes his for the truth. Thus, under the regime of the reality principle, he produces a parody of romance or of speculative thinking, a parody that displays in an undisguised form the libidinal drives that motivate our heroic longings.

It is instructive to note that, in purifying his heroic fantasies of their egotistical character, the artist must in some measure undo the work of the scientist in his previous undermining of the social imagination. Once the culture of the reality principle has taken hold, sanity demands that one should keep fantasy confined to the private recesses of the psyche, where its libidinal origins will not embarrass. But the artist learns to mimic the socially objective quality of religion, philosophy, and romance and, by a kind of camouflage, to produce an effect that is like theirs even though it takes full account of the reality principle. He thus regains the level of the social in imagination. This is the secret of his success. But given that the artist's success depends upon disguising the private to imitate the social, it is obvious that psychoanalysis, which unmasks this secret, stands in a somewhat hostile relation to art.

The artist, the scientist, and the paranoid stand as the last three incarnations of the father-hero, the sole representatives of the heroic to survive in the intellectual regime of modern culture. The artist plays the hero in a make-believe world disguised to look like the one in which we live, the paranoid retreats into a world of his own device, and the scientist becomes a hero by renouncing imagination, narcissism, pleasure, and the ideal. The scientist takes for his aim the mastery of the real world, and he, like the heroes of the past, exacts great sacrifices to further his cause. It is by this process of heroic renunciation that civilization has matured and grown, harnessing greater and greater energy by means of instinctual sacrifices exacted by great leaders, until the power of collective repression achieved a mastery of the physical world that made the modern individual into a "prosthetic god," with all the advantages and hazards of that position.[35]

TWO

Paranoid Logic

I am actually not at all a man of science, not an
observer, not an experimenter, not a thinker. I am
by temperament nothing but a conquistador—an
adventurer, if you want it translated—with all the
curiosity, daring, and tenacity characteristic of a
man of this sort.   —Freud to Fliess

The psychoanalytic history of the human species that I have reconstructed
from Freud's works in order to expose the historical dimensions of his
theory of paranoia would not now be recognized by most Freudians as valid.
It rests upon scientific principles that were suspect even in Freud's day and
have since fallen into the antique. Freud's speculative abandon in the
domain of the instincts was already a source of dissent within the movement
during his lifetime. Though his theoretical activities continued into the
fourth decade of the twentieth century, they remained within the framework
of late nineteenth-century romantic biology. Lamarckian evolution,
Fechner's law, Fliess's theories of sexual cycles, the 'bio-genetic' doctrine
that 'ontogeny recapitulates phylogeny', these errant principles themselves
now look, even to the Freudian, like narcissistic projections or 'secondary
revisions' imposed upon the data in order to provide an intellectual context
satisfying to the mind's sense of coherence.[1] Freud himself raised the
possibility that the myth of the primal father and its historical sequels
might be taken for a narcissistic fantasy of his own: "Is not a hypothesis
such as this a relapse into the mode of thought which led to myths of a
creator and to the worship of heroes, into times in which the writing of
history was nothing more than a report of the deeds and destinies of single
individuals, of rulers or conquerors?"[2]

Saving Freud from his bio-historical hero-worshipping projections has
meant having to recast his theory entirely in psychological terms and
concentrating its explanatory force in that sphere. The psyche described by
Freud is thus removed from the flow of history and becomes a universal

constant. When the latter-day psychoanalyst looks out from this fixed perspective onto the spectacle of human diversity, he or she sees cultures and segments of cultures still swaddled in narcissism, still devoted to the exorbitant fancies of animism and religion. And he or she sees the culture of science, grounded in the reality principle and making it for the first time conscious of its own operation. But now these differences of culture and history appear to be undergirded by a common psyche that goes all the way down to the bottom of human nature, with its bedrock in the Oedipus complex. History is the product of this psyche and its needs rather than the other way around. And if history seems to accomplish a psychological development, that is only because it can, through the efforts of science, be brought to achieve in emulation the movement of individual psychology from the pleasure principle to the principle of reality. The continued force of psychoanalytic thinking rests upon these adjustments, which have severed Freud's connections with the disreputable elements of his theoretical family background.

It is with such genealogical problems in mind that I have attempted to return Freud's theory of paranoia to its context in what he called the *'Urzeiten'*, the "primaeval ages of the human family which had long vanished from men's conscious memory."[3] Just as Freud found a kernel of historical truth in the father projections of religion, leading him to unearth the primal crime, so it may be possible to find a kernel of truth in Freud's own theory of history. The archaic elements of Freud's bio-history—involving the primal father, the brothers of the clan, and the epic poet—cannot be reclaimed by any simple operation. But when it comes to the myth of the heroic scientist we are on solid historical ground. No one can doubt that science has indeed fought a heroic campaign to achieve its place in modern culture, or that in the process it has exacted great renunciations. Nor has Freud misled us when he says that the scientific revolution was fought as a struggle against the social imagination and the authority of tradition. Although such considerations may have been of little or no importance for the early heroes in the Freudian pantheon, figures such as Leonardo and Copernicus, they were of primary importance for later apologists of science, and especially those in the central empiricist and positivist tradition. Freud's portrayal of the scientific method as a means of overcoming the 'omnipotence of thoughts', the 'narcissistic' or megalomaniacal bases of tradition, is a direct descendant of Bacon's critique of those 'idols of the mind' that, by the impetus of self-infatuated speculation, stand as the chief obstacles to knowledge. The positivist trend in philosophy was from Bacon's time forward a crusade of repression. Its intent was to leave the products of tradition behind and to establish a mode of progress both intellectual and social. This movement gathered spectacular momentum in England during the period of the Restoration, making headway against its special targets, Scholastic intellectualism and Protestant enthusiasm. By the 1740s, it had largely conquered the pre-existing religious culture in England and taken its place at the center of the secular order of bourgeois capitalism, liberalism, and individualism.[4] In Catholic Europe, these intellectual, social, and political developments were slower, more difficult, and more violent, progressing and relapsing by revolutionary outbursts. As a liberal Jewish scientist in imperial, Catholic Vienna, Freud was a militant participant in this anti-traditional movement, one of the great fighters of its late battles.[5]

Freud was correct in his description of the early aims of some of the scientific reformers, and he did not overestimate the impact of the scientific movement upon culture. What is questionable in his account is the assumption that this impact was an inevitable consequence of the results of scientific discovery. It was the knowledge that the earth moves and that species evolve, Freud would have us believe, that produced the isolation, frustration, and fragility of the modern psyche and made it the victim of neurosis and paranoia; religion was the only protection against these conditions, and science had put the salubrious narcotic out of reach. In the personified abstraction 'science', Freud aggregates the cultural effects of scientific method as an exemplary discipline, science as an interest embodied in institutions, the knowledge produced and disseminated by means of science, and science as a way or set of ways of thinking about the world. He thus effortlessly obscures the ideological impulses of the early proponents of science and its political uses in the secular order of modernity; what is perhaps most important, Freud's uncomplicated view of the agency of science makes it impossible to recognize the conflicted aspect of modern intellectual culture itself, for what he assumes is that there was only one way to interpret the results of science. But this is hardly the case. It is all too clear that modern science, in addition to being a potent method of investigating the physical world, has also been an ideological instrument or, indeed, an ideology in itself. The psychological effects of scientific discovery can only be understood through the mediating ideological agencies of culture.

Freud would be the first, of course, to recognize the selfish and dominating motives of the scientist. He declared his own nature to be that of a "conquistador."[6] What he would deny is that things could be otherwise, the employment of science as an instrument of power following directly from the narcissistic character of the human being. But this self-suspicion is, paradoxically, an ideological stance, and one that cannot be taken upon faith. It is the purpose of this study to suggest that the emergence of the paranoid as a central figure in modern culture and the psychic economy of 'narcissism' and suspicion that seems to surround this figure can best be explained in historical and cultural terms. They are concomitants of the scientific and philosophical discourse of 'reality' and the heroic efforts of the individuals who made it prosper, advertising the new science as a liberating force that would allow humankind to leave behind the childish fancies of its past. Freud's notion that individuals in mental development move from the operations of the 'pleasure principle' to the 'principle of reality' appears to be a projection or, rather, an injection of this scientific and historical ideology into the domain of the psyche. It is a translation into psychological terms of the imperative to escape from the mystifications of the ideal into the realm of the senses, an imperative by means of which modern culture originally established its polemical identity. (I preserve the term "projection" here not in its psychoanalytic acceptation but to denote false extrapolations of the local, the transitory, and the ideologically self-serving onto the permanent and the universal.)

If the hypothesis I have stated holds, a curious circularity now appears in Freud's historical and psychological scheme. The great and damning evidence upon which he relies for the demonstration of his theory of civilization is the identity in form of, on the one hand, religion and metaphysics and, on the other hand, mental illness. Religion is for Freud a psychological alternative to neurosis and paranoia: he understands "neurosis as an individual religiosity and religion as a universal obsessional neurosis";[7] paranoia has the form of a philosophical system. With this pair of doubles, religion and madness, in view, modernity could be described with perfect economy in psychoanalytic terms as a transition from one form of narcissistic projection to another. And yet Freud believed, as we have seen, that neurosis and paranoia were by-products of the very theory of reality he was seeking to propound. 'Science' itself had brought these forms of pathology into existence. So the evidence in favor of Freud's theory, indeed its seemingly self-evident quality, depended, in fact, upon the activity of previous scientists in their struggle to secure the dominance of what Freud took to be his own theoretical framework. The circular movement is evident. Science succeeded in discrediting traditional forms of thought first by producing their psychological double in the form of madness, then confronting them with this double and conflating the two. Scientific culture stood, then, as superior to the culture of the past because it could admit its kinship with its paranoid double, while the representatives of traditional culture could not.

Freud claimed that his account of human bio-history was grounded in the observation of patients in therapy. The analysis of Adolf Grünbaum has shown that the vicious circularity I have identified in Freud's theory of modernity is also at work in his reasoning about the interpretation of clinical data.[8] It was in clinical practice that Freud placed the burden of proof for the claims of his method to scientific demonstration. He considered the measure of the validity of psychoanalytic interpretations to be their success in producing therapeutic results in his patients. Here once again, just as in Freud's historical narrative, the intervention of the scientist and the injection of his theory into practice *as an explanation* precedes the evidence supposed to confirm it. In fact, it actually produces that evidence. Given the authority that belongs to the psychoanalyst and the suggestibility of the patient, who has placed his or her trust in that authority, entering a highly charged 'transference' relationship based upon it, it is no wonder that the analyst should be able to produce in the mind of the patient a conviction of the truth of psychoanalytic dogma.[9] The persuasiveness of psychoanalytic diagnoses in the minds of patients appears still less reliable as evidence when we consider that, in Freud's own view, it was scientific culture, construed in Freud's broad manner, that had brought modernity's typical forms of mental illness into being in the first place. Their appearance among modern people, he believed, was due to the efforts of the historical forerunners of the analyst in amassing the formidable cultural authority of science.[10] What is remarkable is the scant success that psychoanalysts have enjoyed in using their expertise to remediate what they themselves think of as the destructive effects of the scientific worldview upon their patients.

At this point we might expect the skeptical reader to have accumulated a number of objections. "Freud," such a reader might protest, "attributed the emergence of neurosis and paranoia in modern culture to the destruction of the traditional ideological bases of society, and especially religion. Now, after the discoveries of Copernicus, Newton, Darwin, and their successors, was it not necessary to renounce Christian theology, the medieval cosmos, biblical chronology, and, indeed, the entire panoply of mythological explanations? And does not such a renunciation adequately account for the psychological complaints of the modern soul?"

It is impossible to disagree with the reasonable skeptic that the discoveries of Copernicus, Newton, and Darwin, among others, left the medieval cosmos and biblical chronology in shreds. We can no more regret the loss of belief in these notions than we can imagine returning to animistic spiritualism. It is easy to agree as well that the results of scientific inquiry have, in a sizable segment of the population of the West and increasingly elsewhere, undermined religious belief, and that there is in such a process an exorbitant psychological cost. But the ideologists of modernity did not limit themselves to the exposing of long-cherished errors. They exacted a renunciation greater than this: their attack eventually came to focus upon the power and integrity of thought itself. Even as they gained an immense prestige by making available unprecedented new knowledge of the workings of the physical world, they cemented their position of authority with a new model of the psyche; and this new model, in return for the promised gains of empirical science, exacted an unprecedented renunciation for the operations of thought. For the new science, truth, or 'reality' as Freud would say, became a commodity one could acquire only by subtracting the contribution of the human mind, which is to say, by repression. The new science was founded upon a suspicion of the very faculties that made it possible. It was to the codification of this ideology of suspicion, and not to science per se, that Freud made such a signal contribution.

Freud believed that the reality principle demanded heroic repressions which at first only great scientists could make. In fact, these repressions were so exorbitant that none of the theorists of modern scientific skepticism could possibly accomplish them. For in the view of Freud, the repression demanded by the worldview of science is nothing less than total. As we have seen, "The moment a man asks about the meaning and value of life, he is sick, since objectively neither has any existence."[11] Freud's diagnosis condemns all of us to the category of the mentally ill. In the light of such a diagnosis, Freud's defense of the heroism of science in its struggle against human megalomania acquires a distinctly hollow and, at the same time, paranoid aura. For if his view is correct, there is no heroism that is not paranoid, no reason for action more justifiable than a megalomaniac's delusion. The heroism of psychoanalysis lies in facing just this fact, that the products of reason are no better than a paranoia. "Repression," Freud observed in one of his early letters, "is the withholding of belief." The withholding of all belief requires, in this sense, an absolute repression.

"Very well," replies the skeptic, "perhaps it is true that scientific culture in general, and Freud in particular, maintain a heroic stance in the pursuit of knowledge, and that this heroic stance cannot be justified from within their own mode of thought. Ethical values have no justification— this is what the scientist believes, yet he goes on justifying his science, insisting that it is superior in human dignity to the illusions fostered by religion and metaphysics. When the narcissistic scientist looks into the mirror and sees his heroic face, he should recognize and acknowledge the paranoid. Instead, he insists that he is simply right. All this may be true, but it would not do to make too much of it. For the embarrassment of the scientist itself falls within the sphere of the ethical life—in other words, into that very sphere he has declared to be without meaning. If the scientist cannot free himself from this disease of meaning that he calls narcissism, this shows only that he is human. Human beings have a way of finding reasons for the unreasonable. As Nietzsche put it, human beings would rather will nothing than not to will at all. This only suggests more evidence in favor of the psychologist's claim that our irrationality is fundamental."

The resistant reader would be justified in this admonition if the inconsistency of the theorist of science were limited to considerations of the ethical, the sphere of 'meaning and value'. The heroic advocacy of science would then appear as a form of paranoia, but so would my objection to it. Each of us would be looking for ethical content in a domain of experience that the scientist understands to be mere narcissistic projection. The scientist could preserve intellectual consistency simply by admitting that the reality principle has no ethical significance whatever, and that, from an ethical standpoint, there is no reason why anyone should have bothered to discover it.

The inconsistency of the scientist, however, is not limited to that defense of the value of science which shows the narcissistic excess of his activity. For the pursuit of scientific investigation itself falls under the description of narcissism. Within the vocabulary of his discipline, Freud attempts fully to objectify the activity of the intellect, to set it at a distance, and to assess its transformations and displacements with a calculus of the irrational: the distribution of 'mental energy' is traced through 'economic' exchanges, charted by means of a 'topography', and made the subject of a 'dynamics'. We have already seen the protean flexibility of 'narcissism' as a term of analysis, how it can provide the unifying element in a drama that includes the Quixotic paranoid, the man who created him, his infatuated admirers, generations of readers, and the psychoanalyst himself. What makes this 'uncanny' effect possible is that narcissism is a general term for intellectual interest per se. It is, therefore, a piece of terminology no more precise or explanatory than a phrase like "the nature of thought." We might as well appeal to Plato's intellectual Eros, as Freud, in fact, sometimes did. The difference, of course, between thought considered in its erotic vocation for truth, as Plato considers it, and Freud's conception of narcissism is that for Freud the activity of thought can be understood almost entirely in terms of physical processes internal to the organism; its relation to truth, or the world, is secondary to this more fundamental determination. It leaves, then, no psychological or intellectual grounds for its own analytic activity. Under the auspices of neurophysiology, which studies the instrument of cognition, Freud practices a psychological reductionism that abolishes its contents, in the process denying the validity of all but a few human motives in relation to which the others remain mere forms of disguise.

"Very well, then," let our skeptic now concede, "it may be true that the most extreme and rigorous reductionists like Freud do encounter a difficulty putting forth their arguments in such a way as can stand up in the face of their own anti-intellectualist assumptions. But it does not seem that you yourself have succeeded in escaping the orbit of Freudian reductionism. For you are still using the concept of 'repression'. Whether or not the repression was caused by the findings of science or by a particular interpretation put upon those findings, the use of the term 'repression' implies an economy of intellectual energy, and such an economy can only be physical. 'Repression' is inseparable from reductive psychology."

Once again the skeptic sounds a useful warning. And upon this point it is necessary to be most clear. I am not proposing the mechanism of repression, or renunciation, as a way of explaining the visibility of paranoia in modern culture. Repression does not precede and produce the phenomenon. Rather, paranoia and repression are constituted together as part of the discourse of 'reality' upon which modern philosophical culture is based. Paranoia did not come into existence as a term until the mid-nineteenth century, but the attitude toward thinking that it implies was fundamental to the discourse of modernity from the seventeenth century onward. This discourse treats the products of thought with profound suspicion. It seeks to ground all knowledge in the evidence of the senses, but it believes that even those rudimentary instruments of experience do not provide us with a true object of knowledge. For this tradition, claims to substantial knowledge of physical objects or to objective moral knowledge gain the status of what Freud called 'projection'. To believe in them is to be, ultimately, no different from the paranoid. This attitude was understood by some of its originators—Locke and Hume in particular—to be prejudicial to the claims of science, but by the time of Freud it had become integrated into the scientific Weltanschauung he exemplifies, potently combined, strangely enough, with a faith in mechanistic explanation with which it is quite incompatible.

The concepts of paranoia and projection, therefore, are themselves instruments of repression, and that repression consists of nothing other than the psychological effects of accepting paranoia as a self-description. It is not simply that mental objects are being lost: the psyche is being asked to give up all objects, all claims to authority and truth. In its inevitable failure to do so, it is submitted to the logical and psychological stress of self-contradiction and self-frustration. Let us continue taking Freud as our example of this problem. Freud's psychology begins with a negation of thought. He reduces mental contents to the functioning of a physical Eros. This allows him to produce an account of the processes of thought that can be accepted as a physical description. But in doing so, Freud introduces into his own discourse the very paranoid logic he attempts to diagnose. The root of this logic is what we might call the reductionist's impasse. We have already encountered this phenomenon in the Freudian negation of the ethical; but the psychological implications of a general reduction of thought are so important that the matter is worth stating more fully. The reductionist wants to say that the results of thought are determined by their relation to some other form of cause besides that of logical implication. Let us assume in this case that the reduction is of the psychological, Freudian type. The reductionist argues, then, that the thinking agent is driven by motives that are irrational, unconscious, and uncontrollable, motives that can be altered only insofar as the agent needs to be engaged with his or her surroundings. Only with reference to these psychological forces can intellectual discourse be understood. But once this argument has been proposed, it too, of course, must be ascribed to irrational, unconscious, and uncontrollable motives, thus serving as its own refutation. The reductionist establishes a form of inquiry that can have brilliant results as long as it is applied to the discourse of others. But it cannot keep from turning back upon itself. It constantly encounters a single stubborn exception: like the original Narcissus, it cannot escape the reflection of its own image.

The psychological difficulties that beset the paranoid are immediately reflected in the logical impasse of reductionism. It duplicates both the paranoid's excessive claim to his own worth and his hostility toward others who refuse to accept that claim. The reductionist begins with an aggressive negation of the integrity of the thought of others, by means of this gesture resolving the very substance of discourse into elements foreign to itself. At the same time he asserts the force of his own discourse by means of this universal negation. Making a withdrawal from all intellectual commitment, he establishes illusion and error as universal structures. He inhabits, then, a world deserving of his suspicion. But when it comes to the certitude of his own claim, the reductionist makes himself an exception. His discourse must preserve its object while depriving all others of theirs. Reductionism depends upon the preservation of this inequality. In order to succeed, it must apply one method of procedure, a friendly one, to the validation of its own claims, and another, hostile method to the claims of others. By the very structure of its logic, then, it gives rise to a psychology of heroism and defensiveness, privilege and resentment, for the exceptionalism of the reductionist can never be justified, not even at the most desperate redoubt, when the heroic debunker asserts his entitlement on the basis of his ability to demystify himself. Reductive thinking divides the intellectual world into self and other, and sets them in hostility to each other. Here is the true model of the narcissistic gesture of withdrawal that Freud described as the dynamic force of progress operating in human history.

In the treacherous disequilibrium, then, of the reductionist position do we find the hazards to which the theory of paranoia provides both a description and an example. Psychoanalysis takes its character from the attempt to maintain this supremely productive self-contradiction. It is not narcissism but the theory of narcissism that creates the paranoid phenomena. Freud's paranoid unself-consciously takes his thoughts to be a part of reality. Freud too takes them to be a part of reality—not his own, but the paranoid's. Wherever he looks, the psychologist discovers that narcissism has extended its projections, in forms energetic and menacing. Such projections must then be submitted to a process of deflation and demystification equally energetic and aggressive. But the distance the analyst has opened between his own thought and that of the paranoid permits the establishing of no stable difference—only a reflection, an image of a self-image already in the negative. For the psychologist too is a narcissist. He cannot prevent himself from manifesting projections and presuppositions and narcissistic investments of his own. He is barely closer than his patients to having an unimpeded grasp upon 'reality'. His single hope is that he can bring others to accept the reality principle, which is to say, to share his dilemma on his terms. Such a venture must succeed or fail on the basis of power, prestige, and authority. So the scientist, as a last avatar of the primal father, defends his place in history, admitting at the same time that his claim to knowledge has no other motive than the selfish and unequal competition for narcissistic libido, the zero-sum game of Eros, which he believes to have been the stimulus to human progress all along.

In fairness to Freud it must be stated at this point that he explicitly disclaimed the reductionist position, insisting that the psychological motives that lead to the framing of scientific propositions have nothing to do with whether they are true or false. He maintained a researcher's faith in observation, and, though he admired Nietzsche, he resisted the temptations of Nietzsche's still more radically reductive psychology. But the psychology Freud constructed out of his observations left little place for rational deliberation. Such reason as we can sustain within ourselves comes from a tenuous balance of irrational elements. Our ego remains a servant to the unconscious, and human fate lies more in the determinations of our inner workings than in relation to the outside world, which engages our interest largely in response to the promptings of desire. We are all sick, deluded, frustrated. The aberrations of the neurotic and the paranoid merely show us our own tendencies exaggerated and clarified. What appears to be caricature in them is actually the truest image of the human situation.

Freud did not hesitate to draw the reductionist implications of his findings. He believed that philosophy would have to recognize the new relation between mind and body that the discovery of the unconscious had brought into relief. He also believed that the character of philosophy made it peculiarly susceptible to psychoanalytic interpretation:

Philosophical theories and systems have been the work of a small number of men of striking individuality. In no other science does the personality of the scientific worker play anything like so large a part as in philosophy. And now for the first time psycho-analysis enables us to construct a 'psychography' of a personality. It teaches us to recognize the affective units—the complexes dependent on instincts—whose presence is to be presumed in each individual, and it introduces us to the study of the transformations and end-products arising from these instinctual forces. It reveals the relations of a person's constitutional disposition and the events of his life to the achievements open to him owing to his peculiar gifts. It can conjecture with more or less certainty from an artist's work the intimate personality that lies behind it. In the same way, psycho-analysis can indicate the subjective and individual motives behind philosophical theories which have ostensibly sprung from impartial logical work, and can draw a critic's attention to the weak spots in the system. It is not the business of psycho-analysis, however, to undertake such criticism itself, for, as may be imagined, the fact that a theory is psychologically determined does not in the least invalidate its scientific truth.[12]

This description of 'psychography' contains Freud's most ambitious claim to the power of diagnosing other intellectuals through their creations. At the same time, Freud recognizes a modest and judicious limit when he observes that there is one process by which psychoanalysis scrutinizes a philosophical system for its symptomatic significance and another by which the intellectual significance of the 'system' must be assessed. The problem with this seemingly reasonable division of labor, however, is that the coherence and self-consistency that make a system a system are the very characteristics that signal the determinations of 'narcissism' or the 'pleasure principle'. If these characteristics can be accounted for entirely on a psychological basis, there seems little need for a further application to reality: "A system is best characterized by the fact that at least two reasons can be discovered for each of its products: a reason based upon the premises of the system *(a reason, then, which may be delusional)* and a concealed reason, which we must judge to be the truly operative and the real one" (emphasis added).[13] Such statements leave no doubt that the "truly operative and real" reasons are the psychological ones. The rest are pretexts.

Freud had no hesitation about consigning religion, myth, metaphysics— all of past culture, in other words—to the categories of unconscious wish-fulfillment, superstition, illusion, and paranoia:

In point of fact I believe that a large part of the mythological view of the world, which extends a long way into the most modern religions, is nothing but psychology projected into the external world. The obscure recognition (the endopsychic perception, as it were) of psychical factors and relations in the unconscious is mirrored— it is difficult to express it in other terms, and there the analogy with paranoia must come to our aid—in the construction of a supernatural reality, which is destined to be changed back once more by science into the psychology of the unconscious. One could venture to explain in this way the myths of paradise and the fall of man, of God, of good and evil, or immortality, and so on, and to transform metaphysics into metapsychology. The gap between the paranoic's displacement and that of the superstitious person is less wide than it appears at first sight.[14]

Transforming metaphysics into metapsychology so that its kinship with superstition and paranoia can be recognized—it would be hard to achieve a neater formulation of the psychoanalyst's project than that. There are some qualifying phrases. Freud refers to "a large part of the mythological view of the world," not all of it. But we have already seen that he is willing to draw very few real limits to the scope of psychoanalytic power. The unconscious has a structural integrity, a wholeness and completeness of its own that *mirrors*, as Freud says, that of mythological thought. The reader will recall that Freud credited animism with having embodied the most complete system of explanation because it provided the most perfect reflection of the psychological. Part of his intention was to make it evident that there are no intellectual structures standing outside the field of narcissistic projection. All must be "transformed into metapsychology," transformed, that is, in a way that provides the original ideas with new contents which utterly change their meaning and relation to reality. The reductive ambition of psychoanalysis respects no limits at all.[15] For its 'narcissistic' gaze, two complete worlds, of mind and reality, mirror each other with a mutually ironizing reflection.

What we have in the theory of psychoanalysis is the example of a discourse so radically suspicious that it admits no grounds for its own authority. Yet it goes on, in grandiose, paranoid style, asserting its authority nonetheless. Psychoanalysis, then, undergoes the vicissitudes of its own self-negation, vicissitudes which, though they may be of an abstract and logical kind, lead us quickly to the problems of social authority, of our relations to the past and to each other. The social and historical implications range far beyond the issues of method in social science, extending into the domain of our psychological experience itself. As I will show in a later chapter, Freudian science could draw upon deep reserves of suspicion at the heart of modern culture, not only in the scientific method but in modern views of philosophy, history, and politics. Long before Freud, modern intellectuals had been living out the contradictions he articulated in his theory and suffering the consequences of an excessively suspicious view of the world.

THREE

Paranoid Psychology

> After all, you are psychoanalysis in person!
> —Sándor Ferenczi to Freud

Recent thinking about the psychology of paranoia has tended strongly to discourage Freud's contention that it has a single cause or represents a single condition. 'Paranoia' now accompanies a broad range of conditions, rarely, if ever, occurring in a pure form. The range begins with people who have rigid and suspicious personalities yet function more or less successfully in society, and extends to psychotic patients with megalomaniacal or messianic delusions. Diagnostic terms stretch from mere 'paranoid personality' to 'schizophrenia, paranoid type'.[1] Paranoia is "a *syndrome:* a constellation of symptoms which tend to occur together but which can be caused by many different factors and can even be seen as a secondary accompaniment of other illnesses, such as organic diseases."[2] Paranoia may develop in relatively normal people in times of stress or depression. It is best understood as a 'slant',[3] an 'outlook', a 'style', a 'mode of thinking'.[4] It can be usefully placed in a typology alongside other 'neurotic styles': the 'obsessive-compulsive', the 'hysteric', 'the impulsive'.[5] Most paranoids manage to hold jobs and to conceal their condition much of the time. They are no more likely to be found in an asylum than in society, where they may exert considerable influence:

The paranoid individual may significantly affect the course of history itself, as did Hitler and [John Wilkes] Booth. He may be involved in many areas of the community: obstreperous citizen, cunning politician, delusional clergyman with excessive religiosity. His influence may be as calamitous as that of the paranoid assassin or as subtle as that of the embittered office worker who feels mistreated and plants seeds of discontent in his co-workers. There may be no adverse effects; the researcher who is actively delusional may be able to perform scientific experiments with great skill and perhaps may even be aided by the withdrawal of social contact which gives him ample time to spend in the laboratory.[6]

Taking up this flexible application of the term 'paranoia', it will not be necessary to equate Freudian psychology strictly with any form of psychosis, but merely to see that it represents an example of the 'paranoid slant' in its most elaborate and self-conscious form. In the work of Freud, paranoia achieves the status of a worldview with its own self-generating logic, building upon the already well-developed trend of suspicion in modern culture—that culture which, in proclaiming itself to be modern, defines itself in suspicious rejection of the past. If the argument of the foregoing chapter is correct, the psychological description of paranoia is itself both a symptom and a cause of suspicion. Freud's own involvement with the theory exceeded any ordinary sense of intellectual commitment. In fact there is reason to suspect, as E. M. Thornton has argued, that Freud's personal paranoia went well beyond a mere 'paranoid slant', that it involved psychotic distortions of reality. If Thornton is correct, Freud's paranoia had a physical cause: his addiction to cocaine.[7] Thus to the logical vicissitudes of reductive thinking and the cultural momentum of suspicion we might add the somatic and psychological effects of cocaine addiction. While I emphasize primarily the first and second of these causes, the third should nevertheless be kept in mind.

Besides expanding the categories of paranoid behavior, later analysis has also enriched the description of paranoid thinking and thus will be of help as we move from our analysis of the intellectual origins of the paranoid worldview to the manifestation of its characteristic symptoms in the discourse of psychoanalysis and the scientific persona of Freud. David Swanson and his collaborators[8] identify seven fundamental characteristics:

1. *Projection*. This is the "sine qua non of the paranoid mode" (8). Projection is the mistaking of one's own mental states for external reality. The formulation is essentially Freud's, closely linked with the concept of narcissism. Swanson gives the favorite Freudian example of primitive animism, in which objects are thought of as having "good souls," to illustrate this tendency of thought (10). Paranoids project their self-critical tendencies outward onto others, seeing them as aggressive and threatening. Unable to accept blame, they prefer to accuse others of their own faults.

2. *Hostility*. The paranoid sees the world around him as fundamentally hostile, and his conviction that this is so makes him sensitive to every apparent slight or trace of animus directed his way. Naturally, his attitude ensures that the world around him will cooperate with his delusions by responding negatively to his rigid, defensive behavior.

3. *Suspicion.* The paranoid is hyperalert, fully mobilized at all times to defend himself against threat. He loses his appreciation for the normal social context by scanning it constantly for hints of malice, transforming his environment into a manifold of signs: "His interest is not in the apparent world, but in the world behind the apparent world, to which the apparent world only gives clues. Thus, the subject matter of his interest has to do with hidden motives, underlying purposes, special meanings, and the like. He does not necessarily disagree with the normal person about the existence of any fact; he disagrees only about its significance."[9] Paranoia is fundamentally, as Freud put it, an "interpretative delusion."[10]

4. *Centrality.* The paranoid senses that all eyes are focused upon him. He assumes that the people around him are as much preoccupied with him as he is with them. He frequently makes errors of *reference*, supposing that remarks innocently directed elsewhere are actually about him.

5. *Delusions.* The delusions of paranoids tend to have a stable, systematic character. They may contain a grain of truth and often considerable plausibility, making this condition proverbially the most methodical madness (16).

6. *Loss of Autonomy.* The paranoid is obsessed with controlling his own actions and reactions, and he fears the interference of others. The sense of being controlled by forces outside oneself, often malign or hostile supernatural powers, is a major tendency of paranoid delusion.[11]

7. *Grandiosity.* The paranoid tends to exaggerate the sense of his own power and worth. Many observers take this as a form of compensation for a more fundamental sense of inferiority.

As we now take up the subject of Freud's intellectual stance and personality as they are revealed in his theory, in his attitude toward his colleagues, his opponents, and the world at large, we shall see that each of these symptoms, with the possible exception of delusion, is abundantly evident. It may seem surprising, to begin with, that the founder of psychoanalysis should be thought guilty of the cardinal sin of *projection,* for did he not extend suspicion even to his own thoughts and motives? Partisans of psychoanalysis will tell us that this was his greatest achievement. But is it not rather the case that this suspicion, and the profound hostility that underlies it, was the very substance of Freud's great projection? The fact that Freudian suspicion respects no limit, the fact that it is total, betrays its projective, non-empirical character, to use the Freudian vocabulary, or, stated more broadly, betrays that it is a product of compulsive rhetoric and personal imperative rather than observation. From this derives the nihilating, aprioristic simplicity that, in the thought of others, Freud habitually diagnoses as the sign of projection and 'secondary revision'. For the psychoanalytic mind, nothing is what it seems. Every human act must be reduced within the code of suspicion.

Employing the theory of narcissism, with its properly 'uncanny' power, Freud keeps in play the freedom of the mind to master the world around it while acknowledging nothing beyond its own reflection. Whereas the narcissistic consciousness of religion or metaphysics sees itself positively reflected in the world that it 'projects', the Freudian recognizes the reflection of his wishes with mistrust. For both, nevertheless, the play of such wishes is coextensive with the psychological domain itself, which means that the psychoanalyst can master this domain without having to surrender attention to anything that is foreign to his own sense of order and desire. All he has to do is to reverse the significance of each symptom of mental life, unmasking each pretense of idealism and bringing to light its subterranean connections with Eros and aggression. The interpretive force of suspicion cannot be resisted; it is a holistic 'presupposition', as Freud would say; there is nothing in the mental life that it cannot translate into its proper terms. It never fails to discover in the behavior of others the charm of self-delusion, the mistaking of desire for reality, and the temptation to credit the honesty of conscious motives. It never fails to recognize itself. No counter-evidence can discourage it because there is no single detail that can resist being translated into its code of suspicion. Narcissism is universal. So, in its mastery of the full range of narcissistic projections, psychoanalysis creates a universe of suspicion no less extensive and satisfying to the mind's reflected glory, and no less persuasive for its internal coherence, than those forms of culture it credits to the 'omnipotence of thoughts'. For good reason, Freud recognized the kinship between the animist and the psychoanalyst. Both capitalized upon the human capacity for self-infatuation.

The totalizing power of suspicion is a formidable weapon in the hands of a rhetorician like Freud, who has the skill to evoke in his readers an immediate sense of self-recognition. He asks that we reinterpret our actions in an ironic and suspicious light, but in return we experience a thrill of comprehension. We derive a sense of mastery even in recognizing the nature of our unfreedom. It is no slight to Freud's rhetorical gifts, furthermore, to recognize that suspicion is the most contagious of all attitudes next to simple fear, and that paranoia is the one communicable mental disease.

The triumph of Freudian rhetoric was made all the easier because psychology, more than any other science, admits the hazards of suggestion. It seeks to illuminate the workings of an instrument of which all of us can have but one example directly in view. Of this example, we are the sole observer, which makes it so much the more striking to us when another can seem to anticipate our inner experience. And when it comes to judging whether or not the theory in question adequately accounts for the functioning of our mental instrument, we must use that very same instrument to determine the outcome. Only careful controls make it possible for scientific research to succeed in the face of these difficulties. But psychoanalysis relies for its confirmation not upon controlled experiment but upon success in the therapeutic situation. Its practitioners themselves undergo therapy before taking up the work of analysis, so that their first confirming experiences of the treatment have to do with their own symptoms, anxieties, and problems. For these reasons, it is by no means evident that the people who make this form of therapy a daily pursuit are more likely to evaluate the theory in an objective light than the general public.

The fact that Freudian suspicion has the simplifying appeal of a projection helps to illuminate one of the central psychoanalytic myths—the myth that an intellectual commitment to psychoanalysis demands a libidinal sacrifice. One of Freud's assumptions is that the psychoanalyst differs from the paranoid in being able to rechannel his narcissistic libido into scientific investigation, or to achieve simple renunciations, whereas the paranoid, unable to cope with his repressed desire, regresses to a primitive, narcissistic state. Paranoids "love their delusions as they love themselves. That is the secret," Freud once wrote, the implication being that, for such natures, self-love comes before the attachment to reality.[12] This is where the scientist is superior, in his renunciation: thus Freud's strange boast to Sándor Ferenczi, "I have succeeded where the paranoiac fails."[13] Here is one regard, then, in which Freud insists upon a distance between the scientist and the paranoid. But history has not borne out Freud's view that embracing psychoanalysis requires psycho-erotic, or 'narcissistic', renunciation. Even though psychoanalytic doctrine exacts a drastic form of intellectual repression, it nevertheless seems to make some kind of satisfying psychological return. For contrary to psychoanalytic dogma, the movement has commanded an attraction for the popular mind, a depth of commitment among its adherents, and a level of acceptance among intellectuals all of which exceed what is justified by the scientific validation of the theory. Taken in broad strokes it seems to be, for many people, a compelling, almost irresistible body of doctrine. Those who believe it vastly outnumber those who understand it. It is the allure, the charisma of psychoanalysis that needs to be explained, not the imaginary resistance it evokes.[14] And there seems no better way to explain this allure than to recognize its profound appeal to the mind's sense of what should be.

Freud's theory offers, then, after all of his disclaimers, the same pleasure and attraction he imputed to the religious and philosophical systems he mocked; psychoanalysis and metaphysics cannot be distinguished upon psychological grounds. But it would be negligent of the character of psychoanalysis to portray its sole appeal as that of philosophical generality. Psychoanalysis can legitimately claim to have brought its gaze to the level of everyday life. And here we see the full, paranoid development of the *interpretive system of suspicion.* For no aspect of behavior is too trivial for its consideration: in the most trivial signs it finds the deepest significance. Nothing can be too small, or too large, for its attention: dreams, jokes, works of art, neuroses and psychoses, totemism and religion, group psychology, civilization itself—Freud reinterpreted the entire range of human experience. Inheriting a culture that had stripped the world of significance, he discovered a new kind of significance in every aspect of life that had ever once had a meaning. This is what gives psychoanalysis what Ernest Gellner called its "world-filling exhaustiveness."[15] Even superstition turns out to hold a certain psychological truth.[16] For the psychology of the unconscious, nothing is accidental. The unconscious is original providence. The significance that it conceals is not a true design but the need for design, not an ideal that dominates appetite but a necessary and pragmatic urge to conceal raw appetite and selfishness from our fellow human beings and from ourselves—to patch up the gaps of the world with the tattered rags of philosophy (to paraphrase one of Freud's favorite lines of Heine).[17] It is our need for disguise that justifies suspicion, psychoanalysis tells us, and our fear of knowing this truth that makes it profound.

In a rare moment when Freud was attempting to restrain his tendency toward mistrust, he confessed that "the psychoanalytic habit of drawing important conclusions from small signs is . . . difficult to overcome."[18] To comprehend the depth of Freud's habit-forming science of suspicion, and with it the microscopic focus of its scrutiny, it is enough simply to recall the subjects treated in the first ten chapters of *The Psychopathology of Everyday Life:* The Forgetting of Proper Names; The Forgetting of Foreign Words; The Forgetting of Names and Sets of Words; Childhood Memories and Screen Memories; Slips of the Tongue; Misreadings and Slips of the

Pen; The Forgetting of Impressions and Intentions; Bungled Actions; Symptomatic and Chance Actions; and Errors. Freud taught us in these chapters to discover the aggressive, self-serving motives that were so boldly and conspicuously displayed in the heroic origins of human culture, now still at work in every stray and covert motion of the intellect. Inadvertency, ignorance, failure in this view are never insignificant but, rather, signs for the adept. It is a strip tease of the unconscious: "Every change in the clothing usually worn, every small sign of carelessness—such as an unfastened button—every trace of exposure, is intended to express something which the wearer of the clothes does not want to say straight out and for which he is for the most part unaware."[19] A slip of the tongue avoids a shameful topic; a forgotten word leads back by association to some narcissistically wounding idea; a broken appointment conceals a hidden reluctance out of vanity or greed, an accidental injury a self-punitive or superstitiously sacrificial wish; even randomly chosen numbers hold a secret significance. How many of Freud's minor errors does he trace to his own greediness for fees or scientific credit (205)!

Paranoia hardly seems an aberration in this context, and Freud, as usual, does not deny the resemblance between his own operations and those of the paranoid. Rather, he gives generous credit to paranoid insight:

A striking and generally observed feature of the behaviour of paranoics is that they attach the greatest significance to the minor details of other people's behaviour which we ordinarily neglect, interpret them and make them the basis of far-reaching conclusions. . . . The category of what is accidental and requires no motivation, in which the normal person includes a part of his own psychical performances and parapraxes, is thus rejected by the paranoic as far as the psychical manifestations of other people are concerned. Everything he observes in other people is full of significance, everything can be interpreted. How does he reach this position? Probably here as in so many similar cases he projects on to the mental life of other people what is unconsciously present in his own. In paranoia many sorts of things force their way through to consciousness whose presence in the unconscious of normal and neurotic people we can demonstrate only through psycho-analysis. In a certain sense, therefore, the paranoic is justified in this, for he recognizes something that escapes the normal person: he sees more clearly than someone of normal intellectual capacity, but the displacement on to other people of the state of affairs which he recognizes renders his knowledge worthless. (255–56)

The paranoid applies to others the suspicion that he, in his grandiose delusion, so thoroughly deserves. And Freud knows that all of us actually deserve this suspicion, for none of us is truly different from the paranoid. And once Freud has given us this insight—possessed in a worthless form by the paranoid, in scientific form by himself—we are ready to recognize the common egocentrism of humanity and to share the paranoid's suspicion in all of its exquisitely detailed and systematic elaboration. The passage I have quoted speaks for itself. What Freud says of the paranoid would be true of Freud if only we were to substitute for the paranoid's projection of unconscious knowledge the psychoanalyst's conscious and deliberately contrived self-conception, which leads him to recognize in his own behavior and those of others only that which is worthy of suspicion.[20] And for the psychoanalyst, of course, everything we do is worthy of suspicion, except for those actions that are overtly selfish, violent, or libidinally driven. These things alone can be trusted to present their true aspect to the observer.

With such an attitude toward individual human beings, how threatening must humankind appear to Freud in the mass. In his ingenious case histories, like the analysis of "Dora" or of the "Wolf Man," he exercised the interpretive instruments of psychoanalysis to decode complexes of symbols and motives that could never have been uncovered, or imagined, by the patients themselves. These narratives compel by strangeness and complexity. The unconscious imitates the movements of a tragic fate, turning every evasion of the will to its own use, with results both pitiful and fearful. But when it moves from the Oedipal genre, the analysis of individual minds and fates, to the life of social institutions and the emotional sources upon which they depend, the Freudian narrative becomes a simple morality play. Here the paranoid's *hostility toward the workings of society* is fully developed and justified. Every appearance of good must be exposed as unconscious hypocrisy, every commitment to public interests and to social institutions must be recognized for what it is—a disguise for narcissistic gratification or a painful instinctual concession. To go beneath the surface of social existence and convert each appearance to its opposite, to demystify every claim of social value, hauling it up from the depths of collective delusion onto the horizon of analysis, this method gives to Freudian science its simple and dramatic appeal. With respect to the idealized aspects of culture, the method achieves its most glamorously paradoxical results. Here is Freud, for instance, on the psychological origins of social justice:

What appears later on in society in the shape of *Gemeingeist, esprit de corps,* 'group spirit', etc., does not belie its derivation from what was originally envy. No one must want to put himself forward, everyone must be the same and have the same. Social justice means that we deny ourselves many things so that others may have to do without them as well, or, what is the same thing, may not be able to ask for them. This demand for equality is the root of social conscience and the sense of duty. It reveals itself unexpectedly in the syphilitic's dread of infecting other people, which psycho-analysis has taught us to understand. The dread exhibited by these poor wretches corresponds to their violent struggles against the unconscious wish to spread their infection on to other people; for why should they alone be infected and cut off from so much? why not other people as well? And the same germ is to be found in the apt story of the judgement of Solomon. If one woman's child is dead, the other shall not have a live one either. The bereaved woman is recognized by this wish.

Thus social feeling is based upon the reversal of what was first a hostile feeling into a positively-toned tie in the nature of an identification.[21]

It is in passages like this that Freud's programmatic intentions become clear. Only on the level of the individual can the true motives of human behavior be understood. Adherence to the social is a disguise: the good for human beings lies in private satisfaction alone. Social commitments depend upon paradoxical transformations of selfishness into harmony, greed into generosity, society being held together by illusions of justice and solidarity that benefit the strong and gratify the resentment of the weak. The portrait of the syphilitic tormented by an unconscious spite that can make its way into consciousness only as a painful form of altruism, this is suspicion taken to a level of daring that must be considered marvelous. Freud's conviction that social life consists of nothing beyond such self-punishing distortions of aggression leads to an outlook identical with paranoia. The syphilitic altruist is unforgettable, but perhaps Freud's midrash on the judgment of Solomon stretches credulity even further; for surely it is by a strange logic that, of the three adult characters in the story, the bitter and resentful bereaved becomes the example of the social spirit, while the mother's willingness to sacrifice must in the end be attributed, I suppose, to a narcissistic investment in her own child.

There is only one fact that keeps psychoanalytic suspicion from reaching the elevation of paranoid psychosis—the fact that the psychoanalyst, unlike the full-blown paranoid, does not entirely exempt himself from the domain of suspicion. His suspicion does not rest on private grounds: it ascends to the level of the universal. The psychoanalyst is thus, in a sense, even more suspicious than the paranoid, less restricted in the form of his projection, so that it returns upon himself. He recognizes his own narcissistic character, his own false idealism and ambitious motives, as well as those of others. He sees himself as being dominated and driven by an other, an unconscious, which he recognizes as his true self, making the polite, idealistic character of his social persona admittedly a disguise. Yet, by the peculiar logic of suspicion, the analyst turns these recognitions into an advantage for his theory and another source of its grandiose appeal. He portrays human consciousness as an ironized form of heroism, or narcissism, yet the very acceptance of the irony implicit in the Freudian concept of narcissism is itself a test of strength. In the bravery of self-recognition, of self-suspicion, it turns back toward the truly heroic. Ironic heroism becomes heroic irony.

Psychoanalysis proposes itself as an audacious investigation that begins in renouncing and ends in vanquishing all forms of idealizing consciousness. The spirit of quest and conquest energizes all of Freud's writing. To see it we need look no further than the Virgilian motto at the head of *The Interpretation of Dreams*: "If I cannot move the upper regions, then I will move the lower."[22] Freud particularly liked the metaphor of the depths, the underworld, to signify the adventurous territory of psychoanalytic research. By taking us into the depths, the analyst forces us to a double acknowledgment. First, confronted with the denizens of the unconscious, we are forced to acknowledge what we are not: we are not the bearers of angelic intelligence, beings of reason, as our narcissism prompts us to believe. At the root of mental activity lies not the spirit but the sexual drive and its instinctual rivals. In its negative force, the "blows to human megalomania" administered by psychoanalysis show a likeness in form to those earlier blows Freud attributed to Copernicus and Darwin. But this is just the first. Psychoanalysis bids us, now, to confront what we are. It shows us in the mechanism of the unconscious the origins of all of our narcissistic projections—projections of heroism, of meaning, of beauty and divinity. Once we have accepted that they are such, mere symptoms of self-infatuation, we must endure the further humiliation of realizing that there is no way to escape from them. The cosmos built up by a primitive narcissistic imagination remains within us, an interior cosmos, still vital with its charge of sexual energy and still exercising its sway over the direction of our efforts. It is the difficulty of these recognitions that gives heroic force, or, rather, paranoiac *grandiosity*, to the psychoanalytic worldview. This difficulty is also what gives value to psychoanalysis as a therapy, for only with a guide like Freud could ordinary souls make the Virgilian journey to the inner underworld and face the private demons of that place.[23]

It is essential to psychoanalytic heroism that the distinction it claims is almost entirely of a relative character. A claim to genuine heroism, to high motives and enduring values, would, according to its way of thinking, be a relapse into narcissism and unself-conscious delusion. Solely in relation to the weakness and naiveté of others can the psychoanalytic hero feel the exhilaration of his self-exalting irony. The ultimate value of his knowledge lies in the superior strength that it demands. It was his sense of the great significance of comparative strength in the realm of inquiry that gave opportunity for Freud's constantly grandiose, heroic postures. Here we must enter the consideration of Freud's own personality.

Long before he brought psychoanalysis into existence, Freud struggled with his need for heroic admiration. From the period of his engagement to Martha Bernays, he was looking forward to the attention of his biographers, who would write the story of "The Development of the Hero." [24] The young Freud found it difficult to cope with the recognition that he might not be a genius, and could be heartened to have his friend Breuer recognize his inner resolve: "He told me he had discovered that hidden under the surface of timidity there lay in me an extremely daring and fearless human being. I had always thought so, but never dared tell anyone." [25] Arriving at his theory of the unconscious, Freud was jubilant to pronounce himself the "conquistador." Through all of the struggles with his errant followers, his need to prove his heroic nature only increased; thus he wrote to Ferenczi toward the end of the World War, "I am still the giant." [26] As much as any paranoid, Freud identified himself, in his nature and in his intellectual form of daring, with the most exalted figures of history: the biblical Joseph, [27] Moses, [28] Oedipus, [29] Alexander the Great, Hannibal, [30] William the Conqueror, Columbus, Leonardo, Copernicus, Kepler, Cromwell, Danton, Napoleon, Garibaldi, Darwin, Bismarck, and, inadvertently, even Zeus. This was the company in which he habitually posed. [31]

Yet beneath all of Freud's self-aggrandizement there was a powerful and gnawing sense of inferiority and of thwarted ambition, a sense of being resisted and disliked. During his studies with Charcot in Paris, he oscillated between grandeur and desperation. "I consider it a great misfortune," he wrote to his fiancée, "that nature has not granted me that indefinite something which attracts people. I believe it is this lack which has deprived me of a rosy existence. It has taken me so long to win my friends. I have had to struggle so long for my precious girl, and every time I meet someone I realize that an impulse, which defies analysis, leads that person to underestimate me. This may be a question of expression or temperament, or some other secret of nature, but whatever it may be it affects one deeply." [32] Freud repeated the sentiment twenty years later to Carl Jung:

"You are better fitted for propaganda," he wrote to his collaborator, "for I have always felt that there is something about my personality, my ideas and manner of speaking, that people find strange and repellent, whereas all hearts are open to you."[33]

Freud's defensive stance had a powerful effect upon psychoanalysis as an institution, giving rise to a peculiar, hermetic form of social organization.[34] Its unusual exclusivity and cultishness reflected Freud's hostile and suspicious attitude toward the world at large. Psychoanalysis became in his hands both a theory of the psyche and a separate scientific movement. Its dual nature made it a unique development in modern scientific culture: Freud and his followers repudiated the ecumenical tradition of science carried down from the Enlightenment.[35] The Psychoanalytic Association was a throwback to the esoteric form of the ancient philosophical academies.[36] Almost from the beginning of psychoanalysis, its founders had recourse to a canon of dogma with the primacy of the libido at its center. Adherence to this dogma separated initiates from the opposing professional community. The exceptionalist and schismatic character of the movement made it susceptible to schisms within its own ranks and led to the fortification of an ever more rigid and defensive orthodoxy. In 1913, after the defection of Jung, Freud's "anointed . . . successor and crown prince,"[37] had shattered the morale of the movement, Freud's English disciple Ernest Jones proposed a secret committee to be established around the person of the master in order to ease the burdens of leadership.[38] Freud was so much taken with the scheme that he suspected it to be a forgotten idea of his own.

"The Committee" was to be held together with bonds of special loyalty. Each of its members promised to share research and responsibility with the leader; each promised as well not to depart from the central teachings of psychoanalysis without discussing his doubts with the others. Jones imagined that such bonds would overcome the normal psychological difficulties that inhibit group cooperation. The members would "purge away all excrescences of the theory . . . to coordinate our own unconscious aims with the demands and interests of the movement." The Committee would thus have the unity of a single self. "Like the Paladins of Charlemagne," he wrote Freud, its members would "guard the kingdom and policy of their master."[39] Freud celebrated the first meeting of The Committee by giving each of the members a Greek intaglio from his collection, which they then had mounted on rings in imitation of the intaglio of Jupiter worn by their leader. Both Freud and Jones recognized that this was a "boyish" and "romantic" form of behavior. But this did not restrain their enthusiasm. Freud's immediate concern was that "First of all: This committee would have to be *strictly secret* in its existence and in its actions."[40] The self-glorifying and suspicious attitude that produced the Psychoanalytic Association and The Committee proved, like other, intellectual elements of Freudian paranoia, to be self-confirming and self-sustaining. The grandiosity of Freud, Jones, and the others may seem comical and quixotic, but there is no evidence that they saw it in that way.

The founders of psychoanalysis made Freud's theory the basis of an exclusive intellectual and professional commitment with special rituals of initiation; they also employed psychoanalytic theory to explain the world's supposed reluctance to give psychoanalysis an immediate hero's welcome. This reluctance was largely imaginary.[41] In fact, Freud 'projected', in the most uncomplicated sense of the term, his own hostility onto the surrounding intellectual community, imagining that it was peculiarly enraged by his findings. It is an obvious example of paranoid *centrality*. In the mythology of psychoanalysis, the imaginary hostility of the medical establishment was explained through the doctrine of resistance, which held that the repression of libido in the majority of human beings made the theory of libido itself a source of anxiety and thus a cause of resentment. This doctrine gave the early Freudians the advantage of being able to interpret the motives of anyone who might disagree with them. The ire of critics could be cited as proof of the intensity of unconscious repression applied to sexuality, the incredulity of unbelievers as evidence of an unwillingness to endure the wounds to human narcissism exacted by the Freudian system. Even slips of the tongue could be turned against unwitting opponents. The fact that psychoanalysis was greeted with hostility in some quarters was taken to prove that the universal tendency of humankind was to resist its teachings. The lapsing away of prominent disciples illustrated the difficulty of living with these hard truths. Heretics were pitied as weaklings unable to face up to the power of the unconscious, unable to keep themselves from disguising it with it some pale reflection of the ego.[42] And so the embattled internal history of psychoanalysis, combined with a myth of external resistance, became part of the empirical evidence for the validity of Freudian thinking in a way that could never have arisen with a theory generated in the normal research environment. The doctrine of resistance seemed to have been designed as much for polemical as for analytic purposes. Psychoanalysis came to stand for the unconscious itself: the more its imperatives were repressed, the more powerful it seemed to become. The self-confirming value that could be derived from the history of the movement as a

cultural scandal led Freud to perpetuate in retrospect the myth of his early
reception and the extremity of his early isolation. With the doctrine of
resistance, he had successfully imported into science the style of the avant-
garde, which feeds upon the appearance of rejection, outrage, and the
breach of bourgeois manners. His "movement" represents the most potent
and long-lasting of all the self-advertising cultural provocations of the early
twentieth century.[43]

Science was the one form of heroism toward which Freud never gave a
hint of suspicion. He was aware, of course, of the treachery that can
motivate claims of difficulty: "Perhaps men simply pronounce that what is
more difficult is higher, and their pride is merely their narcissism aug-
mented by the consciousness of a difficulty overcome."[44] So he explains
the appeal of religious renunciation. It was an insight that, uncharacteristi-
cally, he refrained from applying to himself. Instead, he asserted his
superiority over those who could not accept the hard truths of psychoanalytic orthodoxy.

It must be admitted, though, that whatever benefits the heroic myth
of the founder may have provided to the psychoanalytic movement, the
renunciations that he exacted even from his adherents proved to be exorbi-
tantly great. For Freud's truly paranoid obsession with his autonomy and
originality as an investigator proved to be a constantly divisive element. All
signs among his followers of reluctance to agree with Freud had to be
explained by means of the suspicious logic of the unconscious, revealing
father complexes, narcissistic resistance, or Oedipal hostility, depending
upon the stage Freud's theory had reached.[45] Of one of his adherents,
Freud remarked, "I cannot stand the parricidal look in his eyes."[46]
Disagreement with Freud became a form of psychopathology, and members of the movement were adept at exposing the secret springs of all such
transgressions.[47] The practice of self-interested diagnoses continues among
analysts to this day.[48]

No wonder, then, that so many of the most gifted early psychoanalysts
found themselves unable to continue under these humiliating terms. Freud
had to be the master. It was an imperative of his personality, as he was
well aware, and he did not often choose to resist it. In *The Psychopathology
of Everyday Life*, written before the earliest beginnings of organized psychoanalysis, he reveals that "there is scarcely any group of ideas to which I
feel so antagonistic as that of being someone's protégé . . . the role of the
favourite child is one which is very little suited indeed to my character. I
have always felt an unusually strong urge 'to be the strong man myself.' "

The paranoid requires a perfect autonomy. Of the episode that provoked this remark—an episode in which Freud discovered one of his own heroic projections contaminating the data of analysis—he goes on to note that it is "a good illustration of the way in which the relation to one's own self, which is normally kept back, but which emerges victoriously in paranoia, disturbs and confuses us in our objective view of things."[49] The paranoid within can only be a leader, never a follower. This was how Freud at the height of his power thought of his own relation to others. He had to be the primal father, yet he wondered why his disciples often could not accept his title. As he complained to Abraham, "All my life I have been looking for friends who would not exploit and then betray me."[50]

Freud often derided his collaborators, but he did not want to meet his like among them. In a letter of congratulation to the Viennese writer Arthur Schnitzler, whose form of psychological intelligence had often been compared with his own, Freud speculated that the reason they had never met, though living in the same city, was that Freud was afraid to encounter his Doppelgänger.[51] It was a telling example in the genre of the psychoanalytic compliment: Freud flattered Schnitzler in a self-congratulatory way by asserting the likeness between them, while assuming that this likeness would naturally produce a rivalry.[52] The delusion of the double, it is interesting to note, is a concomitant of paranoia from which Freud on one occasion actually suffered in hallucinatory form.[53]

It is one of the greatest ironies of the psychoanalytic phenomenon that Freud should have based his defense of the cultural value of science upon its ability to overcome the 'over-estimation of thoughts', yet his most egregious failing was in his difficulty establishing the boundary between thought and reality. His absurd exaggeration of hysteria as the cause of physical symptoms, and, indeed, his complete distrust of his patients' understanding of their own experience continues to have clinical consequences to this day.[54] Yet the founder of psychoanalysis was himself by no means free of the tendency to let his obsessively charged preoccupations alter his view of the world around him. He was the victim, for instance, of morbid superstitions and was particularly plagued by significant numbers.[55] The scientist who believed that it was impossible to pick a number at random without there being some subliminal motive for the choice nevertheless could not keep himself from believing that the numbers that appeared around him portended some special significance related to his fears of imminent death.[56] But it was not in numbers, those "persistent persecutors," that Freud found the most threatening reflections of his own intellectual activity; it was in the developments from his theoretical vocabulary made by his own colleagues, developments that frequently looked to the suspicious master like hostile urges in the direction of originality. The need to maintain control over the body of thought known as psychoanalysis presented Freud with the greatest difficulty. His entire career was beset with controversies about plagiarism and originality.[57] There was a constant anxiety about what was his and what was not. And although Freud claimed that others' ideas were of no use to him unless they came at a time when he was ready for them, he proved enormously susceptible to their influence and even noted his own tendency to 'cryptamnesia', by which he 'unconsciously' contrived to forget his intellectual debts.[58] He even came to believe that thoughts can be transferred from one mind to another not only unconsciously but by telepathy![59]

Freud was constantly uneasy with those who pursued the science he had brought into being, and all of his relationships with his followers seem to have involved either a struggle or an open agreement about the proper level of subordination. Of the refractory Carl Jung, Freud confided: "His ambition was familiar to me, but I was hoping, through the position that I had created and was still preparing for him, to force this power into my service."[60] Helene Deutsch reports that "Freud's pupils were to be above all passive, understanding listeners; no 'yes men' but projection objects through whom he reviewed—sometimes to correct or retract them—his own ideas."[61] These yes men, or "projection objects," were spared the necessity of having to say anything! It was likewise for his proper level of submission that Freud (in his slightly shaky English) praised Ernest Jones early in their association: "Let me add that I am glad you are not one of those fellows who want to show themselves original or totally independent every time they do something in writing, but you do not despise to show yourself as interpreter of anothers [*sic*] thoughts. It is a proof that you feel *sure* of your own originality and subordinate easily your personal ambition to the interests of the cause. Indeed you seem to have changed in a most thorough and satisfactory manner."[62]

It was in dealing with the heretics of psychoanalysis that Freud showed the depths of his contempt for others' disagreements, often falling back upon his most self-vaunting rhetoric. In his *History of the Psycho-Analytic Movement*, written to excommunicate Adler and Jung, two arch-dissidents, Freud mocks both of his former collaborators for having succumbed to unconscious resistance, to fear of libido. Shrinking back from the discipline of psychoanalysis, they had lapsed into the false comforts of idealism and system-building. Freud's grandiose and persecuted polemic ends on the following note:

Men are strong so long as they represent a strong idea; they become powerless when they oppose it. Psycho-analysis will survive this loss and gain new adherents in place of these. In conclusion, I can only express a wish that fortune may grant an agreeable upward journey to all those who have found their stay in the underworld of psycho-analysis too uncomfortable for their taste. The rest of us, I hope, will be permitted without hindrance to carry through to their conclusion our labors in the depths.[63]

Vast scholarly energy has been invested in clarifying the relations between the workers in the "underworld of psycho-analysis," with the purpose of showing how the discoverers of the logic of the unconscious failed to use their knowledge in such a way as to overcome the natural human propensities toward competition, selfishness, fear, and jealousy.[64] Most of these studies have been written in a psychoanalytic spirit, using Freud's own concepts to analyze the causes of the divisions within his movement. In doing so, they merely repeat, sometimes in a more even-handed way, the hostile gestures of interpretation that were employed at the time. They demonstrate, therefore, the endless capacity of psychoanalysis to generate and then to capitalize upon suspicion. Even the master is fair game so long as the suspicion is couched in psychoanalytic terms. What has not been sufficiently appreciated, however, is the degree to which the theoretical vocabulary of psychoanalysis creates the perils of dissension to which the movement has been so remarkably vulnerable. In giving credit solely to selfish motives in the event of intellectual dissent from orthodox teaching, it made every extension of the theory not initiated by Freud himself a potential occasion for suspicion. No wonder psychoanalysis, as Freud complained, brought out the worst in everyone.[65]

One of the strangest and most absurd, indeed delusional, aspects of Freud's behavior was his willingness to brand those who would not submit to his authority as paranoids. Freud actually believed that the break-up of his friendship with Wilhelm Fliess had had the power to induce "a dreadful case of paranoia" in his former collaborator.[66] The diagnosis of paranoia helped Freud rationalize the hostility that arose between the two men when Fliess discovered that Freud had carelessly disseminated some of Fliess's ideas about human bisexuality, leading to their publication. Fliess's paranoia was entirely in Freud's imagination![67] As Frank Sulloway reasonably speculates, Freud's cavalier way of disseminating Fliess's intellectual property shows his own desire for revenge against a man he felt had forsaken

him.[68] In the midst of another break-up occurring some years after, Freud
wrote to Jones of Alfred Adler observing, "He is not very far from Paranoia,
his distortions are gorgeous"; a couple of months later he added, "As to the
internal dissension with Adler, it was likely to come and I have ripened the
crisis. It is the revolt of an abnormal individual driven mad by ambition,
his influence upon others depending on his strong terrorism and sadis-
mus."[69] To James Jackson Putnam, an American supporter with whom he
was much less intimate, Freud was equally frank, denouncing Adler as "a
gifted thinker but a malicious paranoiac."[70] His innovations were "para-
noivelties."[71] The malice on Freud's part is apparent, but that does not
mean he did not believe what he was saying. He seems no less sincere in
making these charges than he was in making his claims that psychoanalysis
had encountered extraordinary cultural resistance.

By now it should be clear enough that the primal father Freud discovered
at the bottom of human nature was a thinly disguised version of himself.[72]
This fact could be the subject of uneasy jokes between Freud and his inner
circle, and on one occasion they even celebrated a totem meal in Freud's
honor. In the primal father's absolute mastery of the horde, in his untram-
meled 'narcissism' and perfect freedom from libidinal bondage, Freud was
describing his own relation to his followers, whose worship he enjoyed
apparently without an attachment that could be acknowledged in return.[73]
He even had his own way of monopolizing the women—by taking them
into analysis![74] As we have seen, it was in his work on *Group Psychology*
that Freud gave the fullest description of the psychology of the primal
father and its persistence in the psychology of groups. At the time it was
written Freud had been the leader of his own horde for almost two decades.
The experience had confirmed his belief in his own intellectual narcissism.
Late in his career he even went so far as to disclaim that he had the
temperament of a physician:

After forty-one years of medical activity, my self-knowledge tells me that I have
never really been a doctor in the proper sense. . . . I have no knowledge of having
had any craving in my childhood to help suffering humanity. My innate sadistic
disposition was not a very strong one, so that I had no need to develop this one of
its derivatives. In my youth I felt an overpowering need to understand something of
the riddles of the world in which we live and perhaps even to contribute something
to their solution.[75]

This is a chilling admission from the most famous of therapists. We
might think to ascribe Freud's posture to modesty were it not supported by
a long record of comments in which he expresses distaste for his patients

and for human beings as a group: "In my experience most of them are trash."[76] It is further to be noted that the "overpowering need" to solve "the riddles of the world" discovered by Freud at the core of his nature is hardly a point of modesty. Freud positions himself bravely as a descendant of Oedipus. It is no part of his version of the myth that Oedipus investigated his origins in order to save his people;[77] Freud's Oedipus is, like himself, entirely an intellectual hero. There is also something peculiar in the terms of Freud's disclaimer. It is because Freud has no strong "innate sadistic disposition" that he lacks the qualities of a physician. In other words, physicianly care can only be a disguise for a more fundamental sadism, which must be hypocritically masked from conscious awareness in the guise of affectionate concern. One must be cruel, unconsciously, in order to be kind. Now we can see that Freud's lack of solicitude for humanity is actually a virtue, part of his clear-sightedness, honesty, narcissistic independence, and freedom from animus. What it asserts, with a peculiarly sinister form of self-congratulation, is a primal father's notion of virtue.

To illustrate Freud's performance in the role of primal father, I am going to choose the most extreme example of the Freudian egotistical sublime. It is the example of Freud's treatment of an adherent who remained loyal to him even in the act of suicide, a fact that did not make up in Freud's view for his threatening endowment of talent. The story of Victor Tausk has been insightfully reconstructed by Paul Roazen. Tausk killed himself shortly after his return from service in the World War. One of the circumstances surrounding Tausk's dejection, apparently, was Freud's refusal to analyze him and his subsequent command that Tausk's assigned analyst, Helene Deutsch, humiliatingly his junior in the movement, be withdrawn so that Tausk could not interfere in her analysis with Freud. Freud disliked Tausk because Tausk had a way of developing Freud's own ideas very much in the way Freud himself intended to develop them. Freud came to view Tausk's analysis under the direction of his own analysand as an indirect way for Tausk to get at him. A primal father cannot share his women, so Freud forced Helene Deutsch to choose between himself and Tausk, with disastrous consequences. Tausk's farewell note to Freud shows his concern to defuse any sense of a grudge against the master: "I thank you for all the good which you have done me. It was much and has given meaning to the last ten years of my life. Your work is genuine and great, I shall take leave of this life knowing that I was one of those who witnessed the triumph of one of the greatest ideas of mankind. . . . I have no accusations against anyone, my heart is without resentment. . . ."[78] Freud reported the suicide to Tausk's former lover, his sycophantic devotée, Lou-Andreas Salomé; as a former friend of Nietzsche and lover of Rilke, her adherence to the psychoanalytic movement and attachment to its founder were sources of considerable pride to Freud. The note of triumph over a former rival for Salomé's regard is impossible to mistake:

Poor Tausk, whom you for some time favoured with your friendship, committed suicide on 3.7. He returned worn out from the horrors of war, was faced with the necessity of building up under the most unfavourable circumstances the practice in Vienna which he had lost through being called up for military service, had intended to remarry only a week later—but decided otherwise. His farewell letters to his fiancée, his first wife and to me were all equally affectionate, insisted on his clarity of mind, blamed only his own inadequacy and his failure; they gave therefore no clue as to his last act. In his letter to me he swore undying loyalty to psychoanalysis, thanked me etc. But what was behind it all we cannot guess. After all he spent his days wrestling with the father ghost. I confess that I do not really miss him; I had long realized that he could be of no further service, indeed that he constituted a threat to the future. I had an opportunity of taking a glance or two at the foundations on which his high-flown sublimations rested; and I would have dropped him long ago if *you* hadn't raised him so in my estimation. Of course I was still ready to do anything for his advancement, only latterly I have been quite powerless myself owing to the general deterioration of conditions in Vienna. I never failed to recognize his notable gifts; but they were denied expression in achievements of corresponding value.

For my old age I have chosen the theme of death. . . .[79]

Roazen's account of this episode leaves little doubt that the "father ghost" with whom Tausk was struggling was Freud himself. Tausk's friends "in that tiny subculture" took it for granted that "if Freud dropped a man it could lead to his self-extinction" (156). Tausk was not the only example (156–58). Freud's letter reveals a primal father's superiority, which is responsible to no one. No religious leader's "high-flown sublimations" could have earned a more supercilious dismissal than the supposed unconscious susceptibilities of this unfortunate disciple. It is taken for granted that the future interests of the movement override any individual concern for his welfare; indeed, the meaning of Tausk's existence is altogether identified with his contribution to that future. Freud's sense of destiny justifies the dictates of his pride and fear with a flawless theoretical economy.

What is still more remarkable about Freud's assumption of the primal father's privileges is the way his followers often accepted their subordination and the refusal of respect it entailed in the Freudian horde, even while they recognized the destructive effects that could result. Those who remained faithful to Freud found ways to blame the defectors in every case of tension—these weaklings had failed to understand the dictates of Freud's extraordinary nature. So Helene Deutsch, writing shortly after Freud's death, puts the weight of the blame for the divisiveness of the psychoanalytic movement upon the servile characters of Freud's followers. Here she is speaking primarily of the second generation, which surrounded Freud near the end of his life. Freud she exonerates because of his genius:

Everybody around Freud wanted to be loved by him, but his intellectual accomplishment meant infinitely more to him than the people around him. As an inspired pathfinder he felt justified in regarding his co-workers as a means towards his own impersonal objective accomplishment; and with this end in mind, probably every impulse towards originality, when it subserved other than *objective* purposes, annoyed him and made him impatient. Freud was too far ahead of his time to leave much room for anything really new in his own generation. It seems to be characteristic of every discoverer of genius that his influence on contemporary thought is not only fructifying but inhibitory as well.[80]

This line of apology has been carried to further extremes. K. R. Eissler, one of the leaders of the psychoanalytic establishment, in an astonishing book-length reply to Roazen's work on Tausk, takes the cult of the primal father perhaps to the limit of servile rationalizing. He suggests, first, that Freud's harshness toward Tausk in his letter to Salomé was merely an attempt to avoid the appearance of weakness, and that the English translation of "Der arme Tausk," "poor Tausk," does not do justice to the deep sympathy imparted by the German phrase. His ultimate line of defense, though, is that Tausk was a mere "talent," and a neurotic one at that, whereas Freud was a "genius," a fact that sets him, for Eissler, largely above ordinary obligations. If Freud had become completely insensitive to everything but his greatness and the destiny of psychoanalysis—in other words, if all of his 'libido' had been transferred to his 'superego'—this would be no reproach against a genius:

When a man acts in conformity with his biological state, his behavior may shock us, but it cannot be criticized within the biological frame of reference. Further, if a genius's personality becomes completely engulfed by his superego—that is to say, by his life's mission (which may have occurred in some rare instances, but certainly not in the case of Freud)—then it makes no sense to call the effects of such a transformation 'shocking' and 'ruthless' [as Roazen does], for such a transformation is desirable, admirable, and advantageous to the world at large, whose primary interest is not in the genius's psychological processes but rather in his creation of the highest possible values. From this one could deduce that the more such a person is engulfed by the creative processes, to the point of utter absorption, the more will posterity profit from his mortal days.[81]

It would be hard to imagine a more striking example of the moral hazards of the psychoanalytic vocabulary. Eissler compares what he takes to be the necessary hardship created by Freud's Olympian detachment to the providential selfishness—entirely conjectural—that led the young William Shakespeare to leave his wife and children in Stratford and set off toward London!

When Shakespeare left Stratford, clearly shirking his responsibility to his wife and his three children, he committed an act that would have been reprehensible in anyone else; yet it certainly was an absolute necessity for him to do so, in terms of the subsequent creation of the plays that he gave the world. To be sure, there are talents who abuse this type of behavior, which is proper for the genius, in order to rationalize their own selfish pleasure-seeking actions. In talents, however, such behavior has a meaning that is essentially different from the one it has in the life of a genius. (100)

The mythology of psychoanalysis, with its cult of genius, thus gained for Freud an extraordinary permissiveness toward the dictates of his paranoid personality, a permissiveness that long outlived him. Sixteen years at the head of the psychoanalytic movement hardened and confirmed him in his role as grandiose and suspicious master, and, along with what he learned about dominance and submission in the analytic situation, became the basis, as we have seen, for his theorizing about the psychology of groups. During the battles of his later life Freud comported himself with an Olympian superiority to human feeling, refusing to admit satisfaction in the world's homage, which he had so relentlessly pursued, refusing to utter good wishes to his admirers—this being an unacceptable concession to the 'omnipotence of thoughts'[82]—and declaring any altruism that might have characterized his life to be something mysterious and not necessarily admirable: "Why I—and incidentally my six adult children as well—have to be thoroughly decent human beings is quite incomprehensible to me."[83] Only Freud had the strength—and the entitlement—to live out this much of the wisdom of psychoanalysis. His paranoid suspicion toward the world grew up from a fundamental mistrust of his own nature, which he learned to convert into a supreme intellectual advantage.

In the light of the facts presented here, let us now review Freud's own account of his discovery of psychoanalysis: the naive modesty with which he set his findings forth, the hostile response—imaginary—with which they were received, and the slow recognition of the immense importance that this hostility betokened for his achievement. Now that we have become familiar with the suspicious manner in which Freud habitually treats his own motives, his claim to the unselfish idealism of the discoverer rings distinctly false. Yet there is a strange conviction here too, the conviction of a man whose sense of worth is powerfully sustained by an opposition that is the product of his imagination:

I did not at first perceive the peculiar nature of what I had discovered. I unhesitatingly sacrificed my growing popularity as a doctor, and the increase in attendance during my consulting hours, by making systematic enquiry into the sexual factors involved in the causation of my patients' neuroses; and this brought me a great many new facts which finally confirmed my conviction of the practical importance of the sexual factor. I innocently addressed a meeting of the Vienna Society for Psychiatry and Neurology with Krafft-Ebing in the chair, expecting that the material losses I had willingly undergone would be made up for by the interest and recognition of my colleagues. I treated my discoveries as ordinary contributions to science and hoped they would be received in the same spirit. But the silence which my communications met with, the void which formed itself about me, the hints that were conveyed to me, gradually made me realize that assertions on the part played by sexuality in the aetiology of the neuroses cannot count upon meeting with the same kind of treatment as other communications. I understood that from now onwards I was one of those who had 'disturbed the sleep of the world', as Hebbel says, and that I could not reckon upon objectivity and tolerance. Since, however, my conviction of the general accuracy of my observations and conclusions grew even stronger, and since neither my confidence in my own judgement nor my moral courage were precisely small, the outcome of the situation could not be in doubt. I made up my mind to believe that it had been my fortune to discover some particularly important facts and connections, and I was prepared to accept the fate that sometimes accompanies such discoveries.
I pictured the future as follows:—I should probably succeed in maintaining myself by means of the therapeutic success of the new procedure, but science would ignore me entirely during my lifetime; some decades later, someone else would infallibly come upon the same things—for which the time was not now ripe—would achieve recognition for them and bring me honour as a forerunner whose failure had been inevitable. Meanwhile, like Robinson Crusoe, I settled down as comfortably as possible on my desert island. When I look back to those lonely years, away from the pressures and confusions of to-day, it seems like a glorious heroic age. My "splendid isolation" was not without its advantages and charms.[84]

The reader who has assented to the foregoing analysis of Freudian psychology will hardly need a commentary upon this passage. One can only admire the rhetoric by which Freud creates his grandiose, magical, almost cosmic drama of unself-conscious virtue met with, instead of applause, an unexpected and meaningful silence, a "void" gathering round it, full of disturbing "hints," and then the sudden recognition that the "world's sleep" had been inadvertently troubled, with ominous consequences that would forever set the innocent inquirer beyond the pale of human consideration. So what can he do but decide to believe in himself, gather his "moral courage," which was not "precisely small," and await in "splendid isolation" the verdict of the future? Hostility, suspicion, strange significance, heroic isolation, and embattled self-reliance—all the paranoid vices and virtues are here. One thinks of the desperate Rousseau putting his last hopes in posterity and resigning himself to the company of nature. Robinson Crusoe was his favorite book.

The view of Sigmund Freud that I have set out in this chapter is hardly a flattering one. It must be stated though, once again, that in its essential details it confirms Freud's own view of himself. He recognized the primal father in his nature and insisted upon it; only in his most straightforwardly self-serving moments did he refuse this recognition. Where I differ with psychoanalytic dogma is in the contention that Freud's psyche was typical of humanity in general. It seems to me evident that his peculiarly grand and violent personality was special to him and that his theory is an expression of that personality rather than a rational explanation for it. Yet after all it is important to remember that, in the context of a larger cultural ambiance in which intellectual activity has a generally suspicious and hostile character, individuals can be expected to take up whatever weapons have been provided and use them to the best advantage. Psychoanalytic theory shows the typically paranoid, self-spiting, and hostile psychological dynamic created by reductive thinking. Freud did not shrink from the moral hazards of acknowledging the primal father. He gloried, rather, in the difficulties of paranoid self-recognition. The more difficult the achievement, the higher; the more universal the domain of suspicion, the greater the power of the interpreter. It was this logic, and the superb rhetorical stance that accompanied it, that allowed him to brave the reduction of his own motives to narcissism and the resemblance of his own thought to paranoia. He exploited the difficulties arising from the contradictory, self-undermining logic of his own theory as a test of strength and endurance in the mode of heroic irony. And he despised the stragglers who fell by the way. Like the epic poet in psychoanalytic myth, Freud gained in heroic stature by means of the renunciations he exacted from others.

Let there be no mistake about the kind of explanation that I am proposing in order to illuminate the form of psychoanalytic thought and the source of its allure. I am not turning Freud's idea of paranoia back upon him. That would be merely to repeat his own self-reduction. What I am drawing to attention is the fact that his self-conception, his conception of the human subject, is given in the image of the paranoid, and that this gesture is inherently self-fulfilling. The power of psychoanalysis lies in the ingenious manner in which it permits reductive thinking to extend its authority by means of an absolute psychological suspicion, leading to the construction of a most gratifyingly systematic paranoia. Freud the theorist displays every feature of paranoid thinking. Yet all of these features, so inseparable from Freud's personality, spring with unassailable logic from the premises of his science. In this paranoia we are not dealing merely with a psychologically aberrant condition but, rather, with a self-sustaining intellectual dynamic. It is the prevalence of this intellectual dynamic that causes modern people to see themselves so movingly reflected in personalities like those of Rousseau, Nietzsche, and Freud, allowing these agitated and frequently deluded intellectuals to assume a prominent place in history without embarrassment.

FOUR

Before Freud

[Samuel] Johnson's . . . sense of the working of the
human imagination probably provides us with the
closest anticipation of Freud to be found in psychology or moral writing before the twentieth century.   —W. J. Bate

When Siegfried dreams under the linden tree and
the mother-idea flows into the erotic; when Mime
teaches his pupil the nature of fear, while the or-
chestra down below darkly and afar off introduces
the fire motif; all that is Freud, that is analysis,
nothing else.   —Thomas Mann on Wagner

For seven or eight decades now, it has been impossible to give any writer
credit for psychological insight without making the claim that he or she
anticipated Freud. For the twentieth century Freud represents psychological insight itself—the form of intelligence that looks beneath the surface of
mental life to find the hidden duplicities and depths. All subtlety in this
area belongs to him: he sees truly and fearlessly what others have only
glimpsed, and the insights, intimations, and suspicions of others find their
true grounds in him. Having come to symbolize the transition from a faithful
and metaphysical culture to a skeptical, psychologizing one, Freud is now
the most distinct figure of retrospective anticipation since Christ. As the
practitioners of Christian hermeneutics found in Hebrew scripture the
shadowy types of the Messiah, so Freud stands as the meaning hidden in
previous culture. He discovered within himself the secret significance of
human being, and others took it for truth. Thus we can measure the success
of his vocation. For his adherents, and for many others, modernity in
particular looks forward to his arrival, which remains, nevertheless, an
event entirely original in its character. Freud's messianic incarnation, like
Christ's, is double: not man and God but scientist and patient, analyst and
analysand, the one who suffers and the one who redeems. With the revela-

tion of the Oedipal code, Freud becomes the final hero, the hero who could unmask himself, asserting a paranoid version of psychology in order to display his own 'narcissistic' character and to enjoy the triumph of that attractively disturbing irony. The effect was not solely one of destruction: Freud's aim was to complete the transition to modernity by reintegrating the broken fragments of tradition in a comprehensive psychological myth, with himself at the center. Freud thus gave a most convincing performance in a role which, since Rousseau, has dominated the scene of modernity: the role of the first honest man. The division between heroic analyst and pathetic analysand is fully prefigured in Rousseau: pathetic in the doing and heroic in the telling seems to be the motto of the paranoid intellectual. Freud even claimed to believe that the discovery of psychoanalysis had deprived him of his ability to lie.[1]

With the benefit of scholarship in the last twenty-five years, we can now see that most of Freud's apparent originality derives from his ability to absorb and eclipse his sources. The interest in sexuality and the unconscious, for instance, associated in the popular mind primarily with Freud, were powerful intellectual trends of the time. Few of the elements of psychoanalysis were truly unique. Freud's originality lay in the aspect of synthesis and in the rhetorical skills with which he gave expression to his synthesis. Its immediate horizon was post-Darwinian science and literary culture, of which Freud made brilliant use. He had before him, also, some great exemplars of suspicion: Feuerbach, the inventor of the unmasking critique, whom the young Freud "revere[d] and admire[d] above all other philosophers";[2] Schopenhauer, who proclaimed the force of sexual impulse as an obstacle to truth; and, of course, Marx and Nietzsche.[3] But to understand the triumph of suspicion in the form of psychoanalysis, it is necessary to take account of its ability to absorb and resonate with a wider sphere of reductionist and paranoid thinking in modern culture. Freud capitalized upon the momentum that intellectual suspicion had gathered over four centuries, achieving at once the most profound and the most exhilarating version of paranoid heroics. Psychoanalysis does not merely repeat the gestures of this culture of suspicion: it takes them into its own fabric and makes them the sustaining ingredients, the materials and evidence for its own still grander, still more resolutely suspicious and more inclusive gesture.

To delineate the full context of the modern culture of suspicion would require a book much longer than this one. It would begin, perhaps, with the sense of conspiracy, official corruption, and institutional mistrust inspired from the high Middle Ages by the international organization of the Catholic church. It would take notice of the humanist methods of historical criticism and demystification, which were often applied in suspicion of that organization and which later became the staples of Protestant polemic. Freud recognized his kinship with the Protestant critique; the humanist recovery of the original text from among the self-serving fabrications of early tradition also provided him with a favorite metaphor for the activity of the scientist uncovering the true contents of the unconscious. (It is surprising he never referred to himself as the Lorenzo Valla of the mind.) Modern suspicion grew up also from the atmosphere of the Renaissance court, with its shifting alliances and the playing off of favorites one against another, giving rise eventually to a politics of power most notably expressed in the writings of Machiavelli, and a distinctive psychology as well, chronicled in action in the *Memoirs* of Saint Simon and synthesized in Rochefoucauld's *Maxims.* Psychoanalysis can be considered a systematic attempt to refute Rochefoucauld's claim that the power of suspicion can never equal the power of deception. Finally there is the Reformation itself, which initiated an uncontainable process of religious and political schism, an ideological divisiveness ever more complex and minute in its manifestations, instigating mistrust, political conspiracy, and bloodshed over a century and a half. The rise of the nation-state and of colonialism, with their tendency to set local and central authority against each other, also played its part. All of these tributaries fed into the great current of suspicion that energized the anti-traditional, satiric culture of the late seventeenth and early eighteenth centuries in England and France, and which achieved philosophical embodiment in the writings of Bacon, Hobbes, Locke, Hume, and the philosophes. In this intellectual atmosphere, the stage was set for the great rebellion against society itself figured in the life and writings of the clinically paranoid Rousseau. The romantic cult of originality, which so decisively shaped Freud's thinking and behavior, grew up with this suspicion of the group and of tradition.

In lieu of a thoroughgoing history of suspicion, I have chosen here to explore Freud's affinities with four central elements: the methodological form of suspicion described in the scientific program of Francis Bacon; the epistemological suspicion of the empiricists and, especially, Kant; the progressivist historical suspicion of Comte and Hegel; and the political solipsism of Hobbes. Freud was directly familiar with these, except, perhaps, for Hegel. In the case of Bacon there was admiration at least from the age of twenty-one, when Freud expressed his enthusiasm for Macaulay's

essay on Lord Bacon, which he thought "could not be more perfect."[4] The essay combines suspicion of the person and admiration for the intellectual achievement in a way truly congenial to the eventual Freudian outlook. Freud's devotion to Macaulay, we may add, was not the passing fancy of youth. Fifty years later, asked to name ten "good books," he listed the *Essays* among them, interpreting "good books" to mean books "to which one stands in rather the same relationship as to 'good' friends, to whom one owes a part of one's knowledge of life and view of the world."[5] Freud's fluency in English and his lifelong absorption in English culture, with its progressive, positivist, and Baconian outlook, "where human worth is more respected," must never be left out of view.[6]

It is not to chart influence, though, that I have singled out these figures and these aspects of culture; my intention is, rather, to show how psychoanalysis assimilates the existing varieties of suspicion. They prepare for and, indeed, prefigure the master code of paranoid interpretation; it is only in the context of that preparation that we can understand the messianic impact of Freud.

Methodological Suspicion

Francis Bacon invented the ideology of heroic science in the mode practiced by Sigmund Freud. The first installment of his scientific program, *The Advancement of Learning*, appeared in 1605, the same year that produced Part One of the *Quixote*. Bacon has acquired preeminence among the prophetic voices of modernity. He was the first to envision in a programmatic way the accumulative process of investigation that, just a generation or two after his death, would help transform the manner of scientific inquiry, with unparalleled success. He envisioned the model of modern science as an institution, and he provided it with a program of inquiry based upon experiment and the compilation of knowledge, a rudimentary method of induction, and, most important of all, a model of rhetorical self-justification. The essence of this model is a psychology of suspicion and a vision of the heroic scientist. Indeed, it is no exaggeration to say that the notion of scientific method in its primitive Baconian form is not so much a methodology of science as it is a heroic psychology of suspicion. Freud's peculiar achievement was to give full articulation to this psychology, which was already a crucial element of the rhetoric of Enlightenment science.

Bacon looked back into the history of natural philosophy and saw that human progress had been perpetually hindered by the very tendency Freud calls 'narcissism', the tendency for the mind to confuse its own sense of order with the order of reality: "as an uneven mirror distorts the rays of objects according to its own figure and section, so the mind, when it receives impressions of objects through the sense, cannot be trusted to report them truly, but in forming its notions mixes up its own nature with the nature of things."[7] The distortions of the mind, the Idols "adventitious or innate" to which it becomes enslaved, were numerous, and Bacon attempted a systematic survey. In his view, the mind betrays itself always in the same manner, imagining more order and system in nature than is there to be found. The systems of philosophy, like all fictions, gratify not a hunger for truth but a desire for order on the part of those who make them: "In the plays of this philosophical theatre you may observe the same thing which is found in the theatre of the poets, that stories invented for the stage are more compact and elegant, and more as one would wish them to be, than true stories out of history."[8] The human vocation for knowledge is constantly betrayed by the hunger of the mind to see its own image printed upon the world. The lineage of human inquiry is peopled with a long succession of pretenders to knowledge caught up in 'Anticipations of the Mind' and mistaking them for truth. What Freud was later to call the 'overestimation' of the intellect is the factor that for Bacon explains what he takes to be the perennial disagreement and fruitlessness in the speculations of the philosophers. The spectacle evokes Bacon's trenchant satiric vein:

Another error hath proceeded from too great a reverence, and a kind of adoration of the mind and understanding of man; by means whereof men have withdrawn themselves too much from the contemplation of nature and the observations of experience, and have tumbled up and down in their own reason and conceits. Upon these intellectualists, which are notwithstanding commonly taken for the most sublime and divine philosophers, Heraclitus gave a just censure, saying, *Men sought truth in their own little worlds, and not in the great and common world;* for they disdain to spell and so by degrees to read in the volume of God's works; and contrariwise by continual meditation and agitation of wit do urge and as it were invoke their own spirits to divine and give oracles unto them, whereby they are deservedly deluded.[9]

In passages like this one Bacon begins the attack upon metaphysics from the satiric point of view that fueled the rhetoric of positivism down to the time of Freud and beyond. For both Freud and Bacon, the pretentious sublimity of philosophical reason is the very mark of its self-enthrallment. Metaphysics, with its 'intellectualism', its self-projecting sense of order, creates for itself a nonce-world where its adherents can meet upon the

footing of delusion. "Anticipations," Bacon scoffs, "are a ground sufficiently firm for consent, for even if men went mad all after the same
fashion, they might agree one with another well enough."[10] The only way
to preserve oneself from the glamorous world of deception lies, as Freud
would also say, in the proper submission to the facts: "Those . . . who
aspire not to guess and divine, but to discover and know; who propose not
to devise mimic and fabulous worlds of their own, but to examine and
dissect the nature of this very world itself, must go to facts themselves for
everything."[11] "To the facts themselves," "to the things themselves," this
is the hope of positivism, that it can efface thought itself from the process
of inquiry, just as the experimenter keeps his data from being contaminated
by anticipations of the result.

For Bacon, as for Freud, the mind can only guard itself from its wayward
penchant by regulating its own working with a constant suspicion: "Let
every student of nature take this as a rule, — that whatever his mind seizes
and dwells upon with peculiar satisfaction is to be held in suspicion."[12] It
is not mere laziness that keeps the mind enthralled to its anticipations; nor
is it a simple restlessness that leads the imagination to invent for itself what
the mind cannot properly know. Bacon takes account of these factors, but
they are less essential than the "peculiar satisfaction" of error itself. Error
appeals to Eros, to the body and its needs, the 'libido' as Freud would say,
and this is what gives to it a "peculiar satisfaction":

The human understanding is no dry light, but receives an infusion from the will
and affections; whence proceed sciences which may be called 'sciences as one
would'. For what a man had rather were true he more readily believes. Therefore
he rejects difficult things from impatience of research; sober things, because they
narrow hope; the deeper things of nature, from superstition; the light of experience,
from arrogance and pride, lest his mind should seem to be occupied with things
mean and transitory; things not commonly believed, out of deference to the opinion
of the vulgar. Numberless in short are the ways, and sometimes imperceptible, in
which the affections colour and infect the understanding.[13]

The anticipation of Freud is complete. Narcissism, in the form of "arrogance and pride," keeps the mind from recognizing its affinity with "things
mean and transitory." The same false idealism that Bacon saw as an
obstacle to close experiment would become in Freud's view the obstacle to
the theory of libido. The "intellectualists" are those who cannot do without
the erotic satisfactions of error. Bacon, like his successor, ruefully acknowledges in human nature an almost insuperable obstacle to the discovery of truth—not a mere fallibility in the direction of error, but a "natural

though corrupt love of the lie itself." It is this perfidious form of Eros that gives energy to the life of the mind: "A mixture of a lie doth ever add pleasure. Doth any man doubt, that if there were taken out of men's minds vain opinions, flattering hopes, false valuations, imaginations as one would, and the like, but it would leave the minds of a number of men poor shrunken things, full of melancholy and indisposition, and unpleasing to themselves?"[14] Remove error from the mind and its very substance and vitality seem to have been drained away. Bacon applies this description to a "number of men"; but it must include virtually all of the number who had lived until his time.

It would be impossible to overlook the moralizing tone of Baconian self-justification. Like Freud's, it was moralizing of a defensive sort. The presumption of Bacon's age was somewhat against too close an inquiry into the particulars of physical nature, an activity still associated with alchemy and magic. Bacon defended the inquiring spirit as being licensed in all but those aspects of moral knowledge proscribed in the biblical episode of the Fall; he portrayed the material operations of nature as containing the imprint of God's truth no less than 'Final Causes', which he banished from scientific inquiry. It was also necessary for Bacon to keep from the appearance of hubristic innovation, not an easy task for a man with pretensions to the overturning of all traditional modes of understanding the creation. With the argumentative cleverness of the brilliant lawyer that he was, Bacon employed the myth of the Fall to his advantage, shifting the burden of hubris from natural philosophy to those system-making metaphysicians who would substitute their own worlds for the one created by God:

For we create worlds, we direct and domineer over nature, we will have it that all things *are* as in our folly we think they should be, not as seems fittest to the Divine wisdom, or as they are found to be in fact; and I know not whether we more distort the facts of nature or our own wits; but we clearly impress the stamp of our image on the creatures and works of God, instead of carefully examining and recognising in them the stamp of the Creator himself. Wherefore our dominion over creatures is a second time forfeited, not undeservedly.[15]

According to this view, an addiction to the delusion of power is the one obstacle to attaining true power. Hubris leads to impotence, humility to potency. The knowledge of nature as it is can only come with the renunciation of the false pleasures of human creativity, the worship of self-created Idols. Science is thus a form of submission to God as the maker of the actual world; the valor of this submission speaks in all of Bacon's writing: "Nature to be commanded must be obeyed."[16] It is one of the profound ironies in the history of modern culture that science, beginning with Bacon, was able to appropriate the religious abhorrence of vanity and pride and that it would eventually turn Christian humility back upon religion itself. So began the cult of science-as-repression.

Bacon furnished to the future adherents of science a powerful critique of the abuses of intellect. This critique would be perennially useful in the struggles of the Enlightenment against its cultural enemies, religion and metaphysics. Yet it is important to remember that Bacon's program was not at all that of a skeptic. His intention in bringing to light the sources of confusion that frustrate the efforts of intelligence was not to denigrate intelligence itself but to provide it with the proper "helps," and, in so doing, to establish the practice of science upon a more perfect basis than it had previously found. Suspicion was for him part of a necessary reigning in of the force of imagination; only by such a restraint could the mind attain its true object.

The positive aspect of Bacon's program distinguishes it from previous employments of methodical skepticism. The ancient tradition of the skeptics took as its aim a tranquil withdrawal from the world. It sought peace in the futility of inquiry. Its dialectical subtleties ended with a recognition that nothing could be known, and that the human will, having no true objects of desire, should be satisfied with a detached self-complacency. The arguments of this school, exhaustively summarized by Sextus Empiricus in the third century A.D., could easily be reconciled with the Christian spirit of resignation. Montaigne, Bacon's great literary model, was one of the last representatives of this ancient skepticism in its Christian form and perhaps the greatest manifestation of its proper sensibility, which is one of relaxed contemplation and disorganized curiosity. Bacon, on the other hand, is the inventor of a skepticism both searching and productive, a skepticism not satisfied in itself but destroying in order to create. For it, the difficulties of knowledge make necessary a restless, anxious discernment; the mind must be preoccupied with itself if only to escape from itself. This activist skepticism finds itself always amid formidable difficulties; it is generically desperate and beleaguered, condemned to founder in illusion unless it holds to its fixed goal. Like a hero of romance, wandering in a dark wood, the embattled intelligence has need of a clue in order to escape from its inner and outer enemies:

The universe to the eye of the human understanding is framed like a labyrinth; presenting as it does on every side so may ambiguities of way, such deceitful resemblances of objects and signs, natures so irregular in their lines, and so knotted and entangled. And then the way is still to be made by the uncertain light of the sense, sometimes shining out, sometimes clouded over, through the woods of experience and particulars; while those who offer themselves for guides are (as was said) themselves also puzzled, and increase the number of errors and wanderers. In circumstances so difficult neither the natural force of man's judgment nor even any accidental felicity offers any chance of success. No excellence of wit, no repetition of chance experiments, can overcome such difficulties as these. Our steps must be guided by a clue, and the whole way from the very first perception of the senses must be laid out upon a sure plan.[17]

In this passage, Bacon, with a Freudian militancy, splendidly magnifies the difficulty of the way to truth and the anxiety of the search. Unlike his Scholastic predecessors, he envisions no natural correspondence between the structures of the mind and those of nature. Nature itself is knotted now and tangled, perplexed and askew, a thing quite foreign to the order of intellect, vexed with ambiguity and deceitful resemblance. The one "clue" and "sure plan" is the Baconian method of induction, to be employed along with the regular pursuit of experiment and the systematic compilation of results. By these means Bacon proposed to bring about the "true end and termination of infinite error" (37). About the ease with which this termination was to be achieved, Bacon proved strangely optimistic. Without the Baconian method, were "all the wits of all the ages" gathered together, and all the resources of humankind hereafter dedicated to science, no result would come of it, while, with the proper compilation of "natural and experimental history," "the investigation of nature and of all sciences" would be "the work of a few years."[18] It is typical of paranoid logic that the multiplication of obstacles and intensification of suspicion should bring such a heightening of heroic exhilaration.

The procedures envisioned by Bacon delivered few benefits to the technique of scientific investigation. But his program lent a rhetoric to science that is still the main component of its ideological self-image, a rhetoric of organized suspicion and ostentatious self-scrutiny—above all, of productive humility. It was in this that he sounded the distinctive note of modern intellectual culture. Bacon conjured up all of the enemies of inquiry in order to vanquish them with heroic suspicion. The fundamental object of this suspicion was the temptation from within, and for the first time we see knowledge envisaged as the result of an inner discipline of repression:

For my own part at least, in obedience to the everlasting love of truth, I have committed myself to the uncertainties and difficulties and solitudes of the ways, and relying on the divine assistance have upheld my mind both against the shocks and embattled ranks of opinion, and against my own private and inward hesitations and scruples, and against the fogs and clouds of nature, and the phantoms flitting about on every side; in the hope of providing at last for the present and future generations guidance more faithful and secure. Wherein if I have made any progress, the way has been opened to me by no other means than the true and legitimate humiliation of the human spirit. For all those who before me have applied themselves to the invention of arts have but cast a glance or two upon facts and examples and experience, and straightway proceeded, as if invention were nothing more than an exercise of thought, to invoke their own spirits to give them oracles.[19]

Here we have the voice of the heroic investigator just as it was to be assumed by Freud. The scientific hero knows the difficulties of the way and the enemies within. He knows that the greatest enemy is the oracular confidence of the mind inflated by its own self-intoxicating spirits; he knows that in order to dispel these vapors he must brave the underworld in pursuit of what Bacon likes to call the secrets, the "hidden parts" of nature; and, most importantly, he knows that in order to set this achievement upon a social basis he must accomplish "a true and legitimate humiliation of the human spirit." Heroic self-deflation, science through suspicion, power by means of repression, these are the special marks of the new scientific sensibility and the ones its adherents singled out in order to distinguish themselves from the benighted ages of the past.

At this point the voice of the skeptic might be once again inclined to put in a word. "The point of this discussion," such a skeptic might say, "seems to be that Bacon introduced a fundamentally suspicious attitude toward the products of the mind, that he wanted to set culture upon the basis of suspicion. Wherever he saw the human mind expressing itself in an image of the world, there he was eager to expose a wish masquerading as a truth. True enough—but is this not the essence of the method of science, that it excludes the subjective contribution of the observer from the domain of the observed in order to establish the nature of things in themselves? Here Bacon's, and Freud's, claim that science exacts a necessary renunciation seems impossible to deny." Once again the skeptic speaks with reason. Bacon's strictures against "science as one would" are necessary protocols for the experimental observer. But they cannot serve as an adequate theory of scientific inquiry. For the facts of nature do not speak for themselves. They require interpretation: they cannot be grasped without theory. Knowledge does not come simply by excluding human interest and, indeed, it is doubtful that human interest can in practice ever be entirely excluded. Whether one takes a Platonic view of the scientific method as depending upon the forms of mathematical reason, or whether one takes the pragmatist view, which has become persuasive to many in recent years, it seems impossible to understand the practice of science without giving recognition to the positive contribution of the mind. Once one has done this, one must further recognize that the systematic suspicion of the experimenter protecting his data from contamination cannot be the basis for the general outlook even of a scientific culture.

It is unlikely that Bacon intended to make suspicion a general mode of culture. He did not envision the length of time it would take for science to vanquish the enemies he had set it upon. Nor could he have anticipated that the infinitely flexible polemical instrument he had invented would be turned against new enemies. For him, suspicion was confined to a small area of intellectual endeavor that had been until his time the exclusive domain of "great wits" operating upon too little experience, minds of extraordinary fertility suffering a monastic separation from the real world of the senses. Such monastic confinements could be comfortably reversed without extending the resources of Protestant rhetoric. It would not be long, however, before the Baconian critique was turned against Protestant culture itself.

Despite the conservatism of Bacon's cultural stance, his materialism was of a revolutionary sort. His plan of knowledge depends upon the reduction of all phenomena to the operation of material and efficient causes. Even formal causes are made physical. As for the final causes, the evidence of God's design in nature, these he would leave undisturbed though they have no explanatory value. This thoroughgoing materialism was taken up desultorily by Hobbes, but its most significant development belonged to the French, starting with Gassendi in the seventeenth century; applied to the human body it could become a crude mechanistic determinism, as in La Mettrie's *L'Homme machine.* Kant's transcendental revolution in philosophy, along with the German vogue of Pietism, prevented the materialism of the French Enlightenment from being fully assimilated within German culture until the generation of Feuerbach and Marx. This generation and the next one produced many of Freud's university teachers and mentors in biology and neurophysiology. Their materialism had about it a revolutionary zeal owing to its comparatively recent victory over the Romantic *Naturphilosophie* that had developed out of Kant.[20] Freud shared this zeal, even while his psychology, rooted though it was in psycho-physical mechanics, could evoke resistance, he believed, from those purists who would recognize only immediately physical causes.[21] Freud thought of psychic energy, or 'libido', as a kind of free-flowing charge circulating throughout the body unless 'bound' in some particular complex of ideas, or released through some activity.[22] This view of psychic energy, fundamental to psychoanalysis and its 'dynamics' of repression, sublimation, and displacement, has long disappeared from serious science. But the reductive psychology Freud developed out of it continues to be persuasive for those whose thinking is instinctively reductionist; to hold such a position, one needs a psychology of suspicion that can articulate the experience produced when reductive logic is applied to human thought.

Bacon articulated a new and soon-to-be-fruitful attitude toward the investigation of the material world. At the same time, his method recognized a subjective residue of the mind's activity, which had to be excluded from any investigation before it could succeed. The "mimic and fabulous worlds" of the philosophers could be put down to the foibles of the human intellect working under the pressure of affection and will. In making this diagnosis, Bacon established a kind of rough justice over the "fabulous worlds." But the new territory he had opened, the hereditary kingdom of Error, remained as a challenge to modern understanding. Out of this challenge was to come the science of psychology as we know it. Ours is the first psychology that attempts to understand the workings of the mind as abstracted from any proper object of knowledge or experience. It is the first systematic psychology of error.

Epistemological Suspicion

The first great heirs of Baconian psychology were the empiricists, chief among them Locke and Hume. In their work, the practical interests of science were suddenly pushed to the rear by an access of suspicion more formidable even than that of Bacon. For these writers, suspicion is no longer the adjunct of a scientific method. It is not simply our capacity to gain understanding and control of the world before us that must be regulated by suspicion. Now this very world itself is close to being an illusion. The distinction between the "mimic and fabulous worlds" and the true one becomes increasingly difficult to establish. In classic empiricism, the mind has access to nothing more than the simple elements of sensation and the combinations of its own ideas; there are no verifiable objects, no 'substances' underlying the data given to the senses, only the phenomena themselves passing like shadows as in Plato's cave. The logical outcome of this form of thinking would be an absolute repression of thought, a withdrawal of belief from all possible objects of external knowledge, there being nothing for science, faith, or common perception to be about. It was in recognition of the sheer unintelligibility of existence in the empiricist model that philosophers of this period—most famously Berkeley—resorted to God as a coordinating agent between reality and experience. God, they speculated, acts at each moment to keep the world before us consistently in place—a paranoid solution, surely, but within these operating assumptions, the distinction between the paranoid and the normal is no easier to make than it was for Freud. So John Locke, who did not rely primarily upon this paranoid resource, takes up the doubts of his readers on this very point:

> I Doubt not but my Reader, by this time, may be apt to think, that I have been all this while only building a Castle in the Air; and be ready to say to me, To what purpose all this stir? Knowledge, say you, is only the perception of the agreement or disagreement of our own *Ideas:* but who knows what those *Ideas* may be? Is there any thing so extravagant, as the Imaginations of Men's Brains? Where is the Head that has no *Chimeras* in it? Or if there be a sober and a wise Man, what difference will there be, by your Rules, between his Knowledge, and that of the most extravagant Fancy in the World? They both have their *Ideas*, and perceive their agreement and disagreement one with another. If there be any difference between them, the advantage will be on the warm-headed Man's side, as having the more *Ideas*, and the more lively. And so, by your Rules, he will be the more knowing. If it be true, that all Knowledge lies only in the perception of the agreement or disagreement of our own *Ideas*, the Visions of an Enthusiast, and the Reasonings of a sober Man, will be equally certain.[23]

The fact that such an objection, striking to the heart of Locke's program, should occur well over five hundred pages into even so maddeningly disorganized a work as the *Essay concerning Human Understanding* gives reason to suspect that the answer will not wholly satisfy.[24] On this point, readers will have to form their own opinion. For us the passage is interesting in another regard—for the insight it permits into the practical motives of Locke's system. The danger of this system seems to be that the criteria for knowledge are so subjective and private that the "Visions of an Enthusiast, and the Reasonings of a sober Man" cannot be distinguished. But this danger conceals a hidden advantage, for if the superiority of the "sober Man" over the "Enthusiast" has been somewhat restricted, the "Enthusiast," in the habit of taking greater liberties, suffers a still more radical curtailment. The "Enthusiast" envisioned here is not a generic madman but one of a peculiar stripe: that of the inwardly illuminated Protestant. Along with the "superstitious" Catholic, this figure is one of the two chief targets of Locke's polemic. To recognize the identity of these targets is to understand why Locke should have been so concerned to draw the limits of human knowledge. The effect he desired was a denial of all claims to social and religious authority that might disturb the current establishment.[25]

In order to enforce their suspicion of religion and paternalist authority, the empiricists were willing to reason the world itself out of existence. It was left to Hume to take this train of argument to its logical conclusion. For him, our knowledge is so tenuous that only when we forget our philosophical selves can we engage in the most common beliefs, such as the existence of the body or the external world. Belief is a matter of custom and habit, and is "more properly an act of the sensitive, than of the cogitative part of our natures."[26] Freud shared this view in a less extreme version. For him, our common beliefs about the world, those that go beyond the realm of science, arise when we mistake our own mental habits and feelings for part of the objective world. Such 'projections' of the empirical subject onto the data of experience are, for Freud, a normal, unavoidable part of life: "For when we refer causes of certain sensations to the external world, instead of looking for them, as in other cases, within, this normal proceeding is projection."[27] Or, as Hume would have it, "If we believe, that fire warms, or water refreshes, 'tis only because it costs us too much pains to think otherwise" (270). When Freud asserts that the meaning and value of life have no objective existence, it is the empiricist mode that he is drawing on. 'Meaning' and 'value' in this vocabulary are not simply errors. They have a certain concrete reality, and are, indeed, inescapable; but their reality has nothing to do with the world that they envision. That world is a mere creation of the mind shadowing forth its irrepressible sense of order onto phenomena. According to their own descriptions, empiricist philosophers, achieving the absolute of suspicion, are in this respect like the paranoid—that, leaving the study for the real world, they cannot help seeing more than is *really* there.

The great innovation of Kant was to accept the inaccessibility of things-in-themselves, the failure of the senses to achieve true knowledge, and to reestablish experience not upon the basis of truth but upon the reliability and universality of the subject. The consistency of the world and the coherence of our experience become now attributable to the activity of the mind itself—not imposed haphazard, as for Hume, but governed by an intellectual necessity. The implications of this way of thinking are decidedly unfavorable to a reductionism of the Freudian variety, and to mechanical reductions of any kind, applied to the process of thought. The notion that, in spite of the subjective character of physical experience, it is the same for all of us, provides a somewhat genial regulation of suspicion, holding out the possibility of a new authority in the domain of science. The new, 'transcendental' sanction lays claim to validity but without immediate knowledge, demonstration but without an object. Being removed from the realm of things-in-themselves, it is immune from infection either by metaphysical or theological sources, invulnerable to co-optation either for religious purposes or political ones. Kant's philosophy seems to offer a stable, even hardy variety of suspicion, and, like Bacon's, it is compatible with a positive, productive outlook.

Kant confined the reactionary impulse to discover the order of the mind in nature to the faculty of the aesthetic, or, more broadly, of practical judgment; Freud would subsequently locate the sources of the aesthetic in the unconscious. Attempting to account for the inaccessibility of that region of the mind, Freud explicitly invokes Kantian transcendentalism:

The psycho-analytic assumption of unconscious mental activity appears to us, on the one hand, as a further expansion of the primitive animism which caused us to see copies of our own consciousness all around us, and, on the other hand, as an extension of the corrections undertaken by Kant of our views on external perception. Just as Kant warned us not to overlook the fact that our perceptions are subjectively conditioned and must not be regarded as identical with what is perceived though unknowable, so psycho-analysis warns us not to equate perceptions by means of consciousness with the unconscious mental processes which are their object. Like the physical, the psychical is not necessarily in reality what it appears to us to be. We shall be glad to learn, however, that the correction of internal perception will turn out not to offer such great difficulties as the correction of external perception—that internal objects are less unknowable than the external world.[28]

This is a remarkable passage. Freud first acknowledges—again—the likeness between psychoanalytic and animistic thinking, in that they both seek copies of their own consciousness in the phenomenal world. What saves the psychoanalyst from a naive narcissism is his Kantian suspicion: he recognizes a divide between his own sensations and the external world. This same divide now opens within, between the conscious and the unconscious mind.[29] It is as if the conscious intelligence stands in a space between two screens: one to the outside, where it recognizes the projections of the external world, another to the inside, where it recognizes the forms that the unconscious mind projects upon the surface of conscious awareness. On either side it is removed from reality. The aim of Kant's transcendental turn was to sacrifice immediacy of knowledge of the external world for certainty within the domain of the subject. Within this transcendental domain, the subject gives its own law to nature and to its own will. It was an inward migration intended to establish an unshakable autonomy. Freud upsets this intention by introducing within the enclosed kingdom of the Kantian subject the same division and distance that separate it from the outside world. Opening this new and ungovernable territory, the unconscious, Freud established an internal Other which, as he stated, showed reason that it was not the master of its own house. Freud's description of the unconscious mind leaves no doubt about its foreignness to reason and the 'ego'. The wishes that appear in dreams, he reports,

are first and foremost manifestations of an unbridled and ruthless egoism. . . . The ego, freed from all ethical bonds, also finds itself at one with all the demands of sexual desire, even those which have long been condemned by our aesthetic upbringing and those which contradict all the requirements of moral restraint. The desire for pleasure—the 'libido', as we call it—chooses its objects without inhibition, and by preference, indeed, the forbidden ones: not only other men's wives, but above all incestuous objects, objects sanctified by the common agreement of mankind, a man's mother and sister, a woman's father and brother. . . . Lusts which we think of as remote from human nature show themselves strong enough to provoke dreams. Hatred, too, rages without restraint. Wishes for revenge and death directed against those who are nearest and dearest in waking life, against the dreamer's parents, brothers and sisters, husband or wife, and his own children are nothing unusual. These censored wishes appear to rise up out of a positive Hell; after they have been interpreted when we are awake, no censorship of them seems to us too severe.[30]

This "positive Hell" is the inner life, the life of the will, that stands on the far side of Freud's Kantian subject. From now on the claims of reason to have established its dominion over the will could only be exposed as the disguises that they are, disguises of the unconscious, which always gives the lie to the pretensions of autonomy. Freud's psychology preserved the defensive resources of Kantian subjectivism as a useful hedge against metaphysical assertion, even while he introduced into the Kantian system a still more penetrating and destabilizing suspicion.

Freud's greatest debt to Kant was in the latter's conception of the aesthetic, which became the ultimate home of Bacon's "mimic and fabulous worlds." In accomplishing his transcendental turn, Kant had managed to preserve those powers that had presumed in metaphysical culture to grasp things in the world according to the mind's own sense of fitness. While he deprived them of the reality they had once projected across the divide separating the mind from things-in-themselves, he established for them a domain of their own—the domain of aesthetic judgment. In this domain, the mind could enjoy its own sense of order realized within the elements of the external world as long as it recognized that the sole purpose of this order lay in the pleasure it produced. This was the meaning of Kant's formula for art as the pleasure in 'purposeless purpose', 'finality without end'. Once again Kant's motive was to accept the strictures of suspicion with regard to the external world in order to establish a more reliable, internal dominion for the subject. The special harmlessness of the aesthetic impulse is that it takes no interest in things-in-themselves. It is immune to the temptations of epistemic authority and of moral acquisitiveness. It has no component of 'interest'. Its only pleasure arises from the sense of harmony that the objects of beauty can produce among the mind's own cognitive faculties. Thus Kant preserved the dignity of the projective sense, the 'aesthetic judgment', while containing it strictly within bounds. His analysis of the pleasure of the aesthetic provides within his system the sense that the radically contracted subjectivity he describes still embraces a psychological completeness and contains the wholeness of mental experience. Alongside the aesthetic judgment narrowly defined, Kant also recognized the merely practical uses of the teleological sense he had banished from transcendental reason.

Freud imagines the unconscious mind, in its preference for order, to be very much like the aesthetic realm of Kant; it fulfills itself in those elements of consciousness that resonate with its teleological sense of desire. This sense is created by the repression from consciousness of the narcissistic craving for self-confined order very much as the teleology of Kant was confined to the aesthetic. Once again, however, Freud introduces a new theme of suspicion within the Kantian paradigm. The narcissistic impulse that finds its expression in artistic form is by no means free from the taint of physical desire, as Kant had thought, being nothing other than a disguised product of Eros. And the aesthetic judgment cannot in the Freudian model be considered universal as it was for Kant: as we have seen, the artist gratifies his own narcissistic wishes within a historically conditioned climate of repression. He is free to express his narcissistic fantasies in disguised form because of the repressions conceded by others. These repressions stem originally from social inequalities, and the artist reinforces them even as he gratifies his own libidinal drive. Freud worshipped art and the artist; he considered them as his precursors; but he did not spare them the suspicion he directed toward all human behavior, including, in principle, his own. The idealistic or 'narcissistic', order-seeking aspect of the unconscious is not incompatible with the impulses that make it resemble a "positive Hell."

In general, Freud took into his system the suspiciousness of modern epistemology, the sense of the limits of knowledge which that tradition has erected. His view of the human subject is one of radical self-enclosure. But this self-enclosure does not produce simple, incoherent privacy, as it tended to do for Hume in his most skeptical moments. Nor does it have the resources of cognitive necessity attributed to it by Kant. What it has is the regularity of a physical system, which can be charted, predicted, and, sometimes, adjusted. The phenomena of consciousness are deceptive, but they are deceptive in a way ultimately consistent and predictable once the secret motives of our hypocrisy have been unmasked. The integrity of this physicalizing psychology is guaranteed by the banishing of all motives but those of a total and systematic lustfulness and selfishness to the realm of mere appearances: thus Freud is able to achieve a perfect translation of the appearance of intellectual order into the reality of moral chaos.

Historical Suspicion

The third component of Freudian suspicion is perhaps the most dynamic—historical suspicion. The modern sense of history as a movement of progress in knowledge can be felt stirring in Bacon, for if the Baconian project succeeds in the agenda it has set for itself, before long the advancement of human knowledge will render obsolete all that the past has believed about the natural world. Humanity, in that case, will move from a culture of false intellectual glamour to one of practical power. The ages of the past will stand condemned in comparison with the present. Bacon's psychological distinction between the intellectualist method, based upon 'Anticipations of the Mind', and the true practical science, based upon 'Interpretations of Nature', contains the resources for a historical ideology of progress that Bacon himself did not fully exploit but that his successors would vigorously deploy even down to the time of Freud.[31] For this ideology, the past becomes synonymous with error in all of its forms—superstition and intolerance, enforced by priestcraft, enthusiasm, ignorance, prejudice of every kind, the undisciplined intellect left prey to its own excesses and to all the mystifications of private interest. The present, in this model, is by contrast always an age of true submission to the evidence of the senses and to the facts themselves, freed from the distractions of human desire. The present repudiates the past as a world of fantasy, a world "as one would," to use

Bacon's language, while taking its stand upon the hard, cold ground of the real.

Freud's distinction between the 'pleasure principle' and the 'principle of reality', then, was first a historical distinction. Perhaps the most telling formulation of the idea of a primitive historical 'narcissism' was given by Vico in his account of the metaphysical poetry of the age of giants, which remains for him the imaginative substrate of human culture:

> It is noteworthy that in all languages the greater part of the expressions relating to inanimate things are formed by metaphor from the human body and its parts and from the human senses and passions. Thus, head for top or beginning; the brow and shoulders of a hill; the eyes of needles and of potatoes; mouth for any opening; the lip of a cup or pitcher; the gorge of a river; a neck of land; an arm of the sea; the hands of a clock; heart for center (the Latins used *umbilicus*, navel, in this sense); the belly of a sail. . . . The farmers of Latium used to say the fields were thirsty, bore fruit, were swollen with grain; and our rustics speak of plants making love, vines going resinous, trees weeping. Innumerable other examples could be collected from all languages. All of which is a consequence of our axiom that man in his ignorance makes himself the rule of the universe, for in the examples cited he has made of himself an entire world. So that, as rational metaphysics teaches that man becomes all things by understanding them . . . , this imaginative metaphysics shows that man becomes all things by *not* understanding them . . . ; and perhaps the latter proposition is truer than the former, for when man understands he extends his mind and takes in the things, but when he does not understand he makes the things out of himself and becomes them by transforming himself into them.[32]

This is a perfectly Freudian and Baconian formulation. In Vico's *New Science*, the psychological suspicion of the 'narcissistic' intellect, which is active in Bacon's scientific methodology, becomes part of the basis of a full-blown typology of historical stages, each stage being the embodiment of a different form of thought and virtually a different human nature. Vico's conception of the original race of giants might even have provided an indirect inspiration for Darwin's conception of the primal father.[33] The question of Vico's influence, direct or indirect, need not concern us here. His thinking provides a prescient example of the form of historical suspicion which would be a decisive element of the intellectual climate that gave birth to psychoanalysis.

Vico tended to value the imaginative qualities of the primitive giants who began human culture. The French Enlightenment theorists and practitioners of history, politically engaged against what they took to be reactionary elements in the present, regarded the past with suspicious contempt; every step away from its barbarous practices necessarily accomplished some movement of progress. Such was the attitude of Gibbon, Voltaire, Condorcet, Kant, and their descendants. Kant struck the dominant note when, in the programmatic essay "What Is Enlightenment?" he declared that Enlightenment was the emergence of humanity from childhood. In his essay on universal history, Kant makes explicit the implications of this view of human progress, speculating that "man" is the species that cannot achieve perfection in a single lifetime, as all other creatures do; rather, having departed from the guidance of nature in order to undertake responsibility for himself through reason, mankind will require an evolution through many generations in order to become perfect.[34]

Already in Kant's portrayal of Enlightenment as the maturity of man there is a softening toward the past, for maturity must rest upon its childhood and cannot truly leave it behind. If perfection is the historical fulfillment, or telos, of the human species, then all of the phases required to attain this perfection constitute part of its inner necessity. Kant had already been influenced to some degree by the reversal of historical sympathies accomplished in the writings of Rousseau, where primitive nature suddenly emerges out from under the eclipse of progress to exert a new claim upon the present. For Rousseau, the natural element of the human character becomes a regenerative force that could potentially be called upon to reverse the decadence of civilization. These considerations exerted a decisive influence upon Rousseau's theory of education, which he viewed as an attempt to preserve as much of nature within the child as was possible for a socially useful human being. Rousseau's great polemics on behalf of natural morality initiated the tendency, so pronounced in Freud, to see individual development as a dialectic of progressive and reactionary forces connected with the values of different phases of history. As Freud puts it, "Mankind never lives entirely in the present. The past, the tradition of the race and of the people, lives on in the ideologies of the super-ego, and yields only slowly to the influences of the present."[35]

Dialectical psycho-history was taken to its apogee, of course, by Hegel. Hegel's dialectic was an ingenious attempt to recuperate the meaning of the past from the standpoint of the present, to see in the intellectual life of each past epoch a validity relative to its place in the progressive movement of Mind. In Hegel's thought, each standpoint of intelligence is limited in itself, yet each is necessary to the eventual freedom of self-consciousness. For this reason, it is essential for the individual, in his own Bildung, his own movement toward self-consciousness, to retrace each of these prior stages, in the process recapitulating the intellectual history of humanity. The idea that the individual recapitulates the mental development of the species also became part of Auguste Comte's system of positivism, with its three stages of human development—the 'theological', the 'metaphysical', and the 'positivist', or scientific: "Now, each of us is aware, if he looks back upon his own history, that he was a theologian in his childhood, a metaphysician in his youth, and a natural philosopher in his manhood. All men who are up to their age can verify this for themselves."[36]

In the development of these psycho-historical models an interesting series of transformations has taken place. Bacon's scientific method asserted a distinction between 'intellectualist' and practical science. The distinction began as a psychological one applying to different individuals exercising their intellectual faculties in a different way. With the success of Baconian thinking, this psychological distinction became historical in character. The transition from one form of thinking to another appeared now as a necessary goal for the progress of civilization. Finally, with the rise of historicism of the Hegelian or Comtean kind, the stages of historical progress reenter the intellectual life of the individual as necessary phases of development. What began as a psychological distinction between individuals using different methods of inquiry becomes in the later model a psychological distinction between different periods of each person's intellectual and emotional life.[37] In the Freudian system, as we have seen, the principle that the individual repeats the developmental history of the species is a tenet of biology. It entered Darwinian science through the efforts of Ernst Haeckel, propounder of the law that 'ontogeny recapitulates phylogeny'.[38] Haeckel eventually made this one of the principles of a cosmic philosophy, a progressive historico-physical 'monism', which he deployed in opposition to all of the usual scientific enemies, especially Jesuitical Catholicism.[39] Haeckel's theory enjoyed surprising respectability and influence among biologists into the twentieth century.

In all of its forms, biological or historical, the principle of recapitulation allows the progress of history, with its suspicious overcoming of the past, to make its appearance within the personal development of the individual. It is a historical ideology injected into the sphere of the psyche and thereby falsely universalized. In the Freudian Bildungsroman, the hero struggles to free himself from the reactionary forces of narcissism massed in the unconscious. These forces embody the biological traces of the paternal enemies of the past, the primal fathers and their mythical substitutes, God and his poet-priests. The psychological difficulties that beset the individual at each period of his or her life can be understood as the products of tension between relatively progressive and relatively reactionary psychological elements, just as for Comte or Marx the tensions within any particular historical moment can be understood as the products of conflict between relatively progressive and relatively reactionary social or economic forces. The movement from the pleasure principle to the reality principle is thus a historical and, indeed, a political achievement, as well as a personal one. It is a triumph over fixation in the past, a triumph over the temptations of regression to the rule of the 'ancient pleasure principle':

> The liberation of an individual, as he grows up, from the authority of his parents is one of the most necessary though one of the most painful results brought about by the course of his development. It is quite essential that that liberation should occur and it may be presumed that it has been to some extent achieved by everyone who has reached a normal state. Indeed, the whole progress of society rests upon the opposition between successive generations. On the other hand, there is a class of neurotics whose condition is recognizably determined by their having failed in this task.[40]

It could not be more clear that the "liberation" of the individual is as much a political and social necessity as it is a psychological one. Freud's agonistic psychology must be played out between the ranks of each generation in order for progress to continue. Those like Quixote who succumb to paranoia have tragically or comically betrayed the struggle for progress in favor of the ancien régime.[41]

Freud identifies wholeheartedly with the progress of science; but it would be a mistake to consider him a true cultural optimist. His progressivism is sincere, and even militant, so long as it looks backward toward what has been left behind. But for the present and the future, Freud reverts to his habitual irony, often taken by his admirers as a form of tragic moralism. For him, the psychic forces that draw us backward into the past can never be truly vanquished, not even in individuals who have been subjected to the most thoroughgoing and protracted psychoanalytic discipline and who have achieved the most worthy and admirable characters:

> There are nearly always residual phenomena, a partial hanging back. When an open-handed Maecenas surprises us by some isolated trait of miserliness, or when a person who is consistently over-kind suddenly indulges in a hostile action, such 'residual phenomena' are invaluable for genetic research. They show us that these praiseworthy and precious qualities are based on compensations which, as was to have been expected, have not been absolutely successful.[42]

Here the progressivist psycho-history shows its instrumental aptness for suspicion: the least glimmer of imperfection in a person's character reveals his or her true nature, while betraying that the remaining virtues are a more successfully disguised form of selfishness. So the reactionary elements of character betray the ultimate falseness of the progressive as well. And what is true of the individual is no less true of the mass: "Of all the erroneous and superstitious beliefs of mankind that have supposedly been surmounted there is not one whose residues do not live on among us to-day in the lower strata of civilized peoples or even in the highest strata of cultural society. What has once come to life clings tenaciously to its existence. One feels inclined to doubt sometimes whether the dragons of primaeval days are really extinct" (229). How seamlessly the biological and social strata merge in this elegant mythology.[43]

The bio-historical myth of progress that is the basis of Freud's progressive psychology has its roots, we have seen, in a dubious evolutionary science dubiously applied. When we recall the form of the narrative of bio-history, however, we find that it has a distinctly Hegelian cast to it, a strangely rationalistic, idealizing, and even dialectical character. Freud's thinking, true to what we shall see is its Cervantean tenor, mirrors the form of the purest example of its opposite in order to give it a satiric turn. As it is like animism, so it is like Hegelian philosophy. Hegel's dialectical history begins with an absolute separation between mind and world, subject and object. It moves by a process of negation, a progressive unmasking of error, which shows to the subject its unconscious contributions to what had seemed an objective world existing independently of mind. By this process of negation and ever-widening suspicion, mind eventually comes to recognize that all along it was identical with that outer world, that the strangeness and alterity which that world once presented were the by-products of an insufficiently achieved self-consciousness. Freud's untranslatable maxim describing the mastering of the id by the ego perfectly fits Hegel's concept of negation as self-recognition: *Wo Es war, soll Ich werden* ("Where it [id] was, there shall I [ego] be").[44] Hegel thus envisions the overcoming of the divide between inner and outer that had been put solidly into place by Kant.

Freud's psycho-historical scheme is a perfect inversion of Hegel's. For Freud, history begins with the absolute identity of subject and object represented by the perfect narcissism of the primal father. As with Hegel, the progress of history comes with negation, or repression. And now it concludes with the scientist, who attains the perfect subtraction of his subjectivity from objective reality, the perfect renunciation of his narcissistic confusion of self and world. Freud ends where Hegel began. Both men associated the progressive movement of history with the history of science. For both of them, the scientific perspective they had achieved was in itself the goal of history, being the one standpoint from which its movement could be grasped. But while Hegel saw all of past history as redeemed in the present moment of knowledge, Freud saw the present as the one standpoint from which the futility of the past could be fully appreciated. The present was superior not because it had better access to truth but only because it had transcended the errors of what had gone before. The value of the present lay in the renunciations that had been necessary to achieve it and the science that could keep them in place.

Freud does hold out one utopian promise, which is that, through education, science could eventually become an object of passionate interest for modern people, thus saving them from the impoverishment of emotional life caused by the discrediting of religion. The "effects of repression" would be replaced by "the results of the rational operation of the intellect. In this way," Freud concludes, "our appointed task of reconciling men to civilization will to a great extent be achieved."[45] It was one of the central aspirations of post-Romantic historical thought that the unity of intellect and desire that it discerned in the state of natural life should be recovered on the higher ground of culture. Freud offers this ray of hope in the most tentative terms in *The Future of an Illusion*. He is more powerful, and more distinctly himself, when in *Civilization and Its Discontents* (1930) he alludes to the frustrations that come with the taming of human nature and to the false satisfactions of technology, which, as we have seen, transform man into a melancholy "prosthetic God." The renunciations necessary for cultural harmony turn the violence of human nature inward and lead to increasing guilt. Even by charity we are undone. It is a dark, ironic, and formidably suspicious conclusion for the German philosophy of Bildung, though one, it must be acknowledged, suited to the political currents of the 1930s.

Political Suspicion

Freud made trenchant use of the suspicious potential within the liberal ideology of progress. This ideology, however, became less and less persuasive to him during his lifetime. Freud always maintained his admiration for liberal England; but the politics of his own country did not engage him:

"Politically," he remarked in 1926, "I am just nothing."[46] This is again not surprising given the discouraging climate of the time. It is tempting to say that Freud was 'ambivalent' toward politics and toward the idea of progress; but the use of that term would only draw our attention back to the problems of Freudian logic, its generally 'ambivalent', paradoxical, and contradictory character. It will be more illuminating, perhaps, to consider that along with the hopeful attitude toward science and the admiration for civilization that Freud holds partially in common with the Enlightenment, there is a countervailing element in his thought that also touches a major chord of distinctively modern culture: suspicion as the basis of political authority itself. The source is not hard to locate: Freud is a major exponent of the dark liberalism of Hobbes cast into still deeper shades by the gloomy sciences of Malthus and Darwin. Hobbesian suspicion of human nature is at the root of Freud's attitude toward individuals and toward society.

Hobbes believed that the problem of political life stems not simply from human aggressiveness but from our inability to agree upon the basic political and social realities. His estimate of the human intelligence recognizes the tendency toward self-infatuation that Freud was to call 'narcissism':

> For such is the nature of men, that howsoever they may acknowledge many others to be more witty, or more eloquent, or more learned; Yet they will hardly believe there be many so wise as themselves: For they see their own wit at hand, and other mens at a distance. . . . From this equality of ability, ariseth equality of hope in the attaining of our Ends. And therefore if any two men desire the same thing, which neverthelesse they cannot both enjoy, they become enemies; and in the way to their End, (which is principally their owne conservation, and sometimes their delectation only,) endeavour to destroy, or subdue one another.[47]

The inability of human beings to regulate hope and ambition by the dictates of reason is indeed a formidable obstacle to the security of life. It ensures an endless, unsettled competition. But Hobbes finds an even more difficult obstacle to human well-being prior to the establishment of society: human beings do not agree upon the value of the objects for which they compete, nor even upon the meanings of the words they apply in the judgment of such objects. The terms 'good' and 'evil' are in meaning entirely relative to the pleasure of the individual (39). What we have, then, is a kind of privacy, a self-enclosure of thinking and desire, which ensures that social relations can only be based on force, there being no shared ground of reason upon which human beings could establish their relation to each other. It was this conception that led to Hobbes' impressive description of the unimproved human condition as "solitary, poore, nasty, brutish, and short" (89).

The solution Hobbes envisioned for the dilemma he had posed was a radical and simple one: since human beings could not agree upon the relative strengths of their own powers, the objects of desire, or the meaning of the terms in their moral and political vocabulary, they would have to cede the power to govern themselves to a single authority that would provide the unity necessary to support the state. From that moment, the relativity of value would give way to a single, fixed standard. Justice would for the first time come into existence, there being no right or wrong without civil society to establish them. Individuals would enjoy an equality of power arising out of their common submission to the state. The authority of the state, or 'Leviathan' as Hobbes calls it, does not rest in any higher justification or privileged knowledge. Its authority is practical. Being single, uniform, and indefeasible, it possesses all the virtues of truth: endowed with absolute power, it puts an end to every argument. It is to escape from the 'incommodities' of 'civil war' and to secure these advantages that individual citizens give their unconditional allegiance to the commonwealth. The basis was a kind of covenant, but a covenant that secured only one side, it being incompatible with the nature of the sovereign to submit to an agreement (112). No power could restrict his authority, for it was sustained by power alone; it was the essence of the sovereign to be free and beyond obligation: his people were bound to him without return.

The power of Hobbes' argument is that it takes for the very basis of its understanding the divisive, competitive aspects of human nature that had come so prominently into view in the civil wars of the time. Leaving no suspicion unacknowledged, he seems to meet the problems of politics head on. His solution, though, is a singularly paranoid one, for what it amounts to is that the only remedy for political dissension is that all differences be annihilated in the will of a single, omnipotent person—the sovereign. The sovereign cannot argue or make covenants because there is no basis for overcoming differences of thought or of interest. He cannot recognize any moral, intellectual, or political agency outside himself. His freedom rests in an incapacity for difference or, rather, a capacity to repress difference that cannot be tested by any other agent. The notion is deeply embedded in the radical strain of modern political culture. Such freedom is the sanction of Rousseau's *volonté général*, which, under the 'social contract,' becomes the will of a single collective being deriving its right simply from existence:

"The sovereign by the mere fact that it is, is always all that it ought to be."[48] From the rulings of this power it is technically impossible for the individual to dissent; those who appear to do so must be "forced to be free" (64). Such, also, is the perfect unity of the Marxian proletariat: all differences are reconciled in the paradoxically universal class, which will dissolve all classes.[49] And for Nietzsche the most essential characteristic of the bygone aristocratic class, the mark of its superior strength, was that it recognized no interests or values other than its own; without *ressentiment*, it would be neither for nor against.[50] This was its freedom, to be recovered by the 'overman', or 'superman'. Now let us reread Freud's description of the primal father, that figure whose return from repression is paranoia:

The father of the primal horde was free. His intellectual acts were strong and independent even in isolation, and his will needed no reinforcement from others. Consistency leads us to assume that his ego had very few libidinal ties; he loved no one but himself, or other people only in so far as they served his needs. . . . Here at the very beginning of the history of mankind, was the 'superman' whom Nietzsche only expected from the future. Even to-day the members of the group [in typical group psychology] stand in need of the illusion that they are equally and justly loved by the leader; but the leader himself need love no one else, he may be of a masterful nature, absolutely narcissistic, self-confident and independent.[51]

Freud's primal father is evidently a mythological repetition of 'Leviathan', one of those primeval dragons never wholly vanquished. It is, in other words, a political fiction. The father's freedom comes of moral solitude sustained by absolute power. He can never be bound in love to his followers, and this is what marks him as the leader. He is in the most literal sense a law unto himself. Hobbes' attempt to justify the authority of the state has become for Freud the bedrock of human psychology, with its origins in primeval history. Once again we observe that the unconscious minds of Freud's patients were curiously populated with the intellectual dramatis personae of the seventeenth century.

In cannot be said, however, that Freud's Hobbesian tendencies are inadvertent. He is actually a self-conscious continuator of Hobbes, and his contribution to the Hobbesian tradition is an interesting one. Hobbes' solution to the dilemma of political authority suffers from an obvious weakness. Having denied that human beings possess whatever measure of reason it would take to govern themselves, he advises them reasonably to abrogate their freedom. But of course in order to do so they would need at least a Hobbesian intelligence, and this is just what he has theoretically denied to them: Hobbes' own profound intelligence and certainty of practical judgment seem, then, uncanny and in contradiction with his theory. We find ourselves, once again, confronted with the reflexive dilemma of the reductionist. In the light of this problem, Freud's version of the transition from the war of all against all to the state of civilization bears close examination:

> Such, then, was the original state of things: domination by whoever had the greater might—domination by brute violence or by violence supported by intellect. As we know, this régime was altered in the course of evolution. There was a path that led from violence to right or law. What was that path? It is my belief that there was only one; the path which led by way of the fact that the superior strength of a single individual could be rivalled by the union of several weak ones. '*L'union fait la force.*' Violence could be broken by union, and the power of those who were united now represented law in contrast to the violence of the single individual. Thus we see that right is the might of a community. It is still violence, ready to be directed against any individual who resists; it works by the same methods and follows the same purposes. The only real difference lies in the fact that what prevails is no longer the violence of an individual but that of a community. But in order that the transition from violence to this new right or justice may be effected one psychological condition must be fulfilled. The union of the majority must be a stable and lasting one. If it were only brought about for the purpose of combating a single dominant individual and were dissolved after his defeat, nothing would have been accomplished. The next person who thought himself superior in strength would once more seek to set up a dominion by violence and the game would be repeated *ad infinitum*. The community must be maintained permanently, must be organized, must institute authorities to see that those regulations—the laws—are respected and to superintend the execution of legal acts of violence. The recognition of a community of interests such as these leads to the growth of emotional ties between the members of a united group of people—communal feelings which are the true source of its strength.[52]

Freud has in a sense solved the Hobbesian dilemma, for now the transition from the state of war to civilization is envisioned "in the course of evolution." It is no longer up to the individual intelligence to achieve it; rather, each of us forms a bond with the community as a part of normal development. Might has already disguised itself as right and been inscribed in our nature in the form of a capacity for libidinally charged social ties. It is even possible, Freud speculates, that the scope of communal feeling should expand and become universal, thus putting an end to war. But it is not likely. For politics here becomes an entirely irrational activity, each one of us holding in the unconscious a Hobbesian Leviathan, a primal father still craving for an absolute freedom and moral solitude. The fact that we have repressed this creature does not entirely save us from its promptings. Rather, those who have repressed their own narcissistic tendencies find themselves all the more vulnerable to the demands of the paranoids and other narcissists who act them out. Perhaps this is the juncture at which to wonder, if political discourse is nothing but a disguise for absolute selfish interest, if political life is driven entirely by irrational forces, and if there is no authority other than the authority of power, as Hobbes, Rousseau, Nietzsche, Marx, Freud, and others believe, in what sense can paranoia be called a distortion of reality? Paranoia seems to be abundantly justified, it seems to be a natural and logical development out of this crucial strain of political philosophy of which it provides a faithful psychological reflection.

The partial and skeletal typology of suspicion that I have set out in these pages can only begin to suggest the broad scope of its influence in modern culture. Psychoanalysis holds within itself every element of modern suspicion in a rich sedimentation of historical motifs and ideological gestures. It is apparently not the account of universal human nature that it claims to be, but a complex, ironic psychological allegory of the cultural struggles of modernity. We find in this allegory the enemies we would expect—the models and progenitors of religion, for instance. But we find as well the models for the impulse to destroy religion and the impulse to set up poetry in its place. The destructive and creative figures turn out to be very much alike—primal father, poet, philosopher, scientist, paranoid—all narcissists, all destroying and building over the void. And the psychoanalyst too builds over the void. It is no longer possible to accept the 'biogenetic' principle of recapitulation that held this allegory together. But in fact, what the genealogy of Freud's theoretical framework reveals is a different form of recapitulation. The details of Freud's account of individual development recapitulate not bio-history but the history of modern culture in a powerful apologetic version. This version is by no means novel. Rather, it combines the already existing self-conceptions of modernity in a synthesis of great rhetorical originality. It resonates with the historical experience that modernity has created for itself in living out its heroic contradictions; and it repeats these contradictions in an impressively scientific mode of discourse. In place of the bio-genetic law it might be preferable, when dealing with the interpretation of psychoanalytic concepts, to apply instead a psycho-historical law. Such a law would hold that the phases of individual development as they are described by Freud recapitulate the cultural conflicts of modernity in that same version Freud also transferred onto the primeval past.

Freud achieved the perfect synthesis of scientific, social, epistemological, and historical suspicion. It is this achievement that has made him
seem to so many to be the fulfillment of modern self-understanding, the
author and hero of its gospel. Nietzsche, crying in the wilderness of his
own special void, looked forward to the arrival of such a figure in prophetic
tones, calling, at the beginning of *The Gay Science*, for a "philosophical
physician in the exceptional sense of that word"—Nietzsche often prefers
the exceptional sense—who would "carry [his] suspicion to its limits":

> Every philosophy that ranks peace above war, every ethic with a negative definition
> of happiness, every metaphysics and physics that knows some *finale*, some final
> state of some sort, every predominantly aesthetic or religious craving for some
> Apart, Beyond, Outside, Above, permits the question whether it was not sickness
> that inspired the philosopher. The unconscious disguise of physiological needs
> under the cloaks of the objective, ideal, purely spiritual goes to frightening
> lengths—and often I have asked myself whether, taking a large view, philosophy
> has not been merely an interpretation of the body, and a *misunderstanding of
> the body*.[53]

Freud indeed took this particular suspicion of Nietzsche's to its limits,
and many who have read Nietzsche have prized him because of the way he
seems to have anticipated and prefigured Freud. But after all, the philosophical form of suspicious medicine Nietzsche had in mind was not
new. After Cervantes, Bacon, Hobbes, Rochefoucauld, Swift, Voltaire,
Rousseau, Stendhal, Marx, and Dostoevsky, to name just a few salient
examples, not forgetting the supreme achievement of Nietzsche himself in
the genre of heroic irony, it would seem that suspicion had already attained
all of the psychological refinement and all of the solipsistic self-intoxication
of which it was capable. But it is one of the characteristics of heroic
suspicion that it requires continuous renewal. It is original and restless by
nature, ever in search of more certain grounds for doubt, of bolder, more
challenging and exhilarating methods of self-demystification. It was Freud's
ability to repeat the typical gestures of modern suspicion in a novel,
scientific vocabulary that made him seem for so many to be the last word in
human self-understanding. The unconscious, which he believed himself
the first to explore, did contain more than a few dragons; they were not
primeval, though, in their origin, merely the familiar dragons of modernity
masquerading under the title of universal psychology and given a new
space in which to pose.

FIVE

Freudian Satire

Don't you find it very touching to read how a great
person, himself an idealist, makes fun of his ideals? Before we were so fortunate as to apprehend
the deep truths in our love we were all noble
knights passing through the world caught in a
dream, misinterpreting the simplest things, magnifying commonplaces into something noble and rare,
and thereby cutting a sad figure. Therefore we men
always read with respect about what we once were
and in part still remain.
      — Freud to Martha Bernays on Cervantes

Freud's ability to digest the suspicious logic of his precursors and to
reformulate it in the terms of a science must be accounted one of the great
elements of his success. But it is not the whole of it: his rhetorical genius
must also share a large measure of the credit. Freud's literary gifts and
sensibility have often been acknowledged; but we cannot appreciate the
true character even of his literary achievement without recognizing that in
this aspect of his work, too, Freud was depending heavily upon the well-
established resources of suspicion. Satire was the dominant form of imagination of the culture of suspicion from its beginnings in the seventeenth
century until its transformation by Romanticism late in the eighteenth
century, and it was from this strain of modern culture that the rhetoric of
psychoanalysis took its cast.

I have made the point that Cervantes invented the paranoid character as
an object of literary representation. His accomplishment betrays, no doubt,
a gift of psychological observation, but it is psychological observation at
the service of a satiric purpose. The *Quixote* is a portrait of suspicion
directed, with suspicion, at a distinct object of satire, the "books of
chivalry" popular in Cervantes' day. Freud's psychology has a strikingly
similar character. His powers of psychological observation were employed,
in a spirit of mockery, toward a few constant victims—religion, metaphys-

ics, tradition, and, more ambiguously, bourgeois morality—all upholders, in other words, of idealism. There is always, too, in the Freudian satire, a hero in the role of the scientist, but even he is not exempt from the ironies of the unconscious. Marking the affinities between Cervantes and Freud, we shall be drawing together two of the greatest practitioners of the satiric romance.

Were we to play that game, long popular among literary critics, of looking for anticipations of Freud in writers of the past, it is undoubtedly among the satirists that we should enjoy the highest frequency of success. In what other work than Erasmus's *Praise of Folly*, for instance, could be found a more thoroughgoing and perceptive portrayal of the self-glorifying, self-infatuated nature of the human psyche? Erasmus's Folly is nothing other than that aspect of psychology Freud attempted to explain under the term 'Narzissmus'. Folly's oration in praise of herself shows the emptiness of all human ambition, all glory being vainglory by the rule of illusion. Folly can boast that it is she who makes us glad to be French rather than Irish (what Freud called the 'narcissism of minor differences'), and it is she who enthralls us to the imaginary perfections of our object of love ('a state suggestive of neurotic compulsions') as well as to the foolish diversions of art (a 'mild narcosis'). It is the Folly of infants, and even of fools, that makes us love and care for them, for we see our own folly ('repressed infantile narcissism') reflected in them (13). Those who have no love for themselves cannot be expected to bestow it upon others, yet self-love ('Narzissmus') is the most beneficial Folly, the Folly that keeps us attached to life itself (31). Folly lends her energy to valor and to industry, and leads people to do more than they know how. The uninhibited reign of Folly sustains a life of happy exuberance in primitive ('unrepressed', 'totemistic') societies, in the golden age (of the 'omnipotence of thoughts') before natural philosophy could exert its repressive influence. From the viewpoint of Folly, the rule of philosophy (the 'reality principle') inhibits all the performances of life and drains away all of its charms.[1] To remove Folly would be to undermine the basis of social existence (narcissistic 'group psychology'): "Briefly, no society, no association of people in this world can be happy or last long without my help [the help of Folly]; no people would put up with their prince, no master endure his servant, no maid stand her mistress, no teacher his pupil, no friend his friend, no wife her husband, no landlord his tenant, no soldier his drinking buddy, no lodger his fellow-lodger— unless they were mistaken, both at the same time or turn and turn about, in each other" (22). Erasmus's Folly gives a clear-sighted account both of

her private and her social functions, asserting, as unambiguously as Freud
ever did, that life is driven by the force of self-deception, and society held
together in the bonds of illusion.

There is a limit, of course, to Erasmus's satiric perspective. The *Praise
of Folly* is a great jeu d'esprit, and even within it there is a recognition that
some follies do not deserve to be mocked, the folly of faith being one of
them.[2] But the ultimate differences between the Erasmian and Freudian
views of Folly/Narzissmus make the kinship of their satiric rhetoric all the
more striking. What was needed to narrow the distinction between them,
and to arrive at a fully evolved psychology of suspicion, was a mechanistic
form of physical reduction, and that was amply supplied by later psycho-
satirists, beginning with Cervantes. In the writings of Swift, for instance,
we find most powerfully exposed the subjection of intellectual life to emotions, 'vital spirits', located in the body. Swift is perhaps an even more
uncanny precursor of the Freudian way than Erasmus, and has enjoyed
recognition as such.[3] No other writer before Freud has given more vivid
illustration to the ways in which the operations of thought can undergo the
vicissitudes of physicality. Like Freud, Swift is a master at presenting
moral judgments in psycho-physical images, in works such as "The Mechanical Operations of the Spirit," an effort in the same kind as Freud's
"Obsessive Actions and Religious Practices."

English satire also provided Freud with the example of *Tristram Shandy*,
a novel whose comic hero gives a history of the formation of his character
by every accidental influence, physical and psychological, from the moment
of his birth. Tristram's self-analysis could have been the model for Freud's,
and it is grounded in the empirical and associationist psychology Freud
was eventually to inherit. There is also an affinity of satiric motives,
Sternean laughter being directed toward the staple Freudian enemies: tradition, idealism in any form, and, especially, Catholicism. There is even an
appreciation here for the sexual significance of the nose, which could have
prepared Freud for the theories of Wilhelm Fliess. *Tristram Shandy* was
one of Freud's favorite books.[4]

All of his life, Freud's literary tastes inclined distinctly toward the
ironical, the humorous, and the satiric. Among his favorite authors were
Fielding, Anatole France, Gogol, Mark Twain,[5] Bret Harte, and Lichtenberg.[6] Among novels *Tom Jones* stood alongside *Tristram Shandy* as a
particular favorite.[7] The young Freud also delighted in the clothes philosophy of Carlyle's *Sartor Resartus*, with its metaphysical sense of disguise.[8]
And he treasured Heine's sartorial jibes at the follies of the philosopher:

"With his nightcaps and the tatters of his dressing-gown he patches up the gaps in the structure of the universe."[9] In *The Interpretation of Dreams*, Freud invokes episodes from two satiric works, *Gargantua and Pantagruel* and *Gulliver's Travels*, as authoritative glosses on one of his own megalomaniacal dreams.[10] And the satanic mirth of Faust and Mephistopheles are never far from his mind: allusions to *Faust* are a running subtext throughout the oeuvre, providing bravely ironical statements of a multitude of Freudian views.[11]

After Goethe, it is to the author of the *Quixote* that Freud exhibits the deepest attachment and affinity. As a teenager he learned Spanish in order to read Cervantes, and carried on a ten-year Cervantine correspondence, often in Spanish, with his closest friend, Eduard Silberstein. "We became friends," Freud wrote to his fiancée, Martha Bernays, "at a time when one doesn't look upon friendship as a sport or an asset, but when one needs a friend with whom to share things. We used to be together literally every hour of the day that was not spent on the school bench. We learned Spanish together, had our own mythology and secret names, which we took from some dialogue of the great Cervantes."[12] The Freud-Silberstein correspondence takes the form of the proceedings of the Academie Española, a society of two members, each of the friends signing himself with the name of one of the characters in Cervantes' "Colloquy of the Dogs" (Freud was usually "Cipion"). The letters were directed to "dog in the madhouse of Seville," the two young scholars apparently having transferred the "Colloquy of the Dogs," with its four mad projectors, to the setting of the dialogue between the megalomaniacs narrated by the barber at the beginning of Part Two of *Don Quixote*. Amidst the serious ruminations of youth, Freud kept up this mock-heroic posture in the letters to Silberstein with remarkable persistence; he was continually suggesting new plans for resuscitating the languishing activities of the "A.E.," which threatened to expire "unless we turn writing into a duty attached to the sublime name of the Ac. Española and therefore demanding fulfillment at fixed times and with unswerving devotion."[13] The Academie Española provided Freud and Silberstein with a playful means of expressing the unfulfilled grandiosity of youth in comic form. It offers the first evidence of Freud's preference for secret societies and occult languages. The Academie Española stands, therefore, as the precursor of the Psychoanalytic Association and its secret "Committee," and Freud's Cervantine pastiche as a precursor language to that of psychoanalysis.[14]

Freud's devotion to the *Quixote* long outlasted his friendship with Silberstein. A few years later, during his engagement to Martha Bernays, we find him unable to write her a proper love letter, being too involved in his reading of Cervantes:

Forgive me, dearest, if I so often fail to write in a way you deserve, especially in answer to your affectionate letter, but I think of you in such calm happiness that it is easier for me to talk about outside things than about ourselves. And then it seems to be a kind of hypocrisy not to write to you what is uppermost in my mind: I have just spent two hours—it's now midnight—reading *Don Quixote*, and have really reveled in it. The stories of the indecent curiosity of Cerdenio and Dorothea, whose fate is interwoven with Quixote's adventures, of the prisoner whose story contains a piece of Cervantes' life history—all this is written with such finesse, color, and intelligence, the whole group in the enchanted tavern is so attractive, that I cannot remember ever having read anything so satisfactory which at the same time avoids exaggeration . . . : none of this is very profound, but it is pervaded by the most serene charm imaginable. Here Don Quixote is placed in the proper light through being no longer ridiculed by such crude means as beatings and physical maltreatment but by the superiority of people standing in the midst of actual life. At the same time he is tragic in his helplessness while the plot is being unraveled.[15]

Freud follows up the discussion of Quixote's character with an equally sophisticated appreciation of Doré's romanticized illustrations. Reading these words, it is difficult to avoid the impression that Freud would have found Martha at least easier to write to if she had been a member of the Academie Española. Two weeks later we find him urging Martha to continue her reading into Part Two of Cervantes' novel, which he assures her is less shocking than the first (55). If Freud's identification with Cervantes seems to be an interest Martha cannot share, it nevertheless sometimes furnished him with a language of love that she must have understood: "Before we were so fortunate as to apprehend the deep truths in our love we were all noble knights passing through the world caught in a dream, misinterpreting the simplest things, magnifying commonplaces into something noble and rare, and thereby cutting a sad figure."[16] Freud's identification with the original paranoid was a deep one that was to manifest itself crucially in the intellectual structure of psychoanalysis.

My attempt to clarify Freud's satiric portrayal of the paranoid figure will require three stages. First I will attempt a rudimentary analysis of the Quixote character as an example of paranoid psychology understood in Freudian terms. I shall adopt the common Freudian practice of granting to literary characters a multi-layered psyche, my aim being to point out the features of paranoia that a psychoanalytic reading would fix upon as explanatory. There has not been a sustained psychoanalytic treatment of

Quixote as paranoid.[17] Second, I will reassess this reading from a literary and historical perspective, emphasizing the satirical and social motives of Cervantes' novel. Finally, having integrated the psychoanalytic and satiric dimensions of the *Quixote* to the advantage of the latter, and having dealt with some likely objections, I will return, in the next chapter, to Freud's own masterwork, *The Interpretation of Dreams*, to evaluate it in a new, somewhat Quixotic light.

The Narcissistic Quixote

Midway through Part One of *Don Quixote*, confronting the adventure of the fulling mills, the paranoid knight finds it necessary once more to explain to his peasant squire the nature of his calling:

"Friend Sancho, know that I by heaven's will have been born in this our iron age to revive in it the age of gold, or the golden as it is called. I am he for whom perils, mighty achievements, and valiant deeds are reserved. I am, I say again, he who is to revive the Knights of the Round Table, the Twelve of France, and the Nine Worthies, and he who is to consign to oblivion . . . the whole herd of famous knights-errant of days gone by, performing in these in which I live such exploits, marvels, and feats of arms as shall obscure their brightest deeds."[18]

This passage encapsulates the contents of Quixote's delusion. It has three characteristics that are fundamental for the analysis of paranoia. First, it is heroic, and so akin to the nature of romance, which Freud considered to be an uncensored paranoid construction embodied in the communal imagination. Second, it is envisioned even by its psychotic inventor as a return to an earlier state of perfection, a golden age when the flower of knighthood reigned over an untroubled world. It is thus an archaizing and regressive delusion. So arises its nobility. Taking a Freudian view of the matter, we might find here a remarkable recognition on Cervantes' part of the archaic origins of 'narcissistic' fantasy, of its kinship with all utopias and forms of aristocratic dignity. Third, even though its victim gives every evidence of madness, this madness speaks with eloquence; it has coherence and force. Delusion has seized upon the intelligence and the will of the sufferer and made them subject to a grand error consistently held. It has not destroyed his faculties. When Quixote's attention turns to subjects other than the ones involved in his idée fixe, he speaks with wisdom and grace in a way that continues to amaze his many interlocutors.

The coherence of Quixote's delusion points toward its idealizing character. It is clearly the kind of mental expression Freud would have ascribed

to the 'omnipotence of thoughts'. Quixote continuously confuses his megalomaniac wishes with reality. He is besotted with 'narcissism'. Thus arise the
famous scenes early in the novel in which he takes windmills to be giants,
flocks of sheep opposing armies, and so on. Most sublime and emphatic of
all his follies is his devotion to the non-existent beloved, Dulcinea, that
"being to whom all praise is appropriate, be it ever so hyperbolical" (824).
Dulcinea becomes the object in Quixote's mind of a full-blown erotomania
of the kind that sometimes accompanies paranoia. She is, in herself, merely
an ideal construction, and much of the time Quixote himself seems to be
aware of this:

"You should know, Sancho, if you do not know, that two things alone beyond all
others are incentives to love, and these are great beauty and a good name. These
two things are to be found in Dulcinea in the highest degree, for in beauty no one
equals her and in good name few approach her. To put the whole thing in a
nutshell, I persuade myself that all I say is as I say, neither more nor less, and I
picture her in my imagination as I would have her to be, as well in beauty as in
condition. Helen approaches her not nor does Lucretia come up to her, nor any
other of the famous women of times past, Greek, Barbarian, or Latin."(185)

Dulcinea has been constructed entirely by means of a fantasy logic. She
is a pure projection of 'narcissistic' wish, a Baconian idol brought into
being by intellectual necessity alone. All of her characteristics have been
strictly prescribed by that necessity.[19]

The necessity circumscribing the being of Dulcinea also encompasses
the will of her creator: all of his actions are strictly bound by the code of
chivalry. So sacred and formal are the restrictions imposed by this code
that, when opportunities for the practical display of heroism arise, Quixote
is often too tightly constrained by the protocols of courtly service to take
advantage of them. Before going to the rescue of a landlord who is being
drubbed, he must pompously ask permission of his lady of the moment in
order to act outside her service. Confronted with an aggressive underling,
he finds himself unable to do battle with a person below the rank of knight,
and calls for his squire to take his place (352). Quixote's ritualized behavior
frequently degenerates into the automatism of what Freud would call an
'obsessive-compulsive' routine. In *Totem and Taboo,* Freud observes that
ritual taboos can originate in an aggressive impulse on the part of the ruled
to restrict the behavior of their sacred rulers. As an example, he gives the
treatment of Sancho Panza made governor of an island in *Quixote,* Part
Two, when the peasant-squire, having at last achieved his dream, finds
himself so constrained by a comical set of rules prescribing the behavior of

governors that he scarcely has an opportunity to eat or drink.[20] Apparently, then, a self-punitive element underlies Quixote's delusion as well, causing him to apply to himself the restraint of ritual taboo. In behavior and in thought, Quixote has made himself a prisoner of the ideal.

Quixote may be half aware of the 'projected' quality of his beloved, but this does not make him skeptical about the facts of her existence. He relates to reality as if through the prism of an Aristotelian poetics: he is willing, therefore, to concede the recognition of truth to any aspect of being that accords with his sense of what should be. The suggestion that Dulcinea does not exist seems thus for him somehow beside the point. But Sancho's suggestion that she is not the finest lady in the world moves him to rage:

"Are you not aware, you crude, coarse, vile creature, that, but for the might she infuses into my arm, I should not have the strength enough to kill a flea? Say, O scoffer with a viper's tongue, what do you think has won this kingdom and cut off this giant's head and made you a marquis, all of which I consider as already accomplished and decided, but the might of Dulcinea, who uses my arm as the instrument of her achievements? She fights in me and conquers in me, and I live and breathe in her and owe my life and being to her." (233–34)

Dulcinea possesses for Quixote an absolute existence within the order of his delusory system, and he is willing to defend to the death her place within that system. The guarantees of her excellence and perfect beauty do not consist of any evidence that can be derived about the lady in herself: her proofs reside only in the integrity of the system as a whole. They include Quixote's future triumphs, which exert a force of necessity equal to that of his imaginary triumphs of the past. It is part of the very perfection of Dulcinea as a 'projection' of 'narcissistic' imagination that her person is beyond experience and beyond the inspection of skeptical eyes: "If I were to show her to you, what merit would ye have in confessing a truth so manifest? The essential point is that without seeing her ye must believe, confess, affirm, swear, and defend it" (42). Like the very existence of God, belief in Dulcinea is a test of faith, or of 'narcissistic' potency. She infuses her strength into the being of Quixote; his exaltation of mind furnishes the proof of her exalted nature.

The 'narcissistic' character of Quixote's 'fixation' ensures that his way of thinking and behaving will stand in absolute contradiction with reality. The comic discrepancy between fantasy and reality becomes, then, the fundamental interest of the Quixotic narrative. The narrator begins his account of each of Quixote's episodes with a description of the scene and of the characters who will take part, thus preparing the reader to appreciate the difference between reality and Quixotic delusion.[21] But Quixote himself is not so severely impaired that he cannot perceive the discrepancy between his ideal vision and the reality that confronts him. He oscillates between the two, being propelled forward with ever renewed movements of ambition, and driven backward by ever repeated checks from the real world.

The dialectic of ideal and real is further complicated by the part that others take in the development of Quixote's delusion. His niece provides the fundamental resource of hermeneutic suspicion when she tells him that a swarm of enchanters are interfering with his adventures. Here is Quixote invoking the theory of the enchanters to explain how Dulcinea, whom he has just encountered, could have seemed to him like a saucy village lass:

> "Now, Sancho," he said, "do you see how I am hated by enchanters! And see to what a length they go in their malice and spite against me, when they seek to deprive me of the happiness that would be mine in seeing my lady in her own proper form. The fact is I was born to be an example of misfortune, and the target and mark at which the arrows of adversity are aimed and directed. Observe too, Sancho, that these traitors were not content with changing and transforming my Dulcinea, but they transformed and changed her into a shape as vulgar and ugly as that of the village girl yonder, and at the same time they robbed her of that which is such a peculiar property of ladies of distinction, that is to say the sweet fragrance that comes of being always among perfumes and flowers. For I must tell you Sancho, when I approached to put Dulcinea upon her palfrey—as you say it was, though to me it appeared a she-ass—she gave me a whiff of raw garlic that made my head reel and poisoned my very heart." (477)

This passage illustrates the marvelous complexity of Cervantes' paranoid construction. The act of mediating between real world and delusion is made possible for Quixote by the suspicion he now entertains toward the world as it appears. To the degree that the real world calls Quixote's delusion into question, Quixote, in order to sustain his tenuous intellectual coherence, must call the real world into question. For these two worlds are incompatible; no compromise is possible between them. This fact is apparent to Quixote. Indeed, the incongruity between his sense of what should be and his experience of what is terrifies and galls him to the same degree that it amuses and delights the reader. So arises his slightly self-pitying sense of persecution, a sense which, nevertheless, confirms his grandiose self-image.

The Freudian reader would not understand the relation between these two elements, grandeur and persecution, to be one of mere rationalizing, as if the fantasy of being persecuted were merely a way of confirming and sustaining a megalomaniac self-image. In psychoanalytic terms, the hostility expressed in the persecutory delusion must have a sexual origin, and, more specifically, a homosexual one: it must be a disguised attraction. The homosexual motive does not appear in this passage, and it would be stretching the merely propaedeutic character of my Freudian reading of the text to ferret it out; the resources of the *Quixote* to sustain an interpretation of this kind seem rather scant, Sancho being virtually the only available candidate. But the generically sexual component of the delusion could not be more evident or more amenable to psychoanalytic interpretation. What causes Quixote shame in his meeting with Dulcinea in the person of the "village lass" is her creaturely physicality, which departs radically from the ideal image he holds of his beloved and seems to be the very thing his chivalrous attitude was designed to suppress. We can see the paranoid construction, then, as a denial, a 'repression', of sexual impulses and a return to a 'narcissistic' phase of self-contained omnipotence. In the quoted passage the difficulty of sustaining 'repression' seems to make itself felt. We could augment this line of argument by speculating about the original libidinal incitement for Quixote's quest. Miguel de Unamuno, in his retelling of the life of Quixote, points to Aldonza Lorenzo, a local interest of the character, as the motive for Quixote's retreat from reality; later Freudian speculation has fixed upon his niece and housekeeper.[22] It is significant in this regard that "quixote" refers to the piece of armor that covers the thigh, and therefore suggests a phallic motivation and one of shame.[23]

Whatever the emotional origins of Quixote's suspicion and sense of persecution, they serve him well in the preservation of his system of delusion, making possible an extraordinarily subtle and flexible mode of rationalizing. The "enchanters" can make the real Dulcinea look like a peasant lass, and they can make mere puppets look like historical figures, setting the scene for a paranoid skirmish (575). At one point, Quixote is mystified to find that a magical boat that has appeared in order to transport him to one of his adventures leads him only to a dunking, until he realizes that, "In this adventure two mighty enchanters must have encountered one another, and one frustrates what the other attempts; one provided the boat for me, and the other overturned me. God help us; this world is all machinations and schemes at cross purposes with one another" (590). This interpretation is Quixote's way of achieving what we might call, in Freudian terms, a compromise formation, in which opposing motives of desire and repression both fasten upon a single set of symptoms. Quixote's hermeneutic is as flexible and nimble as Freud's.

In Part Two of the narrative, Quixote's originally simple idealism and sense of heroic opposition gradually give way to a more and more complex involvement in "machinations and schemes," levels of illusion, competition with false Quixotes, manipulation by readers of Part One, and so on. But his paranoid construction remains intact through all of these and through all of the endless series of drubbings, dunkings, and tramplings that ensue. It is only when he is dealt a defeat within the framework of his delusion, by the villager Samsón Carrasco disguised as a rival knight, that Quixote's delusory vocation begins to falter. Embittered by this defeat, which he recognizes as a true and significant one, not to be blamed upon enchanters, Quixote takes all of the responsibility upon himself: ". . . for there is no such thing as Fortune in the world, nor does anything which takes place, be it good or bad, come about by chance, but by the special preordination of heaven; and hence the common saying that 'each of us is the maker of his own Fortune'. I have made mine, but not with the proper amount of prudence, and my presumption has therefore made me pay dearly" (792). Quixote has been, in a sense quite different from the one he intends, the maker of his own fortune. In this scene he is beginning to recognize the limitations upon his heroic powers; but his paranoid sense of the meaningfulness of every element of his experience has not left him. He is still a prey to the 'omnipotence of thoughts', even when no longer the bearer of omnipotence. Psychoanalytically speaking, we might say that the 'narcissistic cathexis' has been transferred from the 'ego' to the 'ego-ideal' or 'superego', so that what was formerly a tendency toward absolute freedom from responsibility, absolute independence of the self, becomes a sense of absolute responsibility, shame, and guilt. The self-punitive trend in Quixote's psychology ends in his death.

There is one final element in Cervantes' portrayal of Quixote that, though not specifically a symptom of paranoia, is nevertheless vital for any consideration of the work that has to do with Freud—the great dream reported by Quixote after his descent into the Cave of Montesinos. Quixote descends into the cave at the end of a rope, and there, falling asleep on a ledge not far from the surface, he experiences a dream that is to him as significant and profound as Dante's vision of the underworld. He glimpses at last the heroes of chivalry he has read about and emulated, and it seems that his hunger for glory and truth will finally be satisfied, at least here in this private world of inspired reverie and visionary insight. The "castle built of clear transparent crystal," "strangely cool" alabaster chambers, these details of human construction from divine materials, signs of a heavenly city, transport Quixote toward a higher kingdom of bliss. The very existence of this dream kingdom is enough to certify the vision as a wish-fulfillment: Quixote, on being wakened, laments the sights that he has lost: "God forgive you, friends . . . you have taken me away from the sweetest, most delightful existence and spectacle that ever human being enjoyed or beheld" (549).

Yet, in spite of this simple expression of joy, Quixote's dreamworld is anything but delightful. Powerful forces seem even here to be working against the full expression of desire, preventing Quixote from imagining for himself the state of heroic bliss he has pursued at such great costs. The enchanters who thwart his heroic ambitions follow him even now. They keep the noble company—Durandarte, Montesinos, the lady Bellerma, and Dulcinea herself—in a state of suspended animation. Durandarte suffers in a permanent state of agitation from the thought that, after his death, his heart was not delivered to his lady, while his friend, Montesinos, reassures him over and over again that his dying request has been fulfilled. Meanwhile the lady carries the mummified heart in an endless procession four days out of seven, making "a great outcry and lamentation, accompanied by deep sighs and bitter sobs" belonging to her damsels (553). It is a super-refined, chivalric version of the torments of Sisyphus and Tantalus, which has been aptly compared with "an existentialist hell."[24]

The scene evokes a certain pathos, but this pathos coincides with a sensation of incongruity, an unexpected lack of decorum and dignity in the behavior of the characters and in the very conditions of the dreamworld itself. Durandarte's heart, for instance, does not enjoy the magical protection from decay that ordinarily attends such relics. After the battle of Roncesvalles, Montesinos tells him, "I sprinkled a little salt on your heart so that it would not smell and I could bring it, if not fresh, at least pickled, into the presence of the lady Bellerma" (552). Here is a strange intrusion of the reality principle. Similarly strange is Durandarte's reaction to the news that Don Quixote has come to attempt his liberation: "if that may not be, then, O cousin, I say, 'patience and shuffle the cards' " (553). The lady Bellerma's monthly cycle is discounted as a cause of her deteriorated condition, it being taken for granted that this would be Quixote's first surmise. Most humiliating of all, when Don Quixote sees Dulcinea in that enchanted land, she is still prevented from assuming her true appearance: she greets him in the form of the peasant lass whom Sancho had passed off as Dulcinea. Her only request to Quixote is the loan of six *reales,* and he is ashamed to admit he can offer only four; the knight suddenly wishes he were, of all things, a Fugger, so that he could relieve her distress. Accepting the four *reales*, the damsel messenger from Dulcinea, instead of curtsying, makes her exit by cutting a caper two yards in the air.

The combination of unexpected pathos and incongruity found in this scene looks forward to surrealist art, and indeed it was a source of inspiration for that most Freudian artistic movement. For our purposes, what is most significant is Cervantes' portrayal of the inner checks that prevent Quixote from realizing, even in dream, the perfect image of his desire. The motif of suspicion represented by the enchanters cannot be separated from his delusions of heroism, both being derived from the same 'narcissistic' regression. The suspicion itself emanates, Freud would tell us, from a repressed wish in disguise. Cervantes' presentation of the inner world of fantasy bears out Freud's understanding of the mind as internally divided against itself, with opposing functions of censorship and evasion, disguise, distortion, and displacement.

Cervantes' portrait of paranoia, we may conclude, has all of the features of the complaint that Freudian psychology has taught us to recognize. It is a madly unqualified form of self-aggrandizing idealism that requires a suspicious overcoming of ordinary appearances and a theory of persecuting enemies to keep it in place. Grandiosity and suspicion animate and sustain each other. The paranoid inhabits a world in which everything is significant and demands decoding with specific relation to him. The delusion includes sexual ideas suitably idealized. And even when the character withdraws entirely into the realm of dream, the inner conflicts that have given rise to his delusion prevent him from having access to his heart's desire. The censorship exercised by the superego makes it necessary for the fulfillment of the most important wish to be accomplished under the disguise of a distortion both incongruous and comical.

The Pretentious Paranoid

The congruence of vision between Freud and Cervantes is remarkable. In order to establish its true significance, though, it will be necessary to consider Quixote's paranoia in something closer to its original context. The central aspect is, of course, the books of chivalry that provide the target for Cervantes' satiric attack. In his eyes, these books employed a ridiculous archaism of form, subject, and style. Their sin was to be not only false but incapable of disguising their falsity. And yet, in spite of all the critical attacks against them, they continued, infuriatingly, to command an audience. The combination of reason and unreason, of coherence and madness, that goes to make up Quixote's paranoid state existed already, for his creator, in the minds of the readers for whom the world of these books could sustain interest. So we can understand both the intelligibility and the social interest of Quixote's delusion: before a paranoid hero can be born, a paranoid text and its readership must provide the world in which he will pursue his adventures. In the books of chivalry, Quixote reads: " 'the reason of the unreason with which my reason is afflicted so weakens my reason that with reason I complain of your beauty;' or again, 'the high heavens, that of your divinity divinely fortify you with the stars, render you deserving of the desert your greatness deserves.' Over this sort of folderol," the narrator goes on to say, "the poor gentleman lost his wits, and he used to lie awake striving to understand it and worm out its meaning, though Aristotle himself could have made out or extracted nothing, had he come back to life for that special purpose" (26). Quixote goes mad in a deliberate attempt to make sense of the madness that sustained the popular fantasy of chivalry.

In order to understand the precise social significance of Quixote's delusion, it will be necessary to clarify the specific nature and motives of his misunderstanding of the literary materials that constitute his idée fixe, and to do so in the context of his own social position. The latter, at least, is not difficult to establish: Alonso the Good, alias Quixote, is an impoverished *hidalgo*, a gentleman, though not a knight, who has too little means to sustain his idleness in anything above grinding poverty and yet is too respectable to work for a living. A *hidalgo* of this sort has no meaningful outlet for ambition; he holds himself above the common only by an act of will.[25] The fragility and irrelevance of such a life, based upon what are already questionable pretensions, make Alonso susceptible to the temptations of grandeur. The form of this grandeur, however, is not his own but that of a borrowed grandeur. And here the social application of satiric psychology becomes evident.

Cervantes tells his reader again and again that the object of his work is to destroy the books of chivalry; yet the precise reason for this choice of a satiric object is not, at first glance, so easy to discern. This becomes evident, as many critics have noted, in the scene of the *auto da fé* in which Quixote's library is subjected to a hygienic purge by the curate and the barber. The reader is surprised, for instance, to find that the *Amadis de Gaul*, the book that provides Quixote with his most constant model of chivalry, is preserved from the flames. The reason for this is that the *Amadis* is the first of its kind, which gives it a certain claim to merit.

Quixote, in his folly, takes it for historical truth, and this is an error, but he also does it an injustice when he fails to distinguish the *Amadis* from its imitations. It has a proper claim to historical originality, while they must be condemned to the flames as derivative. The literary-historical aspect of Quixote's error is further clarified when we see the curate preserving *Orlando Furioso* while condemning its translations into Spanish. Ariosto's sophisticated romance takes into account the historically archaic nature of its materials. It is a mark of Quixote's insanity that he cannot distinguish the naive assertion of *Amadis* and its successors from the suave irony of Ariosto's pastiche. For the madman, they are all woven into the same tissue of historical legend.

At this point, two aspects of Quixote's failure of understanding can be distinguished. He does not have the historical insight to recognize that the world of magic and adventure portrayed in the *Amadis de Gaul* never existed. And he lacks the aesthetic judgment to see that Ariosto's sophisticated romance takes into account the historical anachronism of its subject and therefore makes a claim to validity based upon a sense of irony or aesthetic distance that is itself a product of incipient historical conscious-ness. A cultivated sensibility is capable of reclaiming works like the *Amadis de Gaul:* the sophisticated reader should be able to recognize the aesthetic originality of writing that to the present has the appearance of naiveté. But the sophisticated reader should also be able to detect the absurdity of naive imitations of the romance, imitations that do not recog-nize that the form is artistically retrograde. Thus the true victims of Cervan-tean satire are those authors who persist in vulgar imitation of naive romance. Such writing is popular, and to take it seriously, to enjoy it wholeheartedly, is, for a person of judgment like Alonso the Good, to be the victim of a kind of insanity.

We can see opening here the split between popular and sophisticated appreciation of art, which is one of the signatures of modern culture. It should not be confused with the very different distinction between official and folk culture, both of which are in their spheres more or less indepen-dent.[26] The distinction between high culture and popular culture is based upon a difference in the manner of viewing and appreciating the same forms of imagination: the popular, or vulgar, imagination goes on producing and enjoying forms of official culture that to an aesthetically self-conscious elite have come to appear historically antiquated. Quixote is the living embodiment of this vulgar error.

Quixote's paranoia, then, is made possible by a complex social dynamic that would not have been possible before the emergence of that degree of historical awareness which makes for a separation between elite and popular culture. It involves a failure of aesthetic judgment and of social discrimination. The deep social significance of Quixote's delusion is what made it so very funny to the readers of its time and led to 150 years of imitations in the original, satiric spirit. Quixote's comical humiliation is not the treatment that would greet the victim of an innocent mistake or a meaningless delusion: it is the treatment given to a particular kind of fool, a nostalgic gentleman who tries to revive a form of aristocratic fantasy that can now be taken seriously only by the popular mind. His rise to heroism is a descent into vulgarity. The combination of pretentiousness and self-debasement in Quixote's position makes for the exquisite, subtle, and cruel humor of his predicament, humor of a kind that our egalitarian culture can no longer wholeheartedly enjoy.

Cervantes' special distinction in the history of modern culture is to have imagined the form of a meaningful private delusion, a delusion that at once expresses a recognizable pattern of desire and at the same time shows by its imitative character an unmistakable disconnection from reality. His satiric method depends upon the constant portrayal of discrepancy between the romance that Quixote bears as an inner possession and the outer world that resists it. In the light of the social motives underlying the satiric design, the form of this resistance, again, can hardly be described as innocent. Cervantes' intent is that the self-idealizing pretensions of the paranoid delusion should be confronted with the vulgarity it falsely denies, and this vulgarity finds its expression preeminently in the life of the body — that aspect of our being, in other words, which it is the nature of aristocratic imagination, at the height of its refinement, to disown. In order that the true character of Quixote's delusion be revealed, its false idealism must be reunited with all of the embarrassments of corporeal existence; knightly asceticism must be exposed as a form of self-frustration that serves no other end than to deny the exigencies of physical life.

The objective, then, of Cervantes' portrait of the paranoid Quixote was to expose the social and literary pretensions of vulgar romance. The literary aspect is worth emphasizing. It was not only that the books of chivalry were an affront to Cervantes' sense of class privilege. As an author, Cervantes felt a powerful resentment toward the reading and playgoing public whose tastes fell so far beneath what he was willing to gratify. And so at one point in the *Quixote* we find a judicious character proposing that plays should be subject to a rigid censorship in order to improve the public taste and give work to men of judgment (380). The appeal to censorship should alert us to the factor of repression, and, indeed, the *Quixote* itself may be considered a great gesture of repression, being an attempt to undermine the legitimacy of vulgar imagination. This gesture, however, does not seek to suppress the vulgar aspects of culture. On the contrary, it is a revelation of vulgarity, an unmasking of the disguises of vulgar pretense. In this way it prefigures the psychoanalytic method itself.

Cervantes set out to destroy the books of chivalry because of the vulgarity they represented; in creating Don Quixote, he was creating a living example of this vulgarity. But Cervantes' attitude toward Quixote and toward the books of chivalry was not entirely destructive. He does not rage to annihilate in the manner of a Swift, for he recognizes, as the wise canon in the story—the harshest critic of the books of chivalry—puts it, there is "one good thing" in them: "the opportunity they afforded to a gifted intellect for displaying itself":

"The author may show himself to be an astronomer, or a skilled cosmographer, or musician, or one versed in affairs of state, and sometimes he will have a chance of coming forward as a magician if he likes. He can set forth the craftiness of Ulysses, the treachery of Sinon, the friendship of Euralyus, the generosity of Alexander, the boldness of Caesar, the clemency of Trajan, the fidelity of Zopyrus, the wisdom of Cato, and in short all the faculties that serve to make an illustrious man perfect, now uniting them in one individual, again distributing them among many. . . . The unrestricted range of these books enables the author to show his powers, epic, lyric, tragic, or comic, and all the moods the sweet and winning arts of poetry and oratory are capable of, for the epic may be written in prose just as well as in verse." (375–76)

I have drastically truncated this magnificent passage, but its exhibitionistic profusion cannot be suppressed. It is evident that the satiric romance permits the same display of a "gifted intellect" as the books of chivalry it mocks; indeed, the satiric intellect comprehends at once the books of chivalry and the world they exclude. What we see in Cervantes' novel, then, is not merely an act of social destructiveness but an educative spectacle. Quixote's adventures permit an infinitely elaborate social discrimination in behavior and, above all, in speech, in a world in which prestige manifests itself no longer by martial prowess, nor even simply by wealth, but by intelligence, breeding, sophistication, knowledge, and judgment especially in the use of language. As a paranoid knight, Quixote is the subject of contempt, but as a speaker he is the vehicle for Cervantes' enormous pride of rhetorical facility, breadth of learning, and social discrimination. This pride speaks on every page of the *Quixote*. Quixote's mad social pretension, which is the pretension of the romances themselves, is thus comprehended and transformed in a higher language, a language of art that relieves its vulgarity and redeems it as a worthy source of amusement.

Freudian Satire

How, then, shall we relate the two readings of the *Quixote* set forth in this chapter—the Freudian reading, which sees Quixote's delusion as a disguised form of sexual expression, and the reading that gives priority to Cervantes' satiric motives? Perhaps it is already clear enough that the satiric juxtaposition of idealism with vulgar physicality seems designed to establish just that likeness of origin between repressed, or 'narcissistic', and unrepressed expressions of sexuality that is the fundamental analytic resource of Freudian psychology. This being the case, the psychoanalytic perspective is in danger of being supplanted by a much more simple explanation: the ideal and the body are joined in this romance merely because the way to discredit a false idealism is to connect it with what cannot be idealized, that is to say, with the creatureliness of the human body. Now we can see, for instance, why Cervantes should have named his character after the "quixote" that guards a knight's thigh: it is no hidden clue to unconscious sexual drives animating Quixote's delusion, but rather, merely, a sign of its vulgarity. This is why Cervantes is so eager to show poor Quixote's indignant reaction when he discovers that his enchanted Dulcinea reeks of garlic like a dirty peasant lass. How well the enchanters understand his pretentious heart!

Again, it is Cervantes' satiric motivation, not dream censorship, that explains why, even in his dreams, Quixote cannot achieve a true vision of his heart's desire; in the Cave of Montesinos, instead of being called to rescue Dulcinea from enchantment, he finds her more acutely in need of hard cash than of heroic deliverance.[27] Who would have thought that the knight destined to restore the golden age of chivalry would ever in his life utter the wish to become one of the Fuggers, that family of bankers being the supreme symbol of the new order that had destroyed all Quixote longs to regain. But such is the triumph of the enchanters, those uncanny agents who personify the satiric design of the narrative itself. Their presence suggests no disguised sexual instinct but an overt form of mockery. Further, the heroism and archaism of Quixote's delusion clearly originate not in psychological 'narcissism' but in the romances, the literary materials that provided Cervantes with his object of comic imitation. Humor supplies a perfectly adequate motive. Likewise, Quixote's excessive idealism and ritualistic compulsiveness serve merely to show that his assertion of heroic powers is in fact a comically imitative and slavish form of subjection. Now we can see that, when Freud cites the ritualistic torments of the governor Sancho Panza as an example of the aggressive motives underlying ritual prohibitions, he is not truly furnishing legitimate support for psychoanalytic dogma but merely returning to the satiric origins of his own way of thinking.

Having accounted for the details of the paranoid condition in satiric rather than psychoanalytic terms, what now seems remarkable is how unerringly the psychoanalytic approach has led us to the central satiric motifs and to those alone. Both ways of considering the text direct our attention to idealistic structures of thought and to the elements of physical life that idealism tends to deny. They are so similar, the psychoanalytic and satiric modes, as to make the latter appear redundant. There can be no surprise in the discovery of social animus as the determining factor behind each of the details of Cervantes' paranoid entertainment. What is surprising, however, is that the Freudian explanation of the paranoid condition merely repeats Cervantes' original satiric gesture in more general, 'libidinal' terms. Its aim is to demystify idealism by rejoining it with that vulgar, creaturely reality that is its true and hidden source.

There is one crucial difference, though, between Freud and Cervantes as satirists. The form of activity Cervantes aimed to discourage was one that could, in fact, be eliminated from culture: people could, and eventually did, cease to read and write books of chivalry, even if, to this day, they have not tired of the popular romance. But the 'narcissistic' forms of thinking satirized by Freud are, according to his own view, inseparable from human nature itself. They are, in a sense, normal. By undermining any means to make a strong distinction between 'paranoid' or 'narcissistic' psychology and ordinary thinking, by making paranoid psychology normal psychology, Freud achieved a monumental, nearly irresistible satiric gesture. For once we have accepted that our thought is nothing more than a projection of fantasy, and that no degree of intellectual self-scrutiny can free us from enthrallment to the forces that produce such delusion, we have accepted an essential kinship with Quixote and his paranoid descendants.[28] Both Freud and Cervantes wanted to make it unavoidably clear that our intellectual pursuits, some of them or all of them, are akin both to madness and to vulgarity. The unconscious is constituted of a hidden vulgarity.[29]

Some Objections

At this point the Freudian reader will again, perhaps, be ready to protest at the direction that the argument has taken. My either/or logic will doubtless seem foreign to the spirit of psychoanalytic thinking; armed with the Freudian principle of 'overdetermination', psychoanalysis generally avoids the kind of choice between causes that I have posed.[30] To the devotee of Freud, it will undoubtedly seem as if, by fixing upon humor, popular romance, the social repression of vulgarity, and the literary institution of satire as explanations for Cervantes' depiction of the paranoid character, and then turning these categories back upon psychoanalysis itself, my own analysis has illegitimately evaded the explanatory force of available psychoanalytic concepts, since, indeed, all of the social forms of expression I have mentioned have been accounted for in Freudian terms. "It will come as no surprise," such a reader might observe, "that the heroizing, idealizing tendencies of Cervantes' paranoid should be shared by the books of chivalry attacked in *Don Quixote*, for, as Freud understood, the romance itself is a narcissistic and paranoid structure: 'His Majesty the Ego' is the hero of all popular novels and romances, the same narcissistic ego that triumphs in daydream, in myth, and paranoia. Nor is it any surprise to discover that the ingenuities of humor and satire should take paranoia as a fitting spectacle. Freud's theory of wit recognizes that wit gives expression to repressed sexual motifs just as paranoia does. The reasons why were explained by Freud himself: jokes allude in a clever and unexpected way to ideas that it would be socially unacceptable explicitly to mention. The more 'tendentious' the wit, the more readily it makes us laugh: so we understand both the great libidinal energy invested in the *Quixote* by its creator and the irrepressible response it has evoked for nearly four hundred years. The uncovering of Cervantes' tendentious motives only confirms Freud's insight into malicious humor. Further," this Freudian reader might observe, "Cervantes' presentation of the idealizing, narcissistic books of chivalry under the stigma of vulgarity shows him as a participant in the great repression of human narcissism that was being accomplished in this period by the emerging culture of science. Indeed, his satiric onslaught seems to enact this very repression, as it removes the idea of chivalry and knightly heroism from the legitimate public domain, depriving all but the mad of their narcissistic comforts. The very notion of 'vulgarity' is repressive in Freud's sense of the word. It is no accident, finally, that Freud should have chosen a literary work that appeared within four years of *Don Quixote*, namely

Hamlet, as the key text to illustrate the consequences of the final phase of Oedipal repression. Both *Hamlet* and the *Quixote* exhibit with all the vividness of a discovery the full measure of repression that distinguishes psychological modernity from its narcissistic predecessor. The brilliance with which these works depict the torments of the repressed modern character has made them two of the parent-texts of postmedieval Western culture."

Before answering this wide-ranging series of objections, I should remind my readers that there are many causes for skepticism toward psychoanalysis besides the ones I have proposed in the foregoing chapters, and that my chief interest has been in clarifying the paranoid character of Freud's logic and rhetoric rather than in mounting a full-scale refutation of psychoanalytic theory. For this they should refer to the critical works already cited. This being said, it is a principle of scientific and of historical understanding that, in explaining any phenomenon, one should restrict one's generalizations to the narrowest possible extent and seek always the causes most proximate to the effect. Having shown that Cervantes' paranoid character experiences an idealistic form of delusion because Cervantes was using him as a way of branding a certain type of literature as madness, and that his method of doing this was to link idealism with its opposite, the body, in all of its creaturely manifestations, with the aim of exposing the true vulgarity of this form of idealistic literary fantasy, there is, then, simply no need to offer a further explanation linking idealism, 'narcissism', and sexuality. It is enough to see that the paranoid as idealist is a construction of satiric fancy. By the same token, having observed that Freud's theory of paranoia, and, indeed, his method of interpretation in general, uncannily reproduce the satiric structure of Cervantes' novel, it is far more economical as an explanation of its enduring popularity to suggest that, rather than embodying an insight into universal human nature in all of its transformations, a decipherment of the great code of the mind and body, psychoanalysis is a somewhat unwitting but nevertheless strategically deployed imitation of Quixotic satire universalized in the language of science.

In a previous chapter I made the argument that the logic of the reductionist impasse suffices to account for paranoia as a mode of intellectual operation, making it, therefore, a self-imposed condition. Now we can see the natural affinity between reductionist logic and satire, for it is typical of the satiric persona to include itself within the field of ridicule. Freud seamlessly integrated his reductionist model of the intellectual functions with an all-encompassing, self-encompassing satiric vision couched in potent scientific rhetoric. The heroic irony of the psychoanalytic stance combines, then, the heroic rhetoric of scientific discovery with the irony proper to satiric invention. It makes up for a lack of true scientific value by tapping into the powerful vein of modern resentment against tradition.

Having issued this general reply to the Freudian reader, let us take up in sequence the four psychoanalytic objections to the conclusions I have drawn above:

1. The first is that romances like the books of chivalry are themselves paranoid, narcissistic projections; in that case it would do nothing to discourage the psychoanalytic understanding of paranoia to show, as I have done, that the contents of paranoid delusion have a cultural affinity with popular fantasy satirically depicted. Freud believed romance to be a heroic projection of the ego that gives expression to the child's hostility toward the father; this hostility is born out of his feelings of sexual rivalry over the love of the mother. As I have mentioned, Freud's disciple, Otto Rank, employed this theory to explain the common features of a great range of heroic and religious mythology, his analysis embracing figures as diverse as Sargon, Moses, Oedipus, Perseus, Gilgamesh, Cyrus, Tristan, Romulus, Hercules, Jesus, Siegfried, and Lohengrin.[31] Rank shows in the experience of these figures a common pattern: all of them encounter opposition from their very births and a difficulty in establishing a relation to their true parents; and all of them find it necessary to repudiate surrogate parents in order to achieve their true identities, a process that invariably makes them the center of hostility and resentment; as Rank puts it, with ironic quotation, "A prophet is not without honor, save in his own country, and in his father's house" (66). Freud contributed to Rank's book the central theoretical formulation of the argument linking the structure of myth with the family; it was later published separately under the title "Family Romances."[32] According to his analysis, the 'family romance of the neurotic' develops through the process of a child's liberation from his parents. At first the child's fantasy life centers upon the emulation of his parents: "But as intellectual growth increases, the child cannot help discovering by degrees the category to which his parents belong. He gets to know other parents and compares them with his own, and so acquires the right to doubt the incomparable and unique quality he had attributed to them. Small events in the child's life that make him feel dissatisfied afford him provocation for beginning to criticize his parents, and for using, in order to support his critical attitude, the knowledge he has acquired that other parents are in some respects preferable to them" (237). The intensity of this dissatisfac-

tion, Freud argues, is fueled by ordinary slights received from one's parents, by sibling rivalries, and by the underlying sexual competition within the family. Later it gives rise to daydreams of a heroic character by which the child, seeking to remedy the harm that has been done to his ambitious and erotic interests, escapes from his family altogether. It is to such daydreams that the neurotic and, of course, we may add, the paranoid, becomes especially enthralled:

At about the period I have mentioned . . . the child's imagination becomes engaged in the task of getting free from the parents of whom he now has a low opinion and of replacing them by others, who, as a rule, are of higher social standing. He will make use in this connection of any opportune coincidences from his actual experience, such as his becoming acquainted with the Lord of the Manor or some landed proprietor if he lives in the country or with some member of the aristocracy if he lives in town. Chance occurrences of this kind arouse the child's envy, which finds expression in a phantasy in which both his parents are replaced by others of better birth. (238–39)

This scenario, in which the child is set adream by a chance encounter with the "Lord of the Manor" or other aristocrat, evokes a distinctly bourgeois sense of class aspiration. In the context of Rank's sweeping mythographic survey, its social coordinates seem strangely local and confined. As we shall see, the adult Freud was given to experiencing chance encounters with the great that could set vibrating what he thought of as the 'narcissistic' chords of his personality. Such brushes with petty grandeur seem, however, like poor candidates to explain the origins and mythic potencies of the materials discussed in Rank's study. It is hard to imagine Jesus and Moses having been set upon their paths, even as children, by such means, nor do Gilgamesh, Sargon, Lohengrin, and the rest seem likely products from such a narrow sense of class distinction and parental comparison. Transcending the bourgeoisie does not seem to be the aim of their exertions. Freud shows here the deficiency of his sense of history.

Be that as it may, insofar as children, or adults, can be sometimes wounded by the knowledge that they belong to an inferior class, so that they seek to repudiate their own class in imagination, there seems little need to invoke a natural family trauma or sexual competition to account for the meaning of their fantasies. Differences of class more than suffice to stir the imagination. To propose a universal sexual mythology as a way of accounting for the origins of 'family romance' is once again to choose the least rather than the most economical explanation.

As it happens, Freud has given us an autobiographical account of the scene of his own 'family romance'. It occurred not when he was a very small child but when he was ten or twelve, and involved not simply a recognition of social distinctions but a very pronounced episode of ethnic hostility, with Freud's father as the object. Freud tells the story in *The Interpretation of Dreams* in order to explain how he came to identify himself with "the semitic general" Hannibal in his failed attempt to conquer Rome:

> I may have been ten or twelve years old, when my father began to take me with him on his walks and reveal to me in his talk his views upon things in the world we live in. Thus it was, on one such occasion, that he told me a story to show me how much better things were now than they had been in his days. "When I was a young man," he said, "I went for a walk one Saturday in the streets of your birthplace; I was well dressed, and had a new fur cap on my head. A Christian came up to me and with a single blow knocked off my cap into the mud and shouted: 'Jew! get off the pavement!' " "And what did you do?" I asked. "I went into the roadway and picked up my cap," was his quiet reply. This struck me as unheroic conduct on the part of the big, strong man who was holding the little boy by the hand. I contrasted this situation with another which fitted my feelings better: the scene in which Hannibal's father, Hamilcar Barca, made his boy swear before the household altar to take vengeance on the Romans. Ever since that time Hannibal had had a place in my phantasies. (197)

Among all of Freud's conjectures regarding the psychological sources of his interests, this one seems to me the most telling. It describes one of those moments when a fundamental fact of one's life is brought home in a crystallizing episode that will never be forgotten. As the source of Freud's notion of 'family romance', though, it serves only to confirm that the concept is a blatant projection of local conditions onto universal psychology, and a misuse of experiences from late childhood to explain the early psychology of the child and of the human race.

2. On the question of the nature of wit, the Freudian reader is, again, correct in stating that no follower of Freud would be surprised to learn that the presence of sexual elements could be comically motivated: Freud himself showed that wit exerts its effect by giving verbal expression to sexual themes that would in normal circumstances be deemed socially inappropriate. The question we might ask, though, is does Freud's 'sexuality' itself embody anything other than a satiric conception? Freud never succeeded in attaching a precise meaning to the word 'sexual', which can be applied, he noted, as broadly as to include all things having to do with reproduction and the differences between the sexes, or as narrowly as to the act of intercourse itself. But in the *Introductory Lectures* he ingeniously delineates the common element in the psychological range of the 'sexual':

"First and foremost, what is sexual is something improper, something one ought not to talk about [das Unanständige, das, von dem man nicht sprechen darf]."[33] The sexual is what is socially awkward or repressed. Now this same definition would perfectly circumscribe those things that satiric imagination calls upon in order to discredit by association the things that *can* be properly talked about. If it is the case that in psychoanalytic rhetoric the unconscious is defined by hidden vulgarity, then we can understand why the sexual and the creaturely are its primary constituents, these being the essence of what is 'improper'. With his psychology of the unconscious, Freud was merely repeating a satiric gesture he had learned from Cervantes and from his cultural descendants. The aim of all of his writing was to expose every form of idealism as a manifestation of sexuality, or, as we now can see, vulgarity pretentiously concealed. And the mark of a thing's being sexual in its nature was that one would want to conceal it! Again there appears the vicious circularity that typifies this mode of argument.

Freud well understood and memorably clarified what he called the 'tendentious' character of wit. He was hardly the first to do so, but the model he provided is a useful one. *Jokes and Their Relation to the Unconscious* seems to me of all of Freud's writings the one that has descriptive value. It is impossible to disagree with the observation that jokes depend upon the surprising connection of remote ideas, that the cleverness with which they achieve this surprise is important to their success, but that far more important is the way they touch upon socially unacceptable themes. This model applies, however, equally well as a description of the form of psychoanalytic thinking itself. Wilhelm Fliess once remarked to Freud that his analyses of dreams tended to make them all sound like jokes. Freud agreed that all dreamers, and all unconscious processes, are "insufferably witty."[34] The necessity of this insufferable wit derives, however, not, as he thought, from the facts of psychology but from the rhetoric of the unconscious as he employed it: psychoanalysis is, among other things, a grand system of jokes devoted to the charting of the vulgarly humorous and unsuspected connections between all of those elements of mental life that normally seem most distant from each other. Freud describes comic "unmasking" as "the method of degrading the dignity of individuals by directing attention to the frailties which they share with all humanity, but in particular the dependence of their mental functions on bodily needs. . . . Here, too, are to be placed the efforts at laying bare the monotonous psychical automatism that lies behind the wealth and apparent freedom of psychical functions."[35] One would think that Freud was describing his own science, and it would be hard to imagine a better description. Such "unmasking" of "psychic automatism," "degrading the dignity of individuals," constitutes the very substance of his vocation. "Parody and travesty," he writes, "achieve the degradation of something exalted . . . by destroying the unity that exists between people's characters as we know them and their speeches and actions, by replacing either the exalted figures or their utterances by inferior ones."[36] Is this not a perfect account of the psychoanalytic method, which systematically undermines the unity of character to reveal other, unworthy motives and invisible forces working beneath and through a character's words and actions, changing their very meaning?

It is interesting in this connection to note that, in Freud's work on jokes, some of his own tendentious motives appear most conspicuously. The punch lines of the examples, for instance, are often in the lower-class German accent of Yiddish-speaking East European Jewry *(mauscheln)*.[37] Like the pronouncements of Quixote, they are signal revelations of the 'uncanny' coexistence of wisdom and vulgarity. It was a form of vulgarity from which Freud, as a Jewish professional, specifically desired to set himself apart. Freud's own discourse on jokes becomes, then, both a revelation of disguised vulgarity and a mastering of it in a higher, ostentatiously learned professional vocabulary.[38] The imitation of Cervantes is again precise. All of Freud's writing has this double discursive quality, scientific rhetoric braving the taint of vulgarity while it smirches the targets of its rhetoric with the same. Only in the analysis of jokes does psychoanalytic interpretation become a mode of recovery rather than one of demystification, the joke's intent being to show precisely what psychoanalysis aims to show: the vulgar, or 'sexual', intention hidden beneath the surface. In the form of the joke, psychoanalysis finds its true reflection.

In the next chapter I will be providing a broad range of examples of Freud's satiric practice drawn from his Quixotic self-portrait, *The Interpretation of Dreams*. Here a single clarifying instance, taken from the psychobiography of Leonardo da Vinci, will suffice—Freud's treatment of the smile of Mona Lisa and what it means once we understand the unconscious psychology of its creator. The enigmatic, ambiguous expression on the lips of Leonardo's famous subject has proven an irresistible temptation to modern exegesis. In Freud's amazing narrative, it becomes the emblem of Leonardo's rueful knowledge that his psyche was permanently marked by an experience of the "highest erotic bliss" that occurred in early childhood when he kept sole possession of his peasant mother's love. Mona Lisa's seductively maternal smile now takes its place in a series of oral-erotic fantasies that give distinction to Leonardo's personality and determine his choice of artistic subjects. Beneath the childhood memory of a vulture fluttering its tail upon Leonardo's lips, Freud recognizes a fantasy of fellatio that is itself a substitute for the original fulfillment of Eros at the mother's breast. The painting registers the pain of Leonardo's displacement from his primary object of love and the stunting of his sexual nature into the form of a merely sentimental homosexuality. In this way arises the ambiguity of the image, representing both the memory of supreme pleasure and its loss. Leonardo painted this fatal smile over and over again, unable to escape its significance for his sexual being. Thus what might seem like the most innocent and ideal image of aristocratic feminine beauty becomes a symptom of primal incestuous fantasy once gratified at the mother's breast but now lost, fellatio and frustrated homosexuality, and a pathetic sense of the sacrifice required for the making of an artistic nature. The irony of this discrepancy between the apparent and true meanings of Mona Lisa's smile was by no means lost upon Freud, who, near the end of his analysis, glancing at what he takes to be the decisive influence of Leonardo's work upon subsequent imagination, makes the following observation:

From that time onward, madonnas and aristocratic ladies were depicted in Italian painting humbly bowing their heads and smiling the strange, blissful smile of [Leonardo's mother] Caterina, the poor peasant girl who had brought into the world the splendid son who was destined to paint, to search and to suffer.[39]

In this brilliant, ironic sentence we observe the widening out of Freud's satiric perspective: the smile now decipherable to psychoanalytic intelligence as the symptom of Leonardo's peculiarly ambiguous sexual history, the register of his primitive bodily experience with his unwed, peasant mother, becomes, with the touch of Leonardo's genius, the very model of distinction and piety, the exemplary image of the madonna. Leonardo reveals himself as one of those great practitioners of psychic disguise who can purge the creations of fantasy of all that is individual, making them accessible to others so that they can become the basis of the most ideal and exalted forms of culture. And Freud is, of course, the one who can unmask all such disguises and transformations, who can look behind the surface of aristocratic dignity and pious exaltation and glimpse their vulgar origins in the body, who can discover behind the apparent freedom of artistic creativity a subservience to psychic automatism. And so the unity of character of an entire culture can be degraded and undermined. Yet even this does not exhaust the rhetorical achievement culminated in this startling sentence, for we should not fail to notice that once it has cast its ironic glance upon the Italian madonna and recognized her 'improper', creaturely origins, it manages to reinvest that model, nonetheless, with a genuine maternal pathos—the pathos not of the mother of God but of the mother of genius, "who had brought into the world the splendid son who was destined to paint, to search and to suffer." Psychoanalytic rhetoric thus manages to reabsorb for itself the original vulgar heroism of the Christian story. In so doing it demonstrates again its ability to turn ironic heroism back toward heroic irony and, with beautiful economy, makes psychological necessity the basis for its own uncanny narrative of destiny. And so Freud marks Leonardo as one of his great precursors.

3. The third objection posed by our critic returns to Freud's account of modernity to observe that we can see in Cervantes' text an active repression of narcissism in the form of the books of chivalry and so a confirmation of the theory that paranoia originates in repressed narcissism. Thus *Don Quixote* participates in the destruction of traditional culture by science that produced the modern psyche. I have shown in chapter 2 that this mode of argument is viciously circular. It is worth pointing out here, though, *Don Quixote* having been so often understood as one of the inaugural gestures of modernity, that the skepticism toward the meaningfulness of human experience that distinguishes this novel is limited in its application to the naive conventions of vulgar romance. Cervantes himself was the practitioner of sophisticated romance in a form updated to the contemporary landscape of Western Europe. A number of such romances, of a type akin to Shakespeare's, occur interwoven with the *Quixote* plot in Part One. Cervantes has no difficulty asking the reader to accept the faith in Providence that they require. Still more significant in this vein is Cervantes' last work, *Persiles y Sigismunda*, an example of high romance that was his own favorite among his productions.[40] It was not romance per se, only vulgar romance that he opposed, and on grounds more social than philosophical.

Further, Cervantes' mistrust of reason does not derive from contact with modern science but rather from the Erasmian vein of skeptical resignation to faith that, as we have already seen, gave rise to a form of satirical moralizing distinctly akin in its rhetoric to the Freudian. Skepticism of this kind does draw limits to religious knowledge, but its primary motives are nevertheless religious ones. If any science helped bring Cervantes to his anticipations of modern psychology, it was not the science of Copernicus but the early versions of modern psychology itself, versions that bore the unmistakable psycho-satirical stamp of Erasmian humor toughened with a strand of the ancient skeptical philosophy of Pyrrhonism, which was revived in Spain in the late sixteenth century.[41] Cervantes is thought to have read, for instance, the *Examen de Ingenios* (1575), an early and influential classic of modern medicine by his countryman Juan Huarte de San Juan, in which it is argued that each man has a temperamental mixture of the humors that makes him suited only to one profession. It may be we should understand that Quixote, the "Ingenioso Hidalgo" of Cervantes' title, suffers his delusion merely out of the misfortune of having been born for a profession that could, in his age, be practiced only in fantasy and in books.[42] Such cases were for Cervantes a persistent source of interest: professional delirium appears throughout his writing, including in the hospital ward of the "Colloquy of the Dogs," so loved by the young Freud, where the mad poet, the alchemist, the mathematician, and the "planner" outrival each other in the grandeur of their thwarted ambitions.[43] Huarte de San Juan himself has a strongly satirical bent, one that, true to the Erasmian spirit of Folly, turns back upon itself. With the skeptical reservation typical of Pyrrhonism, he disclaims any certitude that his observations are not governed, like those of his patients, by a private distortion of temper: "I close, inquisitive reader, openly confessing that I am sick and 'out of tune' *[enfermo y destemplado]*, and you might be too, for I was born in such a place [that would cause this]; and we might have happen to us what happened to those four men who, upon seeing a blue cloth, one swore it was red, one swore it was white, one said yellow, and the other said black, and none of them hit the mark, due to the peculiar aberration *[la lesion particular]* of each man's vision."[44] The *Examen de Ingenios* was still being read and translated well into the eighteenth century. The popularity of Huarte de San Juan has been outlasted only by the three greatest masters of Renaissance psycho-satire: Robert Burton, author of the *Anatomy of Melancholy*, Francis Bacon, and Cervantes.[45]

4. Finally, there is the question of *Hamlet*, a work that is indeed closely contemporary with the *Quixote* and that Freud took to be an outstanding psychological symptom of modernity. Freud accomplished one of the decisive gestures of twentieth-century intellectual culture when, in *The Interpretation of Dreams*, he juxtaposed *Hamlet* with Sophocles' *Oedipus Rex* in order to introduce the notion of Oedipal repression. The story of Oedipus represents for Freud the working out of the fundamental human desires — incest and murder of the same-sex parent — which we moderns normally

distrain from consciousness. *Hamlet* too, Freud thought, derives its power from this theme, but with a difference:

> The changed treatment of the same materials reveals the whole difference in the mental life of these two widely separated epochs of civilization: the secular advance of repression in the emotional life of mankind. In the *Oedipus*, the child's wishful fantasy that underlies it is brought into the open and realized as it would be in a dream. In *Hamlet* it remains repressed; and—just as in the case of a neurosis— we only learn of it from its inhibiting consequences.[46]

Freud uses *Oedipus* as a kind of erotic paradigm in order to plot the distortions and displacements of desire in *Hamlet* and in every other psychological expression of the modern character. He takes the wish for revenge against the father as a given for the human psyche, observable without distortion in pre-modern texts, disguised in modern ones. Hamlet's inability to act, therefore, his deficiency in heroism, manifests the general psychic repression of the modern subject.

The philosophical context for Shakespeare's plays has proven notoriously difficult to establish. But one fact seems clear: it was not science that gave rise to melancholia in Hamlet, for the skeptical implications of the physical sciences had not at this point been realized. Hamlet's self-absorption bears, perhaps, a slightly Montaignean tinge, and if so it shares a link with the Pyrrhonistic turn of *Don Quixote*. More certainly, *Hamlet* shows the influence of Renaissance psychology, and a preoccupation with morbid themes that is not as clinical as Cervantes' but takes on the resonance of a more general, cultural discouragement. It participates in the sobriety of Timothy Bright, the preacherly author of the *Treatise on Melancholy* drawn on by Shakespeare, rather than the wit of Huarte de San Juan. Nevertheless, as with Quixote's paranoia, Hamlet's melancholy must be considered primarily in a generic, literary context. Freud was correct that there is a paradigmatic text giving form to the desire that remains unfulfilled in *Hamlet*. It is by no means necessary, however, to seek it in the ancient past: we need look no further than the revenge tragedies still popular on the stage in Shakespeare's day. Hamlet's tendency to delay is surprising not in comparison with the general conduct of human behavior but specifically in the context of the Elizabethan revenge play and its conventions.

Hamlet shares with *Don Quixote* the aspect of generic critique, and this gives rise to the play's literary self-consciousness, as conspicuous in its way as that of the *Quixote*. Shakespeare does not leave Hamlet's generic

inadequacies as a hero unremarked. Rather, he goes so far as to bring the
theater into the action, so that Hamlet himself can observe and even
dramatize his own failure of nerve. After hearing the player declaim upon
the death of Priam, Hamlet reproaches himself bitterly for his "pigeon-
liver'd" behavior:

> O what a rogue and peasant slave am I!
> Is it not monstrous that this player here,
> But in a fiction, in a dream of passion,
> Could force his soul so to his own conceit
> That from her working all his visage wann'd,
> Tears in his eyes, distraction in his aspect,
> A broken voice, and his whole function
> Suiting with forms to his conceit? And all for nothing!
> For Hecuba!
> What's Hecuba to him or he to Hecuba
> That he should weep for her? (II, ii, 544–53)[47]

The heroic action described by the player must be a sore story for
Hamlet: the "rugged Pyrrhus," "horridly trick'd/With blood of fathers,
mothers, daughters, sons" seems an example chosen to rebuke his faint-
heartedness in the shedding of familial blood. But that is not what stimu-
lates his invidious comparison, at least for the moment. It is the player's
emotion, demonstrated in his way of speaking, that shames Hamlet and
makes him feel "unpregnant of [his] cause." Yet, as a piece of rhetoric, his
self-reproachful soliloquy is far more natural and far more convincingly
demonstrative than the speech by the player that calls forth his rebuke.
That it is a soliloquy prevents this fact from registering consciously with
the audience: as the late Harry Levin points out, the formality and theatricality of the player's speech makes Hamlet's performance all the more
real.[48] Hamlet's exasperation at the spectacle of the player's art, at his
masterly self-control and the paradox of his gratuitous emotion, builds,
through typical considering "too curiously," to the magnificent chiastic
sputter of the final quoted lines: "What's Hecuba to him or he to Hecuba/
That he should weep for her?" The rhetoric is here most perfectly pitched
to the situation, character, and moment, without a trace of the pomp and
flourish that Hamlet envies in the player. It exemplifies that superb natural-
ism of expression that Shakespeare had now mastered and was to refine for
a decade more. How different is the rhetoric of the speech that calls forth
Hamlet's admiration, the speech that exhibits his own, not his creator's,
literary values. It is, of course, a dramatic report of that tale told to Dido

by Aeneas of the fall of Troy and the slaughter of his father, Priam, by
Pyrrhus the son of Achilles. As we have seen, the treatment of Hecuba's
grief touches Hamlet to the quick:

> But who—ah, woe!—had seen the mobbled queen
> . . . .
> Run barefoot up and down, threat'ning the flames
> With bisson rheum, a clout upon that head
> Where late the diadem stood, and, for a robe,
> About her lank and all o'erteemed loins
> A blanket, in th'alarm of fear caught up—
> Who this had seen, with tongue in venom steep'd,
> 'Gainst Fortune's state would treason have pronounc'd.
> But if the gods themselves did see her then,
> When she saw Pyrrhus make malicious sport
> In mincing with his sword her husband's limbs,
> The instant burst of clamour that she made,
> Unless things mortal move them not at all,
> Would have made milch the burning eyes of heaven
> And passion in the gods. (II, ii, 498, 501–14)

The player's speech has been the subject of much scholarly debate. No
source for it has ever been established; it may be a parody but, if so, the
object is probably not extant. What can be said about it is that it has a
style and, in part, a vocabulary distinctly formal and archaic, an epic
rather than a dramatic relation to its subject, and that these qualities
suggest a kinship with earlier and more naive products of the Elizabethan
stage. Like Quixote's, Hamlet's taste runs toward the literary antique. He
does not share, however, Quixote's vulgarity, his inability to distinguish
the genuine from the popular, though his "antic disposition" is shot through
with vulgarity. Rather, Hamlet is distinctly fastidious, as can be seen in
his warning to the players about the exaggerations of speech and gesture
that "please the groundlings"; he blames the failure of the Pyrrhus play on
vulgar ignorance: it was "caviare to the general." Hamlet's sense of heroic
rhetoric and emotion is anachronistic and stagy relative to that of his creator
and the audience. It is not quite to be mocked, but it has a gorgeousness
and an other-worldliness about it that make heroic behavior seem unlikely.
Hamlet, proverbially, has become caught up more in the judgment of his
performance than in the action itself. He oscillates in speech between the
high and the low, the antic and sublime, envying now the player's passion
and now Horatio's self-control.

Hamlet's melancholy, then, like Quixote's paranoia, borrows the form of a literary diversion. Its social basis is not the strong discrepancy between elite and popular audiences evident in the *Quixote*, but a tension, perhaps, within the audience, and even within Elizabethan imagination itself, a tension that can be unmistakably felt but that has not produced a distinction of elements.[49] Were we to ask the Freudian question, "What is the mechanism of repression?" the answer would have to be a certain literary and social sophistication in Shakespeare and his audience that permitted them to reflect, with Hamlet but in a slightly different, less conservative spirit, upon the discrepancy he notes between his own inconsequential behavior and the officious dispatch and easy, somewhat pompous demonstrativeness of the conventional revenger. It is the awareness of discrepancy between naive and sophisticated imagination, an awareness active in Shakespeare and dominant in Cervantes, that permits both writers to evoke a complex psychological layering, conflicting aspects of will and desire, and illusion within illusion. To measure Hamlet's psyche against the pattern from which it departs, therefore, we need not appeal to "the secular process of repression" going back to Sophocles. It is enough to observe the growing sophistication of the English stage, from the boisterous revenge plays like Kyd's *Spanish Tragedy* to the sickly sophistication of *Hamlet*, where Shakespeare looks back upon this very development and makes it one of the sources of his art. Hamlet's melancholy is not so much a phenomenon calling for Freudian interpretation as another of the models of Freudian rhetoric: for Freud now appears once again as an imitator of Renaissance literary psychology, exploiting the socially and artistically retrograde elements of literary culture to furnish the patterns of repressed desire and coherent delusion. Whereas Cervantes took the romances of chivalry and Shakespeare the revenge plays to furnish the materials of the inner drama, Freudian satire takes for its performance all of past culture and anything that might conceivably replace it.

If, finally, in light of these observations, it no longer seems plausible to conceive of Hamlet as a frustrated Oedipus, shackled by the chains of civilization and so prevented from acting on his, and our own, primal impulses, it remains to be noted, as have many before, how strange and implausible is the logic that would ask us in the first place to view the figure of Sophocles' Oedipus as an embodiment of erotic freedom. This is difficult to do, when the premise of Sophocles' play requires us to accept from the beginning that the incest and patricide committed by Oedipus are not deliberate acts of pleasure but unwitting ones, in which the agent fails to recognize his own performance. Oedipus' crimes are not unrepressed expressions of the libido; rather, they are unconscious in the simple sense: acts of ignorance. Perhaps, as a reading of Aristotle would suggest, they fit the description of *hamartia*, a 'mistake' or 'missing of the mark', though the precise character of Oedipus' mistake has proven notoriously difficult to identify; perhaps his tendency toward unintended crimes can be attributed to the predestined consequences of ancestral guilt;[50] or might his responsibility, finally, lie in his insistence upon bringing his past into the light of day? What is most difficult to see is how the deeds of Oedipus can be considered occasions of knowing pleasure, or to find just where in the play, as Freud asserts, "the child's wishful fantasy that underlies it is brought into the open and realized as it would be in a dream."

We have seen that wherever Freud encountered the appearance of straightforwardness or simplicity, there he found disguise and unsuspected complication; perhaps we should not be surprised to discover that, when he tells us at last of simplicity, of the key lying behind the complexities of human behavior, we should discover in this key complications Freud himself chose to ignore. It is, then, in fact, perfectly in keeping with the generally paradoxical mode of Freudian contrivance that he should give us as the ultimate symbol of the undisguised transparency of desire a character whose story seems above all others to pose the question of the hidden significance and unpredictable consequences of human behavior. And yet, in spite of subsequent qualifications, it is as a symbol of transparency that Oedipus stands at the center of psychoanalytic myth, at the lowest depths of the unconscious mind and at the historical origins of human consciousness, before all such duplicitous refinements as civilization, repression, neurosis, and paranoia.

For Freud, both Oedipus and his creator represent an uninhibited stage of culture. But it is not as if Sophocles was unaware of the distinction between unimproved and civilized life. In fact, in Sophocles' portrayal, Oedipus, far from representing primitive force, stands rather as the embodiment of the intellectual and social achievements of Athenian civilization, and as a model of the active Athenian described in Pericles' funeral oration. Oedipus is distinctly the product of *Kultur*, of all that sets human beings above nature.[51] His story appears in a perspective still more remote from Freud's when we recall the immediate historical context of Sophocles' play, set on the stage at the beginning of the Peloponnesian War. At this perilous moment, Sophocles presented his Athenian audience with the spectacle of a leader whose very strengths and virtues are his undoing, a leader whose every move has been anticipated by an all-powerful enemy, so that it accomplishes precisely what he studied to avoid. Oedipus finds himself the object of calculated manipulation and incomprehensible justice. He represents the failure of policy in a world governed by Olympian irony, a world in which the consequences of human action are impossible to calculate. A more reasonable interpretation, then, of this figure, chosen by Freud as the central psychoanalytic icon, would make him not so much a hero of desire as an image of paranoia justified.

Freud himself, as the story goes, dreamed from his university days of achieving fame through the solving of riddles, in order to become, like Oedipus, "a man most mighty". He paled when his lifelong fantasy of having these Sophoclean words applied to himself came true on his fiftieth birthday.[52] What is more, he portrayed his own fate in a manner that must remind us of Oedipus: as the bringer of a dangerous form of knowledge, happened upon naively in the course of discovery, setting him, from that moment, beyond the pale of human consideration.[53] For Freud, the true personal significance of the Oedipus myth lay not in sexual ambition but in the quest to uncover what is hidden. The drama of Oedipus remains, therefore, a fitting emblem of Freud's paranoid project, being one of its central imaginative models.

SIX

Freud as Quixote

> It cannot be denied that to interpret and report
> one's dreams demands a high degree of self-disci-
> pline. One is bound to emerge as the only villain
> among the crowd of noble characters who share
> one's life. —Freud

In *The Interpretation of Dreams,* the paranoid logic, psychology, and rhetoric of psychoanalysis, which have been the subjects of the preceding
chapters, combine in perfect harmony. The work takes the form of a
romance, a quest, one that demystifies the object it seeks, then mystifies it
in new ways. It is, first, a great treatise of reduction, in which the contents
of ordinary thought, drawn into the network of dreams, are translated into a
new moral and psychological language, which knows only ambition, suspicion, and deceit. The positing of doubleness in every detail of experience
makes possible an agile and irresistible method of decoding and unmasking. This hermeneutic doubleness arises from the original aggressiveness of the reductive method. It permits not a discovery of meaning where
there had been none, but a destruction of ordinary meaning, a translation
into something else. It is a hermeneutic not of fulfillment but of deprivation,
its aim not to recover but to negate. Only when the unmasking of the
ordinary has been achieved, and the reader has been reoriented in the
inverted world of the unconscious, do new mysteries and new adventures
arise.

With the employment of this method, Freud makes his personal psychology an exemplary one. He himself assumes a double role, playing both
parts in the drama of translation: discoverer of hidden motives and victim
of interpretation. The glory of the one lies in the exposure of the other, the
heroism of the one in the folly of the other. Freud's private and contingent
foibles—the "megalomaniac" foibles of the doctor, the friend, the son, the
colleague—provide Freud the interpreter with the materials of a universal
science of suspicion. And it is not only vanity, primal selfishness, and

exalted egotism that the method of suspicion can detect behind the facade of everyday life, struggling to be expressed in the language of dreams. These dreams and their interpretations are rooted in impulses of the rawest physicality, the most infantile bodily preoccupations. They are an embarrassment to civilized sentiment, yet Freud brings them humorously to the center of the human psyche.

And if this were not enough for the satirist's purposes, the dreams also reveal, or are made to reveal, in Freud's psychology a series of comic infatuations with heroes of the imagination. Freud's megalomaniacal quest, like Quixote's, expresses itself as literary repetition. The true underpinning of Freudian bio-history appears: we repeat the past experience of the human race not through biological memory but through imaginative identification and comical, 'unconscious' reenactment. The satiric form remains intact from *Don Quixote* to *Die Traumdeutung*. We will even be able to observe that the ambivalence of the image of Quixote as it moves from Enlightenment to Romantic culture finds its equivalent in Freud's romance of dreams.

In the foregoing chapter I pointed to a difference between Cervantes and Freud as satiric writers: Cervantes' satire has a specific object whereas Freud's is universal. There is a second difference that will undoubtedly have occurred to the reader: Cervantes is funny and Freud is not. The two distinctions are related: it was by giving his readers a view of the foibles of a discrete individual representing the characteristic temptations and follies of a class that Cervantes furnished the opportunity for laughter; the violence of Freudian scrutiny, on the other hand, is general, and recoils upon the analyst and his readers. It does so not with the amiable self-reference with which the Erasmian Folly acknowledges her contradictions, but with an alienating mechanical reduction applied to concrete personal experience just as it is in the *Quixote*. If there is pleasure here it is not the pleasure of laughter, which sets the ridiculous always at a distance. It would seem, then, as if the analogy between Freud and Cervantes were about to break down at the first level of reflection, the ability to evoke laughter being a sine qua non of satiric writing.[1]

In order to overcome this obstacle we will have to accomplish a certain shift in our perspective on the *Quixote*, to see Cervantes' novel no longer in the original context of his attack upon the books of chivalry but rather as Freud saw it at the turn of the twentieth century. We will have to bring the two authors into the same historical frame. For at the time that the young Freud was erecting his cult of Cervantes, the *Quixote* was no longer read merely as a satiric work. The materials against which its humor was originally directed had long since been forgotten, and the dominant European sensibility had undergone a great reversal of values that set the satiric culture of early modern Europe on its head. As we have seen, the emergence of historical consciousness during this period began as a gesture of negation. Previous culture—the culture of "superstition," "enthusiasm," and false idealism—had been set at a satiric distance, and it was on the basis of this distance that the progress of Enlightenment could be asserted. With the great change in culture marked by the phenomenon of Rousseau, the suspicion and satiric scrutiny that had been directed against the enemies of Enlightenment became general. It now extended to culture per se, to all that was of human making. The conditions of social existence were now viewed as threatening, controlling, falsifying, weakening, or sterilizing. Value migrated into the natural, to those things or aspects of things one could be certain were outside the influence or control of other human beings. With Rousseau, paranoid fear of other human beings became a kind of intellectual norm.

From the perspective of this general suspicion toward culture itself, two opposing states of moral and intellectual being came to be distinguished. The first was an image of the primitive or rural life—simple, unselfconscious, lacking all the social advantages that the Enlightenment and bourgeois capitalism had striven to achieve. This state became an object of nostalgia, being imagined as free from the hostile and selfish motives inculcated by society. The second state was that of the superstitious delusion of traditional culture: from the new perspective, aristocracy, chivalry, romance, even Catholicism, became attractive forms of idealistic fantasy—attractive, of course, in proportion to their impotence. Working in these materials one could discern a benign expression of 'narcissism' *avant la lettre.* Their power to embody a form of self-assertion uninhibited yet transparently illusory made them an exhilarating object of aesthetic identification for the new, universally suspicious consciousness. Romantic imagination also recognized its kinship with madness just as Freud was to do. It felt the profundity of ungrounded fancy, just as it felt the limits suspicion had set for its own. It was, again, a case of naive and sentimental paranoia.

The philosophical implications of Rousseau's revolution in value were developed preeminently in Germany, and it is here that we can see the implications for a reading of the *Quixote.* It is not surprising that the madness of Quixote should acquire a new attractiveness in a culture that had come more and more to regard human thought and human value as individually determined and private, emanating from an internal creative agency—the self—to be reunited with the external world, if at all, only through dialectical transformations nearly ungraspable from the current standpoint of history. Locke, we have seen, humorously imagined that, if ideas stand in relation only to each other, the madman might be envied for the superior liveliness of his internal representations; this becomes a prophetic utterance fulfilled in the new admiration of Quixote's character. The classic statement is by F. W. Schelling:

> One need only think of *Don Quixote* to see the implications of the concept of a mythology created by the genius of an individual. Don Quixote and Sancho Panza are mythological persons extending across the entire cultivated earth, just as the story of the windmill and so on are true myths or mythological sagas. What in the restricted conception of an inferior spirit would have appeared intended only as a satire of a certain foolishness, this poet has transformed by the most fortunate of inventions into the most universal, meaningful, and picaresque image of life. . . . The theme on the whole is the struggle between the real and the ideal. . . the novel of Cervantes is based on an extremely imperfect, indeed daft protagonist, yet one who is simultaneously of such noble nature, and who—as long as the *one* point is not touched—displays so much superior understanding that no outrage can actually disgrace him.[2]

Schelling recognizes that Cervantes' initial motive was a satiric one, but he cannot consider the Quixote character as anything other than a universal myth. Quixote is "noble" in his devotion to the "ideal," and this conception of the "ideal" does not find it discouraging to be set in opposition to what is "real." The comic discrepancy between the real world of Cervantes' novel and Quixote's conception of it becomes for Schelling largely a difference of principle, and the self-interested character of Quixote's delusion is thereby obscured. And just as Schelling detaches Quixote's aristocratic delusion from its original social significance, taking it now at something like the value it claims for itself, so he detaches Cervantes' creative activity from its sources. It is now a "mythology created by the genius of an individual," just the status Freud would later ascribe to art and paranoia. For Schelling, the individual character of Cervantes' myth guarantees its universality. It arises out of no local political or social context, but furnishes, rather, "the most universal, meaningful, and picaresque image of life."

For this Romantic sensibility, then, the figure of the paranoid, first observed for satiric purposes, had become the central protagonist of Western European imagination. His quest, in its detached idealism, was no longer to be laughed at, no longer a spectacle of pretentiousness mortified with cruelty, but an emblem of the human condition itself. In succeeding generations, the admiration for Quixote would only grow more extravagant. He would become the archetype of existential revolt, asserting the superiority of inner vision in the face of an absurd reality. The torments and degradations that he suffered in the satiric spirit of the narrative would be transformed into a true martyrdom. Picasso's famous drawing of Quixote captures the Romantic view: the knight and his horse are conjured out of nothing with the lightest of strokes, yet they dominate the landscape, in scale they approach the sun, while Sancho, the windmills, reality itself, dwindle to insignificance.

The most extreme sanctifications of Quixote were to occur after the period of Freud's encounter with Cervantes. But his admiring attitude toward both the hero and his creator appear unambiguously in the letter to Martha I have already quoted, in which he expresses his pleasure to see Quixote's delusory behavior exposed in the good company it deserves. The young Freud identifies Cervantes with the idealism of his hero: "Don't you find it very touching to read how a great person, himself an idealist, makes fun of his ideals? Before we were so fortunate as to apprehend the deep truths in our love we were all noble knights passing through the world caught in a dream, misinterpreting the simplest things, magnifying commonplaces into something noble and rare, and thereby cutting a sad figure. Therefore we men always read with respect about what we once were and in part still remain." The mature Freud would come to believe that love itself was as much of a 'narcissistic' delusion as Quixote's dream, and to agree with the point of Shaw's "malicious aphorism to the effect that being in love means greatly exaggerating the difference between one woman and another."[3] But he did not, in later years, alter his serious view of Quixote:

Don Quixote is originally a purely comic figure, a big child; the phantasies from his books of chivalry have gone to his head. It is well known that to begin with the author intended nothing else of him and that his creation gradually grew far beyond its creator's first intentions. But after the author had equipped this ridiculous figure with the deepest wisdom and the noblest purposes and had made him into the symbolic representative of an idealism which believes in the realization of its aims and takes duties seriously and taken promises literally, this figure ceased to have a comic effect.[4]

Like his Romantic predecessors, Freud can take Quixote seriously even though he recognizes the satiric design of the narrative and the fact that the character's idealism has the form of a delusion. The knight's wisdom, nobility, and, above all, the sincerity of his belief in his own ideals make him immune to laughter. It is strange to see Freud professing admiration for these qualities, which, in any other form, would evoke his suspicion. Claims to nobility and idealism by his contemporaries filled him with scorn, for he knew these to be the most extreme expressions of human hypocrisy and covert violence, derivatives of unchecked narcissism. In the figure of Quixote, however, these same expressions provide Freud with an exquisite delight and even compel his admiration. The paradox is not difficult to unravel: Quixote's idealism has already been disinfected by Cervantes' satiric treatment; the paranoid quest has been deprived of all title to the realization of its hopes. The only claim it makes is the claim of the psychological—in other words, of consciousness satirically detached from reality.

Freud's great mission was to set all human activity at this same satiric distance. Only then could its ethical qualities, its pathos and strangeness, be appreciated. And so we can distinguish in psychoanalytic rhetoric the same two moments or tendencies that mark the reception-history of the *Quixote*. First there is the satiric moment, the revelation of vulgarity pretentiously concealed. This is the dominant of Freud's register. Then, after the negation, there comes a moment of recovery, of integration with the 'universal', when, within the private, often 'unconscious' workings of the psyche, we glimpse the integrity of the great forms of cultural production of the past, the inverted expressions of religion, superstition, totemism, and myth. We might call this tendency, adopting Freud's own usage, the 'uncanny', stipulating that the repressed materials that return in moments of Romantic glamour come not from 'the unconscious' as Freud understood it but from a scientifically discredited and satirically deflated metaphysical and mythological tradition. The 'uncanny' has good Romantic credentials; in his essay on the subject, Freud quotes with approval Schelling's definition: " 'Uncanny' is the name for everything that ought to have remained . . . secret and hidden but has come to light."[5] Freud's self-portrayal participates in both satiric deflation and Romantic heroism of the 'uncanny' sort.[6] The first bears the mantle of science while the second emerges as an aesthetic aftereffect, helping to preserve the dignity of the scientific demeanor. Only in Freud's masterpiece, *The Interpretation of Dreams*, does the uncanny attain anything like a parity with the satiric; it is not surprising that Freud identified most profoundly with this work and that it remains aesthetically the most satisfying of his productions. In the course of its long narrative, Freud shifts in an agile manner from the role of the suspicious interpreter demystifying the social subterfuge of individual dreams, revealing their shameful and vulgar origins and being harshest upon his own, to a more Romantic persona, whose quest is for universal knowledge, a quest whose end is ever delayed and deferred so that the final mystery of dreams can never entirely be reduced to nothing.

The Romance of Dreams

In August of 1899, just a few months before the publication of the work, Freud was still struggling with the form of *The Interpretation of Dreams*. His correspondent and collaborator, Wilhelm Fliess, urged him to relegate the long summary of previous research on dreams to the back of the volume, but Freud felt that it was necessary to pay an immediate homage to his predecessors. Typically, he was expecting a negative reaction from the critics, and doubtless the slightly arcane character of the topic made him hesitate to proceed without marshaling the precedents for his endeavor, as if he had begun his own labors with these in mind.[7] Freud made a virtue of necessity by giving to the whole the form of a "fantasy-walk" ("Spazierungs-phantasie"), as he informs his friend:

> The whole thing is planned on the model of an imaginary walk. First comes the dark wood of the authorities (who cannot see the trees), where there is no clear view and it is easy to go astray. Then there is a cavernous defile through which I lead my readers—my specimen dream with its peculiarities, its details, its indiscretions and its bad jokes—and then, all at once, the high ground and the open prospect and the question: "Which way do you want to go?"[8]

I have already pointed out the heroic motif of the journey to the underworld suggested in this volume's motto. The plan of *The Interpretation of Dreams*, as Freud announced it to Fliess, makes it clear that his heroic rhetoric was not merely decorative but part of a deliberate strategy, the whole being cast in the form of a romance with Freud as the Virgilian guide leading the reader on the difficult quest for truth. There can be no doubt that Freud, even at this early stage of his psychoanalytic career, took himself seriously in his role as a scientific hero. When he announces at the end of the journey that "dreams are a royal road to knowledge of the unconscious activities of the mind," the structure of his romance is complete, with a stress on the value of the goal (608). Yet, in spite of this seriousness of purpose, the manner of the narrative is predominantly satiric. We hear an echo of Dante in Freud's description of the beginning of the journey, in the "dark wood of the authorities,"[9] but the turn is comical. The "cavernous defile" of the specimen dream presents a challenge, but does so by the embarrassing triviality of its elements, "its peculiarities, its details, its indiscretions and its bad jokes." Only passing through these can the higher ground and the crossroads be reached. *The Interpretation of Dreams* is a satiric romance in scientific form. Like the *Quixote*, it has the wit of psychological curiosity applied with an effect of deflation to the rhetoric of the ideal; it adds to this the uncanny appeal of the satirically repressed materials returning to significance as they did for Cervantes' romantic readers.

The title of *The Interpretation of Dreams*, *Die Traumdeutung*, gives the first hint of its tendency toward the uncanny. *Traumdeutung* is to dreams what "palm-reading" is to palms.[10] For a scientific work, the title is provocatively vulgar and Romantic. Freud spends nearly the first hundred pages reveling in the lore of nocturnal fantasy. We read of the dreams of Xerxes and of the elder Scaliger, of Napoleon and the Marquis de l'Hervey:

In spite of many thousands of years of effort, the scientific understanding of dreams has made very little advance—a fact so generally admitted in the literature that it seems unnecessary to quote instances in support of it. In these writings, of which a list appears at the end of my work, many stimulating observations are to be found and a quantity of interesting material bearing upon our theme, but little or nothing that touches upon the essential nature of dreams or that offers a final solution of any of their enigmas. (1)

We will not find scientific wisdom, it seems, among the experts, only a vast range of opinion, from Aristotle to the present, testifying to the perennial mystery of dreams. Freud's approach is not to narrow the divergence of received opinion by analysis but rather to accentuate difference, with the effect of a satiric anatomy in the style of Burton. The conclusions of scientific researchers like Maury, Delboeuf, and Hildebrandt stand alongside the teachings of ancient authorities—Cicero, Lucretius, Macrobius, and Artemidorus—as well as the philosophical speculations of Kant, Schleiermacher, Novalis, and Schopenhauer. We learn of the oracular power of dreams, of their origins in the divine, the demonic, or in local sensations like the desire to micturate. They can revive the most distant memories or the most recent. In them the moral sense is most active or completely inactive, the experts showing on this point "remarkable shifts and inconsistencies in their opinions" (68). The most important of all the conflicts concerns the question of the value of dreams: Do dreams have a meaning or are they the scattered fragments of mental process deprived of the integrity of waking thought? Dreams here are made the object of the same controversy of value as the one that surrounds the ravings of Quixote.

The experts most drastically diverge, Romantic spirits like the followers of Schelling setting upon "dream-life" the highest value, "clearly an echo of the divine nature of dreams which was undisputed in antiquity"; on the other hand, the members of the hard-headed materialist camp deny any worth to dreams as mental objects (5). Pointing up the difference, Freud ventures upon "a simile from the sphere of psychiatry": "the first group of theories construct dreams on the model of paranoia, while the second group make them resemble mental deficiency or confusional states" (76). The issue of value then comes to this: Do dreams betray the coherence of paranoid delusion, are they as profound as the *Quixote*, or do they justify an entirely satiric attitude? If dreams can be equated with paranoia they can be accepted as objects of the greatest interest and value.

The satirists of dream have some notable points on their side, for dreams do evidence remarkable confusion. The case is stated by Hildebrandt:

"What astonishing leaps a dreamer may make, for instance, in drawing inferences! How calmly he is prepared to see the most familiar lessons of experience turned upside down. What laughable contradictions he is ready to accept in the laws of nature and society before, as we say, things get beyond a joke and the excessive strain of nonsense wakes him up. We calculate without a qualm that three times three make twenty; we are not in the least surprised when a dog quotes a line of poetry, or when a dead man walks to his grave on his own legs, or when we see a rock floating on the water; we proceed gravely on an important mission to the Duchy of Bernburg or to the Principality of Liechtenstein to inspect their naval forces; or we are persuaded to enlist under Charles XII shortly before the battle of Poltava." (56)

So dreams acquire a charming absurdity. In a work entitled *Traumdeutung*, though, it is to be expected that the defenders of dream will have the better of the discussion. And so we find the "sagacious Delboeuf" discovering in dreams the full range of what imagination can accomplish: " 'Le songeur est un acteur qui joue à volonté les fous et les sages, les bourreaux et les victimes, les nains et les géants, les démons and les anges' " (60). For Novalis, dreams exercise a restorative power: " 'Dreams are a shield against the humdrum monotony of life; they set imagination free from its chains so that it may throw into confusion all the pictures of everyday existence and break into the unceasing gravity of grown men with the joyful play of a child. Without dreams we should surely grow soon old; so we may look on them—not, perhaps as a gift from on high—but as a precious recreation, as friendly companions on our pilgrimage to the grave" (83). Finally, it is once again left to Hildebrandt, author of the work on dreams "most perfect in form and the richest in ideas" (67), to state this side of the argument with the greatest eloquence:

"There are few of us who could not affirm, from our own experience, that there emerges from time to time in the creations and fabrics of the genius of dreams a depth and intimacy of emotion, a tenderness of feeling, a clarity of vision, a subtlety of observation, and a brilliance of wit such as we should never claim to have at our permanent command in our waking lives. There lies in dreams a marvellous poetry, an apt allegory, an incomparable humour, a rare irony. A dream looks upon the world in a light of strange idealism and often enhances the effects of what it sees by its deep understanding of their essential nature. It pictures earthly beauty to our eyes in a truly heavenly splendour and clothes dignity with the highest majesty, it shows us our everyday fears in the ghastliest shape and turns our amusement into jokes of indescribable pungency. And sometimes, when we are awake and still under the full impact of an experience like one of these, we cannot but feel that never in our life has the real world offered us its equal." (62–63)

Dreams have now attained the full profundity of Quixotic idealism. Fliess could not have been more wrong-headed when he advised Freud to relegate his anatomy of dreams to an appendix. Freud used it ingeniously to conjure up the fog his new insights would dispel. Keeping the received tradition at an ironic distance, he was yet able to initiate his audience into the romance that had gathered around the subject over the centuries. Freud knew that the skepticism of science toward the meaning of dreams was not entirely appealing to the wider public: "Lay opinion has taken a different attitude throughout the ages. It has exercised its indefeasible right to behave inconsistently; and, though admitting that dreams are unintelligible and absurd it cannot bring itself to declare that they have no significance at all. Led by some obscure feeling, it seems to assume that, in spite of everything, every dream has a meaning, though a hidden one, that dreams are designed to take the place of some other process of thought, and that we have only to undo the substitution correctly in order to arrive at this hidden meaning" (96). Only at the end of his discussion do we find Freud finally enlisting himself in support of the Romantic and vulgar position, the one held by the followers of Schelling and the general public: "I have been driven to realize that here once more we have one of these not infrequent cases in which an ancient and jealously held popular belief seems to be nearer the truth than the judgement of the prevalent science of to-day. I must affirm that dreams really have a meaning and that a scientific procedure for interpreting them is possible" (100). Dreams will turn out, like paranoia, and like the pronouncements of Quixote, to have not only a meaning but a distinct value, once we have established the proper means by which they can be read. The first stage of Freud's literary journey ends with exquisite poise between satire and the uncanny.

Innocence Disallowed

Now we come to the "cavernous defile" of the specimen dream. It is a dream of Freud's own, for only in connection with one of his own dreams, Freud tells us, could he permit himself to reveal the indiscreet contents of dream-life. In order to accomplish his purpose, Freud will have to involve his readers not only in the details of his dreams but also in the waking life that surrounds them and provides their materials: "And now I must ask the reader to make my interests his own for quite a while, and to plunge, along with me, into the minutest details of my life; for a transference of this kind is peremptorily demanded by our interest in the hidden meaning of dreams" (105–6). It is always inviting to be taken into an author's confidence. But before we plunge with Freud into the interpretation of his dreams, it will be necessary first to inquire into the nature of the method itself.

Freud's procedure is to trace each element of what he calls the 'manifest content' of the dream, its surface material as narrated to the analyst, along a chain of associations leading back to the original idea that, theoretically, gave rise to the dream. This idea is the dream's meaning. It must be in the nature of a wish-fulfillment, some egotistical or libidinal impulse that could not appear to the dreamer without causing embarrassment and a disturbance of sleep. Because the wish is 'improper', to recall Freud's definition of sexuality, or in some way not for show, it has been subjected to 'censorship' by a separate agency of the mind. The conflict between these two agencies, wish and censor, produces the discrepancy between the 'manifest' and 'latent' contents of the dream. The manifest content is a disguise permitting the latent wish to evade the attention of the censor and make its way into consciousness.

The glaring deficiencies in Freud's theory of dreams are well known to specialists in psychoanalysis but still too little known to the wider intellectual community.[11] They derive from the circular and question-begging character of psychoanalytic logic. First of all, there is the assumption that in discovering the chain of associations leading from the dream we are retracing the dream back to its cause in an unfulfilled, often sexual, always egotistical wish. It being granted that there must be, at any given point in a person's life, certain central preoccupations, sex being one of the most likely, it is not surprising that, when the mind is allowed to wander starting from any particular idea, it should arrive at one of these preoccupations. This will especially be the case if one is told deliberately not to censor one's thoughts, which is bound to bring normally censored thoughts to the fore. But it does not mean that the preoccupations caused the dream. One could freely associate from a set of objects that someone else had placed on a table and arrive at ideas of sex, but this would not mean that one's ideas of sex had caused the objects to be placed on the table.[12] The process of free association may indeed tend to stray toward the matters that are of greatest interest to us, but what we learn about ourselves from the process in all likelihood will have little to do with the starting point. Freud's attempts to deal with this objection show that he never truly understood it.[13]

If there were any reason to expect that an analysis of the associations sparked by dreams, or by objects on a table, might lead us back to the subjects of our primary concern in the manner of a projective test, it is unlikely that we should arrive there by the psychoanalytic method of dream interpretation. For according to this method, it is up to the interpreter to fill in the gaps of association between the manifest contents and the underlying wish using a combination of details gathered from the dreamer's history and a knowledge of typical symbols, most often having to do with parts of the body involved in sex. The analyst decides which associations are to be pursued and which dropped, which are symbolic and which transparent, and what kind of likeness is to count as a link between one association and another. The number of steps in the chain has no limit, and the analyst decides when the end has been reached. There is so little constraint upon the process that it cannot fail, the difficulties being entirely those of narrative invention. The analyst will get where he is going and find what he is looking for.

In analyzing Freud's interpretations of his own dreams, then, we will not be looking over his shoulder to find a more thoroughgoing psychoanalytic interpretation of the master's psyche, as has so often been attempted.[14] It is rather the narrative of interpretation itself that must become the object of scrutiny. How does this so undisciplined and unconstrained process of analysis succeed in producing coherent and persuasive interpretations of dreams? The answer is, of course, through the resources of suspicion. Dreams, Freud tells us, are never innocent: "All of them are completely egoistic: the beloved ego appears in all of them, even though it may be disguised. The wishes that are fulfilled in them are invariably the ego's wishes, and if a dream seems to have been provoked by an altruistic interest, we are only being deceived by appearances" (267). Dreams must always contain something worth hiding, otherwise they would speak their message plain. Their absurdity guarantees the significance of what is being concealed; and because dreams have always something scandalous, something 'improper' to hide, it will always be worthwhile to inquire into their secrets. It is thus to our need for concealment, undeniable and insistent as it is, that the Freudian narrative appeals.

Now we can see what it means to be taken into Sigmund Freud's confidence with regard to his dreams and those of others: we will be asked to extend our polite sense of hypocrisy to the seemingly opaque phenomena of dreams, so that they can be subjected to a hermeneutics of suspicion. What gives persuasiveness to the method is that the hidden and secret meanings of the dreams are imported from the social context of the dreamer. Since it is assumed that every dream is the fulfillment of an egoistic wish, this wish must have a basis in the reality, conscious or unconscious, of the dreamer's life. Somewhere in his or her history that basis must be found. Accept this and the rest follows, for if one *did* have the egoistic thoughts and feelings Freud imputes to the dream-life, one would undoubtedly want to hide them just in the way he suggests. Granting the basic assumption of the egotism of dreams, the social drama of concealment and disguise Freud builds around them becomes an entirely convincing one.

Interpretations of dreams constructed in this manner reveal the preoccupations and preconceptions not of the dreamer but the interpreter. In the case of Freud, the interpretations reveal the paranoid assumption that social life is a systematic form of deception. The system of distortion that the hidden wish motivating a dream must undergo in order to reach consciousness seems to Freud the exact equivalent of common social behavior:

I will try to seek a social parallel to this internal event in the mind. Where can we find a similar distortion of a psychical act in social life? Only where two persons are concerned, one of whom possesses a certain degree of power which the second is obliged to take into account. In such a case the second person will distort his psychical acts or as we might put it, will dissimulate. The politeness which I practice every day is to a large extent dissimulation of this kind; and when I interpret my dreams for my readers I am obliged to adopt similar distortions. (142)

The details of Freud's analogy bear some examination. Freud takes it for granted that when there are differences of power between one individual and another, this will automatically put the inferior in a position of having to dissimulate, the implication being that positions of power derive only from power. That one might be justified, for instance, in deferring to a professional superior is not imagined; the inferior person pretends to respect the superior solely out of practical exigency. The notion that one might receive ordinary recognition from a superior is equally unimaginable to Freud. This condition is not thought to be an exception but the rule of social life, so that there seems nothing strange about putting it forward as the basis for a scientific inference about the general functioning of the mind.[15] Freud's Hobbesian attitude toward authority is evidently instinctive to him. And he is quick to move from his depiction of the hypocrisy employed by the weak in the presence of the strong to a general admission that even his ordinary politeness is "a dissimulation of this kind." Ordinary social respect, in other words, is a disguise; *The Interpretation of Dreams* betrays the same paranoid view of social existence that we have found in Freud's later sociological writings. Freud claimed to have based his views of human nature and society upon his clinical experience in the interpretation of dreams, but those views were already guiding him when he developed his approach to dreams.

Let us follow Freud's social analogy for the distortion in dreams a little further:

A similar difficulty confronts the political writer who has disagreeable truths to tell to those in authority. If he presents them undisguised, the authorities will suppress his words. . . . A writer must beware of the censorship, and on its account he must soften and distort the expression of his opinion. According to the strength and sensitiveness of the censorship he finds himself compelled either merely to refrain from certain forms of attack, or to speak in allusions in place of direct references, or he must conceal his objectionable pronouncement beneath some apparently innocent disguise: for instance, he may describe a dispute between two Mandarins in the Middle Kingdom, when the people he really had in mind are officials in his own country. The stricter the censorship, the more far-reaching will be the disguise and the more ingenious too may be the means employed for putting the reader on the scent of the true meaning. (142)

In a later passage, Freud adds that in dealing with our superiors we are often led as much to disguise our affects as our true intentions: "the censorship bids me above all suppress my affects; and, if I am a master of dissimulation, I shall assume the *opposite* affect—smile when I am angry and seem affectionate when I wish to destroy."[16]

With this analogy between dream distortion and social hypocrisy Freud was capitalizing upon an ethos of social theatricality that was highly pronounced in fin-de-siècle Vienna. Freud's analogy to political censorship made an even more powerful appeal to local conditions of the period. William Johnston describes the paranoid atmosphere of Freud's Vienna:

Secretiveness blanketed public life, prompting a search for latent meanings behind every event. Whatever seemed inexplicable was attributed to conspirators, whether they be Jews, Czechs, Social Democrats, Protestants, or journalists. . . . When [Freud] spoke of superego censoring id, he knew what press censorship meant: a story would be missing from the front page, unleashing a fresh spate of rumors. Helpless before the bureaucracy, the populace indulged fantasies that belittled the omnipotent personages who manipulated them. Most Austrians harbored feelings of paranoia toward the state.[17]

Under such conditions of pervasive mistrust, it apparently seemed natural to extend the suspicions of the political sphere into the inner territory of the psyche. And so, along with the greater paranoid drift of modern culture, and along with Freud's peculiar endowment of mistrust, there appears in the composition of psychoanalysis the special contribution of Viennese politics. "The stricter the censorship, the more far-reaching will be the disguise and the more ingenious too may be the means employed for putting the reader on the scent of the true meaning." Freud promises his readers a method of interpreting dreams that can keep up even with the Viennese ingenuity of disguise made necessary by the potency of the censor. The more difficult the riddle, the more valuable the interpretation—and so he made the censor's power his own.

Freud's assumption that no dream is innocent, that all are "wolves in sheep's clothing" (183), sets him an exacting task: every appearance of altruism in dreams must be convincingly decoded to reveal an egotistical motive. He does not shrink from this task but confronts it head on, using a dream of his own:

The dream which follows is an instance of really low egoistic feelings concealed behind affectionate worry.
My friend Otto was looking ill. His face was brown and he had protruding eyes.
Otto is my family doctor, and I owe him more than I can ever hope to repay: he has watched over my children's health for many years, he has treated them successfully when they have been ill, and, in addition, whenever circumstances have given him an excuse, he has given them presents. He had visited us on the dreamday, and my wife had remarked that he looked tired and strained. That night I had my dream, which showed him with some of the signs of Basedow's [Graves'] disease. Anyone who interprets this dream without regard for my rule will conclude that I was worried about my friend's health and that this worry was realized in the dream. This would not only contradict my assertion that dreams are wish-fulfillments, but my other assertion, too, that they are accessible only to egoistic

impulses. But I should be glad if anyone interpreting the dream in this way would be good enough to explain to me why my fears on Otto's behalf should have lighted on *Basedow's* disease—a diagnosis for which his actual appearance gives not the slightest ground. My analysis, on the other hand, brought up the following material from an occurrence six years earlier. A small group of us, which included Professor A., were driving in pitch darkness through the forest of N., which lay some hours' drive from the place at which we were spending our summer holidays. The coachman, who was not perfectly sober, spilt us, carriage and all, over an embankment, and it was only by a piece of luck that we all escaped injury. We were obliged, however, to spend the night in a neighbouring inn, at which the news of our accident brought us a lot of sympathy. A gentleman, with unmistakable signs of Basedow's disease—incidentally, just as in the dream, only the brown discoloration of the skin of the face and the protruding eyes, but no goitre—placed himself entirely at our disposal and asked what he could do for us. Professor A. replied in his decisive manner: "Nothing except to lend me a night-shirt." To which the fine gentleman rejoined: "I'm sorry, but I can't do that," and left the room.

As I continued my analysis, it occurred to me that Basedow was the name not only of a physician but also of a famous educationalist. (In my waking state I no longer felt quite so certain about this.) But my friend Otto was the person whom I had asked to watch over my children's physical education, especially at the age of puberty (hence the night-shirt), in case anything happened to me. By giving my friend Otto in the dream the symptoms of our noble helper, I was evidently saying that if anything happened to me he would do just as little for the children as Baron L. had done on that occasion in spite of his kind offers of assistance. This seems to be sufficient evidence of the egoistic lining of the dream. (269–70, emphasis in original) [18]

Now this narrative has an undisputable appeal. It fixes, first, on an unusual detail, Basedow's disease, and traces it by association to a memorable event, the roadway accident. Such contretemps, when there are friends involved, acquire a mythological status, clarifying differences of character in the light of an emergency become comical in retrospect. Freud tells the story with novelistic aplomb and some embellishment. It is understandable, for instance, that he should have replaced the names of the characters with initials, but to set the story in the "forest of N." seems rather a literary flourish, none of the actors being presented in an especially scandalous light. The coachman "not perfectly sober" and the genial "night in a neighboring inn" sound like details out of one of Freud's favorite novels, *Don Quixote* or *Tom Jones*. In the middle of all this bonhomie, the perfidy of Baron L., the man with Basedow's, seems like a striking instance. In Freud's private associative register, it would seem, Basedow's disease must be the sign of a dubious character and therefore a reproach to Otto.

But has Freud proved that the dream betrays a suspicious attitude toward Otto just because in it Otto is endowed with Basedow's disease? Let us accept for a moment Freud's assumption that we can retrace the origins of the dream through association. The dream conflates, or 'condenses', the identities of three men: Otto, Baron L., and Basedow the physician and educator. It is Freud's hostility toward Baron L. that becomes the key to the emotional significance of the dream. He is mistrustful toward Baron L. so he must also be secretly mistrustful of Otto. What reason is there to prefer this interpretation other than Freud's assumption that no dream can be innocent? Why should the perfidious Baron be the key? If, for instance, as Freud asserts, the dream of Otto led him first to remember the Baron, who, like Otto in the dream, had Basedow's, then to remember the nightshirt, which reminded Freud of children and Otto's function with regard to his own children, and then the fact that Basedow himself was an educator, might we not rather conclude that Freud's melancholy about his friend's illness had caused him to identify Otto's character with that of the famous physician and educator, Otto having played such a role in Freud's own family? The dream then would mean that Freud's concern about his friend had caused him to reflect on the importance to the Freud family of Otto's benevolence and expertise, as important as that of Basedow to the general public. In this interpretation, Basedow's character would be the key and not Baron L.'s. It appears that we have answered the question, "Why Basedow's?" The importance of Baron L. has been diminished now, just as Basedow's importance was diminished in Freud's interpretation. Baron L. provides only the link to Basedow's double role as physician and educator, whereas in the original interpretation Basedow had been a mere linking feature between Otto and the Baron. We are limited here, necessarily, to the details Freud chose to sustain his suspicious interpretation. But were it necessary to account further for the inclusion of Baron L., it would not be beyond Freud's ingenuity to suggest that, if Otto's symptoms were significantly similar to those of the Baron, it might be because, in Sigmund Freud's associative register, Basedow's disease does not bring about regrettable consequences, for, in the first instance that came to mind, Basedow's was perhaps a welcome punishment for a disagreeable person. One can be as ingenious on behalf of charity as on behalf of suspicion. But let it be remembered that we have been working within Freud's paranoid assumption that everything in a dream must have a meaning. It would be far more reasonable as a response to Freud's narrative simply to refuse his question "Why Basedow's?" as the invitation to paranoia that it is.[19]

What Freud proved with the interpretation of the dream of Otto was that, for any dream, no matter how innocent on the surface, *one can always find* a suspicious interpretation. Freud took this as a confirmation of his hypothesis that all dreams are egotistical: "applications of psycho-analysis are always confirmations of it."[20] He has not proved, however, that, for any dream, one can *only* find a suspicious meaning. It seems unlikely, in fact, given the freedom of Freud's interpretive method, that there is any dream for which one could not find an altruistic meaning if such a one were desired. It is significant, nevertheless, that Freud's suspicious interpretation makes a better story than my altruistic one, involving, as it does, embarrassing revelations and secrets. And it more perfectly accords with Freud's character. In fact, once we have discovered his secret mistrust of his benefactor Otto, decoded from the language of dream, it becomes difficult to believe in the original account of his innocent and affectionate conscious attitude toward the man whom he "owe[d] more than [he] could ever hope to repay." In the light of Freud's own revelations, this innocence now seems like a rhetorical foil for the underlying duplicity of dreams.

There is a certain irony surrounding the operation I have just attempted, which was to show that Freud's dream does not necessarily betray the egotistical motivation that he claimed. I have had to acquit Freud of necessary guilt in order to convict him of contingent paranoia. In doing so, I have departed from the usual practice of Freud's critics up until the most recent days. That practice has been to extend the founder's self-suspicion far beyond its original bounds, showing his false assumptions, theoretical short cuts, therapeutic eccentricities, personal animus, his hidden motives of all kinds, and generally to portray Freud the doctor in a way more compatible with Freud the patient, yet all the while remaining, on the last page, faithful to his essential grandeur. Freud's reputation has a teflon surface, and it is not hard to understand why. By taking the reader into his confidence and making a show of his own egotism, he got the drift of suspicion decisively on his side. To invite suspicion about his character, his motives, even his scientific achievements, was to confirm his basic outlook. Freud succeeded in making himself always the issue, and it has been supremely difficult for his critics to get beyond him. Even those who admit his failure as a scientist insist upon the greatness of his imagination. To take this view of Freud is to recapitulate the Quixotism of the Romantics. The one escape from it is to see the follies of Quixote/Freud the way Cervantes originally saw them—not as the absolute truth of the human condition but as contingent forms of error, the products of thought gone astray. Only then can the absurd humor of paranoid conceit appear for what it is.

The Vindication of Dreams

Freud's dreams mean what he wants them to mean, what they have to mean if his satirically suspicious psychology is to be vindicated. This will cast the imaginary journey of *The Interpretation of Dreams*, to which we now return, into a different light, as its author "plunges" into the "cavernous defile" of the specimen dream "with its peculiarities, its details, its indiscretions and its bad jokes." The "Dream of Irma's Injection" involves Freud's impromptu examination of a recalcitrant psychoanalytic patient beset, in the dream, with an organic illness. In order to decode this dream, Freud treats his reader to a series of remarkable confessions all having to do with his career: his anxiety about the critical regard of his colleagues concerning the value of psychoanalytic treatment, his emotional preferences among his patients, his second thoughts about having sent a hysterical patient on a trip to Egypt in lieu of therapy, and, most notable, his long-lingering guilt about two deaths that he had caused, both having to do with injections.[21] "It seemed as if I had been collecting all the occasions which I could bring up against myself as evidence of lack of medical conscientiousness" (112). Freud the dreamer plays the role of a comically self-deceptive and resentful egotist. His dream, once it has been decoded, is nothing but an elaborate attempt on the part of Freud's unconscious to shift the burden of responsibility for all of his mistakes onto his patients and fellow doctors, thus disarming all their anticipated reproaches:

The groundlessness of the reproaches was proved for me in the dream in the most elaborate fashion. *I* was not to blame for Irma's pains, since she herself was to blame for them by refusing to accept my solution. *I* was not concerned with Irma's pains, since they were of an organic nature and quite incurable by psychological treatment. Irma's pains could be satisfactorily explained by her widowhood . . . which *I* had no means of altering. Irma's pains had been caused by Otto giving her an incautious injection of an unsuitable drug—a thing *I* should never have done. Irma's pains were the result of an injection with a dirty needle, like my old lady's phlebitis—whereas *I* never did any harm with my injections. I noticed, it is true, that these explanations of Irma's pains (which agreed in exculpating me) were not entirely consistent with one another, and indeed that they were mutually exclusive. The whole plea—for the dream was nothing else—reminded one vividly of the defence put forward by the man who was charged by one of his neighbours with having given him back a borrowed kettle in a damaged condition. The defendant asserted first, that he had given it back undamaged; secondly, that the kettle had a hole in it when he borrowed it; and thirdly, that he had never borrowed a kettle from his neighbour at all. (119–20, emphasis in original)

The first thing to be observed about this passage is that the comical ingenuity of the analysis is attributed in some measure to the dream itself. The dreamer Freud behaves like a satirist, putting, for instance, a ridiculously far-fetched and ingenious medical diagnosis into the mouth of a colleague, in this way discrediting his critical view of Freud. Absurdity in dreams is, for Freud, usually satirical and is the one part of the dream that reveals the latent contents without distortion![22] All that is necessary for the analyst to do is to decode the hidden satire of the dream. Once that has occurred, however, it is the dreamer who becomes the satiric victim, the sequence of apparently absurd and unmotivated details being now unmasked as the disguise for self-serving and derisive wish fulfillments.

The analyst's satiric gesture is a recovery, then, of the original animus of the dream. At the same time we are able to observe the cowardliness of the disguise. The dreamer has adopted a clever, hypocritical way of doing one thing while appearing to do another. In the dream of Irma's Injection, the dreamer Freud emerges as a genuine Quixote, inventing an absurd but ingenious personal mythology in order to shift the responsibility for his failure onto others. (Freud had already observed the shifting of blame as a distinctive element of the paranoid character.)[23] Revealing the Quixote in his own nature, Freud more than makes good all of his former physicianly inadequacies by establishing the value of the language of dreams. This language possesses, of course, merely a psychological, not a communicative value; but Freud sounds like Quixote defending the romances as he exalts the phenomena of dreams to a coherence equal with paranoia:

When, after passing through a narrow defile, we suddenly emerge upon a piece of high ground, where the path divides and the finest prospects open up on every side, we may pause for a moment and consider in which direction we shall first turn our steps. Such is the case with us, now that we have surmounted the first interpretation of a dream. We find ourselves in the full daylight of a sudden discovery. Dreams are not to be likened to the unregulated sounds that rise from a musical instrument struck by the blow of some external force instead of by a player's hand; they are not meaningless, they are not absurd; they do not imply that one portion of our store of ideas is asleep while another portion is beginning to wake. On the contrary, they are psychical phenomena of complete validity—fulfillments of wishes; they can be inserted into the chain of intelligible waking mental acts; they are constructed by a highly complicated activity of the mind. (122)

How easily Freud shifts from the ironic tone in which he addresses Freud the dreamer to the Romantic bravado of Freud the investigator. Dreams themselves undergo a sudden enhancement. Individually they are ridiculous and malicious, but as a genre they strike truer than the Aeolian harp, a typical symbol of Romantic imagination. In a letter to Fliess concerning the house where he dreamed this dream, Freud asked, "Do you suppose that some day one will read on a marble tablet on this house:

> Here, on July 24, 1895,
> the secret of the dream
> revealed itself to Dr. Sigm. Freud."[24]

With Freud it was ever a short step from the ridiculous to the sublime. What had once been grasped by psychology could slip half-humorously back toward superstition and the uncanny.

Freud as Gargantua

Freud worked on the interpretations of his dreams over a five-year period before their publication; his analyses have a dense, interlocking symbolic unity.[25] The central theme is ambition: Freud, the self-professed conquistador, discovers with surprise the intensity of his unconscious desire for promotion and reward: "So far as I knew, I was not an ambitious man" (137). In large measure, the narrative of *The Interpretation of Dreams* revolves around Freud's uncovering the disguises of this supposedly unsuspected ambition, this "absurd megalomania" (215) straining upward from beneath the level of his conscious mind. And for the most part this megalomania, like Quixote's, takes the form of heroic literary identifications. To conduct a minute analysis of Freud's paranoid self-portrait as revealed in his dreams in relation to the content of the dreams themselves would be to go beyond the scope of this study. It will not be necessary, moreover, for as we have seen, the dreams serve largely as matter for Freud's ingenious paranoid interpretations. Our method, rather, will be to expose, largely by quotation, the Quixotic dimensions of the Freudian interpretive venture, as Freud presents himself in a bristling array of illusory heroic identities.

At times Freud's unconscious, like Quixote's, expresses itself directly in the form of literary images, which make their way into Freud's dreams—and his interpretations of them—virtually uncensored. Suffering from 'delusions of inferiority' after a disappointing lecture, Freud had the following dream, given here along with its interpretation:

A hill, on which there was something like an open-air closet: a very long seat with a large hole at the end of it. Its back edge was thickly covered with small heaps of faeces of all sizes and degrees of freshness. There were bushes behind the seat. I micturated on the seat; a long stream of urine washed everything clean; the lumps of faeces came away easily and fell into the opening. It was as though at the end there was still some left.

Why did I feel no disgust during this dream? Because, as the analysis showed, the most agreeable and satisfying thoughts contributed to bringing the dream about. What at once occurred to me in the analysis were the Augean stables which were cleansed by Hercules. This Hercules was I. The hill and bushes came from Aussee, where my children were stopping at the time. I had discovered the infantile aetiology of the neuroses and had thus saved my own children from falling ill. The seat (except, of course, for the hole) was an exact copy of a piece of furniture which had been given to me as a present by a grateful woman patient. It thus reminded me of how much my patients honoured me. Indeed, even the museum of human excrement could be given an interpretation to rejoice my heart. However much I might be disgusted by it in reality, in the dream it was a reminiscence of the fair land of Italy where, as we all know, the W.C.s in the small towns are furnished in precisely this way. The stream of urine which washed everything clean was an unmistakable sign of greatness. It was in that way that Gulliver extinguished the great fire in Lilliput—though incidentally this brought him into disfavour with its tiny queen. But Gargantua, too, Rabelais' superman, revenged himself in the same way on the Parisians by sitting astride on Notre Dame and turning his stream of urine upon the city. It was only on the previous evening before going to sleep that I had been turning over Garnier's illustrations to Rabelais. And, strangely enough, here was another piece of evidence that I was the superman. The platform of Notre Dame was my favourite resort in Paris; every free afternoon I use to clamber about there on the towers of the church between the monsters and the devils. The fact that all the faeces disappeared so quickly under the stream recalled the motto: *'Afflavit et dissipati sunt'* ['He blew and they were scattered'], which I intended one day to put at the head of a chapter upon the therapy of hysteria. (468–69, emphasis in original)

There is little need to comment on this unusual report other than to point out Freud's own acknowledgment of the satiric tradition. Freud shows himself to be what one critic admires as "the bravest sort of hero, a hero of the ludicrous," [26] giving a magnificently comical portrayal of vain self-importance. Like the creations of Rabelais and Swift, it offers the spectacle of a bizarre mixture of kinds: two varieties of excrement, Hercules and the gratitude of female patients, "the fair land of Italy," toilet seats, the aetiology of the neuroses, *Gulliver's Travels*, the cathedral of Notre Dame, and the vanquishing of the Great Armada. Instead of attributing its character to the universal unconscious megalomania, though, may we not simply regard it as the dream of a man who has been reading about Gargantua and Gulliver, and has adopted the satiric point of view? If these characters did not inspire the dream itself, they certainly did inspire the interpretation.

Freud's identification with Hercules, it should be added, does not require hidden motives as an explanation, for, as we have seen, he identified consciously with heroes all his life. It is interesting, also, to observe that Freud had to attempt to discover a tension and division within the affective trends generated from these literary materials in order to produce the typical ambivalence of the Freudian model: "The daytime mood of revulsion and disgust persisted into the dream in so far as it was able to provide almost the entire material of its manifest content. But during the night a contrary mood of powerful and even exaggerated self-assertiveness arose and displaced the former one. The content of the dream had to find a form which would enable it to express both the delusions of inferiority and the megalomania in the same material" (470). Just as Don Quixote, in his satiric predicament, saves the appearances given to him in his delusion by positing a division of supernatural agency between warring enchanters whose activities can account for any apparent contradiction, so Freud rationalizes the satiric incongruity of dreams by positing a division of psychic agency between libido and repression.

This dream and its interpretation show the typical character of Freud's construction of dreams and of himself as dreamer. Between urine and feces he discovers the 'unconscious' derivatives of literary megalomania satirically imagined. Heroism ascends from its vulgar origins. Whereas Quixote's paranoia was constructed from idealizing materials, Freud's megalomaniacal 'unconscious' could be invested with the satiric treatment itself, since the unconscious dwells out of sight of the censor that distinguishes between ideal and vulgar imagination. Freud's unconscious megalomania can resonate, therefore, with more or less genuinely heroic figures like Hercules and also with comic heroes like Gargantua, there being no difference between them in the pre-civilized logic of the unconscious. Many years later, as we have already observed, Freud inserted the scene of heroic urination into the bio-history of the human species when he designated the primitive achievement of controlling the impulse to urinate upon fire as one of the Promethean moments of repression leading to the development of civilization. Gulliver and Gargantua had not lost their hold on Freudian fancy.

Freud as Brutus

In the interpretation of the foregoing dream, literary materials furnish a key used to decode the manifest contents. Symbolic decoding of this kind, however, does not constitute Freud's most common use either of literary materials or of reconstructions of his own experience. More typically the literary elements are inserted into his narratives as part of an event, occupying a fixed position in the train of associations that lead back to the cause of the dream. Even in the preceding example, a reference to the Augean stables and a perusal of Rabelais, with pictures, had occurred during the dream day. It is their embeddedness in the associative substrate of the unconscious, fixed in place as if by trauma, that gives to literary influences their determining power. Whatever Freud discovers in a dream must be traceable to some event. For instance, in seeking the origin of the megalomaniacal tendencies he discovered in a dream about his Uncle Joseph, Freud the naively modest investigator lets his mind wander to ambition-building themes:

What, then, could have been the origin of the ambitiousness which produced the dream in me? At that point I recalled an anecdote I had often heard repeated in my childhood. At the time of my birth an old peasant-woman had prophesied to my proud mother that with her first-born child she had brought a great man into the world. Prophecies of this kind must be very common: there are so many mothers filled with happy expectations and so many old peasant-women and others of the kind who make up for the loss of their power to control things in the present world by concentrating it on the future. Nor can the prophetess have lost anything by her words. Could this have been the source of my thirst for grandeur? But that reminded me of another experience, dating from my later childhood, which provided a still better explanation. My parents had been in the habit, when I was a boy of eleven or twelve, of taking me with them to the Prater [a famous park on the outskirts of Vienna]. One evening, while we were sitting in a restaurant there, our attention had been attracted by a man who was moving from one table to another and, for a small consideration, improvising a verse upon any topic presented to him. I was despatched to bring the poet to our table and he showed his gratitude to the messenger. Before enquiring what the chosen topic was to be, he had dedicated a few lines to myself; and he had been inspired to declare that I should probably grow up to be a Cabinet Minister. (192–93)

Freud goes on to note that "those were the days of the *'Bürger'* Ministry," a period of liberal Jewish political hopefulness, when "every industrious Jewish school-boy carried a Cabinet Minister's portfolio in his satchel" (193). Now it is important to recognize the extraordinary importance Freud ascribes to the episodes narrated in these charming vignettes. What he is saying is that, if they had not occurred, his unconscious mind would not now betray the overpoweringly ambitious character his interpretation reveals. We all, of course, have our heroic susceptibilities, we all share the egotism and hostility of the paranoid; but Freud the dreamer has a special tendency in that direction. Heroic ambition is the dominant of his personality. This is what the dreams reveal to psychoanalysis. And the explanation for Freud's tendency toward ambition lies partly with the activities of strolling poets and old peasant women who tell fortunes. Their influence has worked its way deeply into the substrate of associations in his unconscious. We might think it comic that such whimsical triflings could have given rise, by Shandean misadventure, to the ambition of the great scientist. But once we have accepted that such are the chance and arbitrary determinants of the personality, the effect is uncanny, for suddenly the true significance of poetic heroizing and fortune-telling flattery becomes apparent. The powers of divination to which they lay their claim have, after all, a real basis, lying not in fate but in the source of fate—the unconscious. Superstition is unconscious psychology. Its power to determine the future was, and is, real.

One of the uncanny events to which Freud traces the origins of unconscious ambition in his nature is especially interesting for the purposes of this study, going to the heart, as it does, of Freud's tendency to form passionate friendships that turned into bitter, paranoid grudges. The passage in which it is described, part of the interpretation of a dream, was written before the beginnings of organized psychoanalysis and even before Freud's break with Fliess. Among Freud's collaborators, only Breuer at this point had suffered from his fickleness. In the dream, "Fliess had come to Vienna unobtrusively in July." During an awkward scene with him and another friend, P., Freud utters the phrase, *'Non vixit'*, which makes P. disappear. Freud realizes that P. and possibly others like him are "revenants" who can be willed away at any time. Here is part of Freud's interpretation regarding these details. After a long discussion, he arrives at the crux of the *'Non vixit'*:

It then struck me as noticeable that in the scene in the dream there was a convergence of a hostile and an affectionate current of feeling toward my friend P., the former being on the surface and the latter concealed, but both of them being represented in the single phrase *Non vixit*. As he had deserved well of science I built him a memorial; but as he was guilty of an evil wish (which was expressed at the end of the dream) I annihilated him. I noticed that this last sentence had a quite special cadence, and I must have had some model in my mind. Where was an antithesis of this sort to be found, a juxtaposition like this of two opposite reactions towards a single person, both of them claiming to be completely justified and yet not incompatible? Only in one passage in literature—but a passage which makes a profound impression on the reader: in Brutus's speech of self-justification in Shakespeare's *Julius Caesar*, "As Caesar loved me, I weep for him; as he was fortunate, I rejoice at it; as he was valiant, I honour him; but, as he was ambitious, I slew him." Were not the formal structure of these sentences and their antithetical meaning precisely the same as in the dream-thought I had uncovered? Thus I had been playing the part of Brutus in the dream. If only I could find one other piece of evidence in the content of the dream to confirm this surprising collateral connecting link. A possible one occurred to me. "My friend Fl. came to Vienna in July." There was no basis in reality for this detail of the dream. So far as I knew, my friend Fl. had never been in Vienna in July. But the month of July was named after Julius Caesar and might therefore very well represent the allusion I wanted to the intermediate thought of my playing the part of Brutus.

Strange to say, I really did once play the part of Brutus. I once acted in the scene between Brutus and Caesar from Schiller before an audience of children. I was fourteen years old at the time and was acting with a nephew who was a year my senior. He had come to us on a visit from England; and he, too, was a *revenant*, for it was the playmate of my earliest years who had returned in him. Until the end of my third year we had been inseparable. We had loved each other and fought with each other; and this childhood relationship had a determining influence on all my subsequent relations with my contemporaries. Since that time my nephew John has had many re-incarnations which revived now one side and now another of his personality, unalterably fixed as it was in my unconscious memory. (423–24)

In a later passage, Freud completes the story of his relationship with John:

I have already shown how my warm friendships as well as my enmities with contemporaries went back to my relations in childhood with a nephew who was a year my senior; how he was my superior, how I early learned to defend myself against him, how we were inseparable friends, and how, according to the testimony of our elders, we sometimes fought with each other and—made complaints to them about each other. All my friends have in a certain sense been re-incarnations of this first figure who "long since appeared before my troubled gaze": they have been *revenants*. My nephew himself re-appeared in my boyhood, and at that time we acted the parts of Caesar and Brutus together. My emotional life has always insisted that I should have an intimate friend and a hated enemy. I have always been able to provide myself afresh with both, and it has not infrequently happened that the ideal situation of childhood has been so completely reproduced that friend and enemy have come together in a single individual—though not, of course, both at once or with constant oscillations, as may have been the case in my early childhood. (483)[27]

The *'Non vixit'* dream unquestionably expresses a hostile impulse. Freud's oneiric gift of vaporizing "revenants" with a word makes a good example of the psychological temptation to exchange wish for reality—the 'pleasure principle'—and might have served to illustrate the concept of the 'omnipotence of thoughts'. Around it, though, Freud has woven a remarkable private myth, discovering in his unconscious a need to reenact the murder of Julius Caesar with his best friends as the victims. At least Quixote's literary repetitions were benevolent, however vulgar and besotted they may have been! There is a particularly grandiose vainglory in Freud's idea that he cannot be happy without an enemy. Yet what is the basis for this fantastic self-portrayal? The relationship with John that Freud describes seems for all we know about it perfectly typical for three-year-old children, who fight and reconcile by the hour. It is obviously accessible to Freud's *conscious* mind; there is no reason to think that it should be exercising within him a compulsive psychic automatism. There is nothing 'improper' about it. As for Julius Caesar, are these truly the only lines in literature that express ambivalent emotion? The diligence of literary Freudians has shown otherwise.

All of the materials educed by Freud to interpret his dreams could legitimately serve to cast a light upon his personality. It is, indeed, important to know about Freud that he grew up at a time and in a place where people still believed in great men and heroes, where they remembered prophecies about their children, and middle-class folk dining in public parks would willingly pay to hear compliments extemporized in verse. It is important to know that Freud was part of a repressed minority eager for its political heroes to emerge, and that in preparation for adulthood children of fourteen in his family would perform the plays of Schiller, the popular poet of freedom.[28] A reasonable biographer might mention that Freud had an infant rival and that his sense of their rivalry lasted through his teens. Young Sigmund's view of this rival as an exceptional threat must remind us of his superior position in his own household—that of the privileged and petted eldest son. All this is of note, and some of it undoubtedly played a part in making Freud the ambitious and competitive man he was. But in retelling them this way, one immediately deprives these details of their uncanny interest. They become part of a vague social, ethnic, and family atmosphere, whereas in Freud's narrative they are decisive events, punctual and irreversible, that put us in touch with a most ancient and bewitching drama—the predestined course of the hero, his birth, growth, and early trials magically foretold by prophecy and imaged in dreams. The archaizing character of Freud's theory makes available to him every resource of mythology.

Freud as Hannibal

We have seen a number of ways in which Freud's romance of dreams imitates its satiric models: in the exposure of hypocrisy and duplicity, in the revelation of creaturely vulgarity and grandiose ambition, and in the observation of a private mythology involving historically regressive heroic identifications, often from literature, which determine behavior by a kind of psychic automatism. And we have seen, as well, that all of these comic constructions tend to acquire an uncanny aura that lends romantic appeal to the 'return of the repressed', the historical materials that lie waiting to be activated in the fictive domain of the unconscious. Such are the means by which Freud presents the suspicious quest to understand the egotism of his own nature. The interpretations we have reviewed have been somewhat narrow in focus. The dream of Irma's Injection has to do largely, as Freud says, with "professional conscientiousness." The Gargantua dream derives immediately from literary models and deals specifically with feelings generated during the dreamday, while the dream of Freud as Brutus finds its determinations in a rather unambiguous childhood rivalry. Except for the character of Brutus himself, there is little in these compositions to direct us toward the political and social themes that normally generate satiric energy. Only in the prediction that Freud would be a Cabinet Minister do social and political motifs begin to surface. Yet such motifs appear throughout *The Interpretation of Dreams*. It was through the analysis of dreams of an unambiguously political nature that Freud was able to comprehend his megalomaniacal impulses in psychoanalytic terms. We shall turn to the interpretations of two of these dreams, central to Freud's self-portrait, in order to complete the consideration of his satiric romance.

In a sequence of vivid peripatetic dreams, Freud found himself engaging in yet another Quixotic imitation. Analysis revealed that this time he was Hannibal, glimpsing the conquest of Rome but never approaching the city walls. Hannibal, Viennese schoolboys knew, had his great chance to take the city after the battle of Cannae but failed in boldness. Freud confessed a lifelong desire to set foot in Rome which he had failed to satisfy out of fears for his health. Able to visit the city only in his dreams, he yet did so repeatedly. Meditating on his frustration, a sentence came to his mind that enlightened him as to the meaning of these dreams:

"Which of the two, it may be debated, walked up and down his study with the greater impatience after he had formed his plan of going to Rome—Winckelmann, the Vice-Principal, or Hannibal, the Commander-in-Chief?" I had actually been following in Hannibal's footsteps. Like him, I had been fated not to see Rome. . . . Like so many boys of that age, I had sympathized in the Punic Wars not with the Romans but with the Carthaginians. And when in the higher classes I began to understand for the first time what it meant to belong to an alien race, and anti-semitic feelings among the other boys warned me that I must take up a definite position, the figure of the semitic general rose still higher in my esteem. To my youthful mind Hannibal and Rome symbolized the conflict between the tenacity of Jewry and the organization of the Catholic church. And the increasing importance of the effects of the anti-semitic movement upon our emotional life helped to fix the thoughts and feelings of those early days. Thus the wish to go to Rome had become in my dream-life a cloak and symbol for a number of other passionate wishes. Their realization was to be pursued with all the perseverance and single-mindedness of the Carthaginian, though their fulfillment seemed at the moment just as little favoured by destiny as was Hannibal's lifelong wish to enter Rome. (196–97)

Freud is constructing for himself in this interpretation a paranoid grandi-osity that, for once, has real political coordinates. His desire to be Hanni-bal, like Quixote's aspiration to knight-errantry, stems from a sense of social, not merely psychological, repression. Note that again, as with the speech of Brutus, a series of remembered lines introduces the heroically emulated character: a literary delusion is once more sustained by a hidden, controlling memory supposedly lying beneath the surface of consciousness, betokening the recovery of an uncanny event. Freud's identification with Hannibal is not a thing to be viewed with amusement like his self-justifica-tions in the dream of Irma's Injection, nor is it simply absurd like the megalomaniacal compensations of the Gargantua dream. The forces repre-sented by Hannibal's enemies exerted a menacing influence in Freud's life. They were real, not just paranoid enemies. We have already seen in the discussion of 'family romances' that Freud traced his Hannibal infatuation back to his father's narrative of a scene in which he had been humiliated by a Christian anti-Semite on a street in the town where Freud was born. Now it can be appreciated just how distinctly this scene stands out among the keys to a Freudian dream, being neither comical nor uncanny. However doubtful it may be that Freud's oneiric glimpses of Rome meant that he was Hannibal in the dream, however doubtful that the sense of being Hannibal was actually keeping Freud from visiting Rome, one can well believe that Freud's interest in the "Semitic general" grew out of the social frustrations of his Jewish identity. This factor makes it other than comical that the youthful Freud should have dreamt of replacing his own father with Hamilcar Barca in order to become Hannibal. That the adult Freud, however, should still be suffering from a neurotic limitation in his travel plans because of a childhood identification with Hannibal still working in his unconscious and in his dreams, this is a Quixotic form of behavior quite in keeping with the general tenor of Freudian irony; even the noblest cause of Freud's grandiosity leads in his narrative to a delusory form of heroic imitation. Freud's Jewish partisanship is entirely psychological. It belongs to Freud the dreamer, not Freud the analyst, and its result is not political commitment, nor even sympathy, but a neurotically repressed megalomania.[29] This is how Freud's science demands that he portray his own psychological and moral condition.

I am not suggesting that Freud did not identify with Hannibal in his youth, nor am I suggesting that his identification was not energized by anti-Catholic resentment. Such feelings fall within what is to be expected, and Freud's reports about them are quite believable. What is not believable is that these very understandable emotions were determining his behavior, keeping him from visiting the city of Rome, even as an adult, and doing so in a way that was 'unconscious', when there is nothing here that is hidden from Freud's memory nor anything that one would normally want to hide. For the unconscious resonances, Freud is relying entirely upon his interpretation of the dream. This is where he gets the clue as to the unconscious reasons why he could not visit Rome, though it is unlikely that he had even been aware, till the analysis, that his failure to do so was neurotically determined; until the motif appeared in his dream, he had been satisfied with hygienic reasons as to why he did not, and should not, go there in the summertime. Freud's social and political frustrations made him peculiarly susceptible to heroic fantasy, and he took advantage of this fact by portraying these fantasies as being psychically determined unconscious repetitions. In his 'unconscious mind' he was playing out the roles of figures like Brutus and Hannibal, just as Quixote was playing out the roles of Orlando and Amadis de Gaul. It is this 'unconscious' part of the story that is a literary fiction just as it is in the *Quixote*. Again we must exonerate Freud of unconscious megalomania in order to distinguish the conscious factors of ambition, frustration, and suspicion operating in his character; only then, as well, can we do justice to the literary strategies by means of which

Freud's personal attributes are deployed in the construction of his latent megalomania.

Counter-revolutionary Paranoia

The political interest of the Freudian unconscious appears most vividly, and to greatest comic effect, in Freud's "Revolutionary Dream of 1848." On the dreamday, Freud happened to witness a proudly contemptuous aristocratic gesture at the train station made by the Austrian head of state, Count Thun, who was on his way to Ischl for an audience with the Emperor regarding the divisive German-Czech language problems. "The ticket inspector at the gate had not recognized [Count Thun] and had tried to take his ticket, but he had waved the man aside with a curt motion of his hand and without giving any explanation." Freud remained on the train platform to defend his rights to a reserved compartment from anyone who might challenge them "by exercising some sort of 'pull.' " Meanwhile he was humming a subversive aria from *Le Nozze di Figaro*. Freud's lurking grandiosity had been activated:

The whole evening I had been in high spirits and in a combative mood. I had chaffed my waiter and my cab driver—without, I hope, hurting their feelings. And now all kinds of insolent and revolutionary ideas were going through my head, in keeping with Figaro's words and with my recollections of Beaumarchais' comedy which I had seen acted by the *Comédie française*. I thought of the phrase about the great gentlemen who had taken the trouble to be born, and of the *droit du Seigneur* which Count Almaviva tried to exercise over Susanna. I thought, too, of how our malicious opposition journalists made jokes over Count Thun's name, calling him instead 'Count Nichtsthun' ['Count Do-nothing']. Not that I envied him. He was on his way to a difficult audience with the Emperor, while *I* was the real Count Do-nothing—just off on my holidays. (208–9)

After an exercise of "pull" did deprive Freud of his full traveling privileges, leaving him in a compartment without access to a lavatory, he dreamt his most remarkable and interesting dream, a dream whose contents cross the range of his own political interests and experiences and, after the analysis, seem to touch upon elements from the entire history of modern European political development. We find here the German language problems being addressed in a passionately anti-German speech by Count Thun (or Count Taffe) and also the history of Austrian liberalism telescoped in the association between Emperor Franz Joseph's fiftieth year Jubilee and 1848, the year of upheaval that brought him to power. Combined with this are recollections from Freud's student days: a bitter university debate with Freud as vitriolic materialist, almost getting himself into a duel, and a student revolt led by Freud against a tyrannical German language-master, this theme embellished with images of Henry VIII and of Shakespeare's presentation of the Wars of the Roses. The political novels of Zola are present, and Freud's schoolmate, the politician Karl Adler, makes a veiled appearance. Most interesting are the aggressive satiric elements of the dream, for Freud discovers within it a long series of abusive, scatological, and lubricious puns. It contains, he jokes, "examples of impropriety in all three states of matter—solid, liquid, and gaseous" (213); once more he refers his readers to Rabelais to decipher the meaning. And here again we find Freud's coveted motto about the destruction of the Armada, but now the word *'flavit'* is naughtily associated with *'flatus'*.

Some details of the dream, we are told, are too sensitive to be revealed, for their sexual or political content: "I am unable to deal with it in such detail—out of consideration for the censorship" (214).[30] Freud leaves it unclear whether this censorship is political or psychological. But he does at last give us the general import of the dream: "the analysis of these three [last] episodes of the dream showed that they were impertinent boastings, the issue of an absurd megalomania which had long been suppressed in my waking life" (215). Freud's megalomaniac unconscious had never been displayed with such comical profusion, and we are meant to see how deeply his political imagination is embedded in childish wishes, excremental exhibitionism, and resentful egotism. The merest brush with an arrogant head of state could summon up this primitive, gigantistic nightworld in all of its absurdity, silliness, nastiness, and riot. There is a final humiliation, too, in Freud's confession of megalomania. Its ultimate object of reference is not the various political forces and heroes that it evokes but merely Freud's own father appearing at the end of the dream as an old man in need of a urinal, which his son dutifully provides; Freud the dreamer thus gains his unconscious revenge for an episode in childhood when his father had wounded his sense of ambition by predicting the boy would remain worthless after he had taken the Gargantuan liberty of urinating in the paternal bedroom.

During his youth, it is well known, Freud had been passionately interested in politics, and specifically in the cause of Austrian liberalism. His turn to science was in part a repudiation of political hope in light of the increasingly reactionary drift taken by Austrian affairs after 1873.[31] For Freud, science became the last available avenue of heroic aspiration, and even there he encountered social and political obstacles. His failure to attain a university position at the beginning of his career and his withdrawal into private practice was a step down the social ladder "from the upper medical and academic intelligentsia to which he had gained access in the eighties to a simpler stratum of ordinary Jewish doctors and business-men."[32] Freud's personal situation and his scientific aspirations both had about them more than a touch of Quixotic desperation. But it was a profound liberal despair that put Freud so rigidly into the satiric position with regard to social and political ambition. He hated Hannibal's enemies, yet he could not envision a convincing Hannibal. Even Theodor Herzl, the founder of Zionism, evoked his anxious mistrust. Long after Herzl's death, Freud urged Herzl's son to eradicate the influence of his father from his personality by abandoning politics:

It is your task to rid yourself of all ambition. . . . Your ambitions are poisoning your life. You should finally bury your father within your own soul, which is still carrying him alive. It is he, not anyone else, who is appearing to you in your many dreams. In vain would you dismiss them as unimportant. Your father is one of those who has turned dreams into reality. This is a very rare and dangerous breed. It includes the Garibaldis, the Edisons, the Herzls. . . . I would call them the sharpest opponents of my scientific work. It is my modest profession to simplify dreams, to make them clear and ordinary. They, on the contrary, confuse the issue, turn it upside down, command the world while they themselves remain on the other side of the psychic mirror. It is a group specializing in the realization of dreams. I deal in psychoanalysis; they deal in psychosynthesis.[33]

As this passage makes clear, politics itself is Freud's enemy, politics in the broad sense that embraces even Thomas Edison—in other words, the attempt to change the world.[34] To make this attempt is to seek an enactment of dreams, those very dreams of ambition that Freud had undertaken to banalize, demystify, ridicule, and degrade with psychoanalytic rhetoric. A paranoid urgency energizes Freud's attempt to kill off the last vestiges of Herzl in the soul of his son. Freud's entire achievement seems to be at risk in this battle with the father-ghost; we can hear the bio-historical echoes of the primal father and the poet-priest, the menace in the return of the repressed. What Freud feared most of all was a successful Quixote, a paranoid leader who could persuade others to take his dreams for reality. In this he was responding to what was already a pronounced element of the political rhetoric and behavior of the time, the rise of what Carl Schorske calls the "politics of fantasy," the aestheticizing of political discourse eventually brought to its furthest development under National Socialism.[35]

It was to discourage attempts of the Quixotic type that Freud was willing to make such a display of his own ambitious urges, along with their origins in the trivia of the body and the delusory megalomania of childhood. In order to discredit political activity in a certain form Freud was willing to attempt a total political repression, leaving himself in a position of flagrant Quixotic excess.[36]

Having identified the most vital target of Freudian satire, we are now in a position to appreciate just how complete and how marvelously ingenious was Freud's adaptation of the Cervantean way. Like his Spanish precursor, Freud invented a socially prestigious and exhibitionistic language of ridicule in which dreams and madness could be made meaningful and articulate, could be compelled to reveal the depths of their vulgarity and, at the same time, flaunt their kinship with the idealistic elements of culture; it was also a language like Cervantes' that could at once stand above its objects and reinforce the censorship against them: the exposure of the vulgarity of idealism was a disclaimer and a repression of its pretensions, a supremely aggressive and defensive social gesture. Perhaps we should also attribute to the legacy of Cervantes the easy familiarity with which Freud, like the humble narrator of *Don Quixote*, takes us into his confidence—his confidence game: "It cannot be denied that to interpret and report one's dreams demands a high degree of self-discipline. One is bound to emerge as the only villain among the crowd of noble characters who share one's life."[37]

The Asymptotic Romance

I have been emphasizing the satiric dimension of Freud's dream psychology. There is always, however, in *The Interpretation of Dreams*, a counter-movement, a return to the properly Romantic or uncanny aspect of Freudian rhetoric. In his satiric vein, Freud relentlessly follows out the associations of each fragment of dream-thought; what seems suggestively vague becomes humorously concrete, familiar, and vulgar. The attempt at simplification and reduction is total, even though "respect for the censorship" keeps Freud from performing a full analysis of any of his own dreams. Yet in key moments of Freud's romance there is a drawing back from the goal, which, like all Romantic goals, infinitely recedes; or, to borrow out of context one of Freud's own brilliant phrases, the romance of dreams marks the progress of an 'asymptotic desire': "Das Ewig-Weibliche/Zieht uns hinan." The psychoanalytic method has not stripped the veil from the unconscious; it has not fathomed the deepest secrets but merely put us on the "royal road" to that accomplishment. Freud's Virgilian promise to "move the depths" must remain largely a promise. The unconscious is a property of individuals, each with his or her own private mythology, each keeping his or her own secrets from the censor's gaze. It is also a transcendental reality, largely inaccessible to our view: "The unconscious is the true psychical reality; in its innermost nature it is as much unknown to us as the reality of the external world, and it is as incompletely presented by the data of consciousness as is the external world by the communications of our sense organs" (613). Again we run up against the Kantian limit of Freudian investigation.

Since the unconscious lies at an unsoundable depth, it is rarely that even a single dream can yield up all its secrets:

There is often a passage in even the most thoroughly interpreted dream which has to be left obscure; this is because we become aware during the work of interpretation that at that point there is a tangle of dream-thoughts which cannot be unravelled and which moreover adds nothing to our knowledge of the content of the dream. This is the dream's navel, the spot where it reaches down into the unknown. The dream thoughts to which we are led by interpretation cannot, from the nature of things, have any definite endings; they are bound to branch out in every direction into the intricate network of our world of thought. It is at some point where this meshwork is particularly close that the dream-wish grows up, like a mushroom out of its mycelium. (525)

This passage combines with beautiful and enviable skill two essential Romantic tropes — the trope of imagination as a portal, or, in this case, "navel," into the unknown — brave gesture toward infinity — and the trope of organic complexity, here applied to the origins of desire in consciousness: it grows "like a mushroom out of its mycelium," partaking in the richness and irreducible diversity of the ordinary. It is startling to hear such an affirmative note sounded on the Freudian register. Suddenly suspicion finds relief, and what began as a hostile, reductive inquiry into a domain of mere absurdity and egotism has found itself ultimately moving in the direction of an unbounded imaginative space, the domain of a comfortingly private, individual mythology never entirely to be deflated. Quixote's historical transformation from the lunatic to the sublime is reenacted in each Freudian sounding of the depths of unconscious thought. Charm and power reside even in the absurdity of dreams, and this charm and power are not without their political equivalents in Freud's analogy:

Dreams, then, are often most profound when they seem most crazy. In every epoch of history those who have had something to say but could not say it without peril have eagerly assumed a fool's cap. The audience at whom their forbidden speech was aimed tolerated it more easily if they could at the same time laugh and flatter themselves with the reflection that the unwelcome words were clearly nonsensical. The Prince in the play, who had to disguise himself as a madman, was behaving just as dreams do in reality; so that we can say of dreams what Hamlet said of himself, concealing the true circumstances under a cloak of wit and unintelligibility: "I am but mad north-north-west: when the wind is southerly, I know a hawk from a hand-saw!" (444)

Here the Erasmian Folly-as-Wisdom makes an unexpected return: once again, there is no truly aimless human behavior, no "kissing the hot stove." Even Freud the anti-politician cannot resist endowing dreams with a trace of authentic heroism, portraying the knowledge of dreams as a forbidden knowledge few will have the courage to accept. The brave wisdom that would later be claimed by the analyst first belonged to dreams themselves. It was no accident, then, that for half a century the left avant-garde found in psychoanalysis a congenial instrument and took up the Freudian goal of getting in touch with and unleashing forces of the 'unconscious'; academic radicalism since the 1960s has remained essentially faithful to Freud; and literary critics remain particularly in his debt: no one but Freud could have cured them of the nagging textual frustration imposed upon them by their own self-repressive skepticism struggling with the drives of the academic market. None of this should be surprising when we remember that, after all, psychoanalysis was from the outset a scientific adaptation of the original sensibility of Romantic revolution. It reenacts both the attack upon the metaphysical, aristocratic, and religious tradition that set the stage for the Romantic movement and the uncanny return of the repressed, the opening up of the new, internal territory of imagination, which is the distinctive and potent element of Romanticism itself.

SEVEN

The Charismatic Paranoid

> If you argue with a madman it is extremely proba-
> ble that you will get the worst of it; for in many
> ways his mind moves all the quicker for not being
> delayed by the things that go with good judgement.
> He is not hampered by a sense of humour or by
> charity, or by the dumb certainties of experience.
> He is the more logical for losing certain sane af-
> fections. Indeed, the common phrase for insanity
> is in this respect a misleading one. The madman is
> not the man who has lost his reason. The madman
> is the man who has lost everything else.
>
> —Chesterton

In the first chapter of Part Two of *Don Quixote*, the barber of La Mancha tells the mad knight, now in confinement, a story that bears upon his own:

"In the madhouse at Seville was a man whose relations had placed him there as being out of his mind. He was a graduate of Osuna in canon law, but even if he had been a graduate of Salamanca, it was the opinion of most people that he would have been mad all the same. This graduate, after some years of confinement, took it into his head that he was sane and in his full senses, and under this impression wrote to the Archbishop, entreating him earnestly and in very correct language to have him released from the misery in which he was living. By God's mercy he had now recovered his lost reason, though his relations, in order to enjoy his property, kept him there and, in spite of the truth, would make him out to be mad until his dying day. The Archbishop, moved by repeated sensible, well-written letters, directed one of his chaplains to ask in the madhouse about the truth of the licentiate's statements and to have an interview with the madman himself."[1]

When the chaplain arrives at the madhouse to interview the licentiate, he finds him so rational in his understanding, so convincing in his description of the heartlessness of his relatives and the perfidy of his jailers that, over the protests of the director, he is about to have him released. Only in saying farewell to his fellow lunatics does the licentiate give himself away.

167

One of them, convinced that he is Jupiter, threatens to destroy the town by drought if his rival is allowed to depart. " 'Pay no attention to what this madman has said,' " the licentiate replies, " 'for if he is Jupiter and will not send rain, I who am Neptune, the father and god of the waters, will rain as often as it pleases me and may be needful' " (429). The poor fellow is stripped of his traveling clothes and put back in his cell.

Quixote knows that he is being tested and his hurt reply to the barber is a masterpiece: " 'Is it possible that you do not know that comparisons of wit with wit, valor with valor, beauty with beauty, birth with birth, are always odious and unwelcome?' " He has never claimed to be Neptune, only a man who wants to restore the age of chivalry. With this modesty, Quixote shames the barber to apologize. His reply is a moral victory but it is also, of course, in the contest of wits, a failure. It shows he has not succeeded in understanding the point of the story. By refusing comparison with Neptune rather than with the licentiate, he actually admits his likeness to the madman. The barber's gambit has worked.

Cervantes' brilliant fable points toward a genuine problem for psychology: Recognizing that there are forms of madness in which the powers of reason are preserved, how does one go about making the distinction between the mad and the sane? For Cervantes it is largely a practical, not a theoretical concern. At the end of the novel, Alonso the Good regains his senses and repudiates the inanities of Quixote with shame. There can be no doubt that he is at that point virtually a different man, his Quixotic idealism converted now into genuine piety and resignation. This moment marks Cervantes' renunciation of the satiric point of view, at least with regard to his main character. Whereas up to this point the entire narrative has centered around the humor of madness and the fascination it produces in others, the novel ends with a somewhat awesome renunciation of folly.

There is a satiric turn, though, even here. Quixote's renunciation of his paranoid grandeur puts him suddenly into a position of moral superiority with regard to those around him who have made so much of his delusion: the peasant Sancho in his credulous ignorance and greed; the bachelor Samsón Carrasco, eager to match arms with the mad knight; the aristocrats who, in their desire for entertainment, make a toy of him and his squire; the "idle reader" ["desoccupado lector"], willing spectator of an epic of cruelty-in-idleness; and finally the author himself, who has more than anyone been given over to the spectacle of madness: "For me alone was Don Quixote born, and I for him; it was his to act, mine to write; we two together make but one. . . ." (830). All of these have succumbed to the infatuation exercised by the paranoid character. Alonso the Good has at least the excuse that he was mad, even though with a madness like reason, whereas in the case of the others reason has not kept them from an enchantment with madness very much like madness itself. Mad or sane, the effect of the Quixotic character is to evoke folly in others, to show the confusion of reason and folly essential to a satiric point of view.

Freudian psychology never renounces the satiric point of view; making the distinction between the mad and the sane has been at least as difficult for it to accomplish in theory as in practice. As we have seen, Freud systematically employed the categories derived from his study of mental disease to ordinary behavior, distinguishing them only by the degree of neurotic investment. This makes things particularly awkward with regard to paranoia, where the powers of reasoning, and often the sense of contact with reality—'reality testing' as Freud liked to call it—are not impaired. The theoretician is left searching for other means with which to identify the condition of madness.

The failure of this search is a logical result of Freud's attempt to wield the label of illness as an instrument against forms of thinking and behavior that are universal to the species. Having done so, he cannot use the same instrument as a means of separating himself from the truly mad. The dilemma is, as we have seen, a logical problem of reductionism. All rigorous reductionists face the embarrassment of having degraded their own thinking to an irrational effect. But the psychologist, confronted with the eccentric effusions of paranoia, faces a peculiar embarrassment. Having declared the thought of the paranoid to have an essential kinship with his own, he may find himself face to face with a living paranoid who is willing to exploit this honorary status. The paranoid turns up like a disreputable twin whom the psychologist can neither acknowledge nor disown, the self-satirizing impulse of the reductionist having suddenly given rise to a satiric double in living form. The most famous example of the spectacle of para-noid entitlement is that of Judge Schreber, the psychotic German whose memoirs furnished the materials for Freud's essay on paranoia. The remark-able facts of Schreber's confinement and release and the brilliant descrip-tion that he wrote of his experience have made him perhaps the most discussed of all mental patients. The story of Schreber, along with Freud's response to it, provides the best possible introduction to the difficulties of 'paranoia' as a diagnostic term.[2]

The Pretentious Paranoid Once More

Daniel Paul Schreber was a learned and successful jurist who reached the office of *Senatspräsident* at Dresden in 1893 at the early age of fifty-one. The Court of Appeals over which he presided was the second highest judicial authority in Germany. Schreber was in every way a respected citizen, happily married though childless, a man of formidable intellectual gifts and broad interests including, as the translator of his memoir notes, "natural history, particularly the doctrine of evolution, the natural sciences, astronomy and philosophy."[3] Schreber's account of his illness displays a wide reading in literature, etymology, and the history of religion, a fondness for music, and fluency in Greek, which allowed him to commune with hallucinatory voices in that tongue (3). Eight years before his appointment to the Superior Court, he spent five months in confinement for a nervous illness about which there are few details. Six weeks after taking the position of *Senatspräsident* he again fell ill and this time endured a confinement of nine years. In the early phases of the second confinement he suffered from hypochondriacal ideas, to which quickly succeeded delusions of persecution, then fantastic auditory and visual hallucinations, which made him unresponsive to the world around him. Schreber believed that he was "dead and rotten," a victim of the plague, and that his body was undergoing numerous trials and transformations. He frequently begged for death and attempted suicide. As the medical report on his condition states, "Gradually the delusion took on a mystical and religious character, he communicated directly with God, devils were playing their games with him, he saw 'miracles', heard 'holy music', and finally even believed that he was living in another world." He refused food in order that 'God's omnipotence' should not be disturbed by the attendants, and as a result had to be forcibly fed (268).

By November 1894, Schreber began to emerge from his extreme state of withdrawal and to reveal the delusory ideas that had taken possession of his mind. He believed the people around him were effecting harmful changes in the "Order of the World" and that both he and God were threatened. Under the influence of these delusions, Schreber would engage in loud, meaningless laughter and compulsive pounding on the piano. His excitement seemed to be stimulated in part by a belief that the world had come to an end and that all of what he saw around him was, as he says in his memoirs, on a "fleeting improvised" basis. He would bellow repetitive curses at the sun—"the sun is a whore" (270)—and accuse it of cowardice, of hiding from *Senatspräsident* Schreber. He applied to himself the name Ormuzd (269). During this period Schreber was manageable during the day, but at night his outbursts were so noisy that he had to be isolated. He became convinced he was being transformed into a woman, had his mustache shaved off, and began displaying feminine breasts (270).

In the spring of 1897 another great change came over Schreber. He suddenly resumed contact with the outside world and gradually began to take up many of his old interests. He was once more a refined, courteous, and judicious gentlemen, a true judge who retained the use of his formidable intellectual powers. He was still subject to the same set of fixed delusions of a cosmic drama involving himself, God, and his former physician, Dr. Flechsig; spasms and attacks of bellowing still impaired his demeanor; but he was largely self-possessed. In the language of psychiatry, his delusory system had 'crystallized', it had become stable and been integrated with his personality. He was once again capable of intellectual work and his current doctor, Dr. Weber, entertained him regularly as a dinner guest at his family table in the asylum at Sonnenstein. His conversation was as edifying as Quixote's. "Whatever matters were discussed," Weber states in his report,

—naturally apart from his delusion—whether they touched on state administration and law, politics, art or literature, social life or anything else, in all Doctor Schreber showed keen interest, detailed knowledge, good memory and correct judgment, and in ethical matters as well an attitude which one can only agree with. Equally he was well-behaved and amiable during light conversation with the ladies present and his humor was always tactful and decent; during the harmless table talk he never brought up anything which should not have been introduced there but during medical visits. (279–80)

During this period, Schreber began to make notes about his delusory system and, in 1900, undertook to write an account of his "nervous illness," a term he preferred to "mental illness." His first purpose in doing so was to make his behavior comprehensible to his family and those around him in the event that he should return to private life. But as he made progress, he reports in his preface, the value of publication impressed itself upon him: "I believe that expert examination of my body and observation of my fate during my lifetime would be of value both for science and the knowledge of religious truths" (31). Schreber's *Memoirs of My Nervous Illness* (*Denkwürdigkeiten eines Nervenkranken*, 1903) provides an unparalleled example of logic working in the service of madness. In it, Schreber displays remarkable powers of exposition, giving a fluid and more-or-less orderly account of his vast and absurd system of fantasy, which centered upon the idea that "soul murder" had been committed upon him by his former physician, Flechsig, perhaps with the cooperation of God; this act, being contrary to the "Order of the World," had put the universe in danger, and only by means of Schreber's "unmanning," his transformation from a man into a woman, could it be preserved.

Schreber's *Memoirs* cannot be summarized with fidelity. Coherent summary is bound at once to impose more order upon his delusions than they justify and at the same time remove from them that curious circumspection with which Schreber conveys his fractured and tenuous ideas. In his introduction he appeals to the reader's patience, noting the generic difficulty hindering the transmission of supernatural truths, which run up against the limit of the human intellect:

To make myself at least somewhat comprehensible I shall have to speak much in images and similes, which may at times perhaps be only *approximately* correct; for the only way a human being can make supernatural matters, which in their essence must always remain incomprehensible, understandable to a certain degree is by comparing them with known facts of human experience. Where intellectual understanding ends, the domain of belief begins; man must reconcile himself to the fact that things exist which are true although he cannot understand them. (41)

To communicate the substance of things unseen, Schreber resorts to the cautions and indirections that accompany all religious apology. It is hard to doubt in the presence of his careful explanations that there was a core of hallucinatory experience around which these had accumulated, or 'crystallized', and that the process by which this experience was integrated into the fabric of Schreber's general outlook resembles to some degree what occurs in mystical theology.

The likeness does not make the doctrine expressed in the *Memoirs* plausible. Their author believes that for years he has spoken with the sun in human words, that he has been forced to take over God's task of controlling the weather, and that his "nerves" are in communication with those of multitudes of other souls (47). His mind has become a late battlefield of the Reformation, subject to Catholic proselytizing and Jesuit intrigue, mixed with Jewish conspiracies. He could mention, he says, hundreds if not thousands of the names of souls who had been in contact with his: Catholics who expected him to instigate a religious revival, Jesuits, bishops, monks, nuns, and "the Pope himself," who was "the leader of a peculiar 'scorching ray' ":

On one occasion 240 Benedictine Monks under the leadership of a Father whose name sounded like Starkiewicz, suddenly moved into my head to perish therein. In the case of other souls, religious interests were mixed with national motives; amongst these was a Viennese nerve specialist whose name by coincidence was identical with that of the above-named Benedictine, a baptized Jew and Slavophile, who wanted to make Germany Slavic through me and at the same time wanted to institute there the rule of Judaism. (71)

Schreber's delusions maintained, in spite of the conflicting religious and national interests warring within his soul, a certain fidelity to German nationalism.[4] The "nerve-language," he tells us, "the so-called 'basic language' " employed by God to communicate with purified, or "tested," souls, is a "somewhat antiquated but nevertheless powerful German, characterized particularly by a wealth of euphemisms (for instance, reward in the reverse sense for punishment, poison for food, juice for venom, unholy for holy, etc.)" (49–50). He considers the Germans to be God's chosen people, "possibly since the Reformation, perhaps ever since the migration of nations," succeeding the "old Jews," "old Persians," "Greco-Romans," and Franks (50). Exquisitely sensitive, Schreber's illness resonates with every form of cultural agon, every historical resource of paranoia as we have traced it here: the conflicts between religions and between nations, the tension between religion and science, which is a constant preoccupation, and also differences of class, which express themselves in imaginary rivalries between ancestors of his "soul-murderer," Flechsig, and earlier members of the Schreber family, graced with the title "Margraves of Tuscany and Tasmania" (55). Schreber even imagines soul-conflicts between his doctors, in which "Dr. von W." (presumably this is Weber) appears to get the best of Flechsig because of the former's "aristocratic traits," which give his soul greater "organizing talent" than that of Flechsig and so make it often more radiant (111).

Schreber's mind is overtaxed with foreign influences against which he can scarcely defend himself. The greater his nerve potency, or "voluptuousness," the more attractive he becomes to weaker souls, which are drawn to him even from distant stars, and which, having given him their nerve potency, turn into "little men." We are back with Gulliver in Lilliput. "On some nights," he reports, "the souls finally dripped down onto my head, in a manner of speaking, in their hundreds if not thousands, as 'little men' " (84). At other times, he makes the conjecture that

on a distant star, probably by using part of my nerves, the attempt was actually made to create a new human world ("new human beings out of Schreber's spirit," as it has been called innumerable times since then, mostly meant in a mocking spirit). It remains a mystery how the necessary time for this was to be found. . . . These "new human beings out of Schreber's spirit"—physically of a much smaller stature than our earthly human beings—were said to have already achieved a fairly remarkable degree of culture, to have kept small cattle proportionate to their own size etc. I myself was said to have received divine veneration as their "National Saint" so to speak, as if my physical posture (particularly in the "pen" of Pierson's Asylum) were of some significance for their faith. Those of their souls which had ascended to a state of Blessedness after death were said to have attained to rays of fairly substantial vigor. (111–12)

"Little men" could also be instruments of torture, "little Flechsigs, little von W.'s," constantly interfering with his eyes and calling him "wretch" (137). The multiplicity of forms in which Schreber experienced interference with his thoughts by other "souls" or "rays" led him, or his voices, to develop a colorful phenomenological vocabulary in which to describe his ideational disturbances, or "miracles."[5] It was his inability to free his thoughts from the voices that Schreber experienced as the greatest torment. He uses the clinical term 'compulsive thinking,' *'Denkzwang'*, to describe this ordeal, which he understands as a moral imposition upon his basic human freedom:

One can only get an idea of the *enormous infringement of man's most primitive rights* which compulsive thinking constitutes and of how my patience was tested beyond all human conception, when one pictures a human being behaving to another human being in human language in the way that rays behave to me to this day in the nerve-language. Imagine a human being planting himself before another and molesting him all day long with unconnected phrases such as the rays use towards me ("If only my," "This then was only," "You are to," etc.). Can one expect anything else of a person spoken to in this manner but that he would throw the other out of the house with a few fitting words of abuse? I also ought to have the right of being master in my own head against the intrusion of strangers. (275n, emphasis in original)

These pathetic words express the essence of Schreber's difficulty—having to be in his head, so to speak, without being the master of it. All of Schreber's bellowing and pounding upon the piano were a way of defending himself, a "counter-action" as his physician states, "against the hallucinations and disturbances of feeling" (270). Quixote, too, is sometimes reduced to bellowing by the unjust torments of the enchanters (346–47).

"Counter-actions" such as bellowing were not quite Schreber's only resource. He did derive a certain moral comfort within his delusory system from the conviction that, according to the "Order of the World," he was in the right and the victim of an injustice perpetrated by God. Schreber held to the very un-Lutheran theological position that the nature of things embodies a form of necessity that even God cannot contravene: "While still in Flechsig's Asylum when I had my first glimpses of the miraculous harmony of the Order of the World, and also suffered wounding humiliation and was daily threatened by horrifying dangers, I coined this phrase for the rays: *there must be an equalizing justice and it can never be* that a morally unblemished human being with feet firmly planted in the 'Order of the World' should have to perish as the innocent victim of other people's sins in the struggle carried on against him by hostile powers" (214). Schreber justifies himself in opposition to God, but the fact that he must put God in default causes him great anxiety.

In the peculiar form of casuistry that he employs in exculpation of God, Schreber calls upon the Darwinian thinking which had occupied his interest before the onset of his disease. This passage is typical of his apologetic style:

From the human point of view, which on the whole still dominated me at that time, it was in consequence very natural for me to see my real enemy only in Professor Flechsig or his soul . . . and to regard as my natural ally God's omnipotence, which I imagined only Professor Flechsig endangered; I therefore thought I had to support it by all possible means, even to the point of self-sacrifice. It occurred to me only much later, in fact only while writing this essay did it become quite clear to me, that God Himself must have known of the plan, if indeed He was not the instigator, to commit soul murder on me, and to hand over my body in the manner of a female harlot. But I must at once repeat what I expressed at the end of Chapter II, so as not to confuse other people's religious ideas and feelings; however abominable the whole plan was bound to appear to me, subjectively speaking, I must nevertheless acknowledge that it originated in that instinct of self-preservation, as natural in God as in every other living being—an instinct which as mentioned in another context . . . forced God in special circumstances to contemplate the destruction not only of individual human beings but perhaps of whole stars with all the created beings upon them. In the nineteenth chapter of the first book of Moses we are told that Sodom and Gomorrah were destroyed by a rain of brimstone and fire, although of their inhabitants there were some, even though very few, "righteous" men. Besides, in the whole domain of the created world, no one considers it immoral when—as long as it does not contravene the Order of the World—the stronger conquers the weak, a people of higher culture expel from their abode one of a lower culture, the cat eats the mouse, the spider kills the fly, etc. In any case, the whole idea of morality can arise only within the Order of the World, that is to say within the natural bond which holds God and mankind together; wherever the Order of the World is broken, power alone counts, and the right of the stronger is decisive. In my case, moral obliquity lay in God placing

Himself outside the Order of the World by which he Himself must be guided. . . . I am inclined to regard the whole development as a matter of *fate*, in which neither on God's nor on my part can there be a question of moral infringement. On the contrary, the Order of the World reveals its very grandeur and magnificence by denying even God Himself in so irregular a case as mine the means of achieving a purpose contrary to the Order of the World. All attempts at committing soul murder, at unmanning me for purposes *contrary to the Order of the World* . . . (that is to say for the sexual satisfaction of a human being) and later at destruction of my reason, have failed. From this apparently so unequal battle between one weak human being and God Himself, I emerge, albeit not without bitter sufferings and deprivations, victorious, because the Order of the World is on my side. (77–79)

Not only is Schreber vindicated by the "Order of the World," he is even willing to regard all of the sufferings imposed upon him by the injustice of "soul murder" as contributing to an ultimate good: "It need hardly be said what incalculable gain it would be for mankind if, through my personal fate, *particularly as it will be shaped in the future*, the foundations of mere materialism and of hazy pantheism would once and for all be demolished" (79, emphasis in original). Whatever else one might wish to say about Schreber's delusion, it is superbly moral in its character. Its Quixotic idealism has precisely the form of a philosophical or religious system, but the core of delusion it seeks to support gives it the quality of a parody. Indeed it is quite a good parody of a familiar variety of modern faith that goes out of its way, as far as it can, to take into account the results of the physical and anthropological sciences while maintaining a core of religious belief.

Once he had regained the state of relative lucidity in which he produced the *Memoirs*, Schreber discovered that he had been placed under 'tutelage' by the state because of his permanent mental incompetence. Believing himself fully recovered, Schreber petitioned to have this tutelage lifted, but to his surprise it was confirmed by a decree of August 1900. This decree would have prevented Schreber from leaving the asylum and from publishing his *Memoirs*, a step that was opposed by his family for reasons succinctly stated by Dr. Weber:

When one looks at the content of his writings, and takes into consideration the abundance of indiscretions relating to himself and others contained in them, the unembarrassed detailing of the most doubtful and aesthetically impossible situations and events, the use of the most offensive vulgar words, etc. one finds it quite incomprehensible that a man otherwise tactful and of fine feeling could propose an action which would compromise him so severely in the eyes of the public, were not his whole attitude to life pathological, and he unable to see things in their proper perspective, and if the tremendous over-valuation of his own person caused by lack of insight into his illness had not clouded his appreciation of the limitations imposed on man by society (283).

Such restrictions could not be accepted by Schreber when matters of the highest seriousness were at stake. Moreover, the question of his competency was to him one of honor. For this reason he took the initiative to appeal the court's decision, not leaving the details of the case to counsel but taking a decisive part in the proceedings himself. His petition to the court is an impassioned defense of his motives. "One cannot miss," he insists, "the moral seriousness which pervades my whole work and which seeks no other goal but the achievement of truth" (308–9). Of this the court eventually became convinced, and, in the light of Schreber's brilliant handling of his own case against the opposition of the public prosecutor, it declared him competent to live in society and manage his own affairs even though it recognized that he was clearly insane.[6]

Schreber's appeal to the court, a document as remarkable in its way as the *Memoirs*, adopts a double strategy.[7] Schreber begins by attacking the problem of his delusions head on, portraying the difference between himself and his physician as a typical conflict between rationalism and faith. The medical reports, Schreber complains, "start a priori from the tacit assumption that everything I reported in my Memoirs or otherwise mentioned about the connection which has arisen between God and myself, as well as about divine miracles which happen to my person, rests only on pathological imaginings. If I wanted to give expression to my true feelings on this point of view I could only do it with Huss' cry to the wretched peasants who were carrying wood to his funeral pyre: *O sancta simplicitas!*" (289). The source of his assertions, he goes on to say, is "not personal vanity nor morbid megalomania" but a genuine religious insight (289). One cannot lock up all religious believers as if they were mad.

Schreber continues by offering a number of empirical proofs that his body had been the scene of constant miracles for which science can give no explanation: the remarkable number of broken strings to which his piano was subject, the compulsiveness of his bellowing, which he believed to be unique in human experience, the compulsive grimaces to which his face was susceptible, and the physical transformation of his body into that of a woman (290–95). Finally, Schreber resorts to a kind of *credo quia absurdum* with reference to his delusion itself:

I would then welcome the expert opinion of men of science in the mentioned fields so as to ascertain whether it is probable, even psychologically possible, that a human being of cool and sober mind as I used to be in the eyes of all who knew me in my earlier life, and besides a human being who . . . did *not have a firm belief in God and the immortality of the soul* before his illness, should have *sucked from his fingers* so to speak the whole complicated structure of ideas with its enormous mass of factual detail." (296, emphasis in original)

Schreber stands in wonder at the extravagance of his own creation.

It was not the polemical thrust of Schreber's appeal that is likely to have swayed the court, but rather the second part of his apology, in which he addressed the essential issue at law—that of whether his psychological state would impair his handling of practical affairs. Here the medical expert had cautioned that the foundation of Schreber's thinking in delusion made him fundamentally unpredictable. But Schreber convinced the court with his perfect tact in mitigating the practical consequences arising from his illness that he was indeed the master of his affairs. As for the damage to his reputation that Weber feared from the publication of the *Memoirs*, Schreber countered with devastating good sense that the fear of being thought mad could be no motive for incarcerating him when, as long as he was incarcerated, people would naturally consider him mad in any case. Schreber, furthermore, demonstrated a magisterial confidence that his *Memoirs* would make their impact without any exertions upon his part: "In this my point of view is like Luther's: 'If it is man's work it will perish; if it is the work of God it will last' " (302).

The Judge disdains the idea that his religious convictions could have any influence upon his conduct of the practical affairs of life: "I could even say with Jesus Christ: 'My kingdom is not of this world'; my so-called delusions are concerned solely with God and the beyond; they *can* therefore *never in any way influence my behavior* in any worldly matter" (301). So deft was Schreber's handling of his own case, showing indeed the legal mind which had brought him such remarkable success before the onset of his illness, that the court found it necessary to pay him tribute:

Dr. Schreber's intellectual powers and the clarity of his thinking had *in no way* suffered by his illness. The way he personally took up the fight against the tutelage under which he was placed and how he carried it through according to plan, the acuity of the logical and juristical operations developed by him, the reasonableness with which he conducted himself, and last but not least the refined measured attitude he showed when in opposition to the medical expert and the Prosecutor— all this affords indisputable proof that in *this* field plaintiff has no need of protection by a guardian; rather in conducting his case he was able to preserve his interests to the full and independently, better indeed than anybody else could have done it in his place. (347)

After this success, Schreber was able to return to private life and to carry through his plans for the publication of the *Memoirs* in a version somewhat expurgated with regard to matters involving his family. It is thanks to Schreber's efforts alone that we possess that remarkable document, written under conditions of the severest distraction, published over the objections of his family and of the state from whose custody the author had first to secure his own freedom.[8]

Freud and Schreber

In the medical report in which he attempts to establish Judge Schreber's insanity and probable unfitness to conduct his affairs, Dr. Weber denies Schreber's contention that the disagreement between them was a disagreement between rationalism and faith: it was not the character of Schreber's beliefs that made them aberrant but the manner in which he had acquired them, going precipitately from agnostic to savior during a phase of extreme psychological dysfunction. Schreber had already raised and refuted this argument; he never denied that he had been ill, only insisted that the fact of his illness did not discredit the insights he had gained (223–24). Dr. Weber also takes up point by point the empirical evidence supporting Schreber's claims that his body was acquiring feminine features, that his bellowings and other symptoms were unique in human history, and so on (319–22). Here Weber is on solid ground; Schreber's theology was subject to refutation only to the degree that it appealed to factual demonstration.

Freud took up the case of Schreber solely upon the basis of the memoir. He did not like dealing directly with psychotics and refused to treat them.[9] This was his only extended discussion of a case of psychotic disturbance. Unlike Dr. Weber, and unlike the court that had given Schreber his release, Freud considered that the illness that afflicted the Judge had terminated "in something approximating a recovery," attributing this achievement on Schreber's part to the fact that "his father-complex was in the main positively toned and that in real life the later years of his relationship with an excellent father had probably been unclouded" (78). In an essay written twelve years after the case history of Schreber, Freud gives an even more remarkable endorsement of Schreber's mental health, citing the "almost complete recovery" that occurred once the Judge was

able to give himself over to what Freud interpreted as fantasies of being
castrated and of becoming a woman in relation to his father:

President Schreber's recovery took its start from his decision to abandon all
opposition to his castration and to accommodate himself to the feminine role
designed for him by God. Following upon this, he became calm and clear in his
mind, was able himself to arrange his dismissal from the asylum, and led a normal
life, with the exception that he devoted some hours every day to the cultivation of
his womanliness, remaining convinced that it would gradually mature to the final
achievement of God's purpose.[10]

The tone is whimsical, quixotic. In Sigmund Freud, Schreber had found
a powerful champion, for in all of Freud's writing about the subject there
speaks an irrepressible admiration for "the wonderful Schreber, who ought
to have been made a professor of psychiatry and director of a mental
hospital."[11] Given Freud's extraordinary respect, and even affection, for
the paranoid memoirist, a sentiment concurrent with his satiric bent, it is
not to be expected that we are going to find here the key to the distinction
between paranoid and ordinary thinking. Such a distinction would be a
relief from heroic irony and therefore foreign both to Freud's personality
and to the nature of psychoanalytic rhetoric. Schreber denied that he was
mad because he knew that he was right about God and his enemies. Freud
denied that Schreber was entirely mad because he was not fundamentally
more deluded than other men and because he could describe his own
delusion with a scientist's precision. Freud's essay on Schreber, which
starts out as an attempt to define the paranoid condition, find its distinguishing symptoms, and diagnose its causes, finally evades the problem of
definition in favor of satiric and comical identification with the paranoid
himself.

I have already set out the basic elements of Freud's psychology of
paranoia in my discussions of the *Quixote*. The root motive of the problem,
according to Freud, lies in an originally narcissistic homosexual wish that
must be repressed from consciousness. In the case of Schreber, the object
of the wish was his own father, who appears in his delusory system disguised as his former doctor, Flechsig, and as God. The necessity by which
the "Order of the World" demands that Schreber become a woman and that
he should preoccupy the sexual interest of God through his "nerve rays"
masks Schreber's true wish that these things should be so with reference to
his father.[12]

The presence of the repressed homosexual motive may be an important
component in Freud's conception of paranoia but it cannot be the defining

symptom; it occurs in other illnesses as well and also in the psychology of those who are not ill. In search of the distinguishing marks of paranoia, then, Freud first turns his attention to the mechanisms by which the paranoid symptoms are formed. The most striking of these, as we have seen, is 'projection': "An internal process is suppressed, and, instead, its content, after undergoing a certain kind of distortion, enters consciousness in the form of an external perception. In delusions of persecution the distortion consists in a transformation of affect; what should have been felt internally as love is perceived externally as hate" (66). Projection seems to be a likely candidate for the identifying, 'pathognomonic' symptom of paranoia; it had been Freud's first candidate to play that role, as we can see from his early letters to Fliess;[13] but now Freud reflects that it is not present in all cases and that it, too, exercises a role in normal functioning: "For when we refer causes of certain sensations to the external world, instead of looking for them, as in other cases, within, this normal proceeding is projection" (66). Projection, far from being a sign of paranoia, is indispensable for everyday life. Here once again is the essential satirically reductive positivist gesture.

Faced with this obstacle, Freud abandons the path of the symptoms, making a promise—unkept—to take up the subject elsewhere, and turns to the mechanisms by which the paranoid's repression is brought about. He divides the process into three parts: 'fixation', the lagging behind of an instinctual component at an earlier stage of development than the rest; 'repression' proper, an active exclusion from consciousness by the ego of the now aversive trends; and finally, 'irruption', or the 'return of the repressed', which brings about a retrograde movement to the point of fixation (67–68). Freud suggests that just as there are multiple points of development at which the libido may become fixated, so there may be a similar multiplicity in the mechanisms of repression and irruption. Paranoia offers an especially dramatic withdrawal and 'return of the repressed', for the world of the paranoid actually seems to disappear, to be annihilated or reduced to mere appearance. Schreber believed that the people and things around him were contrived by God, "miracled up" ("angewundert"), "fleetingly improvised" ("flüchtig hingemachte") to conceal the "destruction of the world" ("Weltuntergang"). He had arrived through the process of delusion at a perfect Berkeleyan solipsism and occasionalism.[14] The "end-of-the-world phenomenon" is caused by a total withdrawal of libido into the ego and a corresponding regression to the narcissistic stage of development. Elsewhere Freud compares this withdrawal to an amoeba retracting its pseudopodia.[15] It occurs "silently": "we receive no intelligence of it, but can only infer it from subsequent events. What forces itself so noisily upon our attention is the process of recovery, which undoes the work of repression and brings back the libido again on to the people it had abandoned" (71). This is the 'return of the repressed', and it occurs in the form of a delusion, though it is actually an attempt at recovery, "a process of reconstruction" in which the paranoid rebuilds anew the world that has been destroyed.

By dividing the process of repression in its temporal dimension, separating fixation, repression, and return, Freud endeavored to distinguish the disruptive and re-integrative aspects of the disease. This strategy was not without its awkwardness, for in Schreber's case the delusions of persecution had developed before the destruction of the world, not subsequently as the theory requires. The process of rebuilding seems to have actually preceded the catastrophe. Freud saves appearances with a set of stages in which "partial detachments" occur in a complex series of military engagements between Schreber's fixations and resistances, until the "forces of repression" achieve a final "victory" in the annihilation of the world, leaving the self to stand as the lone survivor (72–73). What we are left with at the end of all this is that the paranoid makes a peculiar choice of fixation—at the narcissistic stage—and that the means of repression and return are equally peculiar and distinct from those of other neurotics. But there is little to help us in distinguishing just what in the paranoid's manner of thought makes him different from those who are not paranoid.[16] The system of delusions by which Schreber achieves the 'return of the repressed' does not itself seem to have a pathological character. It represents an attempt to make sense out of his experience given the presence of certain alien elements in consciousness. It hardly seems different from other narcissistic 'projections' or 'secondary revisions'. We are no closer than we were with Dr. Weber's simple categorical diagnosis in accomplishing the task of distinguishing what makes a person's thinking process deserve the label of paranoia. All we have is the inferred cataclysmic event, the 'end-of-the-world phenomenon', and the reconstruction or system of delusion that succeeds it, preserving the effects of the "profound internal change" in the form of hostile projections.

There is one passage in Freud's essay, however, that does help us to situate him a little more precisely with regard to the 'end-of-the-world phenomenon'. In need of an illustration for the nature of the paranoid's world-annihilating gesture of withdrawal into delusion, Freud turns not to the annals of medicine but to his favorite work of literature, Goethe's *Faust*. We have already observed Freud's deep affinity with this work, whose main character is the epitome of the modern hero and his characteristically modern paranoid problem—that of accommodating heroic urges within the banal reality of scientific and bourgeois culture. We have seen that Freud invoked Faust's "In the Beginning was the Deed" in order to emphasize, in the last sentence of *Totem and Taboo,* the historical authenticity of the primal crime. The line is drawn from an early scene in Goethe's drama, in which Faust, attempting to rewrite the Gospel, moves from "In the Beginning was the Word" to "In the Beginning was the Sense" to "In the Beginning was the Force" to "In the Beginning was the Deed" (1224–37). In doing so he traverses the path from Johanine logos-theology through Enlightenment empiricism and mechanist dynamics to the Romantic philosophy of will. By such a movement, Freud suggests, the primal brothers freed themselves from the idealism of narcissistic enthrallment in order to attain the reality of action. In his discussion of Schreber, Freud refers to a similar Faustian moment. In Act One of *Faust,* just before entering his pact with Mephistopheles, Faust makes another gesture of liberation, uttering the following curse:

> My curse I hurl on all that spangles
> The mind with dazzling make-belief,
> With lies and blandishments entangles
> The soul within this cave of grief!
> Accursed, to start, the smug delusion
> Whereby the mind itself ensnares!
> Cursed, brash phenomenal intrusion
> That blinds the senses unawares!
> Cursed, what in lying dreams assures us
> Of name and glory past the grave!
> Cursed, pride of ownership that lures us
> Through wife and children, plow and slave!
> Accursed by Mammon, when his treasure
> To deeds of daring eggs us on,
> For idle self-indulgent leisure
> Spreads a luxurious divan!
> Cursed be the balsam of the grape!
> Cursed, highest prize of lovers' thrall!
> A curse on faith! A curse on hope!
> A curse on patience, above all! (1587–1606)

In this famous passage, Faust again reenacts the Enlightenment's annihilation of traditional, religious, and metaphysical culture and at the same time curses the results: the mind recognizes itself as a slave of "make-believe," of "smug" self-delusion; it recognizes the phenomena of the natural world as no more than a source of distraction and confusion; and, given these recognitions, heroism, family life, love, even greed and intoxication lose their allure, nor can the Christian virtues offer consolation. Such is the disenchantment of the modern world. Faust's curse does not arise out of mere psychological distress. It expresses the causes of that distress, and, indeed, it seeks to master them by embracing the impoverishment of the world with a destructive movement of the will. Its desperate hope is to set itself above destruction by a more total destruction. As Faust so Freud.

It is the next event of the poem that Freud invokes in his discussion of the case of Schreber, quoting the response of the chorus of spirits to the Faustian "Curses which free him from the world":

> Woe! Woe:
> You have destroyed it,
> The beautiful world,
> With mighty fist;
> It crumbles scattered,
> By a demigod shattered.
> . . . .
> Mighty one
> Of the earth's sons,
> In splendor perfect it,
> see it rewon,

In your own breast re-erect it! (1607–12, 1617–21)

"And the paranoid builds it again, not more splendid, it is true," Freud goes on to say, "but at least so that he can once more live in it. He builds it up by the work of his delusions" (70–71). As Faust and the modern psyche, so the paranoid. At a later point in the essay, Freud notes that we are constantly detaching libido from people and objects without falling ill. Faust's curse, he says, resulted not in paranoia nor in neurosis but "simply in a certain general frame of mind" (72). This "general frame of mind" ("eine besondere psychische Gesamtstimmung")[17] is none other than that of modern Romantic and psychological culture itself. It has come about by a historical process of negation and reconstruction identical to what is described in Freud's account of paranoia. It is this history that, in psychoanalytic theory, is recapitulated in the development of the individual. The event of cosmic destruction to which the paranoid's withdrawal gives testimony was a real historical event located at the beginning of the modern movement, and the 'system' that he projects in order to replace that world is none other than the interior reconstruction of the cosmos achieved in Romantic subjectivism, a reconstruction permeated with and grounded in suspicion. The words Freud addresses to the condition of the paranoid, then, might be applied to the edifice of Romantic culture as a whole:

> Such a reconstruction after the catastrophe is successful to a greater or lesser extent, but never wholly so; in Schreber's words, there has been a profound internal change in the world. But the human subject has recaptured a relation, and often a very intense one, to the people and things in the world, even though that relation is a hostile one now, where formerly it was hopefully affectionate. (71)

It would be impossible to demonstrate more vividly my 'psycho-historical law' that the ideas of development in Freudian psychology involve a recapitulation not of a foundational human experience of maturing but of episodes in the history of modern culture.

Freud was aware that the essay on Schreber was somewhat inconclusive, a fact reflected in the title of the work, "Psycho-Analytic Notes on an Autobiographical Account of a Case of Paranoia (Dementia Paranoides)." Making comical use of Schreberian language, he explained to Jung, his close collaborator at the time, that "the piece is formally imperfect, *fleetingly improvised,* I had neither time nor strength to do more."[18] Perhaps it was this sense of incompleteness which led Freud to the unusual dramatic flourish that brings the essay to a close when, having described the flagrant profusions of Schreber's paranoid fantasy, the psychoanalyst steps forward to admit the similarities between paranoid thinking and his own theory.[19] One of the singular features of Schreber's system, Freud observes, is that the spiritual transactions that take place between Schreber, other souls, and God have a character oddly physical, even sexual (45). They occur through the medium of "nerve rays," or "rays of God," which are of the same nature in human beings and in God. The power of "Blessedness" or "voluptuousness" in the nerves of the human body exerts such attraction that at times even God becomes vulnerable to them. The similarity with psychoanalytic doctrine gives occasion to the following remarks:

> Since I neither fear the criticism of others nor shrink from criticizing myself, I have no motive for avoiding the mention of a similarity which may possibly damage our libido theory in the estimation of many of my readers. Schreber's "rays of God," which are made up of a condensation of the sun's rays, of nerve-fibers, and of spermatozoa, are in reality nothing else than a concrete representation and external projection of libidinal cathexes; and they thus lend his delusions a striking similarity with our theory. His belief that the world must come to an end because his ego

was attracting all the rays to itself, his anxious concern at a later period, during the process of reconstruction, lest God should sever his ray-connection with him, — these and many other details of Schreber's delusional formation sound almost like endopsychic perceptions of the processes whose existence I have assumed in these pages as the basis of our explanation of paranoia. I can nevertheless call a friend and fellow-specialist to witness that I had developed my theory of paranoia before I became acquainted with the contents of Schreber's book. It remains for the future to decide whether there is more delusion in my theory than I should like to admit, or whether there is more truth in Schreber's delusion than other people are as yet prepared to believe. (78–79)

This passage shows Freud at his wittiest and wiliest, striking the attitude of the fearless knight of truth who spares himself no embarrassment in his scientific quest; then maintaining his dignity through the fantastic parade of Schreber's vocabulary; offering a witness as to his priority of discovery over Schreber; and finally, with a humorous equability, leaving it to the future to decide matters between the brilliant paranoid and himself. Freud does not by any means discourage the perception that his theory resembles a paranoid fantasy. He is concerned only about his claim to precedence. The offer to summon witnesses is made with some seriousness: Freud could never resist a challenge to his originality. In this case, the fact that he rises to the challenge has the unusual effect of certifying the paranoid as a rival thinker grappling with the same problems as himself. Once Freud had asserted the priority of his insights, the fact that they resembled Schreber's delusory structures only served in his mind to confirm them.

I have mentioned that Freud paid a compliment to animism as the most complete psychological system of explanation. The paranoid shares the animist's uninhibited projection of narcissistic structures, and this gives to his 'endopsychic perceptions' an opportune completeness like that of the animist. In making a point of the similarity between his thinking and Schreber's, Freud was thus paying himself an ironic compliment. It was as much as to say that he had heeded the "call to introspection" to the degree that he could see as fully within what the animist and the paranoid could project without; he had achieved for himself the translation of external, narcissistic culture into psychological terms.

Freud's willingness to present the paranoid's insights on something like an equal footing with psychoanalysis, his acceptance of Schreber as more or less cured, and his wish that Schreber could have a clinic of his own, all of this has a distinctly humorous, fantastic quality.[20] It is certainly not what is normally expected of a scientist. But the irony that runs through these cunning passages is, indeed, what we would now expect given what we have seen to be the generally reductive and satirical character of psychoanalytic thinking. Psychoanalysis tells us that things are not what they seem, and this recognition carries with it always an irony. Freud explained the genius of Leonardo da Vinci by purporting to uncover his sublimated homosexuality and narcissistic investments. The paranoid Schreber, himself something of a genius, is found to exhibit the same tendencies only with a different outcome. And so too with Freud. All of them are subject to the working of the same hidden forces, the same unconscious patterns and displacements. The power of the psychoanalytic model resides in its conquest of the normal and the psychotic using the very same terms.

Schreber, like Quixote, is a hero. He is a hero without a world, a hero who has had to "miracle up" his world, but he maintains a hero's self-possession even amidst his delusions. This is what makes him a powerful instrument in the hands of Freud. Freud's satiric victory lies in his ability to erase the psychological difference that separates Schreber from ordinary heroes. In order for the psychoanalytic victory to be complete, even Schreber's likeness with Freud must be acknowledged. But along with the slightly malicious glee evident in Freud's remarks, the sense of triumph over official psychiatry, for instance, which makes Freud want to install Schreber at the head of his own mental hospital, there is another distinctive tone, a comical grandiosity distinctly Quixotic in flavor. The comical grandeur of the paranoid sheds a reflected glory upon his psychoanalytic student.

It is evident from Freud's correspondence that Jung was the ideal audience of the essay on paranoia, and its author could not have been disappointed with the envious reaction of his colleague: "Only now that I have the galleys can I enjoy your Schreber. It is not only uproariously funny but brilliantly written as well."[21] Jung was well prepared for the humorous spirit of this "fleetingly improvised" document. The comical resources of Schreberian heroism had been a staple of his correspondence with Freud for some time. During the period of Freud's work on paranoia, we find the two researchers adopting the "Grundsprache," Schreber's "basic language," as a private idiom in which they could share their sense of superiority over their critics, competitors, and colleagues. In Freud's employment, the "basic language" can be cleverly witty; writing to Jung on vacation from Lake Constance, he confides: "Since I can no longer get along with Bleuler at all after having abjured his faith in abstinence, I have instructed Binswanger to maintain the necessary *nerve-contact* and sound all those conches that might allure Bleuler" (342). The "basic language" can be crudely derisive, as applied to a critic who had compared the Freudians with Bottom in *A Midsummer Night's Dream* awaking from his dream to find himself with the head of an ass: "His unconscious at least knows this much, that Puck has already '*miracled*' the ass's head on to Ziehen and Oppenheim" (307). Most strikingly, the "basic language" provides a sly, malicious medium for adolescent comments on the romantic life of a close collaborator, Pfister, about whose liaison Freud comments: "It so happens that '*a bird loaded with corpse poison*' has been *miracled up* into existence, which as the rules require bears a girl's name and is gently luring him into the ways of the ungodly. I know this charming little bird. But it seems that she only wants to lure him out of his cage, not to marry him. Still, the main thing is to lure him out. If she succeeds, Pfister can count himself happy" (450). It is remarkable how adolescent and strange the behavior of the founder of psychoanalysis and his "successor crown-prince" could still be regarding women and sex.

Freud's use of Schreberian resources has a caustic quality distinctly out of keeping, it must be noted, with Schreber's gentle manners. In fact, these deployments of the "basic language" all have what Freud in his theory of wit calls a 'tendentious' aspect: their impact as humor is intensified by the animus of the two scientists against their adversaries and their sense of superiority toward their friends. The "basic language" serves for Freud and Jung just the same function as the Cervantine pastiche of the Academie Española served for the adolescent Freud and his friend Silberstein, providing a grandiose mode of secret complicity, a precious folie à deux. As the Cervantine pastiche furnished a model for the language of psychoanalysis, the "basic language" was its comic double. At this point in the relationship of Freud and Jung, the vocabulary and theory of psychoanalysis had become a ground of struggle between the two men, a complex symbolic expression of their sense of competition.[22] The "basic language" provided humorous relief from the aggressive, reductive character of the orthodox vocabulary, which, as Jung himself came to feel, was often a covert vehicle of attack.[23] In another letter, Freud, speaking in a "grandfatherly" capacity, advises Jung not to be too hard on his pupil Honegger:

It is unreasonable of you, I think, to expect his working methods to be as independent of the human libido as yours: we agree that he belongs to a later generation, that he has had little experience of love thus far, and is in general of softer stuff than you. We would not want him to be a copy of yourself. He will be far more useful to you as he is. He possesses a fine receptivity, psychological flair, and a good sense of the "basic language." (327, emphasis in original)

Jung's responses show a less comical enthusiasm and a more pious infatuation with the paranoid idiom:

I was touched and overjoyed to learn how much you appreciate the greatness of Schreber's mind and the liberating ἱεροὶ λόγοι [sacred words] of the basic language. I am still very intrigued by the fate of those unfortunate corps brothers who were *miracled up to the skies* and are described as *"those suspended under Cassiopeia."* The Manichaeans (Schreber's godfathers?) hit on the idea that a number of demons or "archons" were crucified on, or affixed to, the vault of heaven and were the fathers of human beings. (356, emphasis in original)

Freud responds, "I share your enthusiasm for Schreber; it is a kind of revelation. I plan to introduce 'basic language' as a serious technical term—meaning the original wording of a delusional idea which conscious- ness . . . experiences only in distorted form" (358). Freud never carried out this intention. But obviously he found the "hieroi logoi" of the basic language no less "liberating" than did his colleague.

It would, of course, be possible to interpret Freud's infatuation with Schreberian heroism in psychoanalytic terms. Freud once raised the topic of 'hysterical paranoia', a paranoia generated by imitation of another para- noid.[24] We have seen that it takes but a small extrapolation of Freudian theory to imagine that the paranoid would exert some of the same fascina- tion as other narcissistic characters do for those who have repressed their own narcissism. And history, of course, testifies to the power of paranoid infatuation. Freud was conscious of what he took to be strong homosexual currents working in his psyche, discovered through the analysis of his friendship with Wilhelm Fliess. He interpreted Fliess's behavior after their break-up as showing how a homoerotic 'cathexis' could be converted into paranoia; it taught Freud the necessity of sublimating this homoerotic energy into different channels, such as the pursuit of knowledge. In his essay on Leonardo da Vinci, which was also a self-exploration, we have seen that Freud attributed Leonardo's superhuman powers of natural inves- tigation to the homosexual libido he had invested in scientific curiosity.[25] As with Leonardo's, Freud's own victory over the libido had been won only after a difficult struggle. In spite of the putative success of his post- Fliessian sublimation, it was an accepted fact between Freud and the members of his inner circle that the episode with Fliess continued to exert a baleful influence on Freud's behavior, making him perennially mistrustful and wary of intimacy. Ferenczi writes of Freud's "justified distrust of people (even of friends—after the *Fliess* case)."[26]

An episode in Freud's relations with Ferenczi during the period when he was writing the Schreber essay casts an interesting light upon his way of understanding and experiencing the temptations of paranoia and homosexual attachment in his own personality, and gives a sense of the atmosphere in which the essay and the letters to Jung quoted above were written. Ferenczi, despite his knowledge of the Fliess trauma, felt a strong need for greater personal intimacy with Freud. He acted out this need in what Freud called an "infantile" way during a vacation when he refused to collaborate with Freud in composing the Schreber essay, having taken umbrage at Freud's request that he play the part of the secretary.[27] Ferenczi was further wounded by Freud's failure to rebuke him, and issued a plea for openness between the two men, an openness based upon psychoanalytic understanding: an "apparently cruel but in the end only useful, clear-as-day openness, which conceals nothing, could be possible in the relations between two psychoanalytically-minded people who can really understand everything and, instead of making value judgments, can seek the determinants of their psychological impulses" (218). In making this plea, Ferenczi disclaimed any pretense to idealism: "You once told me that psychoanalysis was only a science of facts, of indicatives that should not be translated into imperatives—the latter are paranoid. According to this conception there is no psychoanalytic worldview, no psychoanalytic ethics, no psychoanalytic rules of conduct. I also know of no ethics other than those of pure reason; but the extension and expansion of reason into hitherto unconscious areas has also had a very significant influence on the worldview and behavior of nonparanoids" (220). And so, on behalf of nonparanoids, Ferenczi pleads for the special truthfulness psychoanalysis should permit:

I believe that you underestimate much too much the ennobling power of psychoanalysis if you don't believe that it makes people who have completely grasped its meaning absolutely worthy of trust. . . . Please don't misunderstand me. I really don't want to 'reform' society. I am not a paranoiac. I would only like to see *thoughts* and *speech* liberated from the compulsion of unnecessary inhibitions in the relations of psychoanalytically-minded men. —

Unfortunately—I can't begin, you have to! After all, you are psychoanalysis in person!" (220)

Freud's reply begins rather frostily: "It is remarkable how much better you can present yourself in writing than in speech."[28] He then admits his weakness in failing to scold Ferenczi for his behavior, a weakness he also feels in correcting his sons: "I am also not that psychoanalytic superman whom we have constructed, and I also haven't overcome the countertransference. I couldn't do it, just as I can't do it with my three sons, because I like them and I feel sorry for them in the process." Having admitted his failure properly to act the part of the father toward Ferenczi, Freud now does rebuke him for failing to act upon his psychoanalytic understanding of Freud's behavior:

> Not only have you noticed that I no longer have any need for that full opening of my personality, but you have also understood it and correctly returned to its traumatic cause. Why did you thus make a point of it? This need has been extinguished in me since Fliess's case, with the overcoming of which you just saw me occupied. A piece of homosexual investment has been withdrawn and utilized for the enlargement of my own ego. I have succeeded where the paranoiac fails. (221)

Freud's reply makes it abundantly plain that for him the stability of his mind lay in his success at resisting the hidden influence of Fliess, and, furthermore, that he was not about to allow anyone else to gain sufficient intimacy to threaten him as Fliess had done. Ferenczi's plea for openness smacks both of paranoid idealism and of a more direct expression of those homoerotic impulses presumed to be the unconscious sources of paranoia; Freud rejects the need for both of these. By disclaiming the temptation to paranoia, he rejects the need for intimacy with other men, intimacy that can only have a homoerotic basis. When we see Freud responding with such enthusiasm, then, to the humorous extravagance of the paranoid Schreber, there can be no doubt from the psychoanalytic point of view that he was indulging in a kind of literary flirtation with the forbidden. And when we consider that the theme of the Fliess trauma, as discussed between Freud and his colleagues, was indeed a very intimate and private one, and one with immediate consequences for their own relations with Freud, it becomes all the more clear that the writing of the Schreber essay, and the correspondence and discussions surrounding it, may well have evoked in Freud powerful feelings that he associated with Fliess. The rejection of Ferenczi, according to the psychoanalytic logic, would be a natural repudiation on Freud's part of a homosexual temptation.

A psychoanalytic explanation of Freud's infatuation with Schreber would also undoubtedly emphasize his own admission to Jung, about the Schreber essay itself, that "in working on it I have had to fight off complexes within myself (Fliess)," (380) referring no doubt to that "piece of unruly homosexual feeling," as he put it, that Fliess could still evoke.[29] The Schreberian charm would not have had to rely, furthermore, upon the distant libidinal resonance of Fliessian grandiosity to inspire Freud's hilarious identification, nor upon Ferenczi's respectful pleas for attention. Freud was currently replaying the Fliessian drama with Jung himself, who managed to call up that same "piece of unruly homosexual feeling," on one occasion even causing Freud to faint in his presence. Freud would soon proudly be offering to "occupy [his] unemployed libido elsewhere."[30] It was in vain that Jung assured him "nothing Fliess-like was going to happen. . . . Except for moments of infatuation, my affection is lasting and reliable."[31] No doubt it was within the strong stimulus of Jung's prestigious and masculine intellectual presence that Freud was incited to revisit the Fliessian debacle, to achieve the ultimate portrayal of himself as Leonardo and of Fliess as Schreber, and to set the attractiveness of the paranoid figure at a comic distance where it could be safely acknowledged. We might set into this context, too, Freud's infatuation with the *Quixote*, which derived its early emotional charge from his friendship with Silberstein; it should be remembered, also, that Freud subsequently attempted to enlist his future wife in the cult of Quixote, an attempt that apparently failed, probably because his wife did not share the adolescent intellectual grandiosity that sustained the emotional bond between the two young men. All this would be good psychoanalysis, it seems to me, and also—but for the implications of the theoretical vocabulary—perfectly acceptable as an account of Freud's subjective experience. We do not need a theory of unconscious homoerotic motives to recognize that Freud's most gifted friends excited in him powerful feelings of admiration and rivalry, and that these feelings colored his literary as well as his scientific pursuits.

The recognition that the Schreber case had a highly charged personal and possibly sexual significance for Freud by no means binds us to the psychoanalytic vocabulary for our understanding of it. In fact, it is important to notice once again how that vocabulary determined the shape of the relations between Freud and his followers. We can see, for instance, in Freud's exchange of letters with Ferenczi, the inhibiting effect of the psychoanalytic doctrine that all social ties have a sexual character. In order for Ferenczi to make a simple appeal for Freud's confidence, he had first to overcome Freud's mistrust of friendly intimacy and his conviction that it can arise only from unreliable homosexual impulses. We find Ferenczi, therefore, advancing an extraordinary claim for the "ennobling power of psychoanalysis" and feeling, quite naturally, that in doing so he was in danger of appearing to lapse into idealism, which is the disguised expression of homosexual libido. Psychoanalytic theory, of course, undermines the legitimacy both of idealistic and of personal claims to the worth of social ties. Ferenczi's gambit, then, was doomed from the start.

It turned out of course in any case that Freud had not the slightest interest in claiming the special social benefit, the capacity for perfect openness, that psychoanalysis might be imagined to confer upon 'nonparanoids'. He had succeeded in eradicating the need for such openness in himself. Freud set himself apart from the paranoid, then, not by being able to achieve social ties on a realistic footing but by being able largely to extinguish them. No wonder he preferred the ironic languages of Schreber and Quixote—as well as his own esoteric theoretical code—to open demonstrations of emotion or the sharing of confidence. Again, the psychoanalytic theory of homosexual libido looks now more like an expression of Freud's subjective experience and personal need rather than an explanation for them. Freud considered paranoid characters, including Fliess and other psychoanalytic dissenters, to be guilty of projecting their repressed libido in the form of persecutory megalomania, whereas Freud's accusations of paranoia were evidently motivated by his inability to control his own powerful and unrepressed emotions! Not long after this period, Freud did permit himself to enter into a special social bond with his disciples, as the totemistic chief of The Committee, where his position of masterly reserve was not to be breached.

I have permitted myself to wander here a little way down the path of psychological speculation in order to glimpse what may have been another of the personal motives projected by Freud onto universal psychology through the theory of paranoia. The motives in question were neither unconscious nor were they necessarily sexual: they were Freud's difficulties in governing his conscious emotional attachments, which made him prefer to interact with his friends through complex symbolic vehicles, powerfully expressive and compelling languages of irony and suspicion. By such means, Freud was able to command extraordinary loyalty and at the same time to preserve his dominance and distance within a small circle of admirers set grandiosely and suspiciously apart from the outside world. We can see, then, that the vocabulary of suspicion had for Freud a protective as well as an aggressive dimension. Again it is impossible not to admire the ingenious way in which he adapted to his own needs and purposes the mode of reductive, satiric thinking he acquired from his early literary pursuits. Freud carried the habit of intellectual Quixotism into science. He wielded it aggressively against his cultural enemies, and used it to keep a safe distance from his friends and colleagues. He lived it and applied it with rigorous consistency to his own experience. And so it is not surprising to see him, finally, in his *pas de deux* with Schreber, participating in the same foolish spectacle as the many admirers of Quixote. Like the bachelor Samsón Carrasco, Freud gets up on his horse to join with Schreber/Quixote in a friendly joust.

Having recognized the vanity of all heroic ambitions, Freud could abandon himself to the charm of paranoia in literary form because, in its absurdity, it seems to acknowledge the disreputable sources of heroism. It does not need to be unmasked; and yet, for all of its improbable pretensions, it maintains the conviction of the truly heroic finding itself naively opposed to an external reality not of its own making. In fact, paranoia offers the truest and most complete psychological spectacle of heroism that can be imagined. Only in error does the pattern of the mind reveal itself in its entirety. Truth is always complexly involved with other truth; error stands out like a shadow against the background of what is known and shows the form that cast it. The psychoanalyst exhibits a peculiar susceptibility to the glitter of erroneous heroism because only there can be found a coherent and sympathetic reflection of his own satiric grandeur; it is a trait he inherits from the empirico-romantic culture that produced him.

Schreber is for Freud the supreme rhetorical ally. His condition displays the cunning involvement of reason in madness: the judge's juridical aplomb, his theological fertility, his casuistical brilliance, and his powers of psychological observation, all of these are humorous triumphs for the Freudian method and reflective of its own qualities. Schreber, for all of his madness, evokes in Freud a self-consciously comical but yet still enthusiastic admiration. He alone gives expression to the content of the heroic consciousness without disguise and without irony. And so, for the psychoanalytic mind, the "basic language" in which Schreber speaks the "holy words" has a "liberating" force of expression. Far from any notion to distinguish himself from Schreber, Freud is more than content to bask in the romance and comical reflection of his glamour.

More Recent Formulations on Paranoia

Perhaps it will seem that, having concluded my analysis with Freud's ludicrous treatment of his kinship with Schreber, I have given an unfair emphasis to what is most eccentric in Freud, to a personal whimsy rather than an essential aspect of psychoanalytic thought. In order to remove this false impression, I wish briefly to show that separating the paranoid from the sane has not proven any easier for the descendants of Freud than it was for Freud himself. Let us take for an instance the Jesuit psychiatrist W. W. Meissner, who has invested prodigious and admirable care in the attempt to understand what he calls the 'paranoid process', the deviant way in which paranoid patients go about trying to make sense of the world.[32] Like Freud, Meissner is committed to the significance of the fact that what the paranoid does in constructing a system of beliefs is no different from what occurs in the ordinary person's attempt to interpret experience:

The problem is that the data that reality provides are never so complete, so unambiguous, or so definite that such patterns of meaning are forced upon the human mind. The evidences are often unavailable, thus leaving a certain discontinuity in experience. The evidences that are available are often of varying degrees of clarity and certainty, and involve elements that can only be inferred or conjectured—the thoughts and intentions of other people for example. (117)

Because meaning is not "forced upon the human mind," a rather hopeful expectation, all of us find it necessary to draw certain large conclusions, 'paranoid constructions', which cannot be strictly limited by the data of experience. Myths, 'systems of belief', and 'systems of value' all come under this category. For Meissner, such constructions do not simply impose significance upon inert experience; nor do they simply offer the means of narrative. Rather, he states, following Bronislaw Malinowski, that such constructions make possible a living interaction with reality motivated by an inner need: "The paranoid construction is . . . a lived reality which expresses and grows out of an inner dynamic life feeling. That inner conviction is what gives meaning to the individual's experience" (120).

Because Meissner believes that the paranoid's form of thinking does not differ in kind from the ordinary, it is impossible for him to draw any hard and fast boundaries between those who are pathologically delusive and the rest of us. The fact that gaps in our knowledge of reality leave us prey to indefensible assumptions puts us, he believes, in a state of embarrassment in the face of an authoritative paranoid like Judge Schreber:

How in fact would one go about disproving Schreber's delusion that he was being transformed into a woman? How would one disprove the Christian assertion of the real presence in the Eucharistic sacrifice? We can recognize that a delusional system is in conflict with reality as we interpret it, but how does one go about proving that our interpretation is sane and that the delusional one is insane and in contradiction to reality? Ultimately we cannot. We can resort to an appeal to consensus or to practical and adaptive exigencies that are consequent on our interpretation rather the delusional one—but these are not matters of evidence. The delusional system as well as the belief system is maintained on the basis of a prior emotional commitment, not on the basis of evidences. (93–94)

The therapist's problem here is that he cannot refute Schreber's claims to transcendent knowledge without asserting the possession of an equally transcendent knowledge. The paranoid has put him in a bind. He cannot quite dismiss the paranoid's system as an inadequate one because he has admitted that he has one just like it, "maintained on the basis of a prior emotional commitment." On the other hand, if he attempts to assert that the paranoid's claims are false, he then seems to take on the kind of authority that only the most notorious forms of narcissistic projection allow.

In Meissner's position the full consequences of Freud's psychological relativism are apparent. 'Paranoia' has become a general term for thought; it is taken for granted that intellectual conviction derives primarily from inner need; there is only one remaining question worth asking: At what point does the inner need become so intense that the person's functioning is impaired? Meissner's problem, then, becomes how to separate the strong, pathological form of paranoia from the weak, normal sort that none of us can escape, and to do so in such a way that his own thinking remains on the weak side of the distinction. He needs another criterion for pathology besides 'paranoia' itself. We do not find in Meissner the whimsical courting of the paranoid that was permissible to Freud. He is not a satirical physician of the soul but a psychiatrist who must deal directly and frequently with paranoid patients in an institutional setting, as Freud never did. Issues such as the proper grounds of confinement are real for him in a way that they were not for Freud.

Meissner's first criterion for distinguishing ordinary belief from paranoia centers upon the anti-social character of strong paranoia: "The mechanisms of belief tend to support the individual's participation and membership in the community, whereas the mechanisms of paranoia tend to isolate and exclude the individual from the real community of objects—the delusional network of suspicious and hostile interactions in a paranoid pseudocommunity is a far cry from meaningful sharing in the community of one's fellows" (95). It is odd how, in this sentence, the paranoid 'pseudocommunity' seems actually to come into existence so that its social advantages, or disadvantages, can be compared with those of a real community. Meissner's attitude is very close to Freud's, expressed in remarks to the Vienna Psychoanalytic Society:

The reformer, as long as he is alone, is considered a paranoiac (lately Richard Wagner). The fact that he has followers protects an individual against being declared ill. Thus, the founding of the Christian religion, for example, is a paranoia of twelve men (the vision of resurrection, etc.). Had the religion not found so many adherents, it would certainly have been judged a morbid fantasy of a few men.[33]

It must be true that the paranoid does not share in a sense of community, and that total intellectual isolation must constitute mental dysfunction; but the idea that the degree of social isolation corresponds to the degree of pathology seems hard to defend, for the endurance of disagreement and rejection constitutes a fundamental intellectual virtue. We need only recall in this regard Freud's account of the early days of the psychoanalytic movement when, so he believed, all the world was united in hostility to his discoveries. His sense of intellectual isolation, threat, and suspicion of betrayal became so intense after Adler and Jung defected from the movement that, as we have seen, Freud and Jones felt the need to establish a secret committee to protect him.[34] All this is evidence of a truly heroic isolation. But can the analyst admit that it tends in the direction of a paranoid cult? Despite the many quarrels, forced exiles, and retreats this arrangement fostered, the members of the movement accomplished a remarkable amount of work. Productivity is not beyond the paranoid's capability, but before we consign the psychoanalytic movement to the domain of pathology, we would at least have to agree beforehand that the theory itself has no merits. I, of course, am willing to draw this conclusion with regard to psychoanalysis, but I am by no means willing to extend it to most other examples in which intellectual isolation leads to the production of significant advances.

Meissner adds to the isolation argument a second one having to do with the fixity of belief or the amount of energy invested in it. Even the scientist, he observes, may verge on paranoia when adherence to a theory prevents him from responding to the correctives of the evidence. We cannot do without the seeking of "meaningful patterns" in experience, yet such patterns can become objects of too rigid a commitment. Thus it is possible to distinguish the normal from the pathological in terms of "quantitative variation rather than qualitative difference":

A dividing line is difficult to draw. Certainly we are more likely to attach the label of paranoia where the manifestations occur in a socially deviant context or in association with other forms of pathology—e.g., schizophrenic decompensation is the commonest example. But the mechanisms can be in operation across a broad spectrum of states of mind of varying degrees of adaptation. Our understanding of paranoid mechanisms and of the genesis of paranoid states must take into consideration that the genetic roots of paranoid states are probably widespread in the social matrix and in fact involve important constructive dimensions of social and personal integration. The same mechanisms that serve the ends of development and adaptation also serve from another perspective as the basis of paranoid forms of adjustment. The pathological distortion is very likely, then, a matter of quantitative variation rather than qualitative difference. (97–98)

The quantitative argument raises as many difficulties as the argument from isolation. For it would seem that as we move higher up the scale of intellectual commitment we should find 'quantitatively' a higher degree of pathology. But in order to accept this, we must consign many of the influential and productive members of society to the sphere of the pathological. Again we might take Freud as our example. His commitment to the fundamental principles of psychoanalysis was a powerful one. He pursued his logic to its extremes, and by the end of his career there were few who could follow him in his most radical theoretical innovations—for instance, that of the death instinct. In the eyes of his colleagues, Freud seemed to have cut himself off from the correctives of the evidence. We have seen that so convinced was he of his powers of interpretation over the thoughts of others that, confronted with the presence of unaccountable information in the minds of his patients, he concluded they must have been reading his thoughts. Thus, in one of his later essays, he postulated the occurrence of thought transference from one unconscious mind to another.[35] 'Quantitatively'—if such things can be quantified—Freud was heavily committed to the theoretical framework of psychoanalysis. In the same way, no doubt, Einstein was heavily committed to the theory of relativity, and, later in his life, heavily committed against quantum mechanics. But is not the power to follow original assumptions and intuitions to their logical conclusions over a long period of time the source of most important theories in the first place? Can we really assign these symptoms to the domain of pathology?

What I have been trying to show is that whether we are drawing a boundary between mentally healthy people and paranoids or between healthy and sick paranoids, the concept of 'paranoid construction' proves useless, for it applies to all thought at all times. And the concomitants of thought with which Meissner associates it are actually intellectual virtues. What Meissner, like Freud before him, is attempting to capture under the name 'paranoia' is simply thought itself, intellectual activity. This is why the clinician must ultimately resort to other evidences of dysfunction, such as the presence of obvious delusion, in order to diagnose mental illness.

We can tell there was something wrong with Schreber, it seems to me, not because he proposed himself as an important spiritual being—such people need not be mad—nor because he had a theory of the cosmos, but because he spent several hours a day bellowing and staring at himself in the mirror while decorated with feminine adornments. He actually thought he was being transformed into a woman, clearly a falsifiable and hallucinatory claim. And about certain things, like the hostile intentions and demonic powers of his doctor, he was in a state of constant error. It is difficult to understand why Meissner cannot accept these as "matters of fact." On all of these points, the good sense of Schreber's doctor, Dr. Weber, cannot be denied.

It is important to note a final irony that arises from this situation—that Meissner's identification of paranoia with religious thinking is a repetition of Schreber's original self-defense! Schreber argued that if his religious conceptions were evidence of insanity, then so were everyone else's. Logically, everyone who believes in divine beings should be behind bars. Schreber is perfectly right that to identify faith with madness is a futile gesture. His own doctor was not guilty of this, but Meissner certainly is. He has inherited from Freud a covertly polemical definition of madness, one that would lose its ideological force if it were applied only to those who actually suffer from mental disease.

Schreber cannot be understood as an overly credulous intellectual or a prophet. It is not the method of his thought that marks him as mentally ill but the way he applies it and, ultimately, the result. In this way, too, can we separate religious figures like Christ or Mohammed from mad prophets like Charles Manson or David Koresh. Religious teachers offer a message that transcends ordinary reality, but they do so in a way that comprehends it. And they generally recognize the difficulties of belief. They can be wrong without being crazy. Paranoids, on the other hand, believe without effort; and however transcendent their conceptions may be, they misinterpret the ordinary. This surely marks them as mad. Only by a kind of feedback do their ravings come into correspondence with reality, as in cases like that of Koresh and his followers; believing that the world is conspiring against them, and following out the consequences of that belief, they make it, in a sense, come true.

What makes paranoia an uncanny phenomenon is that in it we can sometimes see the human powers of logic, observation, and verbal expression working at their full capacities in the service of nonsense. What the paranoid lacks, as Chesterton put it, is "everything except his reason."[36]

Specifically, he shows an entire lack of judgment and of common sense, the knowledge of how to apply reason. What makes the psychologists' response to this phenomenon so odd is that, instead of asking how it is that the powers of observation and logic should have been so cut off from ordinary common sense, they have sought to put the blame upon reason itself. Facing his paranoid double, the psychologist falls back upon his own self-suspicion, and particularly the positivist suspicion of theory, labeled by Freud as 'projection', by Meissner as 'paranoid construction'. The psychologist is willing to recognize his own processes of thought as constituting a form of pathology, and he confirms this diagnosis by finding his own intellectual self-image ironically reflected in the thinking of the mad. By so thoroughly undermining the possibility of knowing the truth, these psychologists preserve no space for the possibility of error. All they have left, then, is one 'paranoid construction' or another.

What are the means of escaping from paranoia? For Meissner, and Freud, their resemblance to Schreber is evidence of a common nature and, as usual in psychoanalysis, this fact is given the most pejorative and suspicious interpretation possible. Both paranoid and theorist are involved in paranoia/thought. No matter how suspicious they may become of it, they cannot escape. In the case of Meissner we have seen the serious researcher attempting to struggle out of the conundrum of 'paranoid construction' that Freudian irony has set for him. The only true way out of it would be to distinguish paranoia from normal thought, so that there could be a form of thought about paranoia that is not itself paranoid. One would have to escape, in other words, from the polemical vocabulary of psychology as it was employed by Freud in his romance with Schreber and through the rest of his work. From a methodological perspective, this should not only be possible but unavoidable, for the whole point of the terms 'madness' and 'sanity' is to establish a difference that will set them in an explanatory relation to each other. If many of the attributes of paranoia belong to the sane as well, this tells us not that sanity is a mild version of paranoia but that paranoia involves a persistent misapplication of the faculties that permit most of us to be sane most of the time. This is in fact what Meissner is attempting to say, but the satirical and suspicious vocabulary of Freud compels him to make the category of disease more fundamental than that of health. Once we give up this prejudicial interpretation, the similarities between normal and paranoid thinking need no longer cause difficulty.[37]

But here, finally, we may note that another way of situating oneself in relation to Schreber has been devised; in considering it we will draw to a close our formal account of the long-term Quixotic effects of Freud's great psycho-satirical romance. The strategy to which I am referring is the one of setting a distance between oneself and Schreber by recognizing his superiority, the superiority that belongs to him as a 'schizophrenic', which is to say, a person who has escaped from the rational, 'paranoid' categories, divisions, and distinctions of thought. If 'paranoia' in the psychologist's vocabulary represents thought itself even in its own suspicion toward thought, schizophrenia, in the vocabulary of the modernist avant-garde, represents the escape from thought into primitive spontaneity and emotion.[38] Thus it becomes, for the paranoid intellectual, an object of ambitious emulation. One example will suffice. In the *Anti-Oedipus* of the French theorists Deleuze and Guattari—an urgent attempt to escape from the prison of Freudian Oedipal consciousness—we read the following eulogy of "Schreber-the-subject," a eulogy that takes Freud's Quixotic infatuation with Schreber to an unimagined level; it begins with the phrase, "*if* we are to believe Judge Schreber's doctrine," an "if" that goes without the very long pause, and perhaps a walk around the block, that it deserves:

Further, if we are to believe Judge Schreber's doctrine, *attraction and repulsion* produce intense *nervous states* that fill up the body without organs to varying degrees—states through which Schreber-the-subject passes, becoming a woman and many other things as well, following an endless circle of eternal return. The breasts on the judge's naked torso are neither delirious nor hallucinatory phenomena: they designate, first of all, a band of intensity, a zone of intensity on his body without organs. The body without organs is an egg: it is crisscrossed with axes and thresholds, with latitudes and longitudes and geodesic lines, traversed by *gradients* marking the transitions and the becomings, the destinations of the subject developing along these particular vectors. Nothing here is representative; rather, it is all life and lived experience: the actual, lived emotion of having breasts does not resemble breasts, it does not represent them, any more than a predestined zone in the egg resembles the organ that it is going to be stimulated to produce within itself. Nothing but bands of intensity, potentials, thresholds, and gradients. A harrowing, emotionally overwhelming experience, which brings the schizo as close as possible to matter, to a burning, living center of matter: [quoting Antonin Artaud] ". . . this emotion, situated outside of the particular point where the mind is searching for it . . . one's entire soul flows into this emotion that makes the mind aware of the terribly disturbing sound of matter, and passes through its white-hot flame."[39]

It would be fruitless to comment upon this passage, which is not a joke. It should be read more than once, to appreciate the "endless circle of eternal return," the "actual lived emotion of having breasts," which none of the persons involved can actually lay claim to, but is indeed, I suppose, different from, rather than resembling, breasts themselves. And so on. The authors are prestigious and influential figures in the French and American academies, one a philosopher, the other a psychiatrist. They have had to choose, it seems, between Freud and Schreber and have taken the hindmost, a decision for which, it must be admitted, some good Freudian precedent can be given. I will only observe that, whether or not they have succeeded in achieving the undifferentiated, "anti-Oedipal" consciousness they ascribe to "Schreber-the-subject" among other equally doubtful models, they have admirably succeeded in capturing his literary style, that unique combination of bodily exhibitionism, proliferating technicality, dogmatic certitude upon the most tenuous matters, and uninhibited fancy. The homeopathic cure for paranoia appears to be schizophrenia, and even Quixote was never so desperate.

Paranoia and Modernity

We began with the question of how it could come to pass that so many of the dominant figures of modern culture should exemplify the paranoid character. Attempting to approach this question starting with Freud's theory of paranoia, we have found that the concept 'paranoia' has a self-inclusive character: to accept Freud's theory of this condition, and all that goes with it, one must accept that one is oneself akin to the paranoid in psychology. And to the degree that one takes up psychoanalysis as a worldview, one tends to resemble the paranoid more and more. But this paranoid that one resembles is nothing other than a construction of the theory itself. The question now arises, once again, as to how this theoretical problem relates to the mentally ill, the real-world paranoids, whose existence in substantial numbers is beyond dispute. They, surely, cannot be mere by-products of a self-recursive intellectual paradigm.

The issue of the causal relation between modern culture and insanity is perilous.[40] In order to support the assertion that modern culture fosters paranoia, we would have first to ascertain that paranoia is more frequent in modern society than it is in pre-modern; the attempt, however, leads to problems of definition, for we would need to have at our disposal from the outset a transcultural description of paranoia, one that could be detached from the modern context. The studies that exist suggest that some psychoses are, indeed, less frequent and less serious in pre-modern societies than in modern ones.[41] Were this the case with paranoia, could we ascribe the paranoid susceptibilities of modern people to their intellectual culture? It is encouraging in this regard that well-educated people seem more suscepti-ble to the disease than those who are not.[42] But could paranoia not be more substantially a result of integration within the demanding superstructure of modern social and economic life rather than a symptom of intellectual culture? Further difficulties follow on from these. If the intellectual culture of modern people is to blame, who counts as 'modern'? Shall we include all of those who live in modern society or only those who share the typical presuppositions of modern thought? These difficulties lead us to the more fundamental one of employing the term 'modern' in a neutral, descriptive way, and of giving to it a fixed and substantial meaning. The quality 'modernity' seems most fittingly ascribed to those elements of culture that proclaim their own deliberate separation from the past, their own suspicion and hostility toward society and tradition, and their own self-consciousness of irrational excess — in other words, their own paranoia. Modernity in this sense *is* self-conscious paranoia. We have not escaped the vicious circle.

If the problem of etiology is too tenuous to pursue, perhaps we can say something more positive about the origins of paranoid symptoms. Some psychiatrists admit a distinction between the 'pathogenic' aspect of a dis-ease, its presumably biological cause, and the 'pathoplastic' aspect, that which determines its psychological content.[43] We could, making use of these terms, assume that a certain percentage of the population will be predisposed to mental illness in any culture, but that the culture in question determines the character of the symptoms. It is an attractive hypothesis, and has an evident basis.[44] We might now see paranoia as a successor in form to earlier mental illnesses that were characteristic of pre-modern Western culture and that evoked their own means of therapy. The mad, of course, have always been recognized and their peculiar mode of existence assigned a distinct value. The sublimity of madness is a theme that was preserved from before the time of Socrates till Erasmus at the brink of the modern. The onset of modernity brought with it, by contrast, a devaluation of madness coinciding with the general devaluation of the human being. A mad person becomes now no longer one inspired, or one possessed, but simply one who has a habitual dispositional tendency radically to err. It is a part of the suspicious character of this intellectual culture to insist upon its kinship with this devalued form of madness, and we might well wonder whether intellectual suspicion could not, by a kind of feedback, have given shape to a distinct mental disease that takes these traits to their extreme. Certainly the current of paranoid logic, psychology, and rhetoric among the makers of modern culture has enhanced the prospects of those given the than in science, that as a theorist he fits his own description of the paranoid, and that his inferences about human psychology are self-fulfilling and self-justifying, yet they hesitate to take the further step of acknowledging that, this being the case, psychoanalysis can simply have no value as a way of thinking about the psychology of human beings. "You have shown psychoanalysis to be one-sided, even monomaniacal," goes one line of this response, "in emphasizing the aggressive, suspicious, and lustful aspects of human psychology, but are these not important, even crucial, in our mental life? Aggression and desire are real. If Freud has explained no more than these, his achievement remains a notable and valuable one; it calls for others to balance and complete it while doing justice to those aspects of psychology Freud overlooked. Does psychoanalysis not remain persuasive and useful as an account of a large part of ordinary behavior?"

This objection would bear weight if we could indeed credit Freud with having understood those aspects of psychology he emphasized. Unfortunately, Freud is in a position rather like that of the philosopher Thales, who declared that the world was made entirely out of water. Thales misunderstood the world *and* he misunderstood water. When Freud reduced all of psychology to the transformations out of one or two central motives, or 'drives', he also misunderstood the behavior he attributed to the force of those drives. In fact the whole idea of 'drives', of human beings discharging themselves like batteries, is by now a pitiful anachronism. Not only did Freud overemphasize aggression and lustfulness, he fatally blurred the distinctions between these and other kinds of feeling and behavior. Making them the only true motives, he naturally misunderstood even these, and left us with a simplifying, rationalizing system in which the psychological universe is falsely reduced to one or two primary elements.

Aggression and lust are, of course, real, and so are many of the other phenomena observed by Freud. Our psychological experience was available to him as it is to the rest of us, and with the concentrated focus of his theory he magnified certain aspects of human behavior and brought them to the fore. My argument has been that his powers of observation were absurdly skewed in the direction of suspicion and that the chief object of his scrutiny, the unconscious, was a scientific fiction. We should not forget, however, that the claim of psychoanalysis to scientific value rests not upon Freud's ability to describe human psychology but upon his success in explaining it. The point of his observations is not merely to illustrate the implications of his theory but to validate it; and here he most egregiously fails. We must separate, then, the mythological persuasiveness of the

Freudian code of interpretation as it can be applied to everyday life from its validation as a scientific theory.

To clarify this point, let us consider Freud's concept of 'anal erotism', or 'anality', which has been firmly established as part of our commonsense moral vocabulary. Freud described a certain character or temperament exhibiting stinginess and stubbornness along with obsessive neatness and cleanliness; he called this the 'anal' character. Now there are, no doubt, people who display this character, and it is an almost irresistible temptation to accept their existence as a confirmation of psychoanalytic theory. But what, exactly, is the theory here? Freud conjectured that these 'anal' characters, in their relentless and obsessive need for control, were like an anus (or, more properly, sphincter) carrying out its mission to regulate the flow of human excrement. He took this likeness to be indicative of a causal connection: 'anal' characters exhibit a fixation in the anal stage of psycho-sexual development, when that organ is the primary locus of erotic plea-sure, and the narrowing and tightening, the making sphincter-like of the character represents an effort to sublimate the extraordinary pleasure some people are supposed to experience at that stage.[45] It is this leap of meta-phorical imagination upon which we are relying when we refer to someone as 'anal', that a person should come to resemble an organ. The explanatory value of the leap, though, derives not from the mere existence of 'anal' characters, nor from our ability to discern a likeness between characters and organs, but from the integration of these observations with Freud's theory of sexual development—the transformations and displacements of the libido, the dynamics of sublimation, repression, reaction formation, and so on. Detached from these, Freud's observation of the similarity between a constriction of the character and the constricted anus becomes a mere piece of whimsy, a combination of sympathetic magic and satiric wit. And once we have recognized the general inadequacy of Freud's theory, neither the wit of his magical materialism nor the convenience of the ready-made armamentarium of derision furnished by the psychoanalytic vocabulary will make up for its lack of explanatory value.

"You criticize Freud," my friendly critic now replies, "both for his credulity in the domain of explanation and, at the very same time, for his excessive skepticism, his too suspicious scrutiny of human attempts to understand and master the world by means of intellect. One moment Freud is too critical and suspicious, the next moment he is not critical enough. Freud can't win. What does it mean, furthermore, given your generally skeptical attitude toward modern scientific culture, that Freud fails to be 'scientific'? Is 'scientific' more than an empty compliment here? What 'science' would you put in place of psychoanalysis? Freud has offered us a powerful hermeneutic model for interpreting the world, one that helps us make sense of things every day. Can you offer something better, something stronger and more compelling than this?"

The skeptical reader is correct to observe that Freud is guilty in my account both of excessive suspicion and of speculative recklessness, but we can remedy this apparent contradiction by distinguishing the objects to which Freud's suspicion and his credulity apply. Freud views the collective achievements of past culture and the motives of all around him with a penetrating suspicion. And this suspicion, we have seen, turns back, with ostentatious self-scrutiny, on his own motives as well. This scrutiny, though, does not apply to Freud the master of suspicion, but only to Freud the dreamer, Freud the well-meaning physician, comic victim of slips of the tongue, naively ambitious professional and clumsy fugitive from the censor's gaze. Like Dante the pilgrim of the *Divine Comedy*, all of the dreamer Freud's imperfections and susceptibilities are on display for the edification and entertainment of the reader. But like Dante the poet, Freud the scientist, orchestrator of this grand romance, stands above scrutiny. Making a show of caution, he builds one fragile inference upon another until a great tottering cosmos of speculation has been erected. Freud the scientist never looks back. His suspicious scrutiny is not methodological but disingenuously moral, and his sins are sins of the unconscious, where none of us, apparently, shall 'scape whipping.

As for the honorific title of the scientist, Freud noisily claimed it for himself, insisting that devotion to psychoanalysis called for the staunchest and most implacable scientific resolve. His claim to be scientific was first a moral claim. While I have shown Freud's scientific pose to be a theatrical effect, my intent has not been to replace Freud's way of thinking about science with a better theory of science. My complaints about the 'scientific' failure of psychoanalysis rely not upon a theory of science but upon what any theory of science must account for—the fact that, in ordinary scientific practice, better explanations cast out poorer ones. This is what scientists attempt to do, to provide better and better descriptions and explanations. Theories of science may disagree about what counts as an explanation, how theory relates to fact and fact to theory, what makes one theory better than another, and even whether or not there is always a common conceptual framework, or 'paradigm', within which rival theories can confront each other. But no theory can seriously call into question the fact that to do science is to seek the best explanation, however tenuously or pragmatically that is conceived. We must grant this much if science is to be possible at all. And the theory of psychoanalysis is simply not, by any measure, the best explanation for the phenomena it attempts to address. At every level Freud's evidence was contaminated with his own interpretive activity. We can see with hindsight that his great persuasiveness lay in providing a new, hidden locus of meaning, the unconscious, and using it as a Cartesian starting point from which the psychological world could be systematically rebuilt after the demolition of the pre-existing cultural order. The potency of this maneuver lies not in explanation but interpretation, in an interpretation grounded upon suspicion.

When it comes to that inevitable question, about psychoanalysis, whether I can offer "something better, something stronger and more compelling" than its hermeneutic system, I must admit that to compete with Freud on this level would be beyond my powers. My modesty must be disingenuous, however, as I do not, of course, believe that we should replace psychoanalysis with another great hermeneutic code. The idea that one can only discredit a way of thinking by replacing it with another *in the same kind* is false; otherwise the doctrine of the Rosicrucians would be still among us, or something like it. It is enough that each of the details brought forward by Freud as evidence for psychoanalysis can be explained on other, more likely terms.

The underlying assumption for those who take up the 'hermeneutic stance' is that all the activities of culture can be understood as forms of interpretation. Interpretation is fundamental to experience itself. There are great complexities here; the hermeneutic philosophy has been put forward by gifted and sophisticated theorists. I may point out, however, simply, that if all of our normal investigative thinking is to be described in hermeneutic terms, then hermeneutics will have to account for the discrediting of theories that do not hold their weight—theories, that is to say, like psychoanalysis. Hermeneutics, in this case, would be an attempt to give an account of the process of inquiry, but it would not alter the results. If, on the other hand, we are going to use the hermeneutic theory to introduce a new, 'hermeneutic' kind of truth, which stands or falls merely on the persuasiveness of the interpretations themselves, then we are on treacherous ground. Two observations will, I hope, suffice to suggest why this is so. First, it should discourage us from overestimating the value of interpretation to realize that all interpretive systems succeed in producing them. The reason for this is that they work upon the products of human intentionality, upon what are already meaningful structures; their privileged objects are texts. They operate by choosing certain features as the key to interpretation and subordinating all others to these. Marxists emphasize themes of class, Nietzscheans power, Freudians the 'drives', and so on. One could do as well *as an interpreter* by choosing the 57th word of each text as the key to significance. The astonishing fertility of medieval religious hermeneutics assures us that there is almost no limit to ingenuity in interpretation, no limit to the number of levels of meaning or to the polysemic fecundity of the sign. This is why theories must stand or fall not by interpretive success but by how well the interpreted data support the underlying explanations when confronted with rival theories. The hard part for the interpreter is explaining why sex, why class, why 57 should be the bass note of all understanding. Freudian readings, then, depend upon the validation of Freud's theory, and not, primarily, the other way around. For this reason, too, psychoanalysis cannot be saved as a form of literary criticism when it fails as an account of human psychology: the hermeneutic code cannot live without the underlying explanatory model. Freud never admitted the limits upon the value of interpretation. Believing that every hermeneutic deployment of psychoanalysis was a confirmation of it, he continued throughout his life to draw assurance from the seemingly uncanny fact that, no matter how bold and speculative his explanatory hypotheses, the interpretations just kept working out.

The strong hermeneutic stance has a second fatal aspect besides the fact that interpretive systems never fail to satisfy their own requirements for success: if there is nothing available to us but rival interpretations, that position is itself nothing but an interpretation. Our attention, then, moves to the next obvious question: Who benefits from the success of this interpretation? On what authority does the hermeneutician certify the hermeneutic stance? Whence derives its generalizing and universalizing privilege? We are back to the paranoid logic we found at the heart of psychoanalysis, the logic that makes inquiry ultimately a war of all against all, producing a situation in which any claim to authority looks like an indefensible excess. The move to the hermeneutic stance in this stronger version involves a shift of vocabularies away from explanation toward interpretation per se; but it remains no less reductive for that.

"Well," my friendly skeptic now replies, "are you not being a bit optimistic estimating the degree to which you yourself have escaped from the Freudian hermeneutic stance? Isn't Freud for you a kind of secret sharer? He is suspicious, but you are suspicious of him. You unmask the unmasking critique, but the unmasking even of an unmasking critique is, itself, an unmasking critique. Wouldn't your argument be more persuasive if, instead of denying all value to psychoanalysis, you admitted your ironic resemblance to Freud?" This objection was put to me by a particularly valued respondent, who, though willing to assent to my characterization of Freud's totalizing mode, was nevertheless perplexed by the unqualifiedly negative character of my assessment of psychoanalysis. My response must be that Freud is categorically suspicious of everyone, while I claim to be suspicious only where a particular cause demands it. And this leads me to be suspicious, or, more properly, skeptical, of him. What choice does one have when one is told, "Be suspicious of everyone"? One can either follow this paranoid advice or react suspiciously and skeptically toward the person who gives it.

It is important to note, also, that my analysis does not take the form of an unmasking critique or a "hermeneutics of suspicion," to use Paul Ricoeur's memorable phrase. Unlike Nietzsche, Marx, and Freud, the paradigmatic practitioners of this mode, I have not attempted to provide a new key to all mythologies. The primary lesson I expect my readers to draw from this work is simply that they should forget what they thought they had learned from psychoanalysis and become skeptical about those suspicious aspects of modern culture developed to their maturity in Freud. The "masters of suspicion," though, have a different aim. They want to implement a hermeneutic system—a whole paranoid view of life—founded on the relation between surface and depth, between accepted appearance and denied reality. They unmask this relation of discrepancy, of social dissimulation and metaphysical trumpery, but, except in the case of Marx, they do not expect to overcome it. The heroism of unmasking lies in recognition and stoical endurance, in the simple acceptance of the truth of suspicion. In the machinery of the unmasking critique, surface and depth hold each other in place and become the repositories of all opposite qualities, leading to a black and white, Hatfields and McCoys view of life. The depth of this vision is the rhetorical foil of its superficiality, its subtlety the by-product of the intricate and ingenious casuistical operations necessary to reduce the welter of phenomena in such a narrow scheme. And at the bottom is, of course, the single, primal cosmological constituent. I do not share this project.

The antidote to this seductive form of suspicion would not be an excessively trusting optimism, I might add, but an attempt to recognize the actual complexity of human existence, to avoid reducing it in the abstract, rigid, and facilely moralizing categories of surface and depth; and, when there are depths—which is to say, complexities—of the moral kind, to confront them, at least in principle, in their contradictory appearances, and to bring what can be known onto the same plane of discussion, rather than attempting to make deceitfulness and contradiction the primary rule of understanding. Freud himself professed an ambition something like this one, but his failure as a therapist led him ultimately to be content, like Captain Nemo, admiring the depths of the undersea world he claimed to have discovered. And this was more or less inevitable given that for Freud deceit was a creature not merely of human fallibility, weakness, or evil but of a hidden structure of the mind. Once he had unmasked what he took to be the mere appearances of conscious, ordinary life, they were not to be confronted but, rather, merely translated in the code of the unconscious, made unreal and ridiculous, esotericized, and reduced to childishness.

"Your analysis leaves Freud with much to answer for," my friendly skeptic properly observes, "yet you have gone out of your way to show that his thinking is a development out of the central strain of modern philosophical and scientific culture. Can all of the great figures you cite be so misguided? If they are, your singling out of Freud seems the product of an extraordinary animus, surely the grudge of an ex-believer. Is this why you feel the need to address Freud with irony and to deny psychoanalysis *any* claim to value? Hasn't it at least opened up fruitful areas of inquiry? Why pick on Freud?" I can, first of all, and with a good conscience, disclaim that I have ever been a devotee of psychoanalysis, though I have participated in other forms of paranoid hermeneutics. My disapproval of Freud is not that of a jilted lover. I picked him from the phalanx of suspicion as a salient and clear example of the paranoid trend of modern culture, and because his treatment of paranoia naturally stood in the way of mine and had, thus, to be confronted. As for the breadth of my critique, which pertains not to science itself but to a suspicious understanding of the process of inquiry that stems largely from modern philosophy, I am by no means the first to suggest that the path of speculation inaugurated by Bacon, Descartes, Hobbes, and Locke, among others, needs to be reevaluated and perhaps done away with. That has long been a refrain among religious perennialists and some conservative humanists, and they have been joined in recent decades by a growing chorus of progressive and radical intellectuals following the lead of William James, Heidegger, Wittgenstein, and others. I might cite Charles Taylor, Richard Rorty, and Alasdair MacIntyre, currently, as among the most trenchant and significant

Conclusion

By way of conclusion, let us enumerate the main points of the argument, along with a few more general implications:

1. Freud was correct in his claim that paranoia has a special connection with modern culture but wrong about the character of that connection. It is not on account of the suppression of religious impulses by science that paranoia achieves its force and visibility in modern experience. Rather, paranoia becomes a viable, even normal stance when intellectual culture depends fundamentally and without limit upon suspicion of the faculties that make it possible.

2. Paranoid psychology is a natural derivative from the contradictions of reductionist logic. Among the many confluent elements of modern suspicion, psychoanalysis develops the suspicious aspects of scientific methodology, empiricist and Kantian epistemology, historical idealism, and Hobbesian political philosophy. Freud's argument that the culture of science had redirected religious energies into neurosis and paranoia is viciously circular, since what it points to as the supposedly indirect cause of suspicion, invisible to consciousness, is a way of thinking founded immediately upon suspicion and, by means of suspicion, proclaiming its modernity. To understand the connection between paranoia and modernity, therefore, we need not resort to 'unconscious repression' and the like; we need only observe deliberate strategies of psychological repression: deployments of suspicious logic and rhetoric in the hands of grandiose and suspicious personalities whose talents, under the regime of paranoia, bring them to the fore.

3. As the leader and chief theorist, analyst, and analysand of psychoanalysis, Freud exhibits the full range of paranoid symptoms: grandiosity, centrality, the perception of hostility in the social environment, irrational fears of persecution, obsessive concern with autonomy and control, massive projection, and the most far-flung possible interpretive system of suspicion.

Freud failed precisely where the paranoiac fails, and succeeded brilliantly where he succeeds.

4. Freud's tendency is not to obscure his paranoid characteristics but to emphasize them and to convince his readers that they share the same characteristics 'unconsciously'. He makes the bravery of acknowledging his paranoid affinities the basis of an advantage through a rhetoric of heroic irony. By generating a fully developed scientific system of suspicion, Freud's psychology becomes both self-fulfilling and self-justifying.

5. Just as Freud is both analyst and analysand, so he is both exponent and victim of paranoid logic. He inherited from his intellectual precursors a powerful ideology of suspicion with a long history of anti-traditional, progressivist deployments. His position as part of a socially repressed ethnic minority in the reactionary and increasingly fascistic environment of the Habsburg empire contributed special animus and energy to the ideological application of his science. The paranoid qualities of Freud's intellectual and social inheritance enhanced the embattled and suspicious aspect of his character.

6. The psychoanalytic interpretive system of suspicion works by making egotism of a megalomaniacal sort the energizing motive of human consciousness. This, for Freud, is the form in which our repressed narcissistic sexuality strives to express itself. Interpretation can cease only when it comes upon the selfish, egotistical motif. The interpretations are self-sustaining and depend upon drama and narrative coherence rather than empirical confirmation.

7. Freudian suspicion does not have the character of worldly wisdom, but is purely a rationalizing form of construction. It does fasten upon aspects of experience that are, indeed, part of everyday life: hypocrisy and social theatricality, self-aggrandizement and self-deception, competitiveness, heroic fantasy, suspicion, resentfulness, childishness, vainglory, lust, and fear. But these become evidence of an 'unconscious' realm of perfect, unqualified, cleverly disguised egotism exercising relentless ingenuity in order to conceal its presence from the conscious mind. The unconscious maintains a Cartesian consistency in its irrational aims, ensuring that nothing we do is without meaning. It is this assumption of perfect consistency in the unconscious mind that permits psychoanalysis to achieve its systematically rationalizing form.

8. The concept 'paranoia' is itself a hostile, satirical invention. It points to the fact that the apparatuses of thought can operate at the highest level of coherence, employing the most exalted means of verbal expression,

while serving nonetheless to sustain a framework of utter delusion. The theorists of paranoia, rather than seeking the fault in the paranoid's deficient application of intellectual powers, take the paranoid's intellectual performance as a spectacle discrediting to the nature of those powers themselves. With reductive exactitude and satiric economy, they include their own activity in the spectacle as well.

9. In constructing his image of the modern, paranoid character, Freud imitated Cervantes' depiction of Don Quixote, providing his subject with an 'unconscious' that consists of vulgar and historically discredited elements of culture. These elements, lodged in the unconscious, become, like Quixote's favorite romances, the models for Freud's own compulsive, delusory, comic repetitions, as described in *The Interpretation of Dreams.*

10. Freud can best be understood as a rhetorician of genius who has taken a satiric image of men and women and made it the norm, applying it even to himself. Calling it rhetoric, as I have done, perhaps obscures the fact that it is not so much a way of writing as a consistently held vision of life. This being the case, Freud actually exemplifies the satiric psychology from which his rhetoric derives. His behavior reflects not only the symptoms of the paranoid character mentioned in number 3 above, but also the infatuation with the paranoid, and the hilarious intoxication with satiric language that are central to the humor of Cervantes' paranoid spectacle.

11. Freud was not the first to make the satiric image of the paranoid into an exemplary vision of the human spirit. The Romantic revaluation of Cervantes' comic hero had already achieved this transformation, creating the idealized Quixote who enchanted Freud in his youth. Freud achieved a psychologizing repetition of the Romantic 'return of the repressed' in which discredited, vulgar elements of culture acquired a new moral and imaginative value.

12. Freudian 'psycho-history' has what is ostensibly a progressive cast. It imagines that each individual recapitulates in his or her psychological development the development of the species, from primal father to modern scientist. This development proceeds by repression, the means by which we leave the past behind. Paranoids and other failed psyches undergo a reactionary reversion to more primitive, historically retrograde states of consciousness. But the true model of repression and return at the heart of the Freudian psyche is not the evolutionary development of the race but the development of modern culture itself. This culture has also undergone the pattern of repression and return—Enlightenment repression and Romantic return. The progressive aspect of Freud's narrative remains potent only

insofar as it applies to the development of science itself. For what Freudian science tells us is that we cannot truly leave the past behind. The primeval dragons remain in the unconscious mind, awaiting their chance.

13. Freud's account of the development of individual psychology from infancy and the 'pleasure principle' to adulthood and the 'principle of reality' is evidently a historical ideology injected onto the domain of the psyche. In becoming adults, we are told, each of us strives to leave behind what is "primitive" in us—what belongs, that is, to other, pre-modern cultures—and reach "civilization." Political critiques of psychoanalysis that emphasize merely its privatizing, depoliticizing characteristics overlook this underlying social and political myth.

14. An inventory of what Freud called the unconscious would have to include the disguised presences of a number of distinguished emigrés from the modern philosophical bestiary. Alongside them we recognize a familiar gallery of human foibles: our social fictitiousness, or tendency toward censorship, concealment, and touching up of our true motives; our wishes that certain doctrines, such as those of religion, should be true; the culturally defined vulgarity of the body and of certain socially disreputable, or "primitive," forms of culture, all satirically envisioned. There is actually nothing hidden or mysterious in any of these, nor any need for an 'unconscious' to explain them, unless one has, of course, a bent for mystery and suspiciousness, a vocation for things hidden, difficult, esoteric, and uncanny.

15. Psychoanalysis accords to each of us a personal mythology, as we struggle with the psycho-historical traces of the conflicts of the past. But in essence what we are offered is a repetition of Freud's own Quixotic psychomythology, his own paranoid quest. What was contingently true of Freud—that he was relentlessly suspicious, competitive, hostile, and heroically embattled—becomes, through the force of his imagination, true for those who are willing to accept the necessity of his assumptions.

16. Having recognized the charismatic appeal of the paranoid figure, an appeal deeply grounded in Romanticism and the culture of irony, we can see why Freud himself exerts such peculiar charisma to this day: when paranoia is the only available form of heroism—all others having been skeptically disallowed—the heroism of irony becomes the last resource of ambition and the last object to admire.

Epilogue

> "Tell me, Sancho my friend, what are they saying
> about me in the village here? What do the common
> people think of me? What do the *hidalgos?* What
> do the *caballeros?* What do they say of my valor, of
> my achievements, and of my courtesy? How do
> they regard the task I have undertaken to revive
> and restore to the world the now forgotten order of
> chivalry?"
> —Quixote

In the late afternoon of August 27, 1979, while descending from the #16 trolley on the outskirts of Amsterdam, I was hailed in French by a man in a tattered jacket leaning on a cane who introduced himself as Rico Julien Marie Lucien, a great and persecuted writer and a political and religious leader of genius. He was about sixty, much the worse for wear, and had the familiar face and beard of Solzhenitsyn except for a gash on the crown of his nose. He carried his possessions and clothing in a bucket that also served him as a stool. Had he spoken to me in English I would have known better than to answer him. In French, however, I was without guile. A Romantic wanderer between college and grad school, I was held immediately in fascination by the paranoid's exalted aura.

France was sick, he told me. "Les communistes, les socialistes, les juifs capitalistes, et Giscard d'Estaing" had calumniated him, shot him in the back, and taken away his two million francs. "On m'a calomnié!" And to prove it he pulled out his shirt-tails and exposed to me his wound, a twisted depression that went deep into the base of his spine. Having been so reduced by his enemies, he was forced to ask me for assistance. Would I lend him 50,000 francs to be repaid by the Canadian ambassador upon demand? I offered ten guilders, which he took for a princely sum. He kissed me vehemently on both cheeks. "Vive les États-Unis! Vive le Canada! Vive la Hollande!" he shouted as if to an audience of admirers, pausing after each outburst for my brother, Ed, and me to second him.

"Your father must be very rich to send you here," he observed. "May I have your watch?" "My father is a bricklayer," I told him. He was delighted. "Un maçon! You know Maurice Chevalier?" Without waiting for an answer he started a song and dance, shuffling flat-footed, singing hoarsely. By this time a dozen cars had pulled up at the red light, and the drivers were looking on with sympathetic amusement at what they took to be my predicament.

But I was absorbed with the fate of my interlocutor, who was on his way to the United States to be given a pension that would allow him to carry on his crusade "comme Jeanne d'Arc, comme Luther!" The Canadian ambassador was going to arrange his trip to America so that he could meet with his great ally, an extraordinary American woman politician whose name and title I could not interpret no matter how many times he repeated them for me. Finally he offered to write it down: "Her excellency, Shirley Temple, celebrated actress of the American cinema, beautiful woman politician with perfect form, emblem of virtue and vigilance. Shirley Temple, I love you!"

I finally extricated myself from Monsieur Lucien by directing him to the *Bureau d'Accueil* where I knew he would receive a doubtful welcome even with his ten guilders, which was only enough for a single night's accommodation. Since my reaction to Monsieur Lucien's behavior is an important part of the story, I am going to quote the end of my diary account of this episode written at the time:

I could only give him ten guilders ($5)—last broken-down day of our trip. He asked me again for my watch. I told him it was the only one we had. He asked for my silver pen. I granted it. I directed him to the station to find a room. He talked feverishly on and on, waiting for the tram. It came three times. —Le prochain, le prochain. Are they talking about me in the United States? —I've heard your name. —Who, the religious or the politicians? —The politicians. —The politicians! What do they say? —I don't remember, but they are talking about you. Perhaps they are awaiting your arrival. How his eyes glowed! —Monsieur Lucien, I said, I know very well that you have many enemies, but if it is possible, I would like to remember you with a photograph. —Une photo! Oui! Attendez! My brother focuses the camera, Monsieur Lucien tucks himself in furiously, we clasp hands, he salutes the air. Snap. —Another. —Yes, of my back! Once again the gaping stigma is shown, the shutter flips as the Dutch onlookers turn away in disgust. We gave him a ticket for the #16, told him it was only good for the next trip (true), loaded him on. He kissed me for the thousandth time on both cheeks, disappeared as I stood there waving him off to the uncertain fate I had pointed him toward. He was still shouting "Vive les États-Unis! Vive le Canada!" and even "Vive la

France!" How I loved this crazy man! In him I had seen that rare idealism which utterly subordinates self to cause. It did not matter the cause was mad. I felt its ennoblement and grieved at the reception I knew the old man of *soixante ans* would get at the station. Poor Don Quixote with no Sancho Panza to look after him! I had let him down and felt wretched. I had betrayed that magnificent smile of his, the uncontainable joy and Gallic exuberance with which he sang Maurice Chevalier. His acquaintance with generosity was familiar, his self-respect and affectionate regard untainted by posture of need. Never a trace of self-pity!

The tale I have told is in its outlines a familiar one to readers of modern literature—the encounter with the "greybeard loon." Yet today when I read these extravagant words from my diary I can still remember the sense I had at the time that the experience was indescribable, that I could not set its details in order, for each of them could only be comprehended from within the glow of Monsieur Lucien's personality and none of them individually could begin to convey that. My pen trembled before the page.

Readers of this book will no longer expect a Freudian interpretation of this episode. They will not expect me to believe that I was experiencing a surge of repressed narcissism evoked by Monsieur Lucien's uninhibited self-exaltation. If I found myself admiring and envying this paranoid, it was because I shared the irony toward my own thinking, the self-conscious suspiciousness that made it possible for Freud to exalt Schreber to the level of a collaborator, and which in turn has made Freud himself an object of infatuation. Well do I remember that summer Eurail trek when I ransacked the Continent for traces of its heroic past, for the sense of struggle with natural and historical necessities that, in my mind, was the source of authentic experience. I had already absorbed the teachings of psychoanalysis, but Freud was not my favorite paranoid. I was, rather, a melancholy Nietzschean, skeptical of all dogmas and conventions, seeing through every philosophy and institution the hidden interests that had thrust them into existence. The only refuge from this suspicious nihilism and heroic irony would come in the form of certain vague epiphanies, blissfully unaccountable vibrations of the atmosphere that could somehow make their way onto the page, *intermittences du coeur* too tenuous and fleeting to be the objects of skepticism or suspicion. I had read with anguish the brilliant passage of *Tristes Tropiques* in which Claude Lévi-Strauss announces that the entire human habitat has been explored and its range of experience established. There was nothing left, as Pynchon would say, but tourism, the Baedeker world, a world not at all up to my heroic literary vocation. I was ready to meet my paranoid alter ego, a man whose heroism was as grotesquely divorced from reality as my own, but who could express it and embody it sincerely, bravely, generously, or so it seemed.

A number of people to whom I have told this story have drawn the immediate conclusion that Monsieur Lucien was gloriously pulling my leg, that he was a con man, and it is hard for me to deny that there was a certain practical element in his delirium. Could he have "sucked it all from his fingers," as Schreber would say? My inclination is to think that if the fellow had that much calculating ingenuity at his disposal, he would have found better employment for it. But whether he was a naive or merely a sentimental paranoid, Monsieur Lucien's routine worked because it was a flawlessly updated version of the Quixote myth. It had the heroizing megalomania and pathetic generosity of soul, calumniating enemies as numerous as the enchanters who bedevil Quixote, and, in Shirley Temple, a suitably idealized and inaccessible feminine object of adoration. Even the praise of the lady was accomplished with Quixotically elevated and pedantic rhetoric (and some strange French): "Son excellence, Madame Shirley Temple, actrice célèbre du cinéma americain, belle femme politique avec du forme parfait [sic], emblème de la virtu et de la vigilance. Shirley Temple, je vous aime bien!" It is to be noted as well that my delight in Monsieur Lucien was so great that, like many of Quixote's admirers, I was willing to mislead him in order to confirm his delusion. The paranoid's charms produce the manipulation that he fears. In the delightful pages of Cervantes there is more to be learned about paranoia than from the laborious productions of psychology. His witty folie à deux has become a folie à deux mondes.

Meeting Monsieur Lucien was an aesthetic pleasure, but it need not have been. My detachment from the spectacle of his paranoia, grounded as it was in my philosophical stance, depended as well upon the fact that I felt no responsibility for the consequences of his condition. I was a tourist and he, it seems, an exile. Things might have been otherwise. By the same token, Monsieur Lucien had no power to impose his mad vision upon me. I did not meet him as a member of a class, part of a community, or the leader of an institution. His powerlessness was necessary to my admiration. We might make the same observation about Schreber in relation to Freud. But the allure of paranoia need not be innocent. How much the comical Monsieur Lucien shares, for instance, with Adolf Hitler: the mad and desperate grandeur, the enemies, including Jewish enemies, the fervid eloquence, and a Quixotic demeanor that could appear comical and Chaplinesque or sublime and entrancing depending upon one's point of view. Hitler even had a crush on a truly inaccessible and ideal object of love—his favorite actress, Shirley Temple. The convergence I am pointing toward has to do not with political programs and their moral value but with psychology and imagination: Does a culture that revels in the ironic heroism of Quixote, Schreber, Nietzsche, and Freud also leave itself vulnerable to the rhetoric and allure of paranoid leaders? Or have I succumbed at the last moment to the intellectual and rhetorical temptations of the uncanny coincidence, those very temptations I set out from the beginning to dispel?

Notes

Introduction

1. On paranoia in America see Richard Hofstadter's seminal observations in *The Paranoid Style in American Politics and Other Essays* (New York: Knopf, 1966).

2. See Leo Braudy, "Providence, Paranoia, and the Novel," *English Literary History* 48 (1981): 619–37.

3. Letter to Marie Bonaparte of August 13, 1937. *Letters of Sigmund Freud*, trans. Tania and James Stern, ed. Ernest L. Freud (New York: Basic Books, 1961), 436. I have replaced Freud's phrase "questions the meaning of life" in the translation with "asks about the meaning of life," which is closer to his intent.

4. The case against Freud developed by scholars in recent years has been trenchantly and provocatively summarized in a number of reviews and essays by Frederick Crews. See *The Memory Wars: Freud's Legacy in Dispute* (New York: New York Review of Books, 1996). See also "The Freudian Temptation," Part One of *Skeptical Engagements* (New York: Oxford University Press, 1986), 1–111. For two excellent, wide-ranging, and highly critical assessments of the value of psychoanalytic doctrine see Allen Esterson, *Seductive Mirage: An Exploration of the Work of Sigmund Freud* (Chicago: Open Court, 1993), and Malcolm Macmillan, *Freud Evaluated: The Completed Arc* (New York: Elsevier Science, 1991).

Just as this book was going to press, Richard Webster's compelling synoptic critique of psychoanalysis, *Why Freud Was Wrong: Sin, Science, and Psychoanalysis* (New York: Basic Books, 1995) appeared.

5. The most penetrating critique of the methods by which psychoanalysts have attempted to validate Freud's theories with clinical evidence has been provided in two studies by Adolf Grünbaum, *The Foundations of Psychoanalysis: A Philosophical Critique* (Berkeley: University of California Press, 1984), and *Validation in the Clinical Theory of Psychoanalysis: A Study in the Philosophy of Psychoanalysis*, *Psychological Issues* 61 (Madison, Conn.: International Universities Press, 1993). In the former Grünbaum concentrates on the problems of epistemic contamination in the data gathered in psychoanalytic sessions, and in the latter on the absence of demonstrated causal connections between these data, even if they could in principle be reliably gathered, and the phenomena they are supposed by the theory to explain.

6. E. M. Thornton, *The Freudian Fallacy: An Alternative View of Freudian*

Theory (Garden City, N.Y.: The Dial Press, 1984). The value of Thornton's analysis of Freud's clinical practice is repeatedly confirmed by the researches of Webster in Part One of his work cited above. See also the provocative article by Peter Swales, "Freud, Fliess, and Fratricide: The Role of Fliess in Freud's Conception of Paranoia," in *Sigmund Freud: Critical Assessments*, ed. Laurence Spurling (New York: Routledge, 1989) 1: 302–30.

7. See the critical comments in Macmillan, 17–18.

8. Louis A. Sass, *Madness and Modernism: Insanity in the Light of Modern Art, Literature, and Thought* (New York: Basic Books, 1992). I tend to locate the affinities between culture and madness in its modern acceptation as stemming from the seventeenth century, just as Freud did. Sass is like Freud in taking the culture of modernity and its psychological consequences more or less at face value, objecting only to the last, most paradoxical modernist and postmodernist ironizing of consciousness. Despite these differences, and despite Sass's phenomenological method, which contrasts with my primary emphasis upon the logical and the rhetorical, I believe that the results of this study are quite compatible with his.

9. Paul Roazen, *Freud and His Followers* (New York: NAL, 1971), 407–8.

10. This is not to imply, of course, that there is anything particularly Jewish about paranoia or about the suspicious trend of thought I address in this book. Freud was tapping into a deep vein at the heart of modern culture, already hundreds of years old and certainly not limited to Jewish intellectuals. If Jews have a distinctive connection with paranoia, it is as prime targets of paranoid hostility and conceit.

Chapter One

1. In this work I have assigned the masculine pronoun both to the paranoid and, by and large, to the psychoanalyst as well. My reasons for doing so are that the paranoid character, as prominently represented in modern culture both in history and literature, is almost exclusively male. This is a fact with interesting and possibly profound implications for our understanding of the historical experience of gender, implications I hope eventually to treat in a wider study of paranoia and modernity. My frequent reference to the psychoanalyst in masculine terms is not meant to ignore the contributions of women psychoanalysts but to focus my scrutiny most sharply upon Sigmund Freud, most of my allusions to "the psychoanalyst" being more or less direct and particular references to him.

2. "Psycho-Analytic Notes on an Autobiographical Account of a Case of Paranoia (Dementia Paranoides)," *S.E.* 12: 71.

3. Freud posits the symptoms leading out of the four negative logical permutations of "I love him," each a different form of denial leading to delusions of persecution, erotomania, delusions of jealousy, and megalomania respectively. "Notes on an Autobiographical Account," *S.E.* 12: 59–65.

4. "On Narcissism: An Introduction," *S.E.* 14: 88–89.

5. *Jokes and Their Relation to the Unconscious*, *S.E.* 8: 90–116.

6. "The uncanny is that class of the frightening which leads back to what is

known of old and long familiar." "The 'Uncanny'," *S.E.* 17: 220. 'Uncanny' experiences include the imaginary becoming real, seeing one's double, the female genitals, burial alive, silence, darkness, solitude, and psychoanalysis (243–46).

7. For a presentation of Freud's historical thinking from this point of view see Robert A. Paul, "Freud's Anthropology: A Reading of the 'Cultural Books,' " in *The Cambridge Companion to Freud,* ed. Jerome Neu (New York: Cambridge University Press, 1991), 267–86, and also "Did the Primal Crime Take Place?" *Ethos* 4 (1976): 311–52.

8. *Moses and Monotheism, S.E.* 23: 101–2. See the editor's footnote (102n) for a list of citations on the concept of archaic memory, which is given its most detailed treatment in this late work.

9. Freud is speaking here of the religious heroes who gave birth to the super-ego, but the point extends to all of the other heroic renouncers who have given impetus to human progress. *Civilization and Its Discontents, S.E.* 21: 141.

10. *Group Psychology and the Analysis of the Ego, S.E.* 18: 135 and 122 respectively.

11. "It seems quite possible that all the things that are told to us today in analysis as phantasy . . . were once real occurrences in the primaeval times of the human family, and that children in their phantasies are simply filling the gaps in individual truth with prehistoric truth." *Introductory Lectures on Psycho-Analysis, S.E.* 16: 371.

12. It is telling that Freud does not imagine the 'primal horde' as a bisexual unit even though he considers the fundamental human psychology to be bisexual. What we find, rather, is a respectable heterosexual patriarchy in which the mothers and daughters are kept from the sons.

13. *Group Psychology, S.E.* 18: 123–24.

14. The psychology of the mothers and daughters, objects both of domination and desire, has in this account left no trace in the human constitution.

15. *Totem and Taboo, S.E.* 13: 143. The page numbers cited parenthetically in this and the next two paragraphs of the text are from this volume.

16. *Totem and Taboo, S.E.* 13: 149.

17. *Group Psychology, S.E.* 18: 136.

18. Otto Rank, *The Myth of the Birth of the Hero and Other Writings,* ed. Philip Freund (New York: Vintage Books, 1932). The central theoretical passage of this book was interpolated by Freud and later published separately under the title "Family Romances," *S.E.* 9: 235–41.

19. *Totem and Taboo, S.E.* 13: 156.

20. *Group Psychology, S.E.* 18: 137.

21. Christianity was, by contrast, a son religion. It represented for Freud a regression in cultural terms, "as regularly happens when a new mass of people, of a lower level, break their way in or are given admission." Christianity reintroduced a vulgar proliferation of deities. But in its doctrine of original sin Freud found a recognition of the historical truth of the primal crime. *Moses, S.E.* 23: 111, 88, and 86 respectively.

22. *Group Psychology, S.E.* 18: 102.

23. *Group Psychology*, *S.E.* 18: 136–37. Freud attributes this formulation to another collaborator, Hanns Sachs. It is, however, an application of Freud's own model of the psychology of art developed with Rank many years earlier. See the discussion of "Formulations on the Two Principles of Mental Functioning" below.

24. *Totem and Taboo*, *S.E.* 13: 77. The page numbers given parenthetically in this and the next three paragraphs of the text are from *Totem and Taboo*.

25. *Leonardo da Vinci and a Memory of His Childhood*, *S.E.* 11: 122–23.

26. *Introductory Lectures*, *S.E.* 15: 284–85. An even stronger statement of this theme is to be found in Freud's small paper, "A Difficulty in the Path of Psycho-Analysis," *S.E.* 17: 135–44.

27. Both the quotations in this paragraph can be found in *Group Psychology*, *S.E.* 18: 142.

28. *Group Psychology*, *S.E.* 18: 142.

29. *Totem and Taboo*, *S.E.* 13: 73–74. At the time this passage was written, Freud had not yet formulated the theory of ego-libido. He is thinking of the ego as an instrument of self-preservation. Later it would have a narcissistic libidinal charge of its own. See "On Narcissism: On Introduction," *S.E.* 14: 75–81.

30. For a detailed analysis of the interchangeable character of religion and neurosis as forms of behavior, see "Obsessive Actions and Religious Practices," *S.E.* 9: particularly 126–27.

31. The theme of repression in the form of sexual restraint as a cause of the modern susceptibility to neurosis is of much less importance in Freud's thinking than the narrative of the successive forms of intellectual culture. Sexual restraint is most pointedly discussed in " 'Civilized' Sexual Morality and Modern Nervous Illness," *S.E.* 9: 179–204. This essay, with its grim portrayal of modern marriage and its neurotic frustrations, has the tang of personal experience and deserves to be better known as an expression of Freud's views about the psychological effects of modern culture.

32. The importance of the Prometheus myth is first mentioned in *Civilization and Its Discontents*, *S.E.* 21: 90n and further developed in "The Acquisition and Control of Fire," *S.E.* 22: 183–93.

33. Editor's Introduction to "Formulations on the Two Principles of Mental Functioning," *S.E.* 12: 215. Parenthetical references for the next three paragraphs are from "Two Principles."

34. "Creative Writers and Day-Dreaming," *S.E.* 9: 153.

35. Freud knew well enough that this "prosthetic God" was not necessarily a contented creature: "When he puts on all his auxiliary organs he is truly magnificent; but those organs have not grown onto him and they still give him much trouble at times. Nevertheless, he is entitled to console himself with the thought that this development will not come to an end precisely with the year 1930 A.D. Future ages will bring with them new and probably unimaginably great advances in this field of civilization and will increase man's likeness to God still more. But in the interests of our investigations, we will not forget that present-day man does not feel happy in his Godlike character." *Civilization*, *S.E.* 21: 92.

Chapter Two

1. For a detailed treatment of Freud's indebtedness to nineteenth-century biology see Frank J. Sulloway, *Freud, Biologist of the Mind: Beyond the Psychoanalytic Legend* (Cambridge, Mass.: Harvard University Press, 1992; rptd. from New York: Basic Books, 1979). Sulloway's view has been countered by Lucille B. Ritvo in *Darwin's Influence on Freud: A Tale of Two Sciences* (New York: Yale University Press, 1990), and subjected to critique by Paul Robinson in *Freud and His Critics* (Berkeley: University of California Press, 1993), 18–100.

2. *Moses and Monotheism, S.E.* 23: 107.

3. *Moses, S.E.* 23: 129.

4. Probably the best account of the outlook of the new scientific culture remains Ernst Cassirer, *The Philosophy of Enlightenment*, trans. Fritz C. A. Koelin and James Pettegrove (Princeton: Princeton University Press, 1951). My own sense of the moral and intellectual disadvantages of this movement has been sharpened by Alasdair MacIntyre, *After Virtue: A Study in Moral Theory* (Notre Dame: University of Notre Dame Press, 1981); Charles Taylor, *Sources of the Self: The Making of the Modern Identity* (Cambridge, Mass.: Harvard University Press, 1989); and by Blanford Parker, *The Eclipse of Analogy: The Origins and Progress of Augustanism* (Cambridge: Cambridge University Press, forthcoming in 1997). I am grateful to Parker for access to his work in manuscript.

5. In 1923, Freud wrote to Romain Rolland, "I, of course, belong to a race which in the Middle Ages was held responsible for all epidemics and which today is blamed for the disintegration of the Austrian Empire and the German defeat. Such experiences have a sobering effect and are not conducive to make one believe in illusions. A great part of my life's work . . . has been spent [trying to] destroy illusions of my own and of mankind." Letter of March 4, 1923. *The Letters of Sigmund Freud*, ed. Ernst L. Freud, trans. Tania and James Stern (New York: Basic Books, 1960), 341. Freud's personal Viennese Jewish experience only intensified the force of his commitment to the ideology of science, with its tendency to define itself in hostile reaction against what had come before. It remained militantly *Protestant*, having built upon the impetus of the religious revolt that preceded it. When Freud's friend, Oskar Pfister, the Swiss minister and psychoanalyst, ventured the opinion that "the Reformation was fundamentally nothing but an analysis of Catholic sexual repression, unfortunately a totally inadequate one," Freud replied that "in the historical sense of which you speak I too can call myself a protestant, and in that connection I recall that my friend Professor von Ehrenfels coined the term 'sexual protestants' for us both." Letters of February 18 and 20, 1909. *Psychoanalysis and Faith: The Letters of Sigmund Freud and Oskar Pfister*, ed. Heinrich Meng and Ernst L. Freud, trans. Eric Mosbacher (New York: Basic Books, 1963), 18–19. On the links between Freud, "the last philosophe," and the Enlightenment critique of religion, see Peter Gay, *A Godless Jew: Freud, Atheism, and the Making of Psychoanalysis* (New Haven: Yale University Press, 1987), 35–68.

6. See the epigraph to this chapter, from *The Complete Letters of Sigmund Freud to Wilhelm Fliess, 1887–1904*, ed. Jeffrey Moussaieff Masson (Cambridge, Mass.: Harvard Belknap Press, 1985), 398.

7. "Obsessive Actions and Religious Practices," *S.E.* 9: 126–27.

8. Adolf Grünbaum, *The Foundations of Psychoanalysis: A Philosophical Critique* (Los Angeles: University of California Press, 1984), 127–72. The key text for Grünbaum's interpretation is the twenty-eighth of the *Introductory Lectures on Psycho-Analysis,* "Analytic Therapy," *S.E.* 16: 448–63.

9. One of the persistent difficulties with Freud's technique was that symptoms could vanish so easily at the beginning of the analysis that it became impossible to distinguish psychoanalysis from hypnosis, which is to say, mere suggestion. The premature disappearance of symptoms became a familiar hurdle for analyst and patient. See Grünbaum, *Foundations,* 130–59.

10. As Henri Ellenberger has shown, the 'transference' relationship by which the psychoanalyst establishes his or her power to intervene in the depths of the patient's psychology has clear analogs in a long succession of techniques by which authorities have exerted their influence to achieve therapeutic effects: shamanism, Christian exorcism, faith healing, Mesmerism, and hypnotism. All of these depend upon the power of suggestion wielded by respected representatives of society, often, like the psychoanalyst, inducing a therapeutic crisis in the patient in order to expel harmful agencies. See *The Discovery of the Unconscious: The History and Evolution of Dynamic Psychiatry* (New York: Basic Books, 1970), 1–109.

If Grünbaum's critique, cited above, is correct, as I believe it to be, neither Freud nor his followers have succeeded in distinguishing the therapeutic effects attributed to the treatment from those of mere suggestion. Freud's formulations on the process of therapy tend to raise this suspicion; for instance, in 1910 he writes: "The mechanism of our assistance is easy to understand: we give the patient the anticipatory idea and then he finds the repressed unconscious idea in himself on the basis of the similarity to the anticipatory one." "The Future Prospects of Psycho-Analytic Therapy," *S.E.* 11: 141–42. It is in the context of the problem of suggestion that we should consider Freud's own assertion that, as psychoanalysis achieved more cultural authority, its power to cure would increase. "Future Prospects," 146–51. For the highly charged political context in which this claim was made, see John Kerr, *A Most Dangerous Method: The Story of Jung, Freud, and Sabina Spielrein* (New York: Knopf, 1993), 285.

11. *Letters,* 436. Translation slightly altered; see Introduction, n3.

12. "The Claims of Psycho-Analysis to Scientific Interest," *S.E.* 13: 163–90.

13. *Totem and Taboo, S.E.* 13: 95–96.

14. *The Psychopathology of Everyday Life, S.E.* 6: 258–59. I have not preserved the original italics in this passage.

15. On the basis of the occasional disclaimers of thoroughgoing reductionism such as the one quoted above in the passage on 'psychography', Professor Grünbaum is willing to acquit Freud of the 'genetic fallacy' by which intellectual positions are reduced to the psychological causes that motivate them. See *Validation in the Clinical Theory of Psychoanalysis: A Study in the Philosophy of Psychoanalysis, Psychological Issues* 61 (Madison, Conn.: International Universities Press, 1993), 257–310. Grünbaum is certainly correct that Freud knew, and stated, the difference between the psychological causes that induce one to believe in the truth of a proposition and the reasons that might sustain one's belief; Freud understood,

also, that the presence of the former do not discredit the latter, unless, of course, the statements in question have to do with 'meaning and value', for there Freud made no scruple about genetic reduction. It seems to me, though, that the true significance of Freud's reductionism lies, as I have already emphasized, in the fact that his way of thinking gives so much weight to *unconscious* irrationality that it does not leave sufficient space for conscious deliberation. It was for this reason that the discovery of the unconscious itself became an act of uncanny heroism. Freud did not shrink from the obligations that his reductive ambition imposed upon him. His own vocation for science had to be accounted for within the logic of the unconscious. And so he traced his scientific ambitions, we shall see, to "unconscious megalomania," and described, in his essay on Leonardo da Vinci (cited above), the entirely arbitrary and fortuitous events of childhood that produce the scientist, allowing Leonardo, in fact, to become the "first modern natural scientist," the first man who could investigate nature without the aid of narcissistic 'presuppositions'. In Freud's system the birth of a scientist requires virtually a miracle.

Chapter Three

1. *Diagnostic and Statistical Manual of Mental Disorders* (Washington: American Psychiatric Association, 1987), 3rd ed. rev., 197–201. In the more recent *DSM-IV* (1994), 'paranoia' occurs only twice. The breadth of the term seems to make it less and less useful to psychiatry.

2. David W. Swanson, M.D., Philip J. Bohnert, M.D., and Jackson H. Smith, M.D., *The Paranoid* (Boston: Little, Brown, 1970), 6.

3. This is Sullivan's term and I find his discussion of the paranoid "dynamism," as he calls it, particularly lucid and interesting. The paranoid's fundamental motive, he observes, is to protect the ego through the transfer of blame (89). See Harry Stack Sullivan, *Clinical Studies in Psychiatry*, ed. Helen Swick Perry, Mary Ladd Gawel, and Martha Gibbon (New York: Norton, 1956), 86–99, 166–81, and passim.

4. Swanson, 7.

5. David Shapiro, *Neurotic Styles* (New York: Basic Books, 1965), 54–107.

6. Swanson, 4. Page numbers given in the following paragraphs on the symptoms of paranoia are all from this text.

7. E. M. Thornton, *The Freudian Fallacy: An Alternative View of Freudian Theory* (Garden City, N.Y.: The Dial Press, 1984). Thornton traces Freud's paranoia directly to the use of cocaine and sees it as a continuing trend long after Freud stopped using the drug: "We have good evidence that Freud's paranoiac tendencies and his 'bitterness with the environment' were still strong well into the second decade of the twentieth century. Coupled with these traits, as is so often the case, was a certain shrewdness that enabled him to turn every situation to his own advantage and to conceal his psychotic tendencies from others. His attacks associated with loss of consciousness lasted until about 1912. Thereafter these attacks were succeeded by minor seizures of the temporal lobe variety. As we have seen, epileptiform seizures were a frequent concomitant of cocaine usage. There is in this pattern the tentative suggestion of continued use of cocaine up until 1912,

after which the major effects of its use were no longer seen, pointing to cessation about this time, but leaving residual brain damage leading to minor attacks till well into his later years" (242–43). As mentioned earlier, I do not have the medical expertise either to confirm or to question this diagnosis.

8. I have chosen Swanson's formulation of paranoid symptomatology because, while reflecting the greater flexibility of post-Freudian treatments of the subject, it nevertheless preserves the essence of the Freudian point of view, with its strong emphasis upon 'projection'.

9. Shapiro, 66.

10. "Further Remarks on the Neuro-Psychoses of Defense," *S.E.* 3: 184.

11. Shapiro, 84.

12. Letter of January 24, 1985. *The Complete Letters of Sigmund Freud to Wilhelm Fliess: 1887–1904*, ed. and trans. Jeffrey Moussaieff Masson (Cambridge, Mass.: Harvard University Press, 1985), 111.

13. Letter to Sándor Ferenczi of October 6, 1910. *The Correspondence of Sigmund Freud and Sándor Ferenczi*, ed. Eva Brabant, Ernst Falzeder, and Patrizia Giampieri-Deutsch; trans Peter T. Hoffer (Cambridge, Mass.: Harvard University Press, 1993) 1 (1908–1914): 221.

14. "But why, then, finally, does psychoanalysis still flourish in pockets of our culture, most notably in the discourse of academic humanists and 'soft' social scientists? A full answer would be complex—embracing, for example, such factors as religious yearnings, envy of mainstream science, a vogue for 'hermeneutic' evasion of empirical tests, the indoctrinating effect of the therapy, the lure of deep certainties and ready-made interpretations, and the persistence of the spirit of unmasking that informs the works of Marx, Schopenhauer, Nietzsche, and Freud himself." This canny enumeration is given by Frederick Crews in *Skeptical Engagements* (New York: Oxford University Press, 1986), 71. In this study, obviously, I have given emphasis to the last factor, which I believe to be central, without denying the importance of the others.

15. Ernest Gellner, *The Psychoanalytic Movement, or, The Coming of Unreason* (London: Paladin, 1985), 4.

16. *Psychopathology of Everyday Life, S.E.* 6: 256–65.

17. See the editor's note, *S.E.* 22: 161.

18. Letter to Sándor Ferenczi of January 23, 1912. *Freud/Ferenczi* 1: 333.

19. *S.E.* 6: 194.

20. Peter Swales has observed how well this description of paranoia applies to Freud himself, and, in addition, that the systems of Freud and his friend and rival Fliess share the same self-projective and self-confirming character. See "Freud, Fliess, and Fratricide: The Role of Fliess in Freud's Conception of Paranoia," in *Sigmund Freud: Critical Assessments*, ed. Laurence Spurling (New York: Routledge, 1989) 1: 315.

21. *Group Psychology and the Analysis of the Ego, S.E.* 18: 120–21.

22. *"Flectere si nequeo superos, Acheronta movebo."*

23. See "Remembering, Repeating, and Working-Through (Further Recommendations on the Technique of Psycho-Analysis II)," *S.E.* 12: 152–56. Mircea Eliade observes that psychoanalytic therapy preserves the pattern of ritual initia-

tion, with its heroic character: "The patient is asked to descend deeply into himself, to make his past live, to confront his traumatic experiences again; and, from the point of view of form, this dangerous operation resembles initiatory descents into hell, the realm of ghosts, and combats with monsters. Just as the initiate was expected to emerge from his ordeals victorious—in short, was to 'die' and be 'resuscitated' in order to gain access to a fully responsible existence, open to spiritual values—so the patient undergoing analysis today must confront his own 'unconscious', haunted by ghosts and monsters, in order to find psychic health and integrity and hence the world of cultural values." *The Sacred and the Profane: The Nature of Religion*, trans. Willard R. Trask (New York: Harcourt, Brace, Jovanovich, 1959), 208, quoted in Stanley Edgar Hyman, *The Tangled Bank: Darwin, Marx, Frazer and Freud as Imaginative Writers* (New York: Atheneum, 1962), 337. See also Henri Ellenberger, *The Discovery of the Unconscious: The History and Evolution of Dynamic Psychiatry* (New York: Basic Books, 1970), 524–25.

24. "As for the biographers, let them worry, we have no desire to make it too easy for them. Each one of them will be right in his opinion of 'The Development of the Hero', and I am already looking forward to seeing them go astray." Letter to Martha Bernays, April 28, 1885. *Letters of Sigmund Freud*, trans. Tania and James Stern, ed. Ernest L. Freud (New York: Basic Books, 1961), 140. The young Freud would have been gratified to learn how closely his future thinking would guide the investigations of his biographers, and everyone else's. This passage, written by a twenty-year-old, betrays to me nothing more than the typical grandiosity of late adolescence—but Freud never outgrew it.

25. Letter to Martha Bernays of February 2, 1886. *Letters*, 202.

26. Letter of December 29, 1917. Phyllis Grosskurth, *The Secret Ring: Freud's Inner Circle and The Politics of Psychoanalysis* (Menlo Park, Calif.: Addison-Wesley, 1991), 73.

27. "Freud lived on terms of natural intimacy with the great figures of the Bible; they were so much part of his inner life that he felt himself to be by turns Joseph, Jacob, and Moses." Marthe Robert, *From Oedipus to Moses: Freud's Jewish Identity*, trans. Ralph Manheim (Garden City, N.Y.: Anchor Press, 1976), 37. See also Leonard Shengold, "Freud and Joseph," in Mark Kanzer and Jules Glenn, eds., *Freud and His Self-Analysis* (New York: Jason Aronson, 1979), 67–86.

28. Ernest Jones, *The Life and Work of Sigmund Freud* (New York: Basic Books, 1953) 2: 364–65.

29. Paul Roazen, in *Freud and His Followers* (New York: NAL, 1971), has chronicled a variety of heroic Freudian identifications: Oedipus (437–38), Alexander the Great (32), Columbus (97), and Bismarck (37–38). See also 29–31. For the occasion on which Freud positioned himself as Zeus in relation to his epigones, see Roazen, *Brother Animal: The Story of Freud and Tausk* (New York: Knopf, 1969), 49.

30. For the famous discussion of Freud's identification with Hannibal see *The Interpretation of Dreams, S.E.* 4: 197. This passage will be discussed in chapter 6 below.

31. For a seminal discussion of Freud's character as a hero, see Frank J. Sulloway, *Freud, Biologist of the Mind: Beyond the Psychoanalytic Legend* (Cam-

bridge, Mass.: Harvard University Press, 1992; rptd. from New York: Basic Books, 1979), 445–95.

32. Letter of January 27, 1886. *Letters*, 199.

33. Letter of September 2, 1907. *The Freud/Jung Letters: The Correspondence between Sigmund Freud and C. G. Jung*, trans. Ralph Manheim and R. F. C. Hull; ed. William McGuire (Princeton: Princeton University Press, 1974), 82.

34. Thornton, 240.

35. See Ellenberger on the repudiation of secret societies and scientific schools at the beginning of the nineteenth century, and the special importance of the founding of the University of Berlin (226–27). Freud's sectarian tendencies caused friction with significant supporters like the influential psychiatrist Eugen Bleuler, who wrote to him in 1911: "In my opinion, this 'who is not for us is against us', this 'all or nothing', is necessary for religious communities and useful for political parties. I can therefore understand the principle as such, but for science I consider it harmful." Letter of December 4, 1911. Quoted in Peter Gay, *A Godless Jew: Freud, Atheism, and the Making of Psychoanalysis* (New Haven: Yale University Press, 1987), 145.

36. Ellenberger, 41–43. After his exhaustive review of the development of dynamic psychiatry, Ellenberger concludes that the institutional form of the psychoanalytic movement was the most original element of Freud's contribution to the field (550).

37. Letter of Freud to Jung, April 16, 1909. *Freud/Jung*, 218.

38. The initial idea was that Freud would personally analyze each member of the group: "We all agreed on one thing, that salvation could only lie in a restless self-analysis, carried to the farthest possible limit, thus purging *personal* reactions away so far as can be done. One of them, I think it was Ferenczi, expressed the wish that a small group of men could be thoroughly analysed by you, so that they could represent the pure theory unadulterated by personal complexes, and thus build an official inner circle in the Verein and serve as centres where others (beginners) could come and learn the work. If that were only possible it would be an ideal solution." Letter of July 30, 1912. *The Complete Correspondence of Sigmund Freud and Ernest Jones, 1908–1939*, ed. Andrew Paskauskas (Cambridge, Mass.: Harvard University Press, 1993), 146. Evidently the idea of the training analysis, which eventually became a standard form of psychoanalytic initiation, arose during this embattled period immediately in response to the need for a more thorough indoctrination of recruits in order to ensure their fidelity. The story of "The Committee" and the bitter struggles that eventually destroyed it is brilliantly told by Phyllis Grosskurth in *The Secret Ring*, cited above.

39. Letter of August 7, 1912. *Freud/Jones*, 149.

40. "What took hold of my imagination immediately is your idea of a secret council composed of the best and most trustworthy among our men to take care of the further development of psycho-analysis and defend the cause against personalities and accidents when I am no more. You say it was Ferenczi who expressed this idea, yet it may be mine own shaped in better times, when I hoped Jung would collect such a circle around him composed of the official headmen of the local

associations. Now I am sorry to say such a union had to be formed independently of Jung and of the elected presidents. I dare say it would make living and dying easier for me if I knew of such an association existing to watch over my creation. I know there is a boyish and perhaps romantic element too in this conception, but perhaps it could be adapted to meet the necessities of reality. I will give my fancy free play and leave to you the part of the Censor." Letter of August 1, 1912. *Freud/ Jones*, 148.

41. See Ellenberger's account of the myth surrounding the hostile reception of Freud's early paper on Charcot (439–42), and also Sulloway, 462–64.

42. The first of these pitiful heretics was the co-discoverer of psychoanalysis, Joseph Breuer. As Thornton observes, Freud's abrupt change in attitude toward Breuer from long-standing admiration and friendship to extreme contempt and aversion represents a typical paranoid episode. Thornton, 179–81.

43. As John Kerr observes, the use of the term "movement" carried the danger of placing psychoanalysis outside the pale of science and into the company of sexual reform or of the already out-moded fad of hypnotism. John Kerr, *A Most Dangerous Method: The Story of Jung, Freud, and Sabina Spielrein* (New York: Knopf, 1993), 290–91.

44. *Moses and Monotheism, S.E.* 23: 118.

45. Often Freud unambiguously equates psychological maturity with the ability to accept psychoanalytic dogma, as can be seen in this comment on a work of Eugen Bleuler: "For all its ambivalence, Bleuler's essay plainly shows his regressive trend. He actually accepts far less than he did two years ago." Letter to Karl Abraham of May 13, 1913. *A Psycho-Analytic Dialogue: The Letters of Sigmund Freud and Karl Abraham, 1907–1926*, ed. Hilda C. Abraham and Ernst L. Freud (New York: Basic Books, 1965), 139.

46. Franz Alexander, "Recollection of Berggasse 19," *Psychoanalytic Quarterly* 9 (1940): 195, cited in Thornton, 239.

47. We find Carl Jung at one point attempting to remonstrate with Freud in order to get beyond the reduction of disagreements to psychological motives: "I am writing to you now as I would write *to a friend*—this is *our* style. I therefore hope you will not be offended by my Helvetic bluntness. One thing I beg of you: take these statements as an *effort to be honest* and do not apply the depreciatory Viennese criterion of egotistic striving for power or heaven knows what other insinuations from the world of the father complex. This is just what I have been hearing on all sides these days, with the result that I am forced to the painful conclusion that the majority of psychoanalysts misuse psychoanalysis for the purpose of devaluing others and their progress by insinuations about complexes (as though that explained anything. A wretched theory!). A particularly preposterous bit of nonsense now going the rounds is that my libido theory is the product of anal erotism. When I consider *who* cooked up this 'theory' I fear for the future of analysis." Letter of December 3, 1912. *Freud/Jung*, 526.

48. For a work that chronicles in detail how rival schools of psychoanalysts interpret each other's intellectual and psychological motives, see Peter L. Rudnytsky, *The Psychoanalytic Vocation: Rank, Winnicott, and the Legacy of Freud* (New Haven: Yale University Press, 1991).

49. *S.E.* 6: 149–50n. This passage was suppressed from all editions after 1924, as is mentioned in the note to the *Standard Edition* where it now appears.

50. "So we are at last rid of them, the brutal, sanctimonious Jung and his disciples. I must now thank you for the vast amount of trouble, the exceptional clear-sightedness, with which you supported me and our common cause. All my life I have been looking for friends who would not exploit and then betray me, and now, not far from its natural end, I hope I have found them." Letter of July 26, 1914. *Freud/Abraham*, 186. As Allen Esterson points out, the final sentence "sounds distinctly paranoid." *Seductive Mirage: An Exploration of the Work of Sigmund Freud* (Chicago: Open Court, 1993), 88n.

51. Letter of May 14, 1922. *Letters*, 339.

52. Perhaps the best psychoanalytic compliment was turned by that agile courtier, Jones. Responding to Freud's recommendation of his daughter, Anna, Jones writes: "I had already fully appreciated what you write about her. She has a beautiful character and will surely be a remarkable woman later on, provided that her sexual repression does not injure her. She is of course tremendously bound to you, and it is one of those rare cases where the actual father corresponds to the father-imago." Letter of July 27, 1914. *Freud/Jones*, 295. Jones was more right than he knew, for Freud had created the father-imago in his own image.

53. Thornton, 238.

54. Thornton, 229. In the mistaking of neuropathic conditions for hysteria, Freud had before him the unfortunate example of Charcot, whose misunderstandings he amplified (47–50). Thornton ascribes many of the symptoms Freud diagnosed as hysteria to the unrecognized effects of epilepsy. There is also the example of Freud's rather willful insistence that Dostoevsky's epileptic symptoms were hysterical in origin, evidence of his neurotic character. See James L. Rice, *Freud's Russia: National Identity in the Evolution of Psychoanalysis* (New Brunswick, N. J.: Transaction Publishers, 1993), 185–88.

55. Thornton, 192.

56. The obsession with numbers is discussed in Freud's letter to Jung of April 16, 1909, in which Freud first describes and then analyzes his earlier attack of superstition: "Some years ago I discovered within me the conviction that I would die between the ages of 61 and 62, which then struck me as a long time away. . . . Then I went to Greece with my brother and it was really uncanny how often the number 61 or 62 in connection with 1 or 2 kept cropping up in all sorts of numbered objects, especially those connected with transportation. This I conscientiously noted. It depressed me, but I had hopes of breathing easy when we got to the hotel in Athens and were assigned rooms on the first floor. Here, I was sure, there could be no No. 61. I was right, but I was given 31 (which with fatalistic license could be regarded as half of 61 or 62), and this younger, more agile number proved to be an even more persistent persecutor than the first. From the time of our trip home until very recently, 31, often with a 2 in its vicinity, clung to me faithfully." *Freud/Jung*, 219. Freud recognized in this behavior a morbid obsessiveness that looks for patterns in chance events (220). Yet he went on to analyze the significance of the numbers, following a chain of associations involving his age when he completed *The Interpretation of Dreams* and his home phone number.

"Moreover, the hidden influence of W. Fliess was at work; the superstition erupted in the year of his attack on me" (219). Freud's interpretation of his numerological obsession seems to me as distinctly paranoid as the attack of superstition that produced it.

57. Roazen, *Brother Animal*, 88–93. See also Roazen's observations on Freud's tendency toward the 'over-estimation of thought', 172.

58. *The Psychopathology of Everyday Life, S.E.* 6: 188–89.

59. "Psycho-Analysis and Telepathy," *S.E.* 18: 177–92. Thought transference and experiments with the occult are a running theme in Freud's correspondence with Ferenczi.

60. Letter to Ferenczi of January 23, 1912. *Freud/Ferenczi*, 333.

61. Helene Deutsch, "Freud and His Pupils: A Footnote to the History of the Psychoanalytic Movement," in Laurence Spurling, ed. *Sigmund Freud: Critical Assessments* (New York: Routledge, 1989) 4: 36.

62. Letter of May 22, 1910. *Freud/Jones*, 58–59 (emphasis in original).

63. *On the History of the Psycho-Analytic Movement, S.E.* 14: 66.

64. All of the biographies deal with the long series of alliances and schisms— Breuer, Fliess, Adler, Jung, Rank, and so on—that marked Freud's career. And they are given special investigation in the works of Roazen, Grosskurth, and Kerr cited above.

65. *Psycho-Analytic Movement, S.E.* 14: 39.

66. Letter of February 17, 1908. *Freud/Jung*, 121.

67. Or, as the research of Swales suggests, Fliess's resentment and hostility toward Freud were in response to Freud's obvious demonstrations of hostility. Freud had confessed unconscious death wishes toward Fliess, and Fliess told members of his family that Freud had even thought of pushing him off a cliff! Swales rather impetuously gives credence to the allegation (311–15).

68. Sulloway, 231.

69. Letters of June 25 and August 9, 1911. *Freud/Jones*, 107 and 112.

70. Letter of August 12, 1912, quoted in Kerr, *Dangerous Method*, 416.

71. Freud liked this joke of Hitschmann's enough to repeat it to Ferenczi in a letter of October 13, 1912. *Freud/Ferenczi*, 423.

72. See Ferenczi's letter of June 23, 1913, in *Freud/Ferenczi* 1: 494, and the discussion in Grosskurth, 60.

73. This point has been made from within the psychoanalytic perspective by François Roustang. He seems to consider its significance to be that Freud did not apply the critique of institutions developed in *Group Psychology and the Analysis of the Ego* to the psychoanalytic movement itself, the upshot being that psychoanalysis goes on suffering from the 'transference' problems that plague all institutions. *Dire Mastery: Discipleship from Freud to Lacan*, trans. Ned Lukacher (Baltimore: Johns Hopkins University Press, 1982), 1–18.

74. Grosskurth makes this observation; Freud's way of coming between his followers and their female attachments manifested itself in his relationships with Jung, Ferenczi, and Jones (59–60). Jones remarked to Freud after reading *Totem and Taboo* that the theory of the primal father seemed to have "an unusual personal significance" for Freud. Letter of June 25, 1913. *Freud/Jones*, 206. I see no

immediate confirmation of Grosskurth's surmise that Jones was referring to Freud's primally paternal way with women, but Freud was analyzing Jones' mistress, Loe Kann, at the time.

75. "The Question of Lay Analysis: Postscript (1927)," *S.E.* 20: 253.

76. Letter of November 9, 1918 to Oskar Pfister. *Psychoanalysis and Faith: The Letters of Sigmund Freud and Oskar Pfister*, ed. Heinrich Meng and Ernst Freud, trans. Eric Mosbacher (New York: Basic Books, 1963), 61–62; quoted in Roazen, *Freud and His Followers*, 146.

77. As Carl Schorske points out, Freud ignores the fact that Oedipus is a king. Carl E. Schorske, *Fin-de-Siècle Vienna: Politics and Culture* (New York: Vintage, 1981), 199.

78. Letter of July 3, 1919, quoted in Roazen, *Brother Animal*, 127.

79. Letter of August 1, 1919. *Sigmund Freud and Lou-Andreas Salomé: Letters*, ed. Ernst Pfeiffer, trans. William and Elaine Robson-Scott (New York: Norton, 1966), 98–99. Salomé's reply expresses dutiful understanding of Freud's impatience with Tausk; she rather chillingly, and disingenuously, mitigates the situation by imagining that death might have provided her former lover a "last supreme libidinal satisfaction" (99).

80. Spurling, 4: 38.

81. K. R. Eissler, *Talent and Genius: The Fictitious Case of Tausk contra Freud* (New York: Quadrangle, 1971), 99.

82. See Freud's letter of June 1935 to Thomas Mann on the latter's sixtieth birthday. *Letters*, 426.

83. Letter to James J. Putnam of July 8, 1915. *Letters*, 309.

84. *Psycho-Analytic Movement, S.E.* 14: 21–22.

Chapter Four

1. "Perhaps . . . my being scarcely able to tell lies anymore is a consequence of my occupation with psychoanalysis. As often as I try to distort something I succumb to an error or some other parapraxis that betrays my insincerity." *The Psychopathology of Everyday Life, S.E.* 6: 221.

2. Letter of March 7, 1875. *The Letters of Sigmund Freud to Eduard Silberstein, 1871–1881*, ed. Walter Boehlich, trans. Arnold J. Pomerans (Cambridge, Mass.: Harvard University Press, 1990), 96.

3. All scholars of Freud and of depth psychology are indebted to the wide and deep researches of Henri Ellenberger. Ellenberger provides a dense and rich summary of his exhaustive account of Freud's borrowings in *The Discovery of the Unconscious: The History and Evolution of Dynamic Psychiatry* (New York: Basic Books, 1970), 534–43.

4. Letter of August 15, 1877. *Freud/Silberstein*, 164.

5. "Contribution to a Questionnaire on Reading," *S.E.* 9: 245–46.

6. Freud even considered relocating to England during his long courtship of Martha Bernays: "The thought of England surges up before me, with its sober industriousness, its generous devotion to the public weal, the stubbornness and sensitive feeling for justice of its inhabitants, the running fire of general interest

that can strike sparks in the newspapers; all the ineffaceable impressions of my journey of seven years ago, one that had a decisive influence on my whole life, have been awakened in their full vividness. I am taking up again the history of that island, the works of the men who were my real teachers—all of them English or Scotch; and I am recalling what is for me the most interesting historical period, the reign of the Puritans and Oliver Cromwell with its lofty monument of that time— *Paradise Lost*, where only recently, when I did not feel sure of your love, I found consolation and comfort. Must we stay here, Martha? If we possibly can, let us seek a home where human worth is more respected." Letter of August 16, 1882. Ernest Jones, *The Life and Work of Sigmund Freud* (New York: Basic Books, 1953) 1: 178.

7. *The Great Instauration,* in *The Works of Francis Bacon,* ed. James Spedding, et al. (Boston: Taggard and Thompson, 1863) 8: 45.

8. *The New Organon, Works of Bacon* 8: 90.

9. "Of the Proficience and Advancement of Learning Divine and Human," *Works of Bacon* 6: 132.

10. *New Organon, Works of Bacon* 8: 73.

11. *The Great Instauration, Works of Bacon* 8: 46.

12. *New Organon, Works of Bacon* 8: 86.

13. *New Organon, Works of Bacon* 8: 82.

14. "Essays or Counsels Civil and Moral," *Works of Bacon* 12: 81–82.

15. "The Natural and Experimental History for the Foundation of Philosophy: or, Phenomena of the Universe: which is the third part of the Instauratio Magna," *Works of Bacon* 9: 370–71.

16. *New Organon, Works of Bacon* 8: 68.

17. *The Great Instauration, Works of Bacon* 8: 32.

18. "Description of a Natural and Experimental History Such As May Serve for the Foundation of a True Philosophy," *Works of Bacon* 8: 354–55.

19. *The Great Instauration, Works of Bacon* 8: 33–34.

20. Jones, *Life* 1: 42–43.

21. "The Resistance to Psycho-Analysis," *S.E.* 19: 215.

22. "In mental functioning something is to be distinguished—a quota of affect or sum of excitation—which possesses all the characteristics of a quantity (though we have no means of measuring it), which is capable of increase, diminution, displacement and discharge, and which is spread over the memory-traces of ideas somewhat as an electric charge is spread over the surface of a body." "The Neuro-Psychoses of Defense," *S.E.* 3: 60.

23. John Locke, *An Essay concerning Human Understanding,* ed. Peter Nidditch (Oxford: Oxford University Press, 1975), 562–63.

24. Locke's reassurances hinge upon the fact that our simple ideas must come from outside since we have not the power to generate them; that, except for substances, or external objects, our complex ideas—from morals to mathematics— are self-constructed and therefore not subject to doubt; and that such small knowledge as we may have of external existence, based upon the regularity of association of simple ideas, is real knowledge, though this seems contradictory to his previous teachings. *Essay,* 563–73.

25. Here I am indebted to Blanford Parker, *The Eclipse of Analogy: The Origins and Progress of Augustanism* (Cambridge: Cambridge University Press, forthcoming in 1997). In Parker's view, the discovery of a neutral standpoint of observation that discredits both Protestant 'enthusiasm' and Catholic 'superstition' is a central motive of Augustan culture.

26. David Hume, *A Treatise of Human Nature*, ed. L. A. Selby-Bigge, 2nd ed. rev. with notes by P. H. Nidditch (Oxford: Oxford University Press, 1978), 183.

27. "Psycho-Analytic Notes on an Autobiographical Account of a Case of Paranoia (Dementia Paranoides)," *S.E.* 12: 66. What Freud means is that our sensations are determined relative to the human sensorium. We refer to an object, for instance, as being blue, as if the color we experience were a part of the object itself, while actually what we see is largely determined by our own faculties. In other cases such as that of pain we recognize that the sensation is due to our contact with an external object and not part of the object itself. All value judgments are 'projections', as for instance when one refers to an object that gives one pleasure as a 'good' thing, as if the cause of one's pleasure were external and part of the thing. Value judgments come to have the same ghostly aspect as the 'secondary qualities' of the Cartesian and empirical philosophies. For an interesting discussion of the attitude toward the subject implied in this position, see Charles Taylor, *Sources of the Self: The Making of the Modern Identity* (Cambridge, Mass.: Harvard University Press, 1989), 161–62.

28. "The Unconscious," *S.E.* 14: 171.

29. Here Freud makes the implausible claim that it will be easier to overcome the discrepancy between what appears to the conscious mind and what appears to the unconscious than it has been to overcome the discrepancy between external sensation and true objects. It is true of course that Freud considered the confirmation for psychoanalytic theories to come from patients' acceptance of the diagnoses offered in therapy, the result being that the crucial division to be crossed was between the patient's conscious and unconscious mind. But Freud seems to be forgetting that even the conscious mind of the patient is for the observer part of the external world.

30. *Introductory Lectures on Psycho-Analysis*, *S.E.* 15: 142–43.

31. The scientific mode of suspicion could draw upon the powerful momentum of historical suspicion that grew from the polemical controversies of the Reformation. As Anthony Kemp has shown, the sectarian form of Protestant historical consciousness is one of the powerful confluent sources of modern suspicion. Its dominant trope is that of return to an original moment of charismatic purity, from which historical time can only mark a falling away into corruption, or the prolongation of a "dark age." See Anthony Kemp, *The Estrangement of the Past: A Study in Modern Historical Consciousness* (New York: Oxford University Press, 1991). Enlightenment historical thinking preserves some of the recourse to primitive value that this paradigm typically employs, as seen for instance in Bacon's resuscitation of the *Wisdom of the Ancients*, the pre-classical philosophers and mythographers unjustly eclipsed by Plato and Aristotle; by means of the same rhetorical instrument, Gibbon idealizes pagan Rome in order to lament its Christian corruption.

32. Thomas Goddard Bergin and Max Harold Fisch, trans., *The New Science of*

Giambattista Vico: Unabridged Translation of the Third Edition (1744) (Ithaca: Cornell University Press, rev. 1968), 129–30.

33. I am grateful for this suggestion to Anthony Kemp.

34. Immanuel Kant, "Idea for a Universal History with a Cosmopolitan Intent" (1784), in *Perpetual Peace and Other Essays on Politics, History, and Morals* (Indianapolis: Hackett Publishing, 1983), 30.

35. *New Introductory Lectures on Psycho-Analysis, S.E.* 22: 67.

36. Auguste Comte, *The Positive Philosophy*, trans. Harriet Martineau (New York: AMS, 1974), 26.

37. Freud even worried about Comte's theory of stages as a threat to his originality. See Ernest Jones' letter of February 6, 1914. *The Complete Correspondence of Sigmund Freud and Ernest Jones, 1908–1939*, ed. R. Andrew Paskauskas (Cambridge, Mass.: Harvard University Press, 1993), 260.

38. For Haeckel's influence on Freud see Lucille B. Ritvo, *Darwin's Influence on Freud: A Tale of Two Sciences* (New York: Yale University Press, 1990), 13–30.

39. See Ernst Haeckel, "Science and Christianity," in *The Riddle of the Universe at the Close of the Nineteenth Century* (New York: Harper and Brothers, 1900), 308–30.

40. "Family Romances," *S.E.* 9: 237.

41. As Alasdair MacIntyre observes, any attempt to describe the natural man inevitably involves the ascription of social characteristics; for this reason, those who attempt to indulge in this type of fiction always fall back for their depiction of the natural human being upon what are actually the ethical norms of some other culture. *A Short History of Ethics: A History of Moral Philosophy from the Homeric Age to the Twentieth Century* (New York: Macmillan, 1966), 17–18.

42. "Analysis Terminable and Interminable," *S.E.* 23: 228–29.

43. As Philip Rieff aptly observes, "Though Freud is commonly thought to have measured neurosis against the ideal of an unimpaired sexual efficiency, it would be more accurate to say that he measured it against an ideal contemporaneity." Philip Rieff, *Freud: The Mind of the Moralist* (Garden City, N. Y.: Doubleday, 1959), 46.

44. *New Introductory Lectures, S.E.* 22: 80. For Hegel's anticipation of the Freudian unconscious, see Lancelot Law White, *The Unconscious before Freud* (New York: Basic Books, 1960), 240.

45. *The Future of an Illusion, S.E.* 21: 44.

46. Max Eastman, *Great Companions: Critical Memoirs of Some Famous Friends* (London: Museum Press, 1959), 129, quoted in William M. Johnston, *The Austrian Mind: An Intellectual and Social History, 1848–1938* (Berkeley: University of California Press, 1972), 240.

47. Thomas Hobbes, *Leviathan*, ed. Richard Tuck (New York: Cambridge University Press, 1991), 87.

48. Jean-Jacques Rousseau, *The Social Contract*, trans. Maurice Cranston (New York: Penguin, 1968), 63.

49. *The Communist Manifesto*, in Karl Marx, *Selected Writings*, ed. David McLellan (New York: Oxford University Press, 1977), 237–38.

50. Friedrich Nietzsche, *On the Genealogy of Morals*, trans. Walter Kaufmann and R. J. Hollingdale (New York: Vintage, 1967), 36–43.

51. *Group Psychology and the Analysis of the Ego, S.E.* 18: 123–24.
52. "Why War?" *S.E.* 22: 204–5.
53. Friedrich Nietzsche, *The Gay Science* (New York: Vintage, 1974), 35.

Chapter Five

1. Desiderius Erasmus, *The Praise of Folly and Other Writings: A New Translation with Critical Commentary,* ed. and trans. Robert M. Adams (New York: Norton, 1989), 33.

2. We should not, then, exaggerate the true intellectual affinities between Freud and Erasmus. I am only pointing to the convergence of satiric motifs. Madness itself does not have for Erasmus the same destitution of value that it has for Freud. It can even be the source of divine insight. See M. A. Screech, "Good Madness in Christendom," in W. F. Bynum, Roy Porter, and Michael Shepherd, *The Anatomy of Madness: Essays in the History of Psychiatry,* 2 vols. (New York: Tavistock Publications, 1985) 1: 25–39.

3. For an account of "Swiftian psychoanalysis" see Norman O. Brown, *Life Against Death: The Psychoanalytic Meaning of History* (Middletown, Conn.: Wesleyan University Press, 1959), 179–201. Brown takes the similarities of perception between Swift and Freud to be evidence of shared insight, particularly about the equivalent, alternative character of bodily expression and religious inspiration recognized in the doctrine of sublimation. I, on the other hand, take the convergence between these two authors to be a result of the direct influence of one satiric intelligence upon another.

4. A letter by Freud to Wilhelm Fliess, November 14, 1897, announcing the discovery two days earlier of what Freud took to be a crucial truth about morality, repression, and the nose, shows Freud's capacity for Shandean wit: " 'It was on November 12, 1897, the sun was precisely in the eastern quarter; Mercury and Venus were in conjunction—.' No, birth announcements no longer start like that. It was on November 12, a day dominated by a left-sided migraine, on the afternoon of which [Freud's boy] Martin sat down to write a new poem, on the evening of which Oli lost his second tooth, that, after the frightful labor pains of the last few weeks, I gave birth to a new piece of knowledge." *The Complete Letters of Sigmund Freud to Wilhelm Fliess: 1887–1904,* ed. and trans. Jeffrey Moussaieff Masson (Cambridge, Mass.: Harvard University Press, 1985), 278.

5. Jack J. Spector, *The Aesthetics of Freud* (New York: Praeger, 1972), 8–9.

6. For Freud's enthusiasm about Harte, see the letter of August 15, 1877, and for Lichtenberg, the one dated December 2 and 6, 1874. *The Letters of Sigmund Freud to Eduard Silberstein, 1871–1881,* ed. Walter Boehlich, trans. Arnold J. Pomerans (Cambridge, Mass.: Harvard University Press, 1990), 164 and 73–76.

7. William E. Johnston, *The Austrian Mind: An Intellectual and Social History, 1848–1938* (Berkeley: University of California Press, 1972), 244.

8. Freud on *Sartor Resartus:* "Under all these funny names . . . lies a profound wisdom, and the motley scraps of folly cover the open sores of mankind and of the tale's hero. What we are told about the philosophy of clothes is part parody and part witty reflection, which starts from the assumption that clothes are a representa-

tion of the manifest and 'physical, behind which the spiritual hides in shame'."
Letter of August 13, 1874. *Freud/Silberstein*, 49–50.

9. "Die Heimkehr": "Mit seinen Nachtmützen and Schlafrockfetzen/Stopft er
die Lücken des Weltenbaus." As Strachey's note indicates, these lines were
favorites with Freud, mentioned in a letter to his future wife, Martha, in 1883; then
in *The Interpretation of Dreams*, dated 1900; in a letter to Jung, 1908; and again,
fifty years after the first, in the *New Introductory Lectures*, *S.E.* 22: 161.

10. *S.E.* 5: 469. Early in *The Interpretation of Dreams*, Freud suggests a scene
from *Gulliver* as a reliable gloss on a patient's dream; in a note added twenty-five
years later he observes that this is a "good example of what an interpretation ought
not to be. The interpreter of a dream should not give free play to his own ingenuity
and neglect the dreamer's associations." *S.E.* 4: 30n.

11. For example: "Das Beste, was du wissen kannst,/Darfst du den Buben
doch nicht sagen." I quote Strachey's note: "Mephistopheles, in Goethe's
Faust, Part One, Scene 4: 'After all, the best of what you know may not be told to
boys.'—These were favourite lines of Freud's. He uses them again on p. 453
below. He had already quoted them in letters to Fliess of December 3, 1897, and
February 9, 1898; and, towards the end of his life, on the occasion of his reception
of the Goethe prize in 1930, he applied them to Goethe himself." *S.E.* 4: 142
and n.

12. Letter of February 7, 1883. *Letters of Sigmund Freud*, ed. Ernst L. Freud,
trans. Tania and James Stern (New York: Basic Books, 1961), 96.

13. He continues: "Hence my proposal amounts to stipulating that every Sun-
day each of us, the two sole luminaries of the A.E., send the other a letter that is
nothing short of an entire encyclopedia of the past week and that with total veracity
reports all our doings, commissions and omissions, and those of all strangers we
encounter, in addition to all outstanding thoughts and observations and at least an
adumbration, as it were, of the unavoidable emotions. In that way, each of us may
come to know the surroundings and condition of his friend most precisely, perhaps
more precisely than was possible even at the time when we could meet in the same
city. Our letters, which, when the year has passed may constitute the ornament of
the A. E. archives, will then be as diverse as our very lives. In our letters we shall
transmute the six prosaic and unrelenting working days of the week into the pure
gold of poetry and may perhaps find that there is enough of interest within us, and
in what remains and changes around us, if only we learn to pay attention." Letter
of September 4, 1874. *Freud/Silberstein*, 57–58.

14. Freud's debt to Cervantes the chronicler of delusion has been noted, and
the "Colloquy of the Dogs" has been identified as one of the models of the
psychoanalytic session! The scholars who have made the connection, however, do
not consider Cervantes primarily as a satirist. See León Grinberg and Juan Francisco Rodríguez, "Cervantes as Cultural Ancestor of Freud," *International Journal
of Psycho-Analysis* 65 (1984): 155–68. J. E. Gedo and E. S. Wolf have given a
psychoanalytic view of Freud's powerful adolescent attachment to Cervantes: "It
would seem that Sigmund Freud entered adolescence still searching for idealized
parental imagoes and that he found what he needed in the writings of Cervantes.
Identification with the great novelist's humor and wisdom concerning his own

grandiosity as well as the unworkable idealizations of his characters apparently permitted Freud to avoid the consequences of acting out in a quixotic manner." This is too sanguine a view of Freud's later behavior. See "Freud's *Novelas ejemplares*," in *Freud: The Fusion of Science and Humanism: The Intellectual History of Psychoanalysis*, ed. J. E. Gedo and G. H. Pollock (New York: International Universities Press, 1976), 110.

15. Letter of August 23, 1883. *Letters*, 45–6.

16. Ernest Jones, *The Life and Work of Sigmund Freud* (New York: Basic Books, 1953) 1: 175.

17. I have been unable to obtain John H. Kirchner, "Don Quijote de la Mancha: A Study in Classical Paranoia," *Annali* [Naples] 9–2 (1967): 275–82.

18. Miguel de Cervantes, *Don Quixote: The Ormsby Translation*, ed. and rev. Joseph R. Jones and Kenneth Douglas (New York: Norton, 1981), 132. On Cervantes, see José Ortega y Gasset, *Meditations on Quixote*, trans. Evelyn Rugg and Diego Marín (New York: Norton, 1961); Salvador de Madariaga, *Don Quixote: An Introductory Essay in Psychology* (Oxford: Oxford University Press, 1935); William J. Entwhistle, *Cervantes* (Oxford: Oxford University Press, 1940); Erich Auerbach, *Mimesis: The Representation of Reality in Western Literature* (Princeton: Princeton University Press, 1957), chap. 14; E. C. Riley, *Cervantes's Theory of the Novel* (Oxford: Oxford University Press, 1964); John Jay Allen, *Don Quixote: Hero or Fool?: A Study in Narrative Technique* (Gainesville: University of Florida Press, 1969); Robert Alter, *Partial Magic: The Novel as a Self-Conscious Genre* (Berkeley: University of California Press, 1975); Marthe Robert, *The Old and the New: from Don Quixote to Kafka*, trans. Carol Cosman (Berkeley: University of California Press, 1977); Americo Castro, *An Idea of History: Selected Essays of Americo Castro*, ed. Stephen Gilman and Edmund L. King (Columbus: Ohio State University Press, 1977), Part One; Alexander Welsh, *Reflections on the Hero as Quixote* (Princeton: Princeton University Press, 1981); Walter L. Reed, *An Exemplary History of the Novel: The Quixotic versus the Picaresque* (Chicago: University of Chicago Press, 1981); Vladimir Nabokov, *Lectures on Don Quixote*, ed. Fredson Bowers (New York: Harcourt, Brace, Jovanovich, 1983); John G. Weiger, *The Substance of Cervantes* (New York: Cambridge University Press, 1985); Ruth El Saffar, *Critical Essays on Don Quixote* (Boston: G. K. Hall, 1986); Michael McKeon, *The Origins of the English Novel, 1600–1740* (Baltimore: Johns Hopkins University Press, 1987), chap. 7; Stephen Gilman, *The Novel According to Cervantes* (Berkeley: University of California Press, 1989).

19. Quixote's occasional self-awareness about the subjective quality of his delusion might seem a departure from the tendency of his mania, but it is actually a startlingly realistic depiction of the mental illness, as the recent work of Louis A. Sass has shown. See Chapter One of *The Paradoxes of Delusion: Wittgenstein, Schreber, and the Schizophrenic Mind* (Ithaca: Cornell University Press, 1994).

20. "The obsessional act is *ostensibly* a protection against the prohibited act; but *actually*, in our view, it is a repetition of it. The 'ostensibly' applies to the *conscious* part of the mind, and the 'actually' to the *unconscious* part. In exactly the same way, the ceremonial taboo of kings is *ostensibly* the highest honor and protection for them, while *actually* it is a punishment for their exaltation, a revenge

taken on them by their subjects. The experiences of Sancho Panza (as described by Cervantes) when he was Governor of his island convinced him that this view of court ceremonial was the only one that met the case." *S.E.* 13: 50–51, emphasis in original. The episode of Sancho the governor was one of Freud's favorite parts of the *Quixote*, the cause of an "idyllic moment" to the over-burdened medical student of 1875 as he reported to Silberstein: "That was at six o'clock and I was sitting alone in my room before a nourishing plateful which I devoured voraciously while reading the magnificent scene in which the noble Doctor Pedro Rescio de Tritea-fuera, which must mean something dreadful in Spanish, has the food taken away from under poor Sancho's nose." *Freud/Silberstein*, 87.

21. Leo Spitzer, "Linguistic Perspectivism in the *Don Quijote*" in *Linguistics and Literary History: Essays in Stylistics* (Princeton: Princeton University Press, 1948), 62.

22. Carroll B. Johnston, *Madness and Lust: A Psychoanalytic Approach to Don Quixote* (Berkeley: University of California Press, 1983), 76–80 and passim.

23. John G. Weiger, *The Individuated Self: Cervantes and the Emergence of the Individual* (Athens: Ohio University Press, 1970), 35.

24. Helena Percas de Ponseti, "The Cave of Montesinos: Cervantes' Art of Fiction," in Jones and Douglas, *Don Quixote*, 987.

25. See Auerbach, 137. In a later chapter, Auerbach crucially qualifies this view of Quixote as a frustrated idealist.

26. Folk culture was often patronized by the upper classes, as Peter Burke observes in *Popular Culture in Early Modern Europe* (New York: Harper and Row, 1978), 23–26. And, as later history has amply shown, its materials and styles can be integrated into official culture. Popular culture, as I observe in the text, is separated from elite culture by a difference in attitude toward the same materials and practices, and this difference is preserved even when popular materials are absorbed into sophisticated artistic practices such as those of the postmodernists.

27. As Diana de Armas Wilson points out, the practice of interpreting dreams as messages about money was a tradition going back to Hellenistic times and the *Oneirocriticas* of Artemidorus from which Freud borrowed the title of *The Interpretation of Dreams*. "Cervantes and the Night Visitors: Dream Work in the Cave of Montesinos," *Quixotic Desire: Psychoanalytic Perspectives on Cervantes* (Ithaca: Cornell University Press, 1993), 67–69. The representation of money in Quixote's dream is not cryptic but overt, as befits Cervantes' satiric purpose.

28. Sander L. Gilman has shown that in presenting his vision of neurotic human nature, Freud was universalizing the qualities of sensuality, femininity, and susceptibility to illness that had been prejudicially applied to Jews. Freud's satiric gesture was a *tu quoque*. Gilman makes the telling point that Freud's presentation of himself as his chief patient was a reversal of the usual model of the healthy physician descending among the sick. Again we find the satirist's self-inclusive irony. See *The Case of Sigmund Freud: Medicine and Identity at the Fin de Siècle* (Baltimore: Johns Hopkins University Press, 1993), 25. James L. Rice finds *The Interpretation of Dreams*, with its many references to Freud's Judaism, and even his criminal Jewish relatives, to be "an ethnic self-affirmation, a historically precocious model of being (in the spirit of Joyce), and least of all a clinical method." *Freud's*

Russia: National Identity in the Evolution of Psychoanalysis (New Brunswick, N. J.: Transaction Publishers, 1993), 6. Yirmiyahu Yovel finds Freud to have deep links with the skeptical and anti-authoritarian Marrano sensibility that originated among Jewish *conversos* in fifteenth-century Spain and that finds its paradigmatic example in Spinoza. *The Adventures of Immanence*, volume 1 of *Spinoza and Other Heretics* (Princeton: Princeton University Press, 1989), 136–66. Cervantes himself may have been a Marrano. See *The Marrano of Reason*, volume 2 of *Spinoza and Other Heretics*, 129. Freud, of course, did not suspect an ethnic link with Cervantes. All of these scholars recognize that Freud had strong ethnic and social motives working within his science. But they do not seem to take these motives as primary, nor as an embarrassment to scientific objectivity.

29. It is interesting to observe that Cervantes' novel could furnish Freud with examples of several of the charismatic types of what he calls 'narcissism', and that, as with Don Quixote, there is a vulgar social nostalgia associated with each of them. As we have seen, Freud believed that women, artists, great humorists, and criminals were among the figures of special attractiveness due to their narcissistic self-absorption, which appeals to the narcissism repressed in normal personalities. Cervantes himself, along with his narrator, can serve as an example of the humorist, though it would be anachronistic to call him an 'artist' in Freud's post-Romantic sense; he participates by the license of mirth in the archaic utopian fantasies of his hero. In the role of the criminal there is Roqué Guinart, not a mere criminal but a kind of Spanish Robin Hood, who bears about him a touch of the golden age in a version slightly more believable than Quixote's. The most striking, however, of the novel's 'narcissistic' figures—aside, of course, from Quixote himself—is Marcela, a girl who, in spite of her extraordinary beauty and wealth, refuses to marry, instead taking up the life of a shepherdess; thus she exposes her charms in a vulgar occupation while nevertheless defending an unapproachable chastity. This combination of beauty and reserve proves an irresistible incitement to masculine admiration and love, which proves so powerful as to be fatal in the case of the "student-shepherd" Grisóstomo, another one of Cervantes' mad Salamancan scholars. As with the paranoid knight, Marcela's appeal depends in great measure upon the social archaism of her fancy, its vulgar heroism. Near the end of his days in Part Two, Don Quixote also considers a pastoral charade as a respite from the more arduous delusions of knight-errantry.

For Freud's discussion of narcissistic allure, see "On Narcissism: An Introduction," *S.E.* 14: 88–89.

30. For a discussion of the use of 'over-determination' see the entry in J. Laplanche and J.-B. Pontalis, *The Language of Psycho-Analysis*, trans. Donald Nicholson-Smith (New York: Norton, 1973), 292–93.

31. Otto Rank, *The Myth of the Birth of the Hero and Other Works*, ed. Philip Freund (New York: Random House, 1932), 14–64.

32. *S.E.* 9: 234–41.

33. *S.E.* 16: 303. Sigmund Freud, *Gesammelte Werke Chronologisch Geordnet* (London: Imago, 1940) 11: 313.

34. Freud, writing on September 11, 1899, replied, "It is certainly true that the dreamer is too witty, but it is neither my fault nor does it contain a reproach.

All dreamers are equally insufferably witty, and they need to be because they are under pressure and the direct route is barred to them. . . . The ostensible wit of all unconscious processes is intimately related to the theory of the joke and the comic." *Freud/Fliess*, 371.

35. *Jokes and Their Relation*, S.E. 8: 202.

36. *Jokes and Their Relation*, S.E. 8: 201.

37. See Sander L. Gilman's enlightening discussion of "Freud and the Jewish Joke," in *Difference and Pathology: Stereotypes of Sexuality, Race, and Madness* (Ithaca: Cornell University Press, 1985), 175–90. Gilman points out that the bigoted notion of the *Ostjude* current at that time both in the popular collections of Jewish stories and in ostensibly scientific works like Otto Weininger's *Sex and Character* (1903) tended to ascribe to the Jew a primitive, sensualistic, and feminine nature, all seen as negatives, and to believe that these characteristics were revealed in the Jew's pretentious but faulty attempts to speak German.

38. Gilman, *Difference and Pathology*, 189.

39. *Leonardo da Vinci and a Memory of His Childhood*, S.E. 11: 114.

40. See the Introduction to Miguel de Cervantes, *The Trials of Persiles and Sigismunda: A Northern Tale*, trans. Celia Richmond Weller and Clark A. Colahan (Berkeley: University of California Press, 1989), 5. As the title makes clear, Cervantes has dislocated his tale to the northern fringe of Europe in order to achieve a setting for romance. If Cervantes' efforts in this genre now seem stilted, there remain the late romances of Shakespeare to assure us that this kind of writing could achieve the highest results even in this period of European culture.

41. Richard Henry Popkin, *The History of Skepticism from Erasmus to Spinoza*, rev. and enlarged ed. (Los Angeles: University of California Press, 1979).

42. Otis H. Green has analyzed the psychology of Quixote's condition systematically in Huartean terms. *Spain and the Western Tradition*, 4 vols. (Madison: University of Wisconsin, 1966) 4: 61.

43. Miguel de Cervantes Saavedra, *Three Exemplary Novels*, trans. Samuel Putnam (New York: Viking, 1950), 210–13. Cervantes was probably writing these tales around the time that Part One of *Don Quixote* was being published.

44. Juan Huarte de San Juan, *Examen de Ingenios* (1575), cited by Maureen Ihrie, *Skepticism in Cervantes* (London: Tamesis Books, 1982), 25. I have added the Spanish in brackets.

45. Cervantes' approach to madness reveals a clinical detachment applied to the onset, progress, and even cure of the disease. This can be seen not only in *Don* but also in the case of the wise student depicted in the *Exemplary Novels* poisoned by a rejected lover, comes to believe that his body is mad fantasy does not alter his powers of understanding. "The Licentiate of Glass" remains reasonable in all *idée fixe*. And yet, in spite of the fragility it upon himself in quixotic fashion to exactitude, the men and women of every *ote*, Cervantes offers paranoia as a satiric

47. Harold Jenkins, ed., *Hamlet: The Arden Shakespeare Edition* (New York: Methuen, 1982).

48. Harry Levin, *The Question of Hamlet* (New York: Oxford University Press, 1959), 161.

49. We may think, for instance, of the affectionately tolerant view of the vulgar audience given in the English theatrical spin-off of *Quixote*, Francis Beaumont's *Knight of the Burning Pestle* (c. 1610).

50. For a most persuasive statement of this point of view see Hugh Lloyd-Jones, *The Justice of Zeus* (Berkeley: University of California Press, 1971), chapter 5.

51. See the discussion in Bernard Knox's superb introduction to *Oedipus the King*, in Sophocles, *The Theban Plays*, trans. Robert Fagles (New York: Viking, 1982), 121–26.

52. "At the presentation of the medallion [inscribed in Greek with Sophocles' line, translated by Freud's colleague Hitschmann as "He divined the famed riddle and was a man most mighty"] there was a curious incident. When Freud read the inscription he became agitated and in a strangled voice demanded to know who had thought of it. . . . Freud disclosed that as a young student at the University of Vienna he used to stroll around the great arcaded court inspecting the busts of former famous professors of the institution. He then had the phantasy, not merely of seeing his own bust there in the future, which would not have been anything remarkable in an ambitious student, but of it actually being inscribed with the identical words he now saw on the medallion." Jones, *Life*, 2: 14.

53. See *Psycho-Analytic Movement*, S.E. 14: 21–22, discussed at the end of chapter 3 above.

Chapter Six

1. Since this chapter was written, Alexander Welsh's elegant study, *Freud's Wishful Dream Book* (Princeton: Princeton University Press, 1994), has appeared, giving a subtle treatment of the veiled humor and other narrative techniques employed in *The Interpretation of Dreams*. For Welsh, it is not so much Freud himself as it is the figure of the dream censor who takes the role of comic protagonist. Nevertheless, Welsh's analysis tends to confirm this one in a number of ways, emphasizing its comic form—"romance or serial comedy" (ix)—the centrality of ambition, and Freud's rhetorical projection of the hypocrisy of everyday life into the fictive domain of the unconscious.

This is also an appropriate place to acknowledge the acute literary analysis of Freud's self-presentation by Mark Edmundson in *Towards Reading Freud: Self-Creation in Milton, Wordsworth, Emerson, and Sigmund Freud* (Princeton: Princeton University Press, 1990).

2. Friedrich Wilhelm Joseph Schelling, *The Philosophy of Art*, ed. and Douglas W. Stott (Minneapolis: University of Minnesota Press, 1989), 234 German Romantic reaction to *Don Quixote* see Lienhard Bergel, "Cer Germany," in Angel Flores and M. J. Benardete, *Cervantes across the Quadricentennial Volume* (New York: Gordian Press, 1969; rptd. Press ed., 1947), 315–52; and Anthony Close, *The Romantic A*

Quixote': A Critical History of the Romantic Tradition in 'Quixote' Criticism (New York: Cambridge University Press, 1977), 29–66.

  3. *Group Psychology and the Analysis of the Ego, S.E.* 18: 140.

  4. *Jokes and Their Relation to the Unconscious, S.E.* 8: 232n.

  5. "The 'Uncanny'," *S.E.* 17: 224. I have translated the German word *'Unheimlich'*, 'uncanny', which Freud's translator gives in the original.

  6. As I observed in note 6 to chapter 1, the list of 'uncanny' experiences includes psychoanalysis itself. *S.E.* 17: 243–46.

  7. As Robert Wilcocks points out, there was something deceptive about Freud's summa of the authorities. Freud's own investigation was conducted largely without the benefit of previous research. He did the reading for the opening survey when all but one of the chapters presenting his own results had been completed. See *Maelzel's Chess Player: Sigmund Freud and the Rhetoric of Deceit* (Lanham, Md.: Rowman and Littlefield, 1994), 281 and 321, n3.

  8. Letter of August 6, 1899. *The Origins of Psycho-Analysis: Letters to Wilhelm Fliess, Drafts and Notes: 1887–1902*, trans. Eric Mosbacher and James Strachey (New York: Basic Books, 1954), 290. I have preferred in this instance the Mosbacher-Strachey version, slightly corrected, to that of *The Complete Letters of Sigmund Freud to Wilhelm Fliess: 1887–1904*, ed. and trans. Jeffrey Moussaieff Masson (Cambridge, Mass.: Harvard University Press, 1985), 365. Here is the original: "Nun ist das Ganze so auf eine Spazlergangsphantasie angelegt. Anfangs der dunkle Wald der Autoren (die die Bäume nicht sehen), aussichtslos, irrwegereich. Dann ein verdeckter Hohlweg, durch [den] ich den Leser führe—mein Traummuster mit seinen Sonderbarkeiten, Details, Indiskretionen, schlechten Witzen—und dann plötzlich die Höhe und die Aussicht und die Anfrage: Bitte, wohin wünschen Sie jetzt zu gehen?" Sigmund Freud, *Briefe an Wilhelm Fliess 1887–1904* (Frankfurt-am-Main: S. Fischer Verlag, 1986), 400.

  9. Leonard Shengold, "The Metaphor of the Journey in 'The Interpretation of Dreams,'" *American Imago* 23 (Winter 1966): 320–21. Shengold notes Jones' communication that Freud was reading Dante during the period in which he wrote *The Interpretation of Dreams*.

  10. Henri Ellenberger, *The Discovery of the Unconscious: The History and Evolution of Dynamic Psychiatry* (New York: Basic Books, 1970), 52. As Sulloway observes, *'Traumdeutung'*, as opposed to the more normal *'Deutung des Traums'*, is analogous to *'Sterndeutung'*. Frank J. Sulloway, *Freud, Biologist of the Mind: Beyond the Psychoanalytic the Legend* (Cambridge, Mass.: Harvard University Press, 1992; rptd. from New York: Basic Books, 1979), 323.

  11. The critique of dreams is closely related to the problems of the 'Freudian slip', which have been ingeniously demonstrated by Sebastiano Timpanaro in *The Freudian Slip: Psychoanalysis and Textual Criticism*, trans. Kate Soper (London: NLB, 1976). On the interpretation of dreams see Allen Esterson, *Seductive Mirage: An Exploration of the Work of Sigmund Freud* (Chicago: Open Court, 1993), 160–66 and 175–90, to which I am much indebted, and also Malcolm Macmillan's pages on the history of the question and its contributors, in *Freud Evaluated: The Completed Arc* (New York: Elsevier Science, 1991), 272–79.

  12. Here I am adapting a remark of Wittgenstein's, quoted in Esterson, 179.

13. Freud's failure to understand the point of this objection to his theory of dreams is evident not only in his response to an imaginary "skeptical reader" in the *Introductory Lectures, S.E.* 15: 109, discussed by Esterson (179–80), but also in his reply to a Herr Rudolf Schneider of Munich in a note added to *The Psychopathology of Everyday Life* in 1920, *S.E.* 6: 250–51n. The question raised by the latter is that of significant numbers, which Freud insisted to be identical with verbal associations and, we may extrapolate, with the elements of dreams. Freud remarks, "The fact that appropriate associations arise to numbers (or words) which are *presented* tell us nothing more about the origin of numbers (or words) which emerge *spontaneously* than could already be taken into consideration before that fact was known" (251n, emphasis in original). Freud cannot be made to appreciate, it seems, that since the theory in favor of the unconscious significance of spontaneously chosen numbers (or the details of a dream) depends upon their ability to produce significant associations, the theory fails if such associations can be produced by any stimulus whatever. Freud's difficulty lies, perhaps, in his peculiar conception of psychic determinism, which, as Macmillan suggests, led him to consider the chain of association between ideas to be unalterable, inaccessible to contamination from outside, and therefore always significant. Macmillan, 55–73.

14. In addition to the major biographies, we may add Mark Kanzer and Jules Glenn, eds., *Freud and His Self-Analysis* (New York: Jason Aronson, 1979); Alexander Grinstein, *Sigmund Freud's Dreams* (New York: International Universities Press, 1980); Carl E. Schorske, "Politics and Patricide in Freud's *The Interpretation of Dreams*," in *Fin-de-Siècle Vienna: Politics and Culture* (New York: Vintage, 1981), 181–207; William J. McGrath, *Freud's Discovery of Psychoanalysis: The Politics of Hysteria* (Ithaca: Cornell University Press, 1986); Didier Anzieu, *Freud's Self-Analysis*, trans. Peter Graham (Madison, Conn.: International Universities Press, 1986); and Paul C. Vitz, *Sigmund Freud's Christian Unconscious* (New York: Guilford Press, 1988).

15. 'The censorship' is offered first as an analogy, and as long as it remained such Freud would be entitled to choose his analogy from any course of life, so long as it served to illuminate the subject. But in this case the analogy quickly becomes the basis for a causal or structural link! "The fact that the phenomena of censorship and of dream-distortion correspond down to their smallest details justifies us in presuming that they are similarly determined. We may therefore suppose that dreams are given their shape in individual human beings by the operation of two psychical forces (or we may describe them as currents or systems); and that one of these forces constructs the wish which is expressed by the dream, while the other exercises a censorship upon this dream-wish and, by the use of that censorship, forcibly brings about a distortion in the expression of the wish" (143–44).

16. The entire passage is worth quoting: "In social life, which has provided us with our familiar analogy with the dream-censorship, we also make use of the suppression and reversal of affect, principally for purposes of dissimulation. If I am talking to someone whom I am obliged to treat with consideration while wishing to say something hostile to him, it is almost more important that I should conceal any expression of my *affect* from him than that I should mitigate the verbal form of

my thoughts. If I were to address him in words that were not impolite, but accompanied them with a look or gesture of hatred and contempt, the effect which I should produce on him would not be very different from what it would have been if I had thrown my contempt openly in his face. Accordingly, the censorship bids me above all suppress my affects; and, if I am a master of dissimulation, I shall assume the *opposite* affect—smile when I am angry and seem affectionate when I wish to destroy" (471, emphasis in original).

17. William M. Johnston, *The Austrian Mind: An Intellectual and Social History, 1848–1938* (Berkeley: University of California Press, 1972), 39.

18. Freud goes on to explain that the suspicious treatment of Otto was not the primary wish-fulfillment behind the dream; it lay, rather, in Freud's opportunity to identify with Professor A., who had gotten his professorship, as Freud hoped to do, late in life: "So once again I was wanting to be a Professor!" (271)

19. For a more fertile demonstration of the ease with which Freudian interpretations can be furnished with counter-examples, see Timpanaro, 44–46.

20. *New Introductory Lectures on Psycho-Analysis*, S.E. 22: 146, applied to this point by Esterson, 161.

21. About one of these cases Freud was touching up the facts. With regard to the cocaine addiction of his friend, Fleischl-Marxow, he twice indicates emphatically that he had never envisioned that his friend would inject the substance subcutaneously. But he was still advising this procedure in print months after the beginning of his friend's fatal addiction. Ernest Jones, *The Life and Work of Sigmund Freud* (New York: Basic Books, 1953) 1: 95–96.

22. "A dream is made absurd, then, if a judgement that something 'is absurd' is among the elements included in the dream-thoughts—that is to say, if any one of the dreamer's unconscious trains of thought has criticism or ridicule as its motive. Absurdity is accordingly one of the methods by which the dream-work represents a contradiction. . . . Absurdity in a dream, however, is not to be translated by a simple 'no'; it is intended to reproduce the *mood* of the dream-thoughts, which combines derision or laughter with the contradiction. It is only with such an aim in view that the dream-work produces anything ridiculous. Here once again *it is giving a manifest form to a portion of the latent content.*" S.E. 5: 434–35, emphasis in original.

23. "The determining element of paranoia is the mechanism of projection involving the refusal of belief in the self-reproach." "Draft K. The Neuroses of Defense (A Christmas Fairy Tale)," enclosed with the letter of January 1, 1896. *Freud/Fliess*, 168.

24. Letter of June 12, 1900. *Freud/Fliess*, 417.

25. James L. Rice, *Freud's Russia: National Identity in the Evolution of Psychoanalysis* (New Brunswick, N. J.: Transaction Publishers, 1993), 47.

26. Stanley Edgar Hyman, *The Tangled Bank: Darwin, Marx, Frazer and Freud as Imaginative Writers* (New York: Atheneum, 1962), 317.

27. I have transposed the translation with the original German of the quotation from the Dedication to *Faust* given in Strachey's text: "früh sich einst dem trüben Blick gezeigt."

28. "Freud's favorite heroes—the Carthaginian general, Hannibal; Marcus

Brutus, the defender of the Roman Republic; and Karl Moor, the protagonist of Schiller's *The Robbers*—all shared a passionate dedication to freedom in the face of threatening tyranny." McGrath, 59.

29. I am speaking here of *The Interpretation of Dreams*. As the years went by, Freud's identification with ethnic Judaism deepened but never took on a religious or political character.

30. Rice has found a host of bawdy and witty implications in the dream analysis, including a suggestion, turning on a dialect play on words, that Count Thun had a number of "public women" serving him at public expense. Rice, 52.

31. For an excellent account of the development of Freud's political interests, see the early chapters of McGrath.

32. Schorske, 185–86.

33. Leo Goldhammer, "Theodor Herzl und Sigmund Freud: Traeume," *Theodor Herzl Jahrbuch*, ed. Tulo Nussenblatt (Vienna: Victor Glanz, 1937), 266–68; cited in Avner Falk, "Freud and Herzl," *Midstream* 23 (Jan. 1977): 3.

34. "Having discovered that he was literally driven by political frustration, Freud set about trying to free himself from the neurotic compulsions associated with the world of politics, and his newly deepened understanding of the human psyche provided him with the necessary resources for this task." McGrath, 228.

35. "Successful Quixote" would be a good way to describe Hitler, of course, and on that basis we might take Freud's intuitions to be prophetic. The great virtue of Schorske's work, though, is in having shown that this aestheticizing way of thinking about politics was endemic to Viennese culture, crossing the full spectrum of rhetoric from anti-Semitism to Zionism. See his chapter "Politics in a New Key: An Austrian Trio." Schorske, 116–80. If Hitler was a successful Quixote, it was not for the reasons suggested by the psychoanalytic critique of politics.

36. Schorske, in the eloquent and justly admired study already cited, has argued, based on the analysis of Freud's political dreams and their interpretations, that, in locating the ultimate meaning of political struggle in relations with the father projected into social life, Freud had "achieved a counterpolitical triumph of the first magnitude. By reducing his own political past and present to an epiphenomenal status in relation to primal conflict between father and son, Freud gave his fellow liberals an a-historical theory of man and society that could make bearable a political world spun out of orbit and beyond control" (203). Politics could now be distinguished, in the language of psychoanalysis, as nothing but a psycho-social form of patricide, and psychoanalysis could plausibly claim to be the science of patricide.

Schorske rightly emphasizes that for Freud science had become the new form of heroism. For its political dimensions, I am much indebted to his analysis. In its details, however, it turns, unfortunately, upon an interpretation of Freud's dreams very much in the Freudian spirit. Schorske finds in Freud a psychological struggle between his Hannibal ambitions to destroy Catholic Rome and his Winckelmann desire for assimilation. Ultimately Freud surrenders his political resistance and gives in to a vision of politics as epiphenomena of the personal, the mark of his surrender to the personal being the reduction of his political fantasies in the "Revolutionary Dream of 1848" to the triumph over his father with the urinal. With that gesture, politics is displaced from the center of Freudian concern. Schorske, like McGrath, gives full recognition to the political and social motives at the heart of psychoanalysis but falls nevertheless under the spell of its scientific aura.

37. *S.E.* 5: 485.

Chapter Seven

1. Miguel de Cervantes, *Don Quixote: The Ormsby Translation*, ed. and rev. Joseph R. Jones and Kenneth Douglas (New York: Norton, 1981), 427–28.

2. Today Schreber's condition might fall under the category of 'paranoid schizophrenia'.

3. Daniel Paul Schreber, *Memoirs of My Nervous Illness*, ed. and trans. Ida MacAlpine and Richard A. Hunter (Cambridge, Mass.: Harvard University Press, 1988; rptd. from London: Wm. Dawson, 1955), 3. This volume contains not only the *Memoirs* themselves but also the documents concerning the trial that decided the issue of Schreber's mental competence. These include the reports to the Court of Appeals by Schreber's doctor, G. Weber, Schreber's own statement as plaintiff, and the court's decision. The page numbers for all of these materials will be supplied in the text.

4. This aspect of Schreber's delusion, like so many others, is an exaggeration of beliefs he had held in the past. See Han Israëls, *Schreber, Father and Son* (Madison, Conn.: International Universities Press, 1989), 161–62.

5. For instance, the "cursed creation of a false feeling" ("verfluchte Stimmungsmache"), the "mood-falsifying-miracle" ("die Stimmungsfälschungswunder"), and the "not-thinking-of-anything-thought" ("der Nichtsdenkungsgedanke"). Schreber, *Memoirs*, 144, 145, and 169 respectively.

6. See the "Judgement of the Royal Superior Country Court Dresden of 14th July 1902," translated in Schreber, 329–56, which, after a summary of both sides of the case as presented before it, begins with the statement, "The Court is in no doubt that the appellant is insane" (342).

7. Schreber, 285–313.

8. Schreber left the asylum in December 1902 and enjoyed almost five years of freedom spent with his wife and adopted daughter. His attempt to regain his official responsibilities failed, but he successfully managed the family affairs and took up his old position at the head of family gatherings, for which he wrote poems as he had in former days. Near the end of 1907 his wife had a mild stroke, and Schreber, feeling the onset of his illness, called for his doctors to take him into custody, where he remained in a psychotic state for four years until his death. These details were not known to Freud. Israëls, 187–201, 211–19.

9. Paul Roazen, *Freud and His Followers* (New York: NAL, 1971), 141.

10. "A Neurosis of Demoniacal Possession in the Seventeenth Century," *Sigmund Freud: Collected Papers*, trans. Joan Riviere (New York: Basic Books, 1959) 4: 457–58. In this case I have preferred Riviere's version to Strachey's, *S.E.* 19: 92. Here is the original: "Der Senatspräsident Schreber fand seine Heilung, als er sich entschloss, den Widerstand gegen die Kastration aufzugeben und sich in die ihm von Gott zugedachte weibliche Rolle zu fügen. Er wurde dann klar und ruhig,

konnte seine Entlassung aus der Anstalt selbst durchsetzen und führte ein normales Leben bis auf den einen Punkt, dass er einige Stunden täglich der Pflege seiner Weiblichkeit widmete, von deren langsamem Fortschreiten bis zu dem von Gott bestimmten Ziel er überzeugt blieb." "Eine Teufelsneurose im siebzehnten Jahrhundert," *Gesammelte Werke* 13: 339.

11. *The Freud/Jung Letters: The Correspondence between Sigmund Freud and C. G. Jung*, ed. William McGuire, trans. Ralph Manheim and R. F. C. Hull (Princeton: Princeton University Press, 1974), 311.

12. "Psycho-Analytic Notes on an Autobiographical Account of a Case of Paranoia (Dementia Paranoides)," *S.E.* 12: 35–58. Freud did not discuss Schreber's relationship with his famous father. This relationship has become a subject of great interest in recent decades, since it was learned that Schreber senior used his children as trial subjects for his somewhat bizarre experiments in child-rearing and physical conditioning. These experiences seem to be a major theme of Schreber's delusions. See, to begin with, William J. Niederland, M.D., *The Schreber Case: Psychoanalytic Profile of a Paranoid Personality*, expanded ed. (Hillsdale, N. J.: Analytic Press, 1984); Morton Schatzman, *Soul Murder: Persecution in the Family* (New York: Random House, 1973); and, most important, the work by Israëls cited above.

13. "The Neuroses of Defense (A Christmas Fairy Tale)," enclosed in a letter to Fliess of January 1, 1896. *The Complete Letters of Sigmund Freud to Wilhelm Fliess: 1887–1904*, ed. and trans. Jeffrey Moussaieff Masson (Cambridge, Mass.: Harvard University Press, 1985), 168.

14. The philosopher George Berkeley, like Schreber, believed that the world around us consists of mere sensations or appearances, which do not necessarily derive from objects with an independent existence except as God establishes them upon each occasion of perception.

15. "On Narcissism: An Introduction," *S.E.* 14: 75.

16. As he was preparing this essay, Freud wrote to Jung suggesting that the remarks on the "choice of neurosis" problem, i.e., the remarks on how the mechanisms of repression relate to the symptoms of different conditions, seemed to serve as a substitute for a truly clarifying conclusion to the essay: "A number of scientific notions I brought with me have combined to form a paper on paranoia, which still lacks an end, but takes quite a step forward in explaining the mechanism of the choice of neurosis." *Freud/Jung*, 353.

17. Sigmund Freud, "Psychoanalytische Bemerkungen über einen autobiographische beschriebenen Fall von Paranoia (Dementia Paranoides), *Gesammelte Werke Chronologisch Geordnet* (London: Imago, 1943) 8: 309.

18. *Freud/Jung*, 380, emphasis added.

19. See Leo Bersani's interesting discussion of this passage and the paradoxes of the theory of 'paranoia' that flow from it in "Pynchon, Paranoia, and Literature," *Representations* 25 (Winter 1989): 100–101. Bersani does not imagine a refusal of the gambit of paranoid reflection as it is offered by Freud and Pynchon, but only a living through of its consequences. This is Pynchon's plight as well. His work seems to me to offer the most perfect working out of the satiric vision of paranoia originated by Cervantes and universalized by Freud.

20. Freud was even willing to see in Schreber's delusion itself a covert irony working against Schreber's father, who was a doctor: "the absurd miracles that are performed on him are a bitter satire on his father's medical art." *Freud/Jung*, 369.

21. Letter of March 19, 1911. *Freud/Jung*, 407.

22. The self-justifications and generally competitive maneuverings of Freud and Jung within the theoretical language of psychoanalysis have been described in great detail by John Kerr in *A Most Dangerous Method: The Story of Jung, Freud, and Sabina Spielrein* (New York: Knopf, 1993).

23. Letter to Freud of December 12, 1912. *Freud/Jung*, 526.

24. Letter to Jung of February 12, 1911. *Freud/Jung*, 391.

25. *Leonardo da Vinci and a Memory of His Childhood*, S.E. 11: 74–75.

26. Letter to Freud of October 3, 1910. *The Correspondence of Sigmund Freud and Sándor Ferenczi*, ed. Eva Brabant, Ernst Falzeder, and Patrizia Giampieri-Deutsch; trans Peter T. Hoffer (Cambridge, Mass.: Harvard University Press, 1993) 1: 219, emphasis in original.

27. See *Freud/Ferenczi* 1: 214–15, n1.

28. Letter of October 6, 1910. *Freud/Ferenczi*, 221.

29. Letter to Ernest Jones of December 8, 1912. *The Complete Correspondence of Sigmund Freud and Ernest Jones, 1908–1939*, ed. Andrew Paskauskas (Cambridge, Mass.: Harvard University Press, 1993), 182.

30. Letter of March 5, 1912. *Freud/Jung*, 492.

31. Letter of March 11, 1909. *Freud/Jung*, 212. This was in reference to Freud's "traumatic hyperaesthesia toward dwindling correspondence"—he would become upset when Jung didn't write to him—which he attributed to his earlier experience with Fliess. Letter of March 9, 1909. *Freud/Jung*, 209.

32. W. W. Meissner, *The Paranoid Process* (New York: Jason Aronson, 1978), and *Psycho-Therapy and the Paranoid Process* (Northvale, N. J.: Jason Aronson, 1986). Page numbers to the first work will be included in the text.

33. Sigmund Freud, remarks from January 29, 1908, in *Minutes of the Vienna Psychoanalytic Society*, ed. Herman Nunberg and Ernst Federn; trans. M. Nunberg (New York: International Universities Press, 1962) 1: 295.

34. Phyllis Grosskurth, *The Secret Ring: Freud's Inner Circle and The Politics of Psychoanalysis* (New York: Addison-Wesley, 1991).

35. "Psycho-Analysis and Telepathy," *S.E.* 18: 173–93.

36. G. K. Chesterton, *Orthodoxy* (New York: Dodd, Mead, 1927), 32.

37. Since this chapter was written, I have had the benefit of *The Paradoxes of Delusion: Wittgenstein, Schreber, and the Schizophrenic Mind* (Ithaca: Cornell University Press, 1994) by Louis A. Sass, which gives what I believe to be the most sensitive and interesting, as well as significant reading of the *Memoirs* to date. Sass's observations complicate, to some degree, the distinctions I have drawn between Meissner's position and my own. Sass observes that even though Schreber is beset by delusory ideas, he frequently recognizes their subjectivity. His observations have the 'incorrigibility' that belongs to reports of inner experience and, therefore, make no claim upon reality; Schreber also employs a kind of mental 'double bookkeeping', by which he sets his illusions and his accurate knowledge about his surroundings in separate, parallel columns of awareness; and his reac-

tions to the material of his delusions is not at all what one would expect a person to display when mistaking such ideas for truth. For these reasons, among others, Sass casts doubt upon the notion of 'reality testing' as the basis of a distinction between ordinary cognition and madness. Instead he shows Schreber's illusory system, remarkably, to be a kind of existential psychological expression of the paradoxes of philosophical solipsism as explicated by Wittgenstein.

Since I cannot hope in this space to do justice to the subtlety of Sass's position, let me be content with observing that both he and Wittgenstein regard solipsism as an error that leads to or accompanies certain illusory or highly subjective forms of attention to the world ('seeing as'). Such an error differs from a simple error of reality testing, but, as the case of Schreber makes clear, it can distract one from reality almost to the same degree. This, along with some ordinary failures of reality testing, is what distinguishes Schreber from philosophical solipsists like Berkeley, Hume, and Schopenhauer. 'Reality' remains, then, an important point of reference for our ethical conviction that he should be considered mad.

Sass's reading of Schreber attempts to move away from the cognitive distinction reality/illusion toward the logical distinction truth/contradiction, and therefore it is much in the spirit of my larger argument about psychoanalysis and its contradictions. And, unlike Freud and Meissner, Sass does not leave himself in the position of being unable to distinguish his own observations from Schreber's.

38. This is the thesis put forward by Louis A. Sass in *Madness and Modernism: Insanity in the Light of Modern Art, Literature, and Thought* (New York: Basic Books, 1992).

39. Gilles Deleuze and Felix Guattari, *Anti-Oedipus: Capitalism and Schizophrenia*, trans. Robert Hurley, Mark Seem, and Helen R. Lane (Minneapolis: University of Minnesota Press, 1983), 19.

40. The issue also goes beyond my expertise. The following discussion has been informed by without coming to the same conclusion as the treatment of schizophrenia and modernity in Sass, 355–73.

41. Post-Freudian psychiatry has tended to regard paranoia as "a special form of schizophrenia, developing in individuals with a relatively well-preserved ego-structure." Christian Scharfetter, "Paranoia," in M. Shepherd and O. L. Zangwill, eds., *General Psycho-Pathology, Handbook of Psychiatry* (New York: Cambridge University Press, 1983) 1: 46.

42. H. B. M. Murphy, "Socio-Cultural Variations in Symptomatology, Incidence and Course of Illness," in Shepherd and Zangwill, *General Psycho-Pathology*, 162.

43. See the discussion of these terms and the problems they raise in Sass, 358 and passim.

44. "The content [of paranoid delusion] is highly determined by the culture, so that in India one can meet relatively many delusions of marital jealousy, in France (in the past?) delusions of high descent, in the USA delusions of being a defrauded inventor, and messianic delusions among the Bantu; whereas these varieties are met much less frequently in most other societies." Murphy, "Socio-Cultural Variations," 162.

45. "Character and Anal Erotism," *S.E.* 9: 167–75.

46. MacIntyre and Taylor have already been cited in the text. For Rorty see *Philosophy and the Mirror of Nature* (Princeton: Princeton University Press, 1981). I do not mean to imply that any of these authors share my view of Freud. Rorty remains particularly captivated by him and, in my view, by many aspects of the epistemological tradition he claims to have left behind.

Works Cited

Alexander, Franz. "Recollections of Berggasse 19." *Psychoanalytic Quarterly* 9 (1940): 195–204.

Allen, John Jay. *Don Quixote: Hero or Fool?: A Study in Narrative Technique*. Gainesville: University of Florida Press, 1969.

Alter, Robert. *Partial Magic: The Novel as a Self-Conscious Genre*. Berkeley: University of California Press, 1975.

American Psychiatric Association. *Diagnostic and Statistical Manual of Mental Disorders*. 3rd ed. rev. Washington, D.C.: American Psychiatric Association, 1987.

———. *Diagnostic and Statistical Manual of Mental Disorders*. 4th ed. Washington, D.C.: American Psychiatric Association, 1994.

Anzieu, Didier. *Freud's Self-Analysis*. Trans. Peter Graham. Madison, Conn.: International Universities Press, 1986.

Armas Wilson, Diana de. "Cervantes and the Night Visitors: Dream Work in the Cave of Montesinos." In *Quixotic Desire: Psychoanalytic Perspectives on Cervantes*, ed. Ruth Anthony El Saffar and Diana de Armas Wilson, 59–80. Ithaca: Cornell University Press, 1993.

Auerbach, Erich. *Mimesis: The Representation of Reality in Western Literature*. Princeton: Princeton University Press, 1957.

Bacon, Francis. *The Works of Francis Bacon*. 15 vols. Ed. James Spedding, et al. Boston: Taggard and Thompson, 1863.

———. "Of the Proficience and Advancement of Learning Divine and Human." *Bacon*, vol. 6.

———. "Description of a Natural and Experimental History Such As May Serve for the Foundation of a True Philosophy." *Bacon*, vol. 8.

———. *The Great Instauration*. *Bacon*, vol. 8.

———. *New Organon*. *Bacon*, vol. 8.

———. "The Natural and Experimental History for the Foundation of Philosophy: or, Phenomena of the Universe: which is the third part of the Instauratio Magna." *Bacon*, vol. 9.

———. "Essays or Counsels Civil and Moral." *Bacon*, vol. 12.

Bergel, Lienhard. "Cervantes in Germany." In *Cervantes across the Centuries: A Quadricentennial Volume*, ed. Angel Flores and M. J. Benardete, 315–52. Dryden Press, 1947. Rptd. New York: Gordian Press, 1969.

Bersani, Leo. "Pynchon, Paranoia, and Literature." *Representations* 25 (Winter 1989): 99–118.

Braudy, Leo. "Providence, Paranoia, and the Novel." *English Literary History* 48 (1981): 619–37.

Brown, Norman O. *Life against Death: The Psychoanalytic Meaning of History.* Middletown, Conn.: Wesleyan University Press, 1959.

Burke, Peter. *Popular Culture in Early Modern Europe.* New York: Harper and Row, 1978.

Cassirer, Ernst. *The Philosophy of Enlightenment.* Trans. Fritz C. A. Koelin and James P. Pettegrove. Princeton: Princeton University Press, 1951.

Castro, Americo. *An Idea of History: Selected Essays of Americo Castro.* Ed. Stephen Gilman and Edmund L. King. Columbus: Ohio State University Press, 1977.

Cervantes, Miguel de. *Don Quixote: The Ormsby Translation.* Ed. and rev. Joseph R. Jones and Kenneth Douglas. New York: Norton, 1981.

———. *Three Exemplary Novels.* Trans. Samuel Putnam. New York: Viking, 1950.

———. *The Trials of Persiles and Sigismunda: A Northern Tale.* Trans. Celia Richmond Weller and Clark A. Colahan. Berkeley: University of California Press, 1989.

Chesterton, G. K. *Orthodoxy.* New York: Dodd, Mead, 1927.

Close, Anthony. *The Romantic Approach to 'Don Quixote': A Critical History of the Romantic Tradition in 'Quixote' Criticism.* New York: Cambridge University Press, 1977.

Comte, Auguste. *The Positive Philosophy.* Trans. Harriet Martineau. New York: AMS, 1974.

Crews, Frederick. *Skeptical Engagements.* New York: Oxford University Press, 1986.

——— et al. *The Memory Wars: Freud's Legacy in Dispute.* New York: New York Review of Books, 1996.

Deleuze, Gilles, and Felix Guattari. *Anti-Oedipus: Capitalism and Schizophrenia.* Trans. Robert Hurley, Mark Seem, and Helen R. Lane. Minneapolis: University of Minnesota Press, 1983.

Deutsch, Helene. "Freud and His Pupils: A Footnote to the History of the Psychoanalytic Movement." *Psychoanalytic Quarterly* 9 (1940): 184–94. Rptd. in *Sigmund Freud: Critical Assessments,* Laurence Spurling, ed., 4: 33–41. 4 vols. New York: Routledge, 1989.

Eastman, Max. *Great Companions: Critical Memoirs of Some Famous Friends.* London: Museum Press, 1959.

Edmundson, Mark. *Towards Reading Freud: Self-Creation in Milton, Wordsworth, Emerson, and Sigmund Freud.* Princeton: Princeton University Press, 1990.

Eissler, K. R. *Talent and Genius: The Fictitious Case of Tausk contra Freud.* New York: Quadrangle, 1971.

El Saffar, Ruth. *Critical Essays on Don Quixote.* Boston: G. K. Hall, 1986.

El Saffar, Ruth, and Diana de Armas Wilson, eds. *Quixotic Desire: Psychoanalytic Perspectives on Cervantes.* Ithaca: Cornell University Press, 1993.

Eliade, Mircea. *The Sacred and the Profane: The Nature of Religion.* Trans. Willard R. Trask. New York: Harcourt, Brace, Jovanovich, 1959.

Ellenberger, Henri. *The Discovery of the Unconscious: The History and Evolution of Dynamic Psychiatry.* New York: Basic Books, 1970.

Entwhistle, William J. *Cervantes.* Oxford: Oxford University Press, 1940.

Erasmus, Desiderius. *The Praise of Folly and Other Writings: A New Translation with Critical Commentary.* Ed. and trans. Robert M. Adams. New York: Norton, 1989.

Esterson, Allen. *Seductive Mirage: An Exploration of the Work of Sigmund Freud.* Chicago: Open Court, 1993.

Falk, Avner. "Freud and Herzl." *Midstream* 23 (Jan. 1977), 3–24.

Freud, Sigmund. *The Standard Edition of the Complete Psychological Works of Sigmund Freud.* Trans. James Strachey. London: The Hogarth Press and The Institute for Psycho-Analysis, 1958.

———. "The Neuro-Psychoses of Defense." *S.E.* 3.

———. "Further Remarks on the Neuro-Psychoses of Defense." *S.E.* 3.

———. *The Interpretation of Dreams. S.E.* 4–5.

———. *The Psycho-Pathology of Everyday Life. S.E.* 6.

———. *Jokes and Their Relation to the Unconscious. S.E.* 8.

———. "Character and Anal Erotism." *S.E.* 9.

———. " 'Civilized' Sexual Morality and Modern Nervous Illness." *S.E.* 9.

———. "Contribution to a Questionnaire on Reading." *S.E.* 9.

———. "Creative Writers and Day-Dreaming." *S.E.* 9.

———. "Family Romances." *S.E.* 9.

———. "Obsessive Actions and Religious Practices." *S.E.* 9.

———. "The Future Prospects of Psycho-Analytic Therapy." *S.E.* 11.

———. *Leonardo da Vinci and a Memory of His Childhood. S.E.* 11.

———. "Formulations on the Two Principles of Mental Functioning." *S.E.* 12.

———. "Psycho-Analytic Notes on an Autobiographical Account of a Case of Paranoia (Dementia Paranoides)." *S.E.* 12.

———. "Remembering, Repeating, and Working-Through (Further Recommendations on the Technique of Psycho-Analysis II)." *S.E.* 12.

———. "The Claims of Psycho-Analysis to Scientific Interest." *S.E.* 13.

———. *Totem and Taboo. S.E.* 13.

———. *On the History of the Psycho-Analytic Movement. S.E.* 14.

———. "On Narcissism: An Introduction." *S.E.* 14.

———. "The Unconscious." *S.E.* 14.

———. *Introductory Lectures on Psycho-Analysis. S.E.* 16.

———. *Group Psychology and The Analysis of the Ego. S.E.* 18.

———. "Psycho-Analysis and Telepathy." *S.E.* 18.

———. "The Resistance to Psycho-Analysis." *S.E.* 19.

———. "The Question of Lay Analysis: Postscript (1927)." *S.E.* 20.

———. *Civilization and Its Discontents. S.E.* 21.

———. *The Future of an Illusion. S.E.* 21.

———. "A Difficulty in the Path of Psycho-Analysis." *S.E.* 22.

———. *New Introductory Lectures on Psycho-Analysis. S.E.* 22.

————. "Why War?" *S.E.* 22.

————. "Analysis Terminable and Interminable." *S.E.* 23.

————. *Moses and Monotheism. S.E.* 23.

————. *Gesammelte Werke Chronologisch Geordnet.* London: Imago, 1943.

————. "Psychoanalytische Bemerkungen über einen autobiographische beschrie-benen Fall von Paranoia (Dementia Paranoides). *Gesammelte Werke Chronolog-isch Geordnet* (London: Imago, 1943) 8: 309.

————. "Eine Teufelsneurose im siebzehnten Jahrhundert," *Gesammelte Werke* 13: 339.

————. "A Neurosis of Demoniacal Possession in the Seventeenth Century." In *Sigmund Freud: Collected Papers*, trans. Joan Riviere, 4: 436–72. 5 vols. New York: Basic Books, 1959.

————. *The Origins of Psycho-Analysis: Letters to Wilhelm Fliess, Drafts and Notes: 1887–1902.* Trans. Eric Mosbacher and James Strachey. New York: Basic Books, 1954.

————. *The Complete Letters of Sigmund Freud to Wilhelm Fliess, 1887–1904.* Ed. and trans. Jeffrey Moussaieff Masson. Cambridge, Mass.: Harvard Univer-sity Press, 1985.

————. *Briefe an Wilhelm Fliess, 1887–1904.* Frankfurt-am-Main: S. Fischer Verlag, 1986.

————. *Letters of Sigmund Freud.* Trans. Tania and James Stern; ed. Ernst L. Freud. New York: Basic Books, 1961.

————. *The Letters of Sigmund Freud to Eduard Silberstein, 1871–1881.* Trans. Arnold J. Pomerans; ed. Walter Boehlich. Cambridge, Mass.: Harvard Univer-sity Press, 1990.

Freud, Sigmund, and Karl Abraham. *A Psycho-Analytic Dialogue: The Letters of Sigmund Freud and Karl Abraham, 1907–1926.* Ed. Hilda C. Abraham and Ernst L. Freud. New York: Basic Books, 1965.

Freud, Sigmund, and Sándor Ferenczi. *The Correspondence of Sigmund Freud and Sándor Ferenczi.* Vol. 1, 1908–1914. Ed. Eva Brabant, Ernst Falzeder, and Patrizia Giampieri-Deutsch. Trans. Peter T. Hoffer. Cambridge, Mass.: Harvard University Press, 1993.

Freud, Sigmund, and Ernest Jones. *The Complete Correspondence of Sigmund Freud and Ernest Jones, 1908–1939.* Ed. Andrew Paskauskas. Cambridge, Mass.: Harvard University Press, 1993.

Freud, Sigmund, and Carl Jung. *The Freud/Jung Letters: The Correspondence between Sigmund Freud and C. G. Jung.* Trans. Ralph Manheim and R. F. C. Hull; ed. William McGuire. Princeton: Princeton University Press, 1974.

Freud, Sigmund, and Oskar Pfister. *Psychoanalysis and Faith: The Letters of Sigmund Freud and Oskar Pfister.* Trans. Eric Mosbacher; ed. Heinrich Meng and Ernst Freud. New York: Basic Books, 1963.

Freud, Sigmund, and Lou-Andreas Salomé. *Sigmund Freud and Lou-Andreas Sa-lomé: Letters.* Trans. William and Elaine Robson-Scott; ed. Ernst Pfeiffer. New York: Norton, 1966.

Gay, Peter. *A Godless Jew: Freud, Atheism, and the Making of Psychoanalysis.* New Haven: Yale University Press, 1987.

Gedo, J. E., and E. S. Wolf. "Freud's *Novelas ejemplares.*" In *Freud: The Fusion of Science and Humanism: The Intellectual History of Psychoanalysis*, ed. J. E. Gedo and G. H. Pollock, 87–110. New York: International Universities Press, 1976.

Gellner, Ernest. *The Psychoanalytic Movement, or, The Coming of Unreason.* London: Paladin, 1985.

Gilman, Sander L. *Difference and Pathology: Stereotypes of Sexuality, Race, and Madness.* Ithaca: Cornell University Press, 1985.

———. *The Case of Sigmund Freud: Medicine and Identity at the Fin de Siècle.* Baltimore: Johns Hopkins University Press, 1993.

Gilman, Stephen. *The Novel According to Cervantes.* Berkeley: University of California Press, 1989.

Goldhammer, Leo. "Theodor Herzl und Sigmund Freud: Traeume." In *Theodor Herzl Jahrbuch*, ed. Tulo Nussenblatt, 266–68. Vienna: Victor Glanz, 1937.

Green, Otis H. *Spain and the Western Tradition.* 4 vols. Madison: University of Wisconsin, 1966.

Grinberg, León, and Juan Francisco Rodríguez. "Cervantes as Cultural Ancestor of Freud." *International Journal of Psycho-Analysis* 65 (1984): 155–68.

Grinstein, Alexander. *Sigmund Freud's Dreams.* New York: International Universities Press, 1980.

Grosskurth, Phyllis. *The Secret Ring: Freud's Inner Circle and the Politics of Psychoanalysis.* Menlo Park, Calif.: Addison-Wesley, 1991.

Grünbaum, Adolf. *The Foundations of Psychoanalysis: A Philosophical Critique.* Berkeley: University of California Press, 1984.

———. *Validation in the Clinical Theory of Psychoanalysis: A Study in the Philosophy of Psychoanalysis.* Psychological Issues, no. 61. Madison, Conn.: International Universities Press, Inc., 1993.

Haeckel, Ernst. *The Riddle of the Universe at the Close of the Nineteenth Century.* New York: Harper and Brothers, 1900.

Hobbes, Thomas. *Leviathan.* Ed. Richard Tuck. New York: Cambridge University Press, 1991.

Hofstadter, Richard. *The Paranoid Style in American Politics and Other Essays.* New York: Knopf, 1966.

Hume, David. *Treatise of Human Nature.* Ed. L. A. Selby-Bigge. 2nd ed. rev. with notes by P. H. Nidditch. Oxford: Oxford University Press, 1978.

Hyman, Stanley Edgar. *The Tangled Bank: Darwin, Marx, Frazer and Freud as Imaginative Writers.* New York: Atheneum, 1962.

Ihrie, Maureen. *Skepticism in Cervantes.* London: Tamesis Books, 1982.

Israëls, Han. *Schreber, Father and Son.* Madison, Conn.: International Universities Press, 1989.

Johnston, Carroll B. *Madness and Lust: A Psychoanalytic Approach to Don Quixote.* Berkeley: University of California Press, 1983.

Johnston, William E. *The Austrian Mind: An Intellectual and Social History, 1848–1938.* Berkeley: University of California Press, 1972.

Jones, Ernest. *The Life and Work of Sigmund Freud.* 3 vols. New York: Basic Books, 1953.

Kant, Immanuel. "Idea for a Universal History with a Cosmopolitan Intent." In *Perpetual Peace and Other Essays on Politics, History, and Morals*, trans. Ted Humphrey, 29–40. Indianapolis: Hackett, 1983.

Kanzer, Mark, and Jules Glenn, eds. *Freud and His Self-Analysis*. New York: Jason Aronson, 1979.

Kemp, Anthony. *The Estrangement of the Past: A Study in Modern Historical Consciousness*. New York: Oxford University Press, 1991.

Kerr, John. *A Most Dangerous Method: The Story of Jung, Freud, and Sabina Spielrein*. New York: Knopf, 1993.

Kirchner, John H. "Don Quijote de la Mancha: A Study in Classical Paranoia." *Annali* [Naples] 9–2 (1967): 275–82.

Knox, Bernard. Introduction to *Oedipus the King*. Sophocles. *The Theban Plays*. Trans. Robert Fagles. New York: Viking, 1982, 115–35.

Laplanche, J., and J.-B. Pontalis. *The Language of Psycho-Analysis*. Trans. Donald Nicholson-Smith. New York: Norton, 1973.

Levin, Harry. *The Question of Hamlet*. New York: Oxford University Press, 1959.

Lloyd-Jones, Hugh. *The Justice of Zeus*. Berkeley: University of California Press, 1971.

Locke, John. *An Essay concerning Human Understanding*. Ed. Peter Nidditch. Oxford: Oxford University Press, 1975.

MacIntyre, Alasdair. *A Short History of Ethics: A History of Moral Philosophy from the Homeric Age to the Twentieth Century*. New York: Macmillan, 1966.

———. *After Virtue: A Study in Moral Theory*. Notre Dame: University of Notre Dame Press, 1981.

Macmillan, Malcolm. *Freud Evaluated: The Completed Arc*. New York: Elsevier Science, 1991.

Madariaga, Salvador de. *Don Quixote: An Introductory Essay in Psychology*. Oxford: Oxford University Press, 1935.

Mandel, Oscar. "The Function of the Norm in *Don Quixote*." *Modern Philology* 35 (Feb. 1956): 154–63.

Marx, Karl. *The Communist Manifesto*. In *Karl Marx: Selected Writings*, ed. David McLellan, 221–46. New York: Oxford University Press, 1977.

McGrath, William J. *Freud's Discovery of Psychoanalysis: The Politics of Hysteria*. Ithaca: Cornell University Press, 1986.

McKeon, Michael. *The Origins of the English Novel, 1600–1740*. Baltimore: Johns Hopkins University Press, 1987.

Meissner, W. W., *The Paranoid Process*. New York: Jason Aronson, 1978.

———. *Psycho-Therapy and the Paranoid Process*. Northvale, N. J.: Jason Aronson, 1986.

Murphy, H. B. M. "Socio-Cultural Variations in Symptomatology, Incidence and Course of Illness." In *General Psycho-Pathology*, vol. 1 of *Handbook of Psychiatry*, ed. M. Shepherd and O. L. Zangwill, 157–71. New York: Cambridge University Press, 1983.

Nabokov, Vladimir. *Lectures on Don Quixote*. Ed. Fredson Bowers. New York: Harcourt, Brace, Jovanovich, 1983.

Neu, Jerome. *The Cambridge Companion to Freud.* New York: Cambridge University Press, 1991.

Niederland, William J., *The Schreber Case: Psychoanalytic Profile of a Paranoid Personality.* Expanded ed. Hillsdale, N. J.: Analytic Press, 1984.

Nietzsche, Friedrich. *The Gay Science.* Trans. Walter Kaufmann. New York: Vintage, 1974.

———. *On the Genealogy of Morals.* Trans. Walter Kaufmann and R. J. Hollingdale. New York: Vintage, 1967.

Nunberg, Herman, and Ernst Federn, eds. *Minutes of the Vienna Psychoanalytic Society.* 4 vols. Trans. M. Nunberg. New York: International Universities Press, 1962.

Ortega y Gasset, José. *Meditations on Quixote.* Trans. Evelyn Rugg and Diego Marin. New York: Norton, 1961.

Parker, Blanford. *The Eclipse of Analogy: The Origins and Progress of Augustanism.* Cambridge: Cambridge University Press, forthcoming in 1997.

Paul, Robert A. "Did the Primal Crime Take Place?" *Ethos* 4 (1976): 311–52.

———. "Freud's Anthropology: A Reading of the 'Cultural Books.' " In *The Cambridge Companion to Freud.* Ed. Jerome Neu. New York: Cambridge University Press, 1991.

Percas de Ponseti, Helena. "The Cave of Montesinos: Cervantes' Art of Fiction." In *Don Quixote: The Ormsby Translation,* ed. and rev. Joseph R. Jones and Kenneth Douglas, 979–94. New York: Norton, 1981.

Popkin, Richard Henry. *The History of Skepticism from Erasmus to Spinoza.* Rev. and enlarged ed. Berkeley: University of California Press, 1979.

Rank, Otto. *The Myth of the Birth of the Hero and Other Works.* Ed. Philip Freund. New York: Random House, 1932.

Reed, Walter L. *An Exemplary History of the Novel: The Quixotic versus the Picaresque.* Chicago: University of Chicago Press, 1981.

Rice, James L. *Freud's Russia: National Identity in the Evolution of Psychoanalysis.* New Brunswick, N. J.: Transaction Publishers, 1993.

Rieff, Philip. *Freud: The Mind of the Moralist.* Garden City, N.Y.: Doubleday, 1959.

Riley, E. C. *Cervantes's Theory of the Novel.* Oxford: Oxford University Press, 1964.

Ritvo, Lucille B. *Darwin's Influence on Freud: A Tale of Two Sciences.* New York: Yale University Press, 1990.

Roazen, Paul. *Brother Animal: The Story of Freud and Tausk.* New York: Knopf, 1969.

———. *Freud and His Followers.* New York: NAL, 1971.

Robert, Marthe. *From Oedipus to Moses: Freud's Jewish Identity.* Trans. Ralph Manheim. Garden City, N.Y.: Anchor Press, 1976.

———. *The Old and the New: From Don Quixote to Kafka.* Trans. Carol Cosman. Berkeley: University of California Press, 1977.

Robinson, Paul. *Freud and His Critics.* Berkeley: University of California Press, 1993.

Rorty, Richard. *Philosophy and the Mirror of Nature*. Princeton: Princeton University Press, 1981.

Rousseau, Jean-Jacques. *The Social Contract*. Trans. Maurice Cranston. New York: Penguin, 1968.

Roustang, François. *Dire Mastery: Discipleship from Freud to Lacan*. Trans. Ned Lukacher. Baltimore: Johns Hopkins University Press, 1982.

Rudnytsky, Peter L. *The Psychoanalytic Vocation: Rank, Winnicott, and the Legacy of Freud*. New Haven: Yale University Press, 1991.

Sass, Louis A. *Madness and Modernism: Insanity in the Light of Modern Art, Literature, and Thought*. New York: Basic Books, 1992.

———. *The Paradoxes of Delusion: Wittgenstein, Schreber, and the Schizophrenic Mind*. Ithaca: Cornell University Press, 1994.

Scharfetter, Christian. "Paranoia." In *General Psycho-Pathology*, vol. 1 of *The Handbook of Psychiatry*, ed. M. Shepherd and O. L. Zangwill, 45–46. 5 vols. New York: Cambridge University Press, 1983.

Schatzman, Morton. *Soul Murder: Persecution in the Family*. New York: Random House, 1973.

Schelling, Friedrich Wilhelm Joseph. *The Philosophy of Art*. Trans. and ed. Douglas W. Stott. Minneapolis: University of Minnesota Press, 1989.

Schorske, Carl E. *Fin-de-Siècle Vienna: Politics and Culture*. New York: Vintage, 1981.

Schreber, Daniel Paul. *Memoirs of My Nervous Illness*. Trans. and ed. Ida MacAlpine and Richard A. Hunter. Cambridge, Mass.: Harvard University Press, 1988. Rptd. from London: Wm. Dawson, 1955.

Screech, M. A. "Good Madness in Christendom." In *The Anatomy of Madness: Essays in the History of Psychiatry*, ed. W. F. Bynum, Roy Porter, and Michael Shepherd, 1: 25–39. 2 vols. New York: Tavistock Publications, 1985.

Shakespeare, William. *Hamlet: The Arden Shakespeare Edition*. Ed. Harold Jenkins. New York: Methuen, 1982.

Shapiro, David. *Neurotic Styles*. New York: Basic Books, 1965.

Shengold, Leonard. "The Metaphor of the Journey in 'The Interpretation of Dreams.' " *American Imago* 23 (Winter 1966): 316–31.

———. "Freud and Joseph." In *Freud and His Self-Analysis*, ed. Mark Kanzer and Jules Glenn, 67–86. New York: Jason Aronson, 1979.

Shepherd, M., and O. L. Zangwill. *General Psycho-Pathology*, vol. 1 of *Handbook of Psychiatry*. New York: Cambridge University Press, 1983.

Spector, Jack J. *The Aesthetics of Freud*. New York: Praeger, 1972.

Spitzer, Leo. *Linguistics and Literary History: Essays in Stylistics*. Princeton, N. J.: Princeton University Press, 1948.

Spurling, Laurence, ed. *Sigmund Freud: Critical Assessments*. 4 vols. New York: Routledge, 1989.

Sullivan, Harry Stack. *Clinical Studies in Psychiatry*. Ed. Helen Swick Perry, Mary Ladd Gawel, and Martha Gibbon. New York: Norton, 1956.

Sulloway, Frank J. *Freud, Biologist of the Mind: Beyond the Psychoanalytic Legend*. Cambridge, Mass.: Harvard University Press, 1992. Rptd. from New York: Basic Books, 1979.

Swales, Peter. "Freud, Fliess, and Fratricide: The Role of Fliess in Freud's Conception of Paranoia." Private publication, 1982. Rptd. in *Sigmund Freud: Critical Assessments*, ed. Laurence Spurling, 1: 302–30. New York: Routledge, 1989.

Swanson, David W., Philip J. Bohnert, and Jackson H. Smith. *The Paranoid*. Boston: Little, Brown, 1970.

Taylor, Charles. *Sources of the Self: The Making of the Modern Identity*. Cambridge, Mass.: Harvard University Press, 1989.

Thornton, E. M. *The Freudian Fallacy: An Alternative View of Freudian Theory*. Garden City, N.Y.: The Dial Press, 1984.

Timpanaro, Sebastiano. *The Freudian Slip: Psychoanalysis and Textual Criticism*. Trans. Kate Soper. London: NLB, 1976.

Vico, Giambattista. *The New Science of Giambattista Vico: An Unabridged Translation of the Third Edition (1744)*. 2nd ed. rev. Trans. Thomas Goddard Bergin and Max Harold Fisch. Ithaca: Cornell University Press, 1968.

Vitz, Paul C. *Sigmund Freud's Christian Unconscious*. New York: Guilford Press, 1988.

Webster, Richard. *Why Freud Was Wrong: Sin, Science, and Psychoanalysis*. New York: Basic Books, 1995.

Weiger, John G. *The Individuated Self: Cervantes and the Emergence of the Individual*. Athens: Ohio University Press, 1970.

———. *The Substance of Cervantes*. New York: Cambridge University Press, 1985.

Welsh, Alexander. *Reflections on the Hero as Quixote*. Princeton: Princeton University Press, 1981.

———. *Freud's Wishful Dream Book*. Princeton: Princeton University Press, 1994.

White, Lancelot Law. *The Unconscious before Freud*. New York: Basic Books, 1960.

Wilcocks, Robert. *Maelzel's Chess Player: Sigmund Freud and the Rhetoric of Deceit*. Lanham, Md.: Rowman and Littlefield, 1994.

Yovel, Yirmiyahu. *The Adventures of Immanence*, vol. 1 of *Spinoza and Other Heretics*. Princeton: Princeton University Press, 1989.

———. *The Marrano of Reason*, vol. 2 of *Spinoza and Other Heretics*. Princeton: Princeton University Press, 1989.

Index

Abraham, Karl, 55
Adler, Alfred, 56
Adler, Karl, 162, 197
Amadis de Gaul (Rodríguez de Montalvo), 109–10
Aristotle, 138; on *Oedipus*, 129; poetics of, 103
Art: origins of myth and the first epic poet, 18–19; and paranoia, 26–27; and pleasure principle, 25–27. *See also* Freud, Sigmund; Narcissism; Psychoanalysis; Romance; Satire
Artemidorus, *Oneirocriticas*, 138, 243 n. 27
Auden, W. H., 212

Bacon, Francis: *The Advancement of Learning*, 69; 'idols of the mind', 29, 102; Macaulay's essay on, 68; modernity, 211; romance in rhetoric of, 73–74; as satirist, 124; suspicion in, 69–77, 80, 81, 83–84, 86, 95; *Wisdom of the Ancients*, 238 n. 31. *See also* Science
Beaumont, Francis, *Knight of the Burning Pestle*, 246 n. 49
Berkeley, George, 78, 181
Bernays, Martha (Freud's fiancée and wife), 99, 100, 135
Bersani, Leo, 252 n. 19
Bleuler, Eugen, 187–88, 232 n. 35, 233 n. 45
Breuer, Joseph, 155, 233 n. 42
Bright, Timothy, *Treatise on Melancholy*, 125
Brown, Norman O., on Swift and psychoanalysis, 240 n. 2
Burroughs, William, 2
Burton, Robert, *The Anatomy of Melancholy*, 124, 138

Caesar, Julius, Freud's identification with, 155–57
Carlyle, Thomas, *Sartor Resartus*, 98
Censorship, theory of, in *The Interpretation of Dreams*, 141–45, 248–49 nn. 15, 16. *See also* Reality principle; Repression; Satire
Cervantes, Miguel de, 5, 95, 98; "Colloquy of the Dogs," 99, 124, 241–42 n. 14; Freud's adolescent cult of, 99–100; "Licentiate of Glass," 245 n. 45; philosophical stance and attitude toward romance, 123–24; *Trials of Persiles and Sigismunda*, 123, 245 n. 40. *See also Don Quixote*; Freud, Sigmund; Satire
Charcot, Jean-Martin, 51
Chesterton, G. K., 167, 199
Civilization and Its Discontents, 89
" 'Civilized' Sexual Morality and Modern Nervous Illness," 226 n. 31
Comte, Auguste, 68; Freud on, 239 n. 37; historical recapitulation theory in, 86–87
Condorcet, Marquis de, 85
Copernicus, Nicholas, 22, 29, 32, 50, 51
Crews, Frederick, on persistence of psychoanalysis, 230 n. 14

Dante, *Divine Comedy*, 137, 207
Darwin, Charles, 32, 90; as Freud's self-chosen precursor, 22, 50, 51; on the primal father, 14, 84; and Schreber, 175
da Vinci, Leonardo, 21–22, 29, 51, 189, 229 n. 15
Deleuze, Gilles, and Felix Guattari, *Anti-Oedipus*, 200–202
Descartes, René, 211
Deutsch, Helene, 8–9, 56, 59, 61
Don Quixote: dreams in, 106–8; Dulcinea

Don Quixote (Continued)
  in, 102–5, 107, 113; enchanters in, 153;
  Freud the dreamer and, 150–53; Freud's
  early love of, 99–100; and Freud's infatuation with Schreber, 192–94; Freud's Romantic view of, 135–36; and *Hamlet*,
  126–28; as inspiration to surrealism,
  108; and M. Lucien, 220–21; narcissistic
  types in, 244 n. 29; paranoid symptoms
  in, 10–11, 101–14; problem of value in,
  138; psychoanalytic reading of, 101–8,
  115–16; psychological accuracy of,
  242 n. 19; Quixote compared with
  Schreber, 171, 174, 187; relation to science and modernity, 69, 123; repetition
  of the myth of, 220–21; romance internalized in, 111; Romantic and existentialist
  readings of, 10–11, 132–35; Sancho
  Panza in, 102–3, 114, 243 n. 20; sanity
  and madness in, 167–69; as satiric
  model of psychoanalysis, 121, 146, 164–
  65; satiric motives of, 96, 108–13; satiric
  procedure in, 113–14; stages of discussion of, 100–101; summary, 215; suspicious hermeneutics in, 104. *See also* Cervantes, Miguel de; Psychoanalysis;
  Romance; Satire
"Dora" (Freud's patient), 48
Dostoyevsky, Fyodor, 95; Freud on, 234 n.
  54; paranoia of his Underground Man, 2

Einstein, Albert, 198
Eissler, K. R., on Freud's right to cruelty,
  61–62
Eliade, Mircea, psychoanalysis and ritual,
  230–31 n. 23
Ellenberger, Henri, pre-psychoanalytic ther-
  apies, 228 n. 10
Ellison, Ralph, 2
Emerson, Ralph Waldo, on society as con-
  spiracy, 1
Erasmus, Desiderius: and Cervantes, 124;
  comparison of satiric perspective with
  Freud's, 97–98, 132, 166, 203, 240 n.
  2. *See also* Narcissism; Satire
Esterson, Allen, on Freud's sense of perse-
  cution, 234 n. 50
Existentialism, in reading of *Don Quixote*,
  10–11

"Family Romances," 17–18, 117–19;
  Freud's own, 159–60. *See also* Romance
Faust (Goethe), 16, 99, 164, 183–85
Ferenczi, Sándor, 51; on ennobling power of
  psychoanalysis, 190–91; and the occult,
  235 n. 59; relations with Freud, 190–93
Feuerbach, Ludwig, 67, 76
Fielding, Henry, *Tom Jones*, 98, 146
Fliess, Wilhelm, 28, 57–58, 98, 120, 136,
  151, 155–56, 235 n. 67; psychological
  influence on Freud, 189–93, 230 n. 20
"Formulations on the Two Principles of Mental Functioning," 24–26
France, Anatole, 98
Frazer, Sir James, on animism (quoted by
  Freud), 19–20
Freud, Sigmund: adolescent cult of Cervantes, 99–100, 241–42 nn. 13,14,
  243 n. 20; anticipated by Bacon, 70–73,
  75; association of acceptance of psychoanalysis with maturity, 233 n. 44; attitude toward Jung, 234 n. 50; author's attitude toward, 211; capacity to absorb
  precursors, 67; and Carlyle, 98, 240–
  41 n. 8; cocaine addiction, 5–7, 42,
  229–30 n. 7; and Comte, 239 n. 37; conscious ideas portrayed as unconscious,
  157–58, 160; contempt for humanity, 59;
  correspondence with Jung about
  Schreber, 187–89; and Dante, 137, 207;
  death wishes toward Fliess, 235 n. 67;
  defensive use of theory of paranoia, 190–
  93; delusions, 55, 253 n. 31; denial of
  own altruism, 58–59; in "Dream of
  Irma's Injection," 149–51; in "Dream of
  Otto's Illness," 145–48; in "Dream of
  Rome," 152–53; duplicity, 249 n. 21;
  and England, 89, 236–37 n. 6; epistemological suspicion, 77–83; and Erasmus,
  98, 240 n. 2; faith in science, 54; 'family
  romance' of, 118–19; favorite authors,
  98–99; fear of a successful Quixote,
  163–64; and Goethe, 99, 241 n. 11;
  grandiosity and heroic identifications,
  50–51, 57, 231 nn. 24, 27, 249–
  50 n. 28; and Heine, 98–99, 241 n. 9;
  historical suspicion, 83–89; and Hobbes,
  90, 92–94; homoerotic impulses, 192;
  hostile use of diagnosis of paranoia, 57–

58; hostile view of society, 49–50; identification with Gulliver, Gargantua, and Hercules, 152–53; identification with Hannibal, 158–61; identification with Julius Caesar, 155–57; identification with Oedipus, 130, 246 n. 52; inability to lie because of psychoanalysis, 67; infatuation with Schreber and its sources, 180, 189–93, 219; sense of inferiority, 51–52; intensity of commitment to psychoanalytic doctrine, 198; Jewish identity, 118–19, 158–61, 227 n. 5, 250 n. 29; materialism of his teachers, 76; methodological suspicion and, 69–77; misdiagnosis of hysteria, 234 n. 54; misreading of *Oedipus the King*, 128–30; monopolizing of psychoanalytic women, 235–36 n. 74; myth of discovery of psychoanalysis, 62–64; in " 'Non vixit' Dream," 155–56; and the occult, 235 n. 59; theory of paranoia, 2–4, 11–13; paranoia and satiric method in treatment of Rank and Deutsch, 8–9; permissiveness toward, within psychoanalytic movement, 60–62; persecution by numbers, 55–56, 234–35 n. 56; personality reflected in exclusiveness of psychoanalytic movement, 52–53, 232–33 n. 40; place in modernity, 66–67; political imagination in "Dream of 1848," 161–64; and political suspicion, 89–94; and politics, 90; as primal father, 58–65, 235–36 n. 74; professional ambition, 162–63, 249 n. 18; projections in psychoanalysis, 43–46; psychological influence of Fliess upon, 189–93, 230 n. 20; Quixotic appeal, 216, 221–22; Quixotic megalomania in, 150–53; Quixotism with regard to Schreber, 192–94; reading of Macaulay, 68–69; relations with Ferenczi, 190–93; as rhetorician, 44–45, 186–87; Romantic view of *Don Quixote*, 135–36; as satirist, 4–5, 96–98, 113–14, 116, 121–23, 150–53, 164; self-portrayal, 3–4, 64, 131–32; sense of rivalry with Schnitzler, 55; "sexual protestant," 227 n. 5; social motives of writing on wit, 121; sources of megalomania of, 154–58; and Sterne, 98, 240 n. 4; subject for later analysts, 57, 148–49; and suicide of Viktor Tausk, 59–61; summary of general argument about, 213–16; suspicion of colleagues and need to dominate, 54–57, 233 n. 42; and Swift, 98–99, 240 n. 3, 241 n. 10; "traumatic hyperaesthesia toward dwindling correspondence," 253 n. 31; use of colleagues as "projection objects," 56; use of own dreams in *The Interpretation of Dreams*, 141. See also *Don Quixote*; Esterson, Allen; Narcissism; Paranoia; Psychoanalysis; Romance; Satire; *and titles of individual works*

Future of an Illusion, 89

Gassendi, Pierre, 76
Gellner, Ernest, 46
Gibbon, Edward, 85, 238 n. 31
Goethe, Johann Wolfgang von. See *Faust* (Goethe)
Gogol, Nicholai, 98
Gospel of John, quoted ironically in *Totem and Taboo*, 16
Group Psychology and the Analysis of the Ego, 58
Grünbaum, Adolf: on circularity of clinical validations of psychoanalysis, 32; on Freud's genetic fallacy, 228–29 n. 15
Guattari, Felix, and Gilles Deleuze, *Anti-Oedipus*, 200–202

Haeckel, Ernst, historical recapitulation theory in, 86
Hamlet: literary self-consciousness in, 125–28; as model of psychoanalytic rhetoric, 128; philosophical context of, 125; as symptom of modernity, 115–16, 124–25. See also *Oedipus the King*
Hannibal, Freud's identification with, 158–61
Harte, Bret, 98
Hegel, Georg Wolfgang von, 68; dialectic of, and psychoanalysis, 88–89; historical recapitulation theory in, 85–86
Heidegger, Martin, 211
Heine, Heinrich, 46, 98–99, 241 n. 9
Heller, Joseph, 2
Hemingway, Ernest, 1

Hermeneutics of suspicion, 208–11; antidote to, 210–11
Herzl, Theodor, 163
Hitler, Adolf: paranoid symptoms, 11, 220; as a successful Quixote, 163–64, 220–21
Hobbes, Thomas, 1, 68, 76, 95, 211; political thought of, 90–94
Hoffmann, E. T. A., delusions of persecution, 1
Huarte de San Juan, Juan, *Examen de Ingenios*, 124
Humanist historical methodology, 68
Hume, David, 36, 68, 77, 83; anticipation of Freud, 79
Hyman, Stanley Edgar, 152

Ibsen, Henrik, 1, 2
Interpretation of Dreams, The, 50, 99, 101, 119, 121, 131–66, 215; "Dream of 1848," 161–64; "Dream of Irma's Injection," 149–51; "Dream of Italy," 152–54; "Dream of Otto's Illness," 145–48, 161–64; "Dream of Rome," 158–61; egotism of dreams, 81; Freud's identification with Julius Caesar, 155–57; Freud's literary megalomania in, 150–53; lay opinion about dreams, 140; Romantic structure of and the 'uncanny', 164–65; satire and the 'uncanny' in, 136–37; sources of his megalomania according to Freud in, 154–55; theory of dream interpretation, 141–49, 248 n. 13; title of, 138; value of dreams, 138–141; wit in dreams, 120, 244–45 n. 34. See also *Don Quixote*; Psychoanalysis; Romance; Romanticism; Satire

James, Henry, Napoleonic delusions, 1
James, William, 211
Jones, Ernest, 52, 56, 58, 197; psychoanalytic compliment, 234 n. 52
Joyce, James, and paranoia of Stephen Daedalus, 2
Jung, Carl, 51–52, 197; attractiveness to Freud, 192; correspondence with Freud about Schreber, 187–89; Freud on expulsion of, from psychoanalytic movement, 234 n. 50; protest about hostile psychoanalytic diagnosis, 233 n. 47. See also Schreber, Daniel Paul

Kafka, Franz, 2
Kant, Immanuel, 68, 76, 79–83, 85, 88, 138, 164, 238 n. 29; "What Is Enlightenment," 85
Kemp, Anthony, on Protestant historical consciousness, 238 n. 31
Kerr, John, on term 'movement', 233 n. 43
Kesey, Ken, 2
Kyd, Thomas, *The Spanish Tragedy*, 128

Lamarckian evolution, 28
La Mettrie, Julien Offray de, *L'Homme machine*, 76
Leonardo da Vinci and a Memory of His Childhood, satiric method in, 121–23. See also Freud, Sigmund; da Vinci, Leonardo
Levin, Harry, on *Hamlet*, 126
Levi-Strauss, *Tristes Tropiques*, 219
Lichtenberg, Georg Christoph, 98
Locke, John, 36, 68, 134, 211; *An Essay concerning Human Understanding*, 78, 237 n. 24; philosophical and political motives of, 77–79
Lucien, Rico Julien Marie, 217–21

Macaulay, Thomas Babington, essay on Bacon, 68–69
MacIntyre, Alasdair, 211; on "natural man," 239 n. 41
Mailer, Norman, 2
Malinowski, Bronislaw, 195
Malthus, Thomas, 90
Mann, Thomas, 66
Marx, Karl: concept of the proletariat, 92; suspicious hermeneutics, 2, 67, 76, 95, 210
Maupassant, Guy de, 1
McGrath, William J., 249–50 nn. 28, 34
Meissner, W. W., on paranoia and normal thinking, 195–200, 253–54 n. 37; on Schreber, 195–96, 199
Melville, Herman, 2
Modernity: allegorically figured in psychoanalysis, 94; of Bacon, 211; connection

with paranoia, 1–4, 33–36, 42, 65,
202–4, 213; critics of, 211–12; *Don Quixote* as symptom of, 69, 123; epistemological suspicion in, 77–83; Freud's place
in, 66–67; *Hamlet* as symptom of, 115–
16, 124–25; historical suspicion in, 83–
89; methodological suspicion in, 69–77;
political suspicion in, 89–94; and primal
father, 27; psychological impact of, 6,
27, 31–34, 226 nn. 31, 35. *See also* Reality principle; Repression; Science
Montaigne, Michel de, Pyrrhonism of, 125

Napoleon, 1, 51, 138
Narcissism: and animism, 186; and character Don Quixote, 13, 101–8, 113–17,
128, 135–36; concept anticipated by
Bacon, 69–72; concept as opportunity for
projection, 43; concept's use in psychoanalysis, 11–13, 34–35, 44–45; and ego-
libido, 226 n. 29; and Erasmian Folly,
97–98; of Freudian theory, 28; Freud's
display of, 67; in Hobbes, 90; in human
bio-history, 11–21; and love, 135; in modernity, 27; in origins of paranoia, 6,
180–82; of primal father, 14–15; range of
narcissistic types in *Don Quixote*, 244 n.
29; and reductionism, 37–70; and religion, 133; repressed, 11–13, 93–94; repression of, in *Don Quixote*, 123–24,
189; of scientist, 49–50; and 'uncanny',
12–13; and 'unconscious', 82–83; and
Vico, 84; and passim. *See also* da Vinci,
Leonardo; Hegel, Georg Wolfgang von;
Pleasure principle; Romance
Newton, Isaac, 32
Nietzsche, Friedrich, 34, 60, 65, 67, 210,
221; concept of the 'superman', 15, 92;
paranoid characteristics, 1, 2; reductionism, 38
Novalis, 138–39
Nozze di Figaro, Le (Mozart), 161

"Obsessive Actions and Religious Practices," 98
Oedipus complex, historical origins of, 13–
14, 16–18
Oedipus the King: Freud's identification with
hero, 51, 59, 130; and *Hamlet*, 124–25;

motivation of, 128–30; and Peloponne-
sian War, 129–30
*On the History of the Psycho-Analytic Move-
ment*, 56–57. *See also Oedipus the King;*
Paranoia
Orlando Furioso (Ariosto), 110

Paranoia: antidote to, 200, 210–11; and
art, 26–27; as caricature of philosophical
system, 23; in Cervantes' "Licentiate of
Glass," 245 n. 45; charm of, 11–13,
133–36, 168–69, 180, 187, 189–94,
215–21, 230 n. 14; as communicable
disease, 44; contemporary thinking on,
41, 254 n. 41; cultural variation in,
254 n. 44; diagnosis of, as hostile rhetorical instrument, 57–58; in *Don Quixote*,
10–11, 101–14; and dream interpretation, 141–45; and dreams, 139; and
Faust, 182–85; Freud's analysis of, as applied to Schreber, 179–87; Freud's identification with, 51, 57–59, 130; homosexual motives in, 104–5; hysterical
paranoia, 189; insightfulness of, 47–48;
and modern political philosophy, 94; and
modernity, 1–4, 31, 33–36, 42, 65,
202–4, 213; and Oedipus, 128–30; and
reductive logic, 31–40, 169; relation to
sanity, 6–7, 114, 167–69, 195–200; and
religion, 2–3, 32, 195–96, 199; and romance, 115; and Romanticism, 134–35;
vs. schizophrenia, 201–2; in Schreber
case, 170–79; summary of general argument about, 213–16; symptoms of, 11–
13, 42–43, 229 n. 3; tentativeness of
Freud's essay on, 252 n. 16; theory of, as
defense for Freud, 190–93; use of term
and its self-fulfilling dynamic, 7, 64–65,
224 n. 3; in Viennese political atmosphere, 144–45; and passim. See also
Don Quixote; Freud, Sigmund; Hermeneutics of suspicion; Hitler, Adolf; Meissner, W. W.; Narcissism; Nietzsche,
Friedrich; Pleasure principle; Primal father; Psychoanalysis; Reality principle;
Romance; Romanticism; Satire; Suspicion
Parker, Blanford, motives of Augustanism,
238 n. 25
Pfister, Oskar, 188, 227 n. 5

Picasso, Pablo, 135
Plato, concept of Eros, 35
Pleasure principle: concept of, 24–26; as historical concept, 31, 216; survival as art in modernity, 25–27
Popular and elite culture, 109–11
Primal father: Darwin on, 14, 84; and his family, 14–16; Freud as, 58–65, 235–36 n. 74; moral solitude of, 92; murder of, 16–17; narcissism of, 14–15; respectable heterosexual patriarchy of, 225 n. 12; survival in modernity, 27
Projection, concept of, 31, 36
Prometheus, myth of sexual repression, 24, 153
Psychoanalysis: adaptation of Kant, 80–83; as allegory of modernity, 94; 'anal erotism', 206; animism, 19–21; application to philosophy, 38–39; applied to Freud by later analysts, 148–49; author's assessment of, 212; and avant-garde, 53–54, 166; censorship in, 141–45, 248–49 nn. 15, 16; circularity of bio-historical theory, 31–32; concept of projection, 238 n. 27; concept of psychic energy in, 76–77; de-historicizing of, by later analysts, 13, 28–29; divisiveness of, 54, 57; dream interpretation in, 141–49, 248 n. 13; and epistemological suspicion, 77–83; and Erasmian satire, 97–98; as expression of Freud's paranoid personality, 43–64; 'family romance' in, 17–18, 117–19; the first epic poet, 17–18; the first epic poet compared with the modern artist, 26; Freud's account of discovery of, 62–64; grandiosity and heroic stance of, 33–34, 50–51; and Hegelian dialectic, 88–89; on heroic fantasy and popular romance, 26; historical origins of paranoia according to, 14; historical recapitulation theory in, 86–88; and historical suspicion, 83–89; hostility in, 48–50; and hypnotism, 233 n. 43; influence of Hamlet on, 128; influence of Rousseau on, 85; institutional exclusiveness of, 52–53, 232 nn. 35, 36; on Leonardo da Vinci, 21–22, 229 n. 15; the libidinal economy of social imagination, 18–19; in literary criticism, 209, 212; moral solitude of the primal father, 92; Moses and

Ikhnaton, 18, 21; murder of the primal father, 16–17; myth of resistance to, 45–46, 52–53; narrative of human bio-history in, 13–24; objections from the point of view of, 115–16, 204–12; origins of religion, 21; as paranoid cult, 197; on 'pleasure principle' and 'principle of reality', 24–26, 31; precursors of psychotherapy, 228 n. 10, 230 n. 23; prefigured in the Academie Española, 99–100; the primal father and his family, 14–16; and problem of suggestion, 45; as projection, 43–46; 'projection' and the 'omnipotence of thoughts', 19–21; on psychology of art, 25–27; on psychology of modernity, 21–27; reductionism in, 37–40; redundancy of, applied to Don Quixote, 113–14, 116; relation of observation and explanation, 205–6; on relations of paranoia, science, and art in modern psychology, 26–27; as romance, 59, 86, 96–97; satiric character and method of, 4–5, 113–14, 116, 119–23, 164, 194, 214–15; satiric influence on subsequent psychology, 196; and Schreber's "basic language," 188; and Schreber's system, 185–86; as science, 206–8; science and history in, 88–89; on scientist's place in cultural history, 22, 29–31; sense of 'centrality' in, 53; concept of sexuality, 119–20; stages of discussion of, 4–5; and stereotypes of Jews, 243 n. 28, 245 n. 37; summary of general argument about, 213–16; suspicious hermeneutics of, 8–9, 40, 44–50, 131–32, 208–10; theory of wit in, 13, 119–21; tragedy, 18; training analysis, 232 n. 38; 'uncanny' in, 13, 133–36, 164–65, 224–25 n. 6; weakness of evidential claims, 5, 32. See also Freud, Sigmund; Narcissism; Paranoia; Pleasure principle; Primal father; Reality principle; Reductionism; Satire
Psychoanalytic compliment, 55, 234 n. 52
"Psycho-Analytic Notes on an Autobiographical Account of a Case of Paranoia (Dementia Paranoides)," 180–87, 252 n. 16
The Psycho-Pathology of Everyday Life, 46–47, 54
Putnam, James Jackson, 58
Pynchon, Thomas, 2, 219, 252 n. 19

Rabelais, François, urinating and megalomania in *Gargantua and Pantagruel*, 24, 99, 152–54

Rank, Otto, relations with Freud, 8; theory of 'family romance', 17–18, 117–18

"Rat Man" (Freud's patient), 20

Reality principle: concept of, 24–25; as historical concept, 31, 216; and repression, 33–34, 97; and science, 25–27

Reductionism: logic of, 37–38; and paranoia, 169; of psychoanalysis, 34–36, 228–29 n. 15; self-inclusiveness of, 116–17, 213. *See also* Science

Religion: Christianity as son-religion, 225 n. 21; Freud as "sexual protestant," 227 n. 5; historical origins of, 16–19, 29, 225 n. 21; and narcissism, 133; as object of Freudian satire, 96–97, 121–23; and origins of modern suspicion, 67–68; as protection against neurosis, 23; Protestantism, 68; relation to paranoia, 2–3, 32, 195–96, 199; repression of, 29–30, 89, 227 n. 5; Romantic view of, 133; and Schreber, 172–73, 176–79; and science, 32–34, 213; and scientific rhetoric, 72–73, 76; as target of Lockean empiricism, 78–79

Repression: concept of, 35–36; in *Don Quixote*, 123–24, 189; heroism of, 23–24; and reality principle, 33–34; of religion by science, 29–30, 33–34; and sexuality, 226 n. 31; and passim. *See also* Modernity; Prometheus; Reality principle; Satire

Ricoeur, Paul, "hermeneutics of suspicion," 210

Rieff, Philip, on Freud's measure of health, 239 n. 43

Rilke, Rainer Maria, 60

Roazen, Paul, 8, 59–60

Rochefoucauld, Duc de la, 95

Romance: in Baconian rhetoric, 73–74; in books of chivalry, 114–17; Cervantes's attitude toward, 123–24; in Dante, 137; in Dante and Freud, 207; in *Don Quixote* and psychoanalysis, 215–16; internalized in *Don Quixote*, 111; naive and sophisticated, 109–13; narcissism of, 115; and paranoia, 4–5, 7, 26; psychoanalysis as, 59, 86, 96–97; repression of, in *Don Qui-*

xote, 123–24; in structure of *The Interpretation of Dreams*, 131–66; and the 'uncanny' in structure of *The Interpretation of Dreams*, 133–36, 164–65. *See also* Art; Satire

Romanticism: aspect of the Committee, 52, 59, 232–33 n. 40; in biology, 28; historicism of, 89; *Naturphilosophie*, 96; and paranoia, 134–35, 215–16; in psychoanalysis, 216; Quixotism of replayed toward Freud, 148; in reading of *Don Quixote*, 10–11, 132–35, 166; in *Totem and Taboo*, 183; in title *Traumdeutung*, 138; view of dreams, 139–41; view of religion, 133. *See also* *Faust* (Goethe); Rousseau, Jean-Jacques; Schelling, Friedrich Wilhelm Joseph

Rorty, Richard, 211, 255 n. 46

Rousseau, Jean-Jacques, 65, 68, 95; *Confessions*, 1; cultural impact of, 132; as first honest man, 67; and freedom, 91; historical thinking of, 85; persecution complex, 1; *Reveries of a Solitary Walker*, 1; *Rousseau, Judge of Jean-Jacques*, 1

Roustang, François, 235 n. 73

Sachs, Hanns, 226 n. 23

Salomé, Lou-Andreas, on Tausk's suicide, 60, 236 n. 79

Sass, Louis A., on normal vs. abnormal thinking, 253–54 n. 37; on schizophrenia and modernism, 6, 224 n. 8

Satire: in Bacon, 124; and concept of sexuality, 119–20; in conflation of normality with insanity, 6–7; in dreams, 150, 162–64, 249 n. 22; in Freud and Cervantes, 132; in Freud's essay on Schreber, 180, 186–89, 194; in Freud's treatment of Leonardo, 121–23; in psychoanalysis, 4, 116, 119–23, 164, 194, 214–15; in Schreber's delusions, 253 n. 20; self-inclusiveness of, 116–17, 243–44 n. 28; social motives in *Don Quixote*, 108–13; summary, 215; in Swift and Freud, 98–99, 240 n. 2; and the 'uncanny' in *The Interpretation of Dreams*, 136–37, 139. *See also* Burton, Robert; Carlyle, Thomas; Cervantes, Miguel de; *Don Quixote*; Erasmus, Desiderius; Fielding, Henry; France, Anatole; Freud, Sigmund;

Satire *(Continued)*
 Goethe, Johann Wolgang von; Gogol, Ni-
  cholai; Harte, Bret; Heine, Heinrich; Hu-
  arte de San Juan, Juan; *The Interpretation
  of Dreams;* Lichtenberg, Georg Christoph;
  Rabelais, François; Rochefoucauld, Duc
  de la; Shaw, George Bernard; Sterne,
  Laurence; Swift, Jonathan; Twain, Mark;
  Voltaire; Wit
Schelling, Friedrich Wilhelm Joseph, 134,
 140; on the 'uncanny', 136
Schiller, Friedrich, 157
Schizophrenia, vs. paranoia, 201–2
Schnitzler, Arthur, 55
Schopenhauer, Arthur, 1, 67, 138
Schorske, Carl E., 173; Freud and liberal
 politics, 250–51 nn. 35, 36
Schreber, Daniel Paul, 5, 169, 220–21;
 Darwinism, 175; Deleuze and Guattari
 on, 200–202; in Freud/Jung correspondence, 187–89; Freud's analysis of,
 179–87; Freud's Quixotic infatuation
 with, 180, 192–94, 219; and Gulliver,
 173; legal defense of, 176–79; life after
 release, 251 n. 8; Meissner on, 195–96,
 199; *Memoirs of My Nervous Illness*, 171–
 72, 179; and Quixote, 171, 174, 187; relations with father, 251 n. 12; and religion, 172–73; Sass on, 253–54 n. 37;
 satire in delusions, 253 n. 20; symptoms
 of mental illness, 170–76. *See also*
 Freud, Sigmund; Paranoia; Psychoanalysis; Religion; Science
Science: Bacon's suspicious methodology of,
 69–76; as crusade of repression, 29–30;
 Freud's faith in, 54; Freud's personified
 abstraction of, 30; generalization in, 116;
 heroism of, 34; and history in psychoanalysis, 88–89; materialism, 76–77; psychological and cultural impact of, according
 to Freud, 21–27, 29–32; and reality principle, 25–27; relation of *Don Quixote* to,
 123–24; and religion, 32–34, 72–73,
 76, 213. *See also* Freud, Sigmund; Paranoia; Psychoanalysis
Sexuality, concept of, 119–20; and repression, 226 n. 31, 239 n. 43
Shakespeare, romances of, 123
Shaw, George Bernard, 135

Silberstein, Eduard, 99–100, 188
Socrates, 203
Stendhal (pseudonym of Marie-Henri
 Beyle), 1, 2, 95
Sterne, Laurence, *Tristram Shandy*, 98,
 240 n. 4
Strindberg, August, grandiosity and persecution complex, 1
Sullivan, Harry Stack, 'paranoid slant',
 229 n. 3
Suspicion: of Bacon, 69–77, 80, 81, 83–
 84, 86, 95; in *Don Quixote*, 104; epistemological suspicion, 77–83; Freud's suspicion of colleagues and need to dominate, 54–57, 233 n. 42; in hermeneutics
 of psychoanalysis, 8–9, 40, 44–50,
 131–32, 208–10; hermeneutics of suspicion, 208–11; in historical thinking, 83–
 89; history of, 67–68; in scientific methodology, 69–77
Swales, Peter, on Freud and Fliess, 230 n.
 20
Swanson, David, 42–43
Swift, Jonathan, 95; and Freudian satire,
 98–99, 240 n. 3, 241 n. 10; Gulliver
 and Schreber, 173; Gulliver's urinating
 and megalomania, 24, 99, 152–53,
 241 n. 10; "The Mechanical Operations
 of the Spirit," 98; paranoia of Gulliver, 2

Tausk, Viktor, Freud and his suicide, 59–
 61
Taylor, Charles, 211
Temple, Shirley, 218, 220–21
Thornton, E. M., on diagnosis of hysteria,
 234 n. 54; on Freud's cocaine addiction
 as cause of paranoia, 5–7, 42, 229–
 30 n. 7, 233 n. 42
Totem and Taboo, 16, 102–3, 183, 235–
 36 n. 74
Twain, Mark, 98

Unamuno, Miguel de, 105
'Uncanny', 13, 224–25 n. 6; in *The Interpre-
 tation of Dreams*, 133–37, 150–51, 158,
 164–66, 224–25 n. 6, 247 nn. 5, 6;
 Schelling on, 136. *See also* Narcissism;
 Romance; Romanticism; 'Unconscious'
'Unconscious': dramatis personae of, 95,

216; and dreams, 141–66; fictitiousness of, 205, 214; Freud's conscious ideas portrayed as, 157–58, 160; and homosexual motives of paranoia, 191; and Kantian transcendentalism, 80–83, 164–65; and literary reenactment in *The Interpretation of Dreams*, 132–66; modes of expression in Freud's dreams, 151; suspicious discovery of, 9, 47–50, 54; vulgarity in, 114, 120. *See also* Narcissism; Paranoia; Pleasure principle; Satire; Suspicion; 'Uncanny'

Valla, Lorenzo, 68
Vico, Giambattista, *The New Science*, 84
Virgil, 50, 137, 164
Voltaire, 95

Wagner, Richard, 66
Wallace, Alfred Russell, 22
Welsh, Alexander, 246 n. 1
Wit: in dreams, 120, 244–45 n. 34; psychoanalytic theory of, 119–21
Wittgenstein, Ludwig, 211, 253–54
"Wolf Man" (Freud's patient), 48